Design America

CONTENTS

Whether You're a First-Time Home Builder or an Experienced Contractor...

...Design America's exceptional home plans and helpful, knowledgeable staff will make your project a complete success!

1 Choose the Design America Home Plan Book that offers plans for the style of home you've always wanted.

The plans in our Design America Series have been created by many of the nation's top architects and designers. No matter what your tastes, you're sure to find several homes you would be thrilled to call your own.

You can select from a wide range of styles, including the hottest new trends in contemporary styling. Design America has them all! We also showcase outstanding plans of affordable homes for those who are building on a budget.

STALLION

In addition to more than 200 home plans included in each Design America book, you'll find a wealth of other helpful information. Companion articles will give you hints on securing construction financing and show you how easy and inexpensive it is to customize your plans.

2 Order a complete set of blueprints.

Design America plans provide you with a complete blueprint package from as low as **$195.00. Blueprints include the following:**

- Exterior elevations of all sides
- Foundation plans and details
- Scaled floor plans
- Locations of electrical outlets, switches & light fixtures
- Plumbing schematic plan (If available)
- Roof & wall sections
- Cross-section view
- Material list and general notes (If available)

It's reassuring to know that Design America's blueprints meet one or more nationally recognized building standards at the time and place they were drawn. If you'd like a preview of one of our home designs, ask us about a Preview Plan of the home. Some plans offer a Preview Plan that shows the exterior elevation drawings of the plan, the floor plan, and kitchen cabinet elevations.

Customize the blueprints you select for a tailor-made home just for you.

From changing siding material to adding a walk-in closet or a room, our design staff will save you thousands of dollars over what you might otherwise pay. For a nominal charge, we can even mirror-reverse the entire plan!

In addition to design customization, Design America also provides assistance in securing construction financing. **Call us today** and we'll be happy to give you more information on this helpful, time saving service.

Our #1 goal is to help you build the home that matches your needs and lifestyle.

Call us toll free **(800) 533-4350** or fax us your blueprint order today at **(800) 344-4293.** Let's get started on your new home!

Real Life Home-Building Experiences

Are you wondering what it's like to build your own home?

Let those who have gone before you share what they have learned.

If you're apprehensive about tackling such a huge project as building your own home (and who wouldn't be?), take heart. People of all levels of experience and backgrounds have successfully built homes for themselves. There are many ways to achieve your goal of a custom-built home. If you wish to avoid as many headaches as possible, hiring an experienced builder to handle all the details is the answer. If you possess a lot of confidence and have the desire to save as much money as possible, acting as your own general contractor is the way to go. There are even those who use a blended approach, hiring a builder to take care of some tasks, and completing the rest themselves. In all cases, the key to success is to do your homework. Doing the proper research first helps to minimize problems down the road. Part of that research is understanding the mistakes others have made so you can learn from them.

Playing the Role of the General Contractor

When you are the general contractor on your home building project, you can expect to have more challenges to deal with than if you hire a builder. Those who have lived through the experience have learned, however, that the snags aren't insurmountable. Sometimes these challenges can be turned into positives and **you can save a lot of money.**

Chuck & Annette Weidner

Chuck Weidner, of rural Harvard, Ill. is a repeat customer of National Plan Service USA,Inc. Twenty years ago he used plans from NPS to build a home in suburban Chicago. In April 1993 he and his wife Annette, following a set of Design America plans, started construction on another home situated on ten acres near the Wisconsin state line. They chose the design, a truly grand Victorian home encompassing over 2,500 square feet with an enormous porch that wraps around more than half of the house. Chuck and Annette are proof that you can play the role of general contractor if you're willing to endure some difficulties. Together, they served as the general contractor on both homes.

Other than five years working in construction (he's a police officer now), Chuck had no experience as a general contractor prior to building the first home. He and Annette taught themselves as they went through the process. What was the most trying part of the whole experience? "Making sure that all the subcontractors got their work done on time," answers Chuck. "Personality conflicts between the subcontractors was the biggest challenge. For example, the carpenters weren't happy with the way the electrician's were doing their work. The sheetrock was delivered at the same same the insulators were here, and it caused some difficulties...you just need to talk to both of them and make some compromises."

Chuck and Annette had the misfortune of buying their lumber shortly after Hurricane Andrew hit southern Florida in the fall of 1992. The demand for lumber for rebuilding caused prices to skyrocket. "The first time we went for bids was in September," explains Chuck, "and then we didn't really finalize it until January or February. The price of just the lumber went up $12,000...that was something we did not plan on."

Despite these problems, work progressed smoothly. The Weidners didn't need to alter their house plans to get the village's approval. There were no construction delays, even for the weather, and the project was completed on schedule. The solution to one particular problem turned out to augment the design of their house. The excavators and laborers were having trouble installing the septic tank because of the slope of the ground. "They had to move the house 15 or 20 feet," explains Chuck, "and that raised the foundation in the back where we now have a walk-out basement."

Weidner Residence

Photo courtesy of Carl Cullen

When you are your own general contractor, finding a construction loan can also be difficult. Banks are hesitant to lend if an experienced builder isn't involved. "We looked at a few banks," says Chuck, "but they all wanted to see a builder." The Weidners eventually financed the construction of their latest home with a home equity loan taken out on their old house.

"The most enjoyable part of the whole experience was seeing everything coming together," says Chuck, "Towards the end, when all the goodies come in such as the trim, cabinets, and flooring…then it starts looking like a house." Another positive outcome was the money Chuck and Annette saved by not hiring a builder. They **estimate their savings totalled $40,000.**

Would he recommend that anyone try being a general contractor? "I would say yes. With a little guidance from someone that's in the trades who knows what the difficulties are…I think anybody can do it." What advice would he give someone who's considering such an undertaking? "Make sure you're working with reputable people, get several bids, and check with the county where you get your permits, because they can make helpful recommendations (when looking for subcontractors)." Chuck mentioned that negotiation skills are also helpful when dealing with the trades.

Obviously, if asked if they would do it again, Chuck and Annette's answer would be yes. And, they would use Design America plans. The Weidners were so impressed with the quality of the plans and service they received that they have recommended Design America plans to other people.

Hiring A Builder

Serving as your own general contractor involves managing all aspects of your home-building project. Building materials must be ordered, and competitive bids must be solicited. A complete work schedule must be created, and deliveries and subcontractors' work must be coordinated. In addition, you have to make sure that the subcontractors (or trades as they are also known) get paid on time so that no mechanic's liens are put on your property. Make sure the necessary building permits and insurance are in place, and it's your responsibility that the plans for your house get approved by the village building authority.

If this sounds too overwhelming, consider hiring a local builder to do this work for you. The builder will take care of as much of the project as you want. If you decide to hire a builder, finding a reliable one is essential. How do you go about finding a reputable builder? And what separates the good builders from the bad ones?

"Word of mouth is the best way to find a builder," says Eric Rossi of Avanti Construction Corp., a builder based in the near west suburbs of Chicago. Rossi has been in the business for 20 years and builds 10 to 15 houses per year in Chicago's western and northwestern suburbs. He recently used a set of Design America plans for one of his homes and was very pleased with the result. "Talk to people. See some spec homes. Go in and see the type of work their doing. Talk to people who have bought their homes and ask them what they think of their house," Ross recommends.

There are various third party sources that you can check out as well. Local attorneys and county offices should be able to provide you with information about the track record of a particular builder. Reporting services such as Dun & Bradstreet can be consulted as well. One especially important item to investigate is whether or not the builders pay their subcontractors on schedule. A sub who doesn't get paid on schedule can place a mechanic's lien on your property preventing you from calling it your own until he gets paid. Every builder has had to fend off mechanic's liens at one time or another, however, the fact that a builder has a few doesn't necessarily mean he isn't doing his job. "That's one of the problems in the business," says Rossi. "Any guy that has a dispute can throw a lien on you. There should be some guidelines, there should be some standards that they have to meet, But there's nothing like that." A builder with many liens from several different subs should raise a red flag. A good builder will avoid all but the most frivolous liens. "I don't let things slide. My tradespeople perform and they get paid, and that's important," Rossi states.

It's a good idea to research and hire your builder early, while you're still in the planning stages, and even before your house plans are finalized. This is important because the builder will offer many helpful suggestions concerning the plans and specs. When it comes time to start construction, the builder may know of a more efficient or cost-effective way to achieve a certain result. The builder can also tell you if there are going to be any problems getting the village's approval for the plans. Good builders will always be doing research and attending trade shows to stay informed on the latest issues in the industry. You should tap into this knowledge as early in the process as possible.

Rossi points out that if your home's interior will be completed during the colder months, your labor costs will be less. This is because less construction takes place during the winter and so there are more plumbers, electricians, etc. available. With more trades competing for fewer jobs, they'll be more likely to offer discounted rates during winter.

Builders such as Rossi have built homes for many people and are full of helpful hints. Rossi recommends locating your financing first, before doing anything else. "The first thing to do is to find out what you're qualified for. You don't want to be looking for a $300,000 home if you've only qualified for $170,000. Then your next step is to find your land." Rossi recommends finding a lot in a location you like and then picking out house plans that fit the lot. Don't select your plans before the lot, and allow enough time for construction. "You've got to figure six to eight months to build a house even though everybody wants it in three," says Rossi.

The best piece of advice that Rossi can give to those building their own home is to choose your builder carefully. Shop around and select a builder based on reputation and the quality of their work.

It's Definitely Worth Building Yourself to Get Exactly What You Want.

Having owned half a dozen different houses and condos, Bob and Judy Sipek decided to build a custom home in a southwestern suburb of Chicago. Bob works as a project manager and Judy is a building manager. "We wanted a new home and so we found a lot we really liked in a nice subdivision and started looking for house plans and a builder," explains Bob. "We ended up going with the builder who built my sister's house because I could see he did quality work. I had been talking to various people and had a ballpark figure of what it would cost. This builder's price was in the ballpark. We knew his work and he could start right away so we went with him." In addition, their builder had built other homes in the same subdivision, and was familiar with local building codes and soil conditions.

The Sipeks chose the NP1348 Chesterton design from the Design America series. A contemporary design, the Chesterton features 1,890 square feet of living area neatly packaged into 1 1/2 stories. The home was built on a 1/4 acre lot. "We started looking at plans about one year before we broke ground," says Bob. "The first plans we chose were from a company in Texas. But then we found out that the plans weren't certified for Illinois and it would've been very costly to modify them to comply." The Design America staff was able to deliver plans certified for Illinois and also incorporated some changes the Sipeks wanted to make. Among other things, they enlarged the first-floor master bath and rearranged some closet space to allow a first-floor powder room to become a third full bath. The Sipeks were somewhat pressed for time, but the Design America staff was able to meet their needs. "The company was good at rushing our changes through in about a week," says Bob.

This was Bob and Judy's first attempt at building a home for themselves, and they enjoyed the experience. Their greatest concern was finding a builder they could trust who wouldn't run into financial trouble during construction and be unable to finish. This concern wasn't great enough, however, to cause them to try their hand at being a general contractor.

The only real problem the Sipeks encountered was a time crunch towards the end of the project. There were some rain delays, and a rather complicated roofline took longer to construct than anticipated. Bob and Judy had to wait an extra six weeks to move in, but delays such as these are common. In fact, allowing enough time for construction is one piece of advice the Sipeks offer first-time home builders. They started researching plans and builders about one year in advance of construction, but really could have used a year and a half. It's also important to match the design of your home with your lifestyle. "When you pick out a floor plan, think about how you live," says Judy. "Since we don't have kids, I wanted every place I need most to be on the main floor, and the rooms that we don't use all the time somewhere else. This house fits just perfectly."

Even with the construction delays and minor problems, the Sipeks agree that building their custom home was well worth it. Neighbors are always saying how much they like the house and Bob and Judy couldn't be happier. **"It's definitely worth building yourself to get exactly what you want**," says Judy. "We plan to retire here."

Sipek Residence

Photo Courtesy of Lewellyn Studio

Make Design America Plans Part of Your Home-Building Experience

Many people have built their own custom homes and so can you! Allow enough research time, solicit bids from a variety of builders or subcontractors, insist on quality work, and choose Design America plans. By following these tips from successful home builders, you'll be well on your way to living in that home you've always wanted. Design America also offers books on building and construction to help you start your project with a solid foundation of knowledge.

Analyze the Blueprints Before Building to Create the Best Possible Home of Your Dreams

Article by Guhner-Jahr Publishing
Build-It & Build-It Ultra

There need be nothing "stock" about a custom home built from pre-drawn mail-order plans. In fact, with imagination and/or professional guidance, thousands of homeowners have modified existing blueprints to create truly personal, character-filled homes. Changes can range from simple facade embellishments, such as articulated door and window casings, to major spatial modifications—for example, combining two small bedrooms to create a grand master suite with a bath and dressing room.

Though dramatic in effect, many custom touches may not even require new architectural drawings. Other, more substantial changes are best accomplished with the help of an architect or other design professional, who can prepare any new drawings that are needed.

In either case, it is critical to consider and decide on any changes early in the process, long before construction begins. Otherwise, any bids you solicit prior to changing the plans will be inaccurate. Worse still, if you ask for modifications during construction, your project is likely to be beset by delays and cost over-runs.

Material Choices

Among the simplest changes are those related to materials. Let's say your plans and specifications call for clapboard siding, but you prefer the more rustic look of wood shakes. Simply select the alternative material, change the specification, and you've personalized your home-to-be. Other easy-to-change materials with a potentially big impact on a home's looks include roofing and the trim around windows and doors.

One step further are changes that affect both materials and design. For example, many two-car garages are designed with a single, large door, but you may prefer the lighter look of two single-width doors. Or, instead of the double-hung windows in the plans, you may opt for the more gracious look of floor-to-ceiling casements.

In many instances it's possible to "test" the visual impact of such changes by sketching in the alternate materials on tracing paper laid over the elevations in the blueprints. These changes should not be treated lightly, however, and if you're unsure, it's a good idea to invest in some professional design help. (For more on the importance of material specifications, see "Specifying Your Dream." page 14.)

Floor Plan Changes

Another area to consider is the floor plan itself. Though today's mail-order house plans are generally well-designed with the needs of modern families in mind, it's often possible to make a change or two in the layout that turns an almost-perfect design into an ideal home for your family. Removing a single wall, for example, might create the large, open living room/dining room you desire. Or, raising the garage's walls and roof by just 4 feet could turn an unfinished storage loft into the spacious home office you need.

Kitchens and baths, which are the most complicated and most used rooms in the house, deserve special attention. A luxurious two-person shower, for example, may better suit your lifestyle than a standard tub/shower combination. Similarly, an expanded kitchen

Article Courtesy of Guhner-Jahr Publishing.

Cornwall
Design No. 104-1315
Design No. 104-1321
Design 72-4258
BREAKFAST AREA
FAMILY ROOM
DEN/OFFICE
LIVING ROOM
KITCHEN
DINING ROOM
GARAGE
FIRST FLOOR PLAN
PLAN NUMBER
1315-1
CHURCHILL
NATIONAL PLAN SERVICE
NPS
LIGHT & VENT.
DOOR, WINDOW
SCHEDULE
FLOOR PLAN
ENTER
MODE

CUSTOMIZE IT !

Small changes on paper can greatly improve your plans, but make sure you decide on any modifications before construction begins.

that can accommodate two sinks and dishwasher may be the perfect solution if you entertain frequently.

Again, you can begin by sketching your ideas on tracing paper laid over the blueprints. If you can't figure out the layout changes needed, seek professional advice from an architect or other design professional.

Working with Pros

If you're confident about the changes you desire but can't quite visualize or draw them, you can hire an architectural draftsperson—perhaps a local architecture student—who can turn your ideas into finished plans and/or elevations. Rates for drafting start at about $25 per hour.

If you need design help or advice about materials—especially if you're considering changes that will affect the house's structure, such as moving or removing walls—seek the services of an architect or other qualified design professional. Registered architects are trained to address both spatial and structural questions. Designers vary more in training and experience; some are best at what was traditionally called decorating, while others are fully adept at space planning.

Many architects and designers will work on an hourly consulting basis, with fees ranging from about $75 to $125 per hour or more, depending on professional accreditation, experience and location.

Kitchen and Bath Specialists

Kitchens and baths are highly specialized design areas, so make sure whatever type of design pro you choose has a lot of experience. One option is to seek out a Certified Kitchen Designer (CKD) or Certified Bath Designer (CBD). To earn this title, professionals must meet special requirements, pass tests and obtain certification from the licensing arm of the National Kitchen & Bath Association

(NKBA). In addition to providing design services, CKDs and CBDs can help you select and can provide materials and products for the kitchen and bath.

Kitchen and bath dealers, many of whom are NKBA members, work out of showrooms that sell cabinets, appliances, bath fixtures and more. Most dealers provide design services and provide products and materials.

Article Courtesy of Guhner-Jahr Publishing

A Custom Home Doesn't Have to be Expensive

It's true. If you're planning on building your next home, it's cheaper to customize your own design and hire your own builder than it is to choose a plan from a large developer who's building a subdivision. Even if you accept the developer's stock plans with no modifications, it will still cost you more than building a custom home from your own plans. And the home need not be large, either. No matter if your dream is for 1300 or 3000 square feet, you'll spend less by designing and building yourself.

Why it Makes Sense to Build Your Own Custom Home

You might be thinking, "But how can that be? Can't those big developers build houses cheaper because of the volume of business they do? Don't they get volume discounts on their building materials?" That might be the case, but they also incur significant costs associated with marketing their developments.

It's easy to see these marketing expenses when you take a look at a new subdivision. Consider the model homes that are built for prospective home buyers to tour. The developer has to pay for the interior designers who decorate the homes as well as for all the custom furnishings and landscaping. The salespeople who work there seven days a week must also be paid. Costly brochures promoting the subdivision must be created, and advertising space in newspapers and on television and radio must be purchased. The developer can recoup some of these expenses when the models are sold, but not all of them because the models are sold at a discount. Much of the cost gets passed on to you, the buyer, making the homes more expensive. By building yourself, using custom plans, you can avoid paying those extra costs and have a more personalized home, too!

What's the Best Source for Customized Plans?

You could hire an architect to draw up your custom plans, but you may end up spending thousands of dollars to get the design you want. A better alternative is to purchase customized plans from Design America and spend only hundreds. Design America has top-quality plans, and the expertise and the willingness to back them up with good customer service. Since we've been designing people's dreams for over 80 years, we know what you're looking for in a home. And because of the volume of our business, we can offer customized plans at prices that are 25 – 50% less than what a professional designer would charge.

Example of plan modification

Please Modify to A 3 car garage w/ dormer
3 car garage

Rendering courtesy of Select Home Designs

FIG 1

Even if your future home is less than a mansion, you'll save money by building yourself with custom plans from Design America

Revised Plans after modifications

Photo courtesy of Select Home Designs

The Customization Process

The first step is to browse through our Design America Series and select the design that comes closest to your idea of a perfect home. Design America has hundreds of different designs to choose from. If the simplified drawings and renderings in our plan books give you enough information, then fax us your request for changes. Just let us know what changes you need as outlined preceeding page (pg.11, fig.1) and our architects will do the rest.

If you'd like to buy a set of plans first, Design America's helpful design staff will discuss any customization options with you at the time of your order. Feel free to ask as many questions as you like. If changes are necessary, you can tell us at the time of your order. Preferably, you should give us the modifications in writing via mail or fax so there is no confusion over any of the details.

Other home plan companies may ask you to mark up a diagram of the home with the desired changes. But NPS believes you shouldn't have to worry about drawing your plans yourself. After all, we're the architects! We'll do the sketching; you just tell us what you want changed. After we evaluate your request, we'll estimate how much the changes will cost **free** of charge and how long they will take. Of course, price and lead time will vary depending on the extent of the modifications.

NPS Can Provide Your Plans in Several Different Formats

If you won't be making any changes to the stock plans you've selected, then you should order your plans in the form of blueprints. Blueprints are non-erasable and non-reproducible so not even minor changes can be made to them by you or your builder. Order these only if you're sure nothing else will be altered. You'll probably need 4 – 7sets for everyone involved in the construction of your new home. You'll want one set for yourself, of course. The village or local government body that's responsible for approving the design will need a set. Your lender will request plans before a loan is approved, and finally, the general contractor will probably need several sets for all of the subcontractors.

If you want to make only very minor changes, ones the contractors can make themselves, then you should order plans that are reproducible. These plans can be erased and redrawn. If you only want to move a wall a few feet or enlarge a walk-in closet, these plans allow the contractor to erase lines and redraw them. Mylar, vellum plans are also reproducible, so you can make as many copies as you need for all the parties involved. Because mylar, vellum plans are reproducible, they are slightly more expensive than blueprints.

The Design America Advantage:

Other home plan companies' service will stop after you've received your modifications of the plans. They'll redraw the plans and send them off to you. But what happens if the village authorities won't approve construction because your plans don't meet local codes or ordinances? This can be a serious problem. And the fewer problems you have when building a house, the better. What good are plans for a home that can never be built? With other plan companies, you're on your own, but not with Design America.

We realize that local building codes may be complex. Our plans are drawn to meet one or more national standards. Sometimes this isn't enough, however. Regional and local authorities often have their own sets of codes that must be met. If you're building in a subdivision, the seller of the lots may impose certain building restrictions or covenants that must be followed. In some cases, you may not fully understand the codes, or some restrictions may get missed. Design America will help you wade through all of this bureaucracy and help you get your plans approved.

"We realize that the homeowner may not be well versed on the technical aspects of dealing with all of the different codes and ordinances," says David Azran, President of National Plan Service USA, Inc. "We see ourselves as being a liaison between the homeowner and the builder. If permitted, we'll actually sit down with the homeowner and builder and discuss what has to be done to get the plans approved." If your plans are questioned by village authorities because of code requirements, Design America will get in touch with the village and find out exactly which parts of the plans need clarification. Then we discuss what must be done with you and make the changes needed to earn the village's approval. One of Design America's customers recently learned the value of this **exceptional service** when a conflict arose concerning the topography of the customer's lot. The local authorities rejected the homeowner's plans because the village felt the home's design was not compatible with a small hill on the site. The builder contended there was no hill, but the village insisted there was. After numerous discussions with the builder and the village, Design America discovered the problem. The village was using out-of-date drawings, and there really was no hill!

Peace of Mind With Your Customized Plans

We're sure you can see the value of Design America's services.This peace of mind is included in the price you pay for your customized plans. So call Design America today, at **(800) 533-4350** and let us assist you in the construction of your new home.

The More Active Your Role in Selecting Materials, Products and Techniques, the Better Your Home

Article by Guhner-Jahr Publishing
Build-It & Build-It Ultra

The best custom homes are carefully tailored to meet their owners' needs and wishes, and nowhere is this more important than in the selection of products, materials and construction techniques. After the workmen leave and you move in, the home will be a complete success only if you're pleased with the wood, glass, metal and stone used to transform your blueprints into a house.

Of course, many of the physical elements that comprise a home are spelled out in floor plans, elevations and allied documents. But some of these specifications may be generic, meaning there are still decisions to make. And even when a specific item is listed, you may prefer a different option—perhaps in-floor radiant heating rather than the forced hot-air furnace shown in the blueprints, or oak interior doors instead of pine.

Though it may seem easier to leave all these details to the contractor, the fact remains that you will live with the results, maybe for a lifetime. So the investment you make now in learning about the options will pay handsome dividends for years. Here's what to consider and how to find information and assistance.

Rendering courtesy of Alan Mascord Design Associates

Dollars and Sense

One of the best reasons to take an active role in product and material specification is to maintain budgetary control over your project. Obviously, the various options in each product category related to the home carry widely differing price tags, and those costs go directly to your home's bottom line.

Upgrade from plastic laminate to granite kitchen counters, for example, and your house may cost $7,500 more. Specify floor-to-ceiling ceramic tile in the baths instead of small tiled areas around the tub, and the additional cost might be $3,000 – $5,000, depending on the specific tile you choose.

Naturally, your total budget for the construction of the house will help to determine your material and product selections. The important point is to consider the many options—and their costs—early in the planning stages, ideally before putting your plans out to bid. That way the fixed price you contract for will reflect the many materials, products and techniques you want for the home, rather than choices the contractor may have made to save time and increase his profit.

If you're ready to solicit bids, but haven't made final decisions on every material, tell the contractors to exclude those elements from their prices. Or, if you have a good idea of what you're willing to spend on, say, flooring, ask them to include a flooring allowance of that dollar amount.

Rendering courtesy of Alan Mascord Design Associates

Filling in the Blanks

Another key concern is to fill in the blanks on all specifications that are treated generically in your plans. Though a complete set of blueprints, materials lists and specification sheets represents a comprehensive set of instructions for building a home, it does not necessarily provide a single choice for every detail.

For example, plans may call for "hardwood flooring" without indicating the type of wood or pattern to use. Or they may indicate the size and position of appliances and plumbing fixtures, but not the brands or model numbers. The same may be true of siding, roofing, windows, heating and cooling equipment, cabinetry, door hardware, even such final details as switchplates. In the end, someone must make the decision between inexpensive knotty pine clapboard and top-quality cedar, or between brand X appliances in black versus brand Y finished in stainless steel. And, taken together, these choices will have a profound impact on what becomes your home. Rather than accept someone else's choice, consider the options available in each instance and select the one that best satisfies your needs, desires and budget.

Upgrades

Even when items are listed specifically in the plans, it's worth analyzing the choices and considering upgrades. In roofing, for example, premium asphalt shingles not only look better than standard products, but also carry 50 percent longer warranties, making them a good value over time. Energy-efficient high-performance window glazing offers similar benefits when life cycle costs are factored in, as do top-quality cabinets built to last for decades.

Other changes relate more to aesthetics, but are just as valid. If you've always wanted goldplated bath fittings, why pay for chrome-plated models? Likewise, if standard-issue oak strip flooring is not your dream for a living room, it makes little sense to pay for it now only to switch to polished maple in a few years. Want classic ceramic mosaics on the bathroom walls? Specify them now rather than remodeling later.

Construction Techniques

The techniques used by a contractor to build your home can greatly affect its quality and the amount of maintenance and repairs you'll face over the years. Though your selection of an experienced, competent builder takes care of much of this question, there are some details worth specifying if you want top quality. Here are some important ones that may or may not be listed in your existing spec sheets:

• Drywall should be affixed with screws, rather than nails, which are more likely to pop. Skim coating all ceiling and wall surfaces with joint compound produces a better looking, more plaster-like finish than simply taping the joints between drywall sheets.

• Vapor barriers should be affixed to studs and joists prior to drywall to prevent condensation in wall cavities.

• An airspace should be left between insulation and roof sheathing so that air can pass freely from eave to roof vents.

• Sills, the horizontal wood members on top of foundation walls, should be cut from pressure-treated lumber so you'll never have to worry about rot.

• Valleys, rakes and eaves—the most vulnerable parts of a roof— should have a waterproof membrane applied under flashing or shingles.

• Wood siding and exterior trim that will be painted should be back primed prior to installation; this will extend the life of a paint job.

• Interior and exterior painting should include a primer and two finish coats, which can outlast a single coat by as much as 50 percent.

Information and Assistance

The specification of products, materials and techniques is a complicated business. But the task becomes much easier if you familiarize yourself with the available options.

You should also shop local lumberyards, home centers, kitchen and bath dealers, lighting stores, etc., to see and price the possibilities. Collect manufacturers' product literature and scour design magazines for ideas as well. If it's a book you're after, we recommend "The Apple Corps Guide to the Well-Built House," by Jim Locke, Houghton Mifflin, 1988.

Rendering courtesy of Alan Mascord Design Associates

If you'd rather spend your money than your time, consider an architect or other design professional on a consulting basis. Working from your budget and preferences, a pro can prepare a detailed spec list for your approval, can analyze a list you've prepared and suggest worthwhile changes, or can present you with a range of good options.

However you proceed, if your aim is the best, most personal custom home possible, make sure work doesn't begin until there's a complete materials list and specification sheet that you understand and with which you're comfortable. Otherwise, you may have to start planning a remodeling soon after you move in.

Article Courtesy of Guhner-Jahr Publishing

Financing the Construction of your Custom Home

by Kevin D. Woodard

Even before you have finalized the plans and site for your new custom home, your thoughts should turn to answering the question, "Where am I going to get the money to fund construction?" Unless you have large sums of cash saved up, you will need to take out some sort of loan to allow construction to begin. A conventional mortgage loan is not the answer at this stage, because you don't yet have a house to mortgage. For some, a home equity line of credit on their existing house can provide the cash they need. For most people wanting to build their own home, however, a *construction loan* is necessary. A permanent mortgage (also known as an *end loan* or *take-out loan*) will come later. This may sound unfamiliar to you, so let's go through the loan acquisition process one step at a time.

1. Select the source of financing

Professionals in the lending industry suggest looking to your current bank first for construction financing. You and your bank are familiar with each other, and the loan officers might already have a good idea of your present financial condition. Banks love to have multiple deposit and lending relationships with their customers and that is a good bargaining chip to have when you are negotiating the terms of your loan. But be forewarned: most banks will not lend to you if you are acting as your own general contractor unless that is how you make your living. Experience in the construction business is everything from the bank's point of view, so plan on hiring an experienced builder to oversee the construction for you unless you have a proven track record as a general contractor.

Other financial institutions can serve as funding sources as well. These include mortgage banks and brokers, and your company pension or savings plan. Retirement plans are often good for providing construction money because of the favorable terms at which you can borrow against your accumulated funds. Another source of funding is the builder himself. Your builder has a revolving line of credit with his bank and can use that to finance the construction of your new home. This arrangement simplifies things because you don't have to go to the trouble of applying for a loan at a bank. But there are disadvantages. A large deposit will be required up front and the interest the builder pays on his credit line will, of course, be passed on to you. You would pay this interest yourself anyway if you were borrowing directly from the bank, but then you would get the benefit of a tax deduction. When looking for possible sources of financing, rely on those who really know the business. Ask real estate attorneys, realtors, and local builders if they can recommend a lender.

2. Determine the type of loan that is best for you

Construction loan plus end loan. This is the most common way to finance the construction of a new home. With this arrangement, you actually get two separate loans to cover your financing needs: one for the construction phase and one for the "live in" phase after the home is built. The construction loan finances all costs associated with

Photo courtesy of Design Basics, Inc.

Photo courtesy of Select Home Designs

building the house. The end loan is nothing more than a conventional mortgage that pays off the construction loan. The construction loan typically has a term of six months to a year and is an "interest only" loan. This means your monthly loan payments include only interest calculated on the amount that you have borrowed. None of your payment goes toward reducing the principal balance. The principal balance is never reduced during the entire term of the construction loan. The interest rate you pay is usually tied to the prime rate and is stated as so many points over prime. The "spread" over prime can be anywhere from 1 to 2 percentage points. The rate will fluctuate as the prime rate fluctuates and may adjust monthly or even daily. Make sure you understand exactly how and on what amount the interest is calculated.

As described below, the loan proceeds are metered out in stages. It's obviously better for the interest payments to be calculated on only that portion of the loan amount that has actually been disbursed. You don't want to pay interest on money that is not even being used yet.

Expect to pay some points when you close on your construction loan. Points are a percentage of the loan amount that must be paid up front. One point equals 1 percent. For example, a one point fee on a $100,000 loan would be $1,000. The lender charges points to cover various expenses associated with administering the loan. It's important to note that these points are not like the optional discount points you can pay on a conventional mortgage. Points on a construction loan are a pure fee for the lender and do nothing to reduce your interest rate. They typically range from 1 to 2.5 points. More points are charged on construction loans than on mortgages, because construction loans are more costly to administer. As an incentive to stay with the same lender for your permanent mortgage, some institutions will let you use .5 point as a credit towards any points you pay on the mortgage.

A down payment will, of course, be required. Lenders usually require at least 20 percent down. This equates to a loan-to-value ratio (LTV) of 80 percent. Don't expect to get your entire loan amount disbursed to you all at once. In fact, you won't actually see any of the money at all unless you are acting as your own general contractor. The funds will be distributed to the general contractor in increments called "draws." The institution advances each draw when a specified stage of construction has been completed. For example, money will be advanced when the foundation is laid and when the framing goes up. A title company usually takes care of the actual disbursements. A representative of the lender or title company will usually inspect the project before each draw to verify that the work is being completed as planned. In addition, you the borrower may be required to sign off on each completed stage before a draw is made.

After the construction phase, when your new home is ready to be occupied, you're ready to take out the end loan. The end loan can come from the same lender as the construction loan or from a different lender.

Combination loan. Unlike the scenario presented above, in this case one loan takes care of all the financing. At the end of construction, the construction loan is simply converted into a permanent mortgage. This can save you money on closing costs since you only have to close once. Of course, you must use the same institution for construction and permanent financing.

Home equity loan. If there is a lot of equity built up in your present house, a home equity line of credit could be used as a construction loan. Equity credit lines usually have minimal paperwork and lower costs associated with them. Up to 80 percent of your home's market value may be available to use for construction financing.

3. Gather information and documents required at the time of the loan application

Here is a list of items that lenders typically require you to provide at the time you fill out a loan application:

Sworn contractor's statement. This document itemizes the contractor's estimate of all costs associated with building your home. It also lists who the subcontractors are and what they will do. It is signed by the general contractor.

General contractor's information letter. This is a form that the lender asks the builder to complete. It asks the general contractor questions about experience, insurance, bonding, etc. It helps the lender evaluate the general contractor.

Detailed blueprints and specs. The bank or other lending institution doesn't want to lend more than about 80 percent of the estimated value of the completed home. Blueprints and specs are needed for making this estimate of market value.

Signed contract between the builder and the individual. This proves you have an experienced builder working for you. It also assures the lender that the house will be built.

Deed to your lot. The lender will not grant you a loan without first knowing that you own the land on which your home will be built. If the lot is mortgaged, you will also need to have on hand all of the relevant loan documents.

Personal financial information. These are the standard items commonly required by all mortgage lenders and serve to verify your income, expenses, assets and liabilities. You'll be required to provide W-2s, paystubs, previous addresses for the past two years, name and address of employer, information on bank accounts, and outstanding loan balances, etc.

4. Close on the loan and start construction

Just as in a closing for a permanent mortgage, there are costs associated with closing on a construction loan. In addition to the points mentioned earlier, there will be recording fees, attorneys' fees, notary fees, etc. Costs such as these can vary from lender to lender, so it's a good idea to compare points and fees when shopping for a construction loan.

It's a lot of work finding construction financing and evaluating all of the options. But it will all be worth it as you watch your custom home take shape.

To help you evaluate your different financing options, Design America now offers a financing referral service. Call Design America today at **(800) 533-4350** to find out more about this new time-saving service.

Photo courtesy of Select Home Designs

A Wealth of Information When You Decide To Build Your Own Home

Now that you've decided to build your own home and have picked the plans ...where do you go? With today's home improvement market booming, you, the consumer, have more choices then ever before. Below are some helpful hints.

LUMBER YARDS

Materials, materials, materials ..How much do I need? ...How much will they cost?...What grade of lumber should I purchase? **Your local lumber dealer is the place to start.** Here you will find a service or lumber desk. The people behind that counter just may be your next best friends. You'll typically find estimators on hand who can provide a "take off", in other words an estimate, from your blueprint or materials list. This will be based on the grade of materials that you specify. Their estimates are typically right on target. Remember that they are in the business of selling lumber. Thus you will find them both helpful and attentive because they want your business.

Although don't expect them to do it while you wait; they usually are working on numerous sets at any given time. This is especially true in early and middle spring when the majority of housing starts take place.

HOME CENTERS

Huge stores, miles of products, and helpful staffs. Although you may be overwhelmed by its sheer size you can find practically anything here. Today's typical home centers can be over 100,000 square feet with full service garden building centers. Here you get both discounted prices and idea centers. These stores have everything for home improvement and more. You ramble past full kitchen and bath displays, order custom blinds, browse through thousands of different wall paper patterns and borders.

HARDWARE STORES

Here is the place to go when things get down to the nitty gritty or you need speed and convenience. When your stuck on a pipe fitting or need specialized fasteners your local hardware store will help you. Hardware store are the one retail outlet where a local and community atmosphere exists. Employees here will help you answer the most difficult questions and help you find the most distinguished nuts and bolts.

A Quick Guide so You'll Know What to Expect Once Construction Begin

Now that you've settled on your plans, the joy of turning your dreams into reality begins in earnest. The wrenching matter of financing needs to be settled, and a patch of land selected. Such decisions can take weeks or even years, depending on your determination and sometimes your luck. But once the time comes to break ground, a house can't be built fast enough.

Constructing a home can take anywhere from six months to one year (or more), depending on a number of factors. The size of the house, number of workers, weather conditions and unexpected—but inevitable—delays, all make a difference. Though the order of work may vary slightly and local building inspection requirements differ, this timetable, spread over a seven-month period, will give you a sense of what to expect and when.

Rendering courtesy of Alan Mascord Associates

Months 1 & 2

- Municipal and state permits obtained
- Site work and excavation
- Pour foundation
- Building inspection of foundation
- Frame floors
- Rough-in electrical and plumbing under floors
- Inspection of rough-in mechanical systems if house is built on slab
- Install first floor subfloor

Months 2 & 3

- Frame walls, roof and ceilings, including all door and window rough openings
- Install remaining subfloors
- Apply exterior wall and roof sheathing
- Rough-in remaining electrical and plumbing lines in wall, ceiling and floor cavities.

Months 3 & 4

- Building inspection of mechanical rough in and exposed structural work
- Apply roof flashing and shingles or other roofing material
- Install windows and exterior doors
- Apply exterior trim (window and door casings, fascia)
- Apply exterior wall finish material (i.e., clapboard, vinyl siding, stucco)

Months 5 & 6

- Install cabinets and countertops
- Apply ceramic tile in baths
- Finish plumbing and electrical work (light switches and fixtures, outlets, install sinks, tubs, etc.)
- Painting and wallpapering
- Install finish flooring

Months 6 & 7

- Install appliances
- Install hardware
- Inspection by homeowner and final touch-up work
- Site cleanup and landscaping
- Final building inspection
- Final payment to contractor
- Move in!

Article Courtesy of Guhner-Jahr USA Publishing

Design America Designers

National Plan Service USA, Inc.
(The publisher of the "Design America" house plan book series)

With a history that dates back to the early 1900's, when it offered do-it-yourself plans to lumber dealers, and individual consumers, the motto of National Plan Service USA, Inc., has become "Turning Your Dreams Into Reality For Over 80 Years."

Based in Bensenville, IL, the in-house staff of registered architects and designers at NPS work to provide consumers with unlimited design possibilities. These designs range from starter homes to luxury designs, with many alternatives to fit virtually any home-building budget. Home plans from NPS can easily be modified to suit a buyer's particular needs and lifestyle. The company offers customization services, as well as general advice and assistance to make the experience of building a new home as pleasurable as possible.

Many NPS designs reflect the regional influences of the northeast and midwestern United States. These solid, time-proven designs incorporate feedback from the thousands of customers who now live in homes built from fully detailed blueprint packages provided by NPS.

DESIGN BASICS, Inc.

Design Basics, Inc. creates home plans for builders nationwide. The company markets its plans,which are designed for single family dwellings, through catalogs and trade publications. The company originated in 1983 when its primary purpose was to design plans for custom home builders in the metropolitan areas. Seeing danger in controlling too much of the local market, the company's focus shifted from designing custom home plans locally to designing plans that were adaptable anywhere. Included in these plans is a construction license allowing the purchaser to build the plan as many times as desired, and a promotional license granting the right to produce the camera-ready art work for promotional purposes. Today, Design Basics is nationally recognized through numerous awards,not only for their designs, but also for achievements in business management,corporate growth, sales, and the development of effective marketing

products. This growth and success, in turn, has helped Design Basics, Inc. define their mission statement, "Bringing People Home." All the design products and services as well as each employee are a part of a culminating effort to help people attain their dream home.

CARMICHAEL AND DAME

It was 1986 when two small-volume builders, Patrick Carmichael and Robert Dame, merged their efforts and began designing and building homes for Houston's upper-end housing market. Carmichael's forte was in finance and business management; Dame's was in translating buyers' ideas into exquisite designs. The blend of their natural talents led them to their design/build firm, Carmichael and Dame. In 1994, with more than 300 designs accumulated, Carmichael and Dame made the decision to market designs nationwide by teaming up with Design Basics, Inc. one of Americas leading home plan design firms.

Carmichael and Dame plans are nothing meticulous, averaging 20-35 pages in length with specifications as detailed as the dimension of every piece of moulding. Unlike most plan services, each of the designs have been built by its own building division, ensuring the structural soundness and buildability of each plan as a result, Carmichael and Dame is able to provide builders and consumers with both technical and construction support throughout the building process. In addition, elegant watercolor renderings are available for each of their designs, as well as a Contract Development package - a complete materials specifications and quantities reference guide. Through itsr products and designs, Carmichael and Dame hope to rekindle the passion for excellence. "One of my dreams is that the craftsman aspect of design will return to the building industry in America as it was before the turn of the century," Dame says. "Our company has tried to do that by providing designs and products with a higher level of detail, craftsmanship, architectural significance and quality."

ALAN MASCORD DESIGN ASSOCIATES, INC.

Founded in 1983, Alan Mascord Design Associates, Inc. has developed an outstanding reputation in the industry for providing innovative, buildable stock plans. Mascord first began working with local builders, providing them with great plans for their projects. Soon it became apparent that these homes could be marketed nationwide;they began a direct mail program to reach builders in other areas. This success led to publishing opportunities and soon the company's plans were being featured in several national magazines.

Always interested in providing the best possible plans available, Mascord has wholeheartedly embraced the Computer Aided Design (CAD) technology. Starting in 1986, everything Alan Mascord Design Associates, Inc. has drawn has been on CAD. This has greatly improved the quality of its drawings and the efficiency of the drafting staff. Mascord, a professional member of the A.I.B.D. and the National Association of Home Builders, has been designing homes for 25 years. "In addition to projects all over the country, many of our homes have been built in Japan by the Mitsui Company, one of the biggest builders in Japan," says Mascord.

MICHAEL E. NELSON AND ASSOCIATES, INC.

At Michael E. Nelson and Associates, Inc. creativity, craftsmanship and technology are combined to form a unique offering in the home plan industry. By utilizing computer-aided drawing technology, Michael E. Nelson and his staff produce accurate and complete designs for individuals, designers and home builders throughout the United States, producing quality designs for over ten years. Michael E. Nelson & Associates' blend of creativity and technology has brought the firm recognition through several national publications and from the American Institute of Building Designers.

A constant quest for customer satisfaction has driven Nelson and Associates to produce a portfolio of plans that meet the needs of a diverse marketplace. The vast collection of plans range from traditional to contemporary, and can be modified to suit the special needs of clients. This collection of plans brings years of experience and insight together to form an invaluable resource to home builders and individuals alike.

VAUGHN A. LAUBAN DESIGNS

Vaughn A. Lauban Designs was established in 1976 incorporating Southern traditional and Creole farmhouse styles into its designs, Vaughn A. Lauban Designs has flourished. The company's home style developed a national market with its "Back to Basics" designs. With stock plans in demand in all 50 states and several foreign countries, Vaughn A. Lauban purchased a small office building, expanded, and remodeled it to reflect this Early American feeling. "We still concentrate on the farmhouse designs, although now with additional designers on staff, Midwestern and European designs are drafted to satisfy a demanding market,"

says Vaughn A. Lauban.

SELECT HOME DESIGNS

With nearly 50 years of experience delivering top-quality and affordable residential designs to

the North American housing market, Select Home Designs is proud to continue that tradition. Since the company's inception in 1948, more than 350,000 new homes throughout North America and overseas have been built from Select Home Design plans. The Select Home Design team, however, is never content to rest on its laurels, and is constantly striving to develop the best new plans for today's lifestyles. With an outstanding collection of proven plans, virtually every architectural style and influence is represented, many featuring the latest design innovations: lavish master bathrooms, dramatic foyers, unique staircase designs, and generous use of outdoor living spaces such as decks, porches and patios. One of the most important features of a Select Home Designs plan is the flexibility it offers- which is always an important factor to consider when building a new home.

FILLMORE DESIGN GROUP

Fillmore Design Group was formed in

1960 by Robert L. Fillmore, president and founder. Over the years, the firm has grown to 12 designers and draftspeople. Fillmore designs are often characterized by their European influences, massive brick gables and high flowing, graceful roof lines". We spend considerable time on detail, particularly brick detail, and we often place a fireplace with decorative brick patterns along the front facade for focus and interest. In fact, this attention to detail extends inside the home and pays off in terms of handsome, finely wrought moulding, cornices, and other interior detailing," says Fillmore. "Each plan is done in our office by one of our experienced designers under close supervision and is checked and rechecked for accuracy before leaving the office," explains Fillmore. "Each plan is carefully thought out, down to the smallest detail by our design group. We pay attention to such items as traffic flow, open rooms with tall ceiling heights and window openings, while at the same time think of furniture placement and wall space. We try to allow plenty of storage areas, large kitchens with good work patterns, luxurious and exciting master baths and spacious master bedrooms." Fillmore Design Group belongs to the American Institute of Building Designers and the National Association of Home Builders. The company's work has been featured in various national publications.

How To Work With An Interior Designer

The preliminaries

People hire interior designers for a variety of reasons. Some people realize that they don't have the skill or imagination to handle the job. Others don't have the time. And still others want an image - "drop-dead" chic, slick contemporary, or "instant-heritage" traditional. They hire a designer known for a particular look who can help them achieve the image they want.

A good interior designer is an interpreter who translates your *tastes* and needs into an environment that is comfortable, functional, and pleasing to look at.

The specifics

Shortly after agreeing to work with you, the designer will probably draw up a contract.

Although there is no set system of fees in the interior design business, most designers charge clients in one of several ways, or in combination:

By the hour: Some designers charge by the hour when the job is small. Others charge by the hour regardless of the scope of the job.

***Flat fee*:** Usually arrived at based on the extent of the work and the amount of time the designer gauges it will take to complete the job.

Percentage: Some designers charge a percentage of what the total job - concept, labor, and materials - will cost, usually 20 to 30 percent, as their design fee.

Mark-up: If not charged hourly, services will be included in the retail price.

It is the designer's responsibility to come up with a plan that fits your budget. If the estimates for the job come in higher than the original budget, it's up to the designer to rework the design so that it stays in line with the amount you originally intended to spend.

Your role

Realize that the interior designer is one of the last custom professionals. The dressmaker, milliner, and bootmaker have all vanished. But the interior designer continues to produce custom one-of-a-kind design work. Custom work takes time.

You should also be aware that the interior designer is an intermediary. He or she relies on a fleet of other professionals - painters, upholsterers and specialized craftsmen - to get the job done. Foul-ups do occur. The sofa may get delayed at the upholsterer's. The painter may get backed up in his work schedule. The custom-dyed fabric that was supposed to be delicate peach could arrive in bright orange. Be prepared for setbacks.

You can sit passively by and let the designer choose everything for you. But, if you get engaged in the process, it will be much more exciting. Most designers welcome the client who shows an active interest as the transformation takes place. Working with the designer to select accent pieces, accessories, and antiques is the best way to become involved in the process, since it allows you to add your personality to the environment the professional is creating. And it's a sure way to be entirely satisfied with the final look of the room.

Carol J. Guess, ISID

Please, Help Us To Help You

In order to ensure that our Design America series best serves your needs, please assist us by filling out the questionnaire below. As a token of our appreciation, we'll send you a **FREE CATALOG** of **Project Plan Ideas**. (Please check the correct responses.)

1. Is this book your
   - ❏ 1st home plan book
   - ❏ 2nd home plan book
   - ❏ 3rd home plan book
   - ❏ ____________ plan book

2. What prompted you to buy this Design America book?
   - ❏ Number of plans offered
   - ❏ Various plan styles
   - ❏ Customization
   - ❏ Looking for building ideas
   - ❏ Book category
   - ❏ Helpful articles

3. How long have you been searching for your dream home plan?
   - ❏ 0 - 6 months
   - ❏ 7 - 12 months
   - ❏ 12 - 24 months
   - ❏ More than two years

4. Would you like information on financing your dream home?
   - ❏ Yes
   - ❏ No

5. Are you looking for land to build on, if so, where?
   - ❏ Yes ______________________
   ____

6. When do you plan to begin construction of your new home?
   - ❏ 0 - 6 months
   - ❏ 6 - 12 months
   - ❏ Within 2 years
   - ❏ Not sure, gathering materials

7. How much do you plan to spend on materials on your new home (excluding land)?
   - ❏ Less than $100,000
   - ❏ $100,000 - $149,000
   - ❏ $150,000 - $199,000
   - ❏ More than $200,000

8. What style of home do you plan on building?
   - ❏ Traditional ❏ Multi Family
   - ❏ Colonial ❏ Country
   - ❏ Contemporary ❏ Vacation
   - ❏ Ranch ❏ Victorian
   - ❏ Other ______________________

9. What additional information could we provide that would make it easier for you to build your dream home? (Please check all that apply)
   - ❏ Rear elevations
   - ❏ Interior elevations
   - ❏ Colored photographs of the homes
   - ❏ Approximate cost to build
   - ❏ More articles related to the home building process.
   - ❏ Other______________________

10. Are you a . . . ?
    - ❏ Consumer ❏ Building Trades
    - ❏ Professional Builder/Contractor

11. In what type of residence do you currently live?
    - ❏ Single family home ❏ Townhouse
    - ❏ Condo / co-op ❏ Apartment
    - ❏ Other

12. The population of the city, town you currently reside?
    - ❏ less than 20,000 ❏ 83,000-100,000
    - ❏ 21,000-41,000 ❏ 101,000- +
    - ❏ 42,000-82,000

13. What is your gross annual household income - before taxes?
    - ❏ Under $30,000
    - ❏ $31,000 - $60,000
    - ❏ $61,000 - $80,000
    - ❏ $81,000 - $100,000
    - ❏ $101,000 +

Mail or fax to: *NATIONAL PLAN SERVICE USA, INC., 222 JAMES ST., BENSENVILLE, IL 60106*

NAME ____

ADDRESS ____

CITY ____

STATE __________ ZIP ______________ PHONE (_____) ____________

PLEASE FAX TO ***1-800-344-4293***

Design America Your Blueprints For Success

Our Blueprint Package contains nearly everything you need to get the job done properly and accurately, whether you're acting as your own general contractor or with help from an architect, designer, builder or subcontractors. Each Blueprint Package is the result of many hours of work by licensed architects or professional designers.

ACCURACY & QUALITY

Our staff of architects and professional designers have developed blueprints to ensure accuracy and quality.

VALUE

Purchase professional quality blueprints at a fraction of their development cost. With Design America, your dream home plan is attainable.

PROMPT SERVICE

Once you've chosen your dream home plan, fax your order to 1-800-344-4293 or call toll free at 1-800-533-4350. Upon receipt of your order, we will process it quickly!

SATISFACTION

With over 80 years of quality service to home plan buyers; past, present, and future, our experience and knowledge have made us a premier home plan company.

ORDER TOLL FREE

1-800-533-4350 or Fax 1-800-344-4293

After you've chosen your home plan package, simply mail or fax the accompanying order form on page 33 or call toll free on our Blueprint Hotline: 1-800-533-4350. We're ready to assist you in building your dream home.

- **HOUSE SECTIONS**
- **DETAILED FLOOR PLANS**
- **EXTERIOR ELEVATIONS**
- **INTERIOR ELEVATIONS**
- **FOUNDATION PLANS**
- **COVER SHEETS**
- **MATERIAL LIST**

Each set of blueprints is a collection of floor plans, exterior & interior elevations, details, cross-sections, diagrams and general notes showing precisely how your house is to be constructed.

Your Plans Will Show:

Cover Sheet

This artist's sketch of the exterior of the house, done in perspective, gives you an idea of how the house will look after it is built. This is only an artistic conception and may vary from actual working drawings.

Exterior Elevations

Drawn in 1/4-inch or 1/8-inch scale show the front, rear and sides of your house. General notes on exterior materials and finishes. A generic site plan may be incorporated in your blueprints.

Foundation Plan

Drawn to 1/4-inch scale, this sheet shows the complete foundation layout including support walls, excavated and unexcavated areas, if any, and foundation details. Specify slab construction, basement, or crawl when ordering.

Detailed Floor Plans

Completed in 1/4-inch scale, these plans show the layout of each floor of the house. All rooms and interior spaces are carefully dimensioned and keys are provided for cross-section details given later in the plans. The positions of all electrical outlets and switches are incorporated in this sheet.

House Sections

Large-scale cut-away views, normally drawn at 3/8-inch or 1/2-inch equals 1 foot, show sections or cut-away of the foundation, interior walls, exterior walls, floors, and roof areas. Additional cross-sections are given to show important changes in floor, ceiling or roof heights or the relationship of one level to another. Extremely valuable for construction, these sections show how the various parts of the house fit together.

Interior Elevations

These large-scale drawings show the design and placement of kitchen and bathroom cabinets, laundry areas, fireplaces, bookcases and other features. Little "extras," such as mantelpiece and wainscoting drawings, plus moulding sections, provide details that give your home that custom touch.

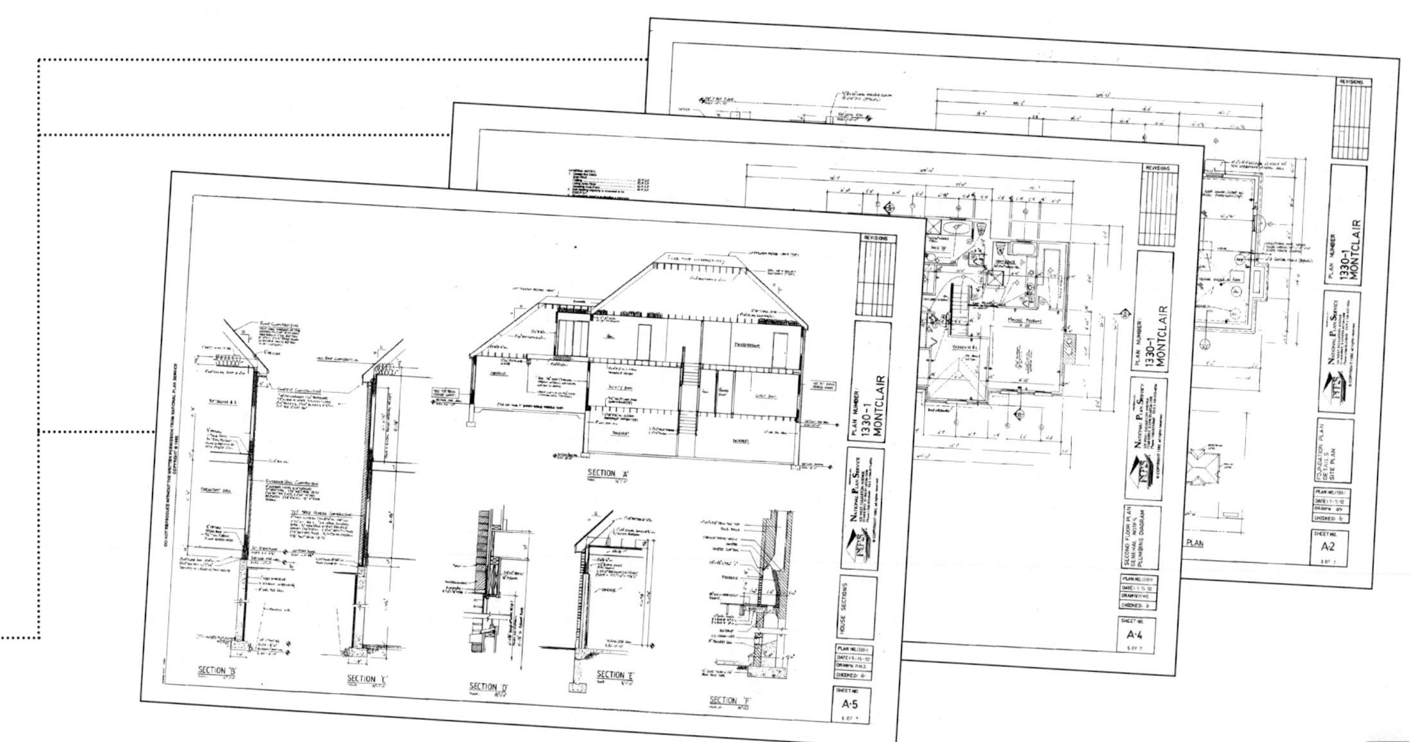

REVISIONS
PLAN NUMBER
1330-1 MONTCLAIR
SECTION 'A'
HOUSE SECTIONS
A-5
A-4
A2

Design America Options and Services

Reversed
As Shown

Reversed Plans

Have you ever thought you've found the perfect home plan only the garage or porch is on the wrong side? The solution to this problem is in reversed, or "mirror image" plans. We can send one full set of "mirror image" plans (although the text will appear backwards) as a master guide for you and your builder.

Financing Your New Home Program

Questions? Call our mortgage specialist at **1-800-533-4350**

Interior Design Services

Looking for the right image for your new home? We can help you with the right interior design image for your new home! Call our interior design expert at **1-800-533-4350**

Modifying Your Design America Home Plan

If you are considering making major changes to your design, we strongly recommend that you purchase our reproducible vellums and use the services of a professional designer, architect or ask our Design America staff. For this valuable service please call **1-800-533-4350 Architectural Dept.**

Our Reproducible Vellums and Mylars Make Modifications Easy

With a reproducible copy of our plans, a design professional can alter the drawings just the way you want. You can print as many copies of the modified plans as you need. And, since you have already started with our complete detailed plans, the cost of expensive professional services will be significantly less. Refer to the price schedule for vellums and mylars.

Don't Forget To Order Your Materials List

Our material list can help you save money. Available at a modest additional charge, the Materials List provides the quantity, dimensions, and specifications for the major materials needed to build your home. You will get faster, more accurate bids from your contractors and building suppliers. Materials Lists are available for most home plans, and can only be ordered with a set of plans. Due to differences in regional requirements and homeowner or builder preferences; electrical, plumbing and heating/ air conditioning equipment specifications are not designed specifically for each plan.

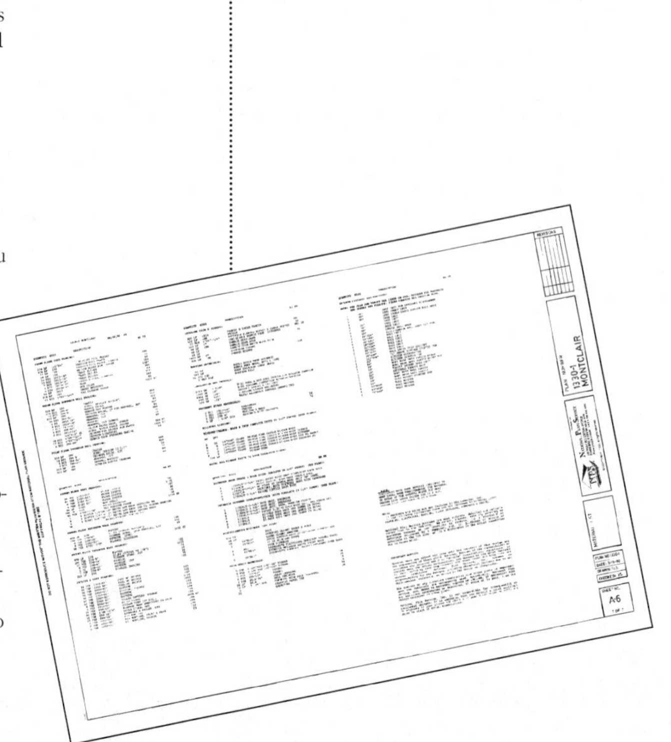

How Many Sets Of Plans Will You Need?

Single-Set Package

We offer this set so you can study the blueprints to plan your dream home in detail. Please NOTE that the Plans in this publication are copyrighted, therefore the plans cannot be reproduced. **Ignoring Copyright laws can be a costly mistake.**

The Standard 4-Set Construction Package

- First set is for yourself.
- Second set is for your builder.
- Third set is for your village or municipality.*
- Fourth set is for your bank.

The Contractor 7-Set Construction Package

- First set is for yourself.
- Second set is for your builder.
- Third set is for your village or municipality.*
- Fourth set is for your bank.
- Fifth set is for a plumbing contractor.
- Sixth set is for a heating contractor.
- Seventh set is for additional bids.

Generic Details for the Home Builder

Because local codes and requirements vary greatly, we recommend that you obtain drawings and bids from licensed contractors to complete your mechanical plans. However, if you want to know more about techniques— and deal more confidently with subcontractors—we offer these remarkably useful detail sheets. Each is an excellent tool that will enhance your understanding of these technical subjects.

Residential Construction Details

Eight sheets feature the essentials of stick-built residential home construction. Detailed foundation options - poured concrete basement, concrete block, or monolithic concrete slab. Shows all aspects of floor, wall, and roof framing. Provides details for roof dormer, eaves, and skylights. Conforms to requirements of Uniform Building code or BOCA code.

$14.95 each

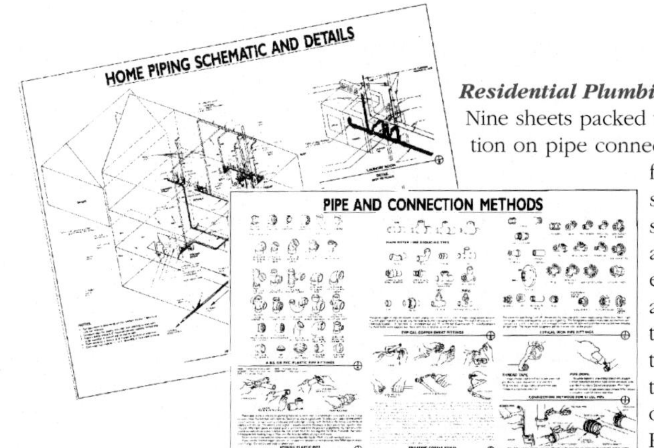
HOME PIPING SCHEMATIC AND DETAILS
PIPE AND CONNECTION METHODS

Residential Plumbing Details

Nine sheets packed with information on pipe connection methods, fittings, and sizes. Shows sump pump and water softener hookups, and septic system construction. Conforms to requirements of National Plumbing Code. Color coded with a glossary of terms. **$14.95** each

Residential Electrical Details

Nine sheets that depict all aspects of residential wiring, from simple switch wiring to the complexities of three-phase and service entrance connection. Explains service load calculations and distribution panel wiring. Shows you how to create a floor plan wiring diagram. Conforms to requirements of National Electrical Code. Color coded with a glossary of terms.

$14.95 each

Detail Plan Prices

Purchase any two (2) sets for only $22.96 or all three (3) for $29.97. See the Order Form on page 33.

Important Shipping Information

Your order is processed immediately. Allow 10 working days from our receipt of your order for normal UPS delivery. Save time with your credit card and our "800" number. UPS must have a street address or Rural Route Box number—never a post office box. Use a work address if no one is home during the day. Please call for international shipping information.

AN IMPORTANT NOTE:

1) All plans are drawn to conform to one or more of the building industry's major national building standards at the time and place they were drawn. However, due to the variety of local building regulations, your plan may need to be modified to comply with local requirements—snow loads, energy loads, seismic zones, etc. We strongly recommend that you consult with your local building officials or local architect for required information on submission of permit documents.

2) Detail plans are generic and do not conform specifically to the house plan that you purchase.

*Multiple sets of documents (blueprints) may be required by your local village or municipality building depts.

1. **Choose your Design America Plan**

2. **Would you like to customize your blueprints to your family's needs and lifestyle?**

   If YES: Talk to one of our blueprints experts at 1-800-533-4350 or in Illinois 630-238-0555

   If NO: Order the design number indicated at the top of the page, determine number of sets needed and specify if you are ordering a plan with foundation options; basement, crawl space, slab, pier.

3. **Upon having made your decision as to the design you wish to purchase, we recommend you order them through the Lumber yard, Home Center, or Hardware dealer who provided you with this book. Your local Lumber yard, Home Center, or Hardware dealer can give you valuable information and suggestions on you new dream home. Or mail, phone or fax us your blueprint order or customization request and we will process your order quickly. For accurate processing of your order please enclose check, money order, cashiers check or Master card/Visa information with the plan design number and order form (Page 33) To:**

NPS Design America, Inc.
Slot A-1
P.O. Box 66973 **DA 1000**
Chicago, Illinois 60666-0973
Ph. 1-800-533-4350 • 630-238-0555
Fax 1-800-344-4293 • 630-238-8885

Blueprint Prices

The cost of having an architect design a new custom home typically runs from 4 to 10 percent of the total construction cost, or from $4,000 to $10,000 for a $100,000 home. A single set of blueprints for the plans in this book ranges from $195 to $720, depending on the size of the house. Working with existing drawings may save you enough money on design fees to enable you to build a deck, upgrade your materials, or design a luxurious kitchen. Please note : garages, porches, decks, and unfinished basements are not included with the total living area, unless noted.

What will it cost to Build?

As noted in one of the articles, it is best to find out how much you can qualify for prior to building. Building cost vary widely from region to region, depending on a number of factors, including local material availability and labor costs, and the finished materials selected.

Foundation Options & Exterior Construction

Depending on your site conditions and region, your home will be built with a slab, pier, pole, crawlspace, or basement foundation. Exterior walls will be framed with either 2 by 4's or 2 by 6's, determined by structural and insulation standards in your area. Consult with your local building official in your area. Most contractors can easily adapt a home to meet the foundation and/or wall requirements for your area.

Service & Blueprint Delivery

Blueprint representatives are available to answer questions and assist you in placing your order. Plans are delivered via U.S. Mail or UPS.

Returns & Exchanges

Blueprints are specially printed and shipped to you in response to your specific order, consequently, requests for refunds cannot be honored.

Local Codes & Regulations

Because of climactic, geographic, and governmental policies set by your municipality, building codes and regulations vary from one area to another. These plans are authorized for your use only on the expressed consent that you oblige and agree to comply with all local building codes, ordinances, regulations, and requirements, including permits and inspections at time of construction.

Architectural & Engineering Seals

With increased concern about energy cost and safety, many cities and states require that an architect or engineer review and "seal" a blueprint prior to construction. To find whether this is a requirement in your area, contact your local building department.

License Agreement, Copy Restrictions & Copyright

When you purchase your blueprints, you are granted the right to use these documents to construct a single unit. All the plans in this publication are protected under the Federal Copyright Act, Title XVII of the United States Code and Chapter 37 of the Code of Federal Regulations. Each designer retains title and ownership of the original documents. The blueprints licensed to you cannot be used by or resold to any other person, copied, or reproduced by any means. The copying restrictions do not apply to reproducible blueprints. When you purchase a reproducible set of mylars or vellums, you may modify and reproduce it for your own use.

AN IMPORTANT NOTE:

1) All plans are drawn to conform to one or more of the building industry's major national building standards at the time and place they were drawn. However, due to the variety of local building regulations, your plan may need to be modified to comply with local requirements—snow loads, energy loads, seismic zones, etc. We strongly recommend that you consult with your local building officials or local architect for required information on submission of permit documents.
2) Detail plans are generic and do not conform specifically to the house plan that you purchase.

*Multiple sets of documents (blueprints) may be required by your local village or municipality building depts.

PRICE CODE*

	A	B	C	D	E	F
BLUEPRINTS (Material List subject to availability)						
One Set of Blueprints	$195.00	$230.00	$275.00	$320.00	$520.00	$720.00
Four Sets of Blueprints	$265.00	$310.00	$355.00	$400.00	$1,020.00	$1,220.00
Seven Sets of Blueprints	$320.00	$360.00	$405.00	$450.00	$1,420.00	$1,620.00
Reproducible Vellum (1 Set)	$480.00	$540.00	$600.00	$675.00	$1,645.00	$1,845.00
Reproducible Mylar (1Set)	$500.00	$560.00	$620.00	$695.00	$1,665.00	$1,865.00
Additional regular sets	$40.00	$40.00	$40.00	$40.00	$180.00	$180.00
Mirror reverse	$40.00	$40.00	$40.00	$40.00	$180.00	$180.00
SHIPPING AND HANDLING 1-7 sets						
Regular U.S.(6-10 days)	$10.00	$13.00	$16.00	$19.00	$22.00	$25.00
Express (2-3 days)	$25.00	$28.00	$31.00	$34.00	$37.00	$40.00
Overnight*	$30.00	$33.00	$36.00	$39.00	$42.00	$45.00
Other**	Call	Call	Call	Call	Call	Call
*Not available on certain plans **For delivery outside U.S.						
MATERIAL LIST *Material list subject to availability						
1-3 copies	$40.00	$40.00	$40.00	$40.00	CALL	CALL
4-7 copies	$45.00	$45.00	$45.00	$45.00	CALL	CALL
PREVIEW PLANS (11" X 17" format)						
1 ea. B/W format*	$15.00	$15.00	$15.00	$15.00	CALL	CALL
1 ea. Colored format*	$40.00	$40.00	$40.00	$40.00	CALL	CALL
*Subject to availability						
DESIGN SHEETS (8.5" X 11" format)						
1 ea. B/W sell sheets	$25.00	$25.00	$25.00	$25.00	—	—
100 qty. ea. B/W sell sheets	$38.00	$38.00	$38.00	$38.00	—	—
200 qty. ea. B/W sell sheets	$58.00	$58.00	$58.00	$58.00	—	—
ARCHITECTURAL RENDERING OF HOME						
B/W 8"X10" PMT Format*	$89.00	$89.00	$89.00	$89.00	CALL	CALL
Colored 8"X10" PMT format*	$115.00	$115.00	$115.00	$115.00	CALL	CALL

*Subject to availability

Step 1.

BLUEPRINTS ORDER FORM

PURCHASED BOOK FROM: ____________________ TOWN: ________________

DATE BOOK WAS PURCHASED: ____________________

NAME: ________________________________

ADDRESS: ________________________________

CITY: ______________________ STATE: _____ ZIP: __________

PHONE #: (   ) ________________

Enclosed is: ❑Check ❑Money Order

Bill: ❑Visa ❑Master Card

Checks Payable to: NPS Design America, Inc.

CARD NUMBER: ____________________

EXPIRATION DATE MONTH/YEAR_____/_____

SIGNATURE

Step 2.

Plan Number ____________________ Price Code________

Foundation Type:____________________
(Many plans offer different options; others are designed to one type of condition).

Number of Sets: ____One Set ____Four Sets ____Seven Sets ____Vellum ____Mylar

Additional Sets: _____ Qty. ($40.00 Price Code A-D; Price Code E-F Call) Prices good for 60 days
Mirror Reverse:_______ ($40.00)
Material List: ________(See List)
Preview Plan Number: ________________ (See List)
Design Sheets: _____1ea. ____100 qty. ____200 qty. of Plan Number:________________
(Check appropriate space)
Architectural Rendering: _____B/W _____Colored (See List) Plan Number:________________

Send Your Order To: NPS Design America, Inc.
Slot A-1 P.O. Box 66973 Dept. DA1000, Chicago, IL, 60666-0973

Order Toll Free 1-800-533-4350 Or 24-Hour Fax Ordering 1-800-344-4293

Step 3.

Detail Plans

______**H801C Construction** @ $14.95 each
______**H802E Electrical** @ $14.95 each
______**H803P Plumbing** @ $14.95 each
Any two (2) - $22.96
Any three (3) - $29.97

Write in dollar figure

$__________Detail plans
$__________Blueprints
$__________Material List
$__________Preview Plans
$__________Design Sheets
$__________Arch Rendering
$__________Shipping & Handling
$__________Sub Total
$__________Sales Tax (IL 6.75%)
$__________**Total**

*Prices may change without notice

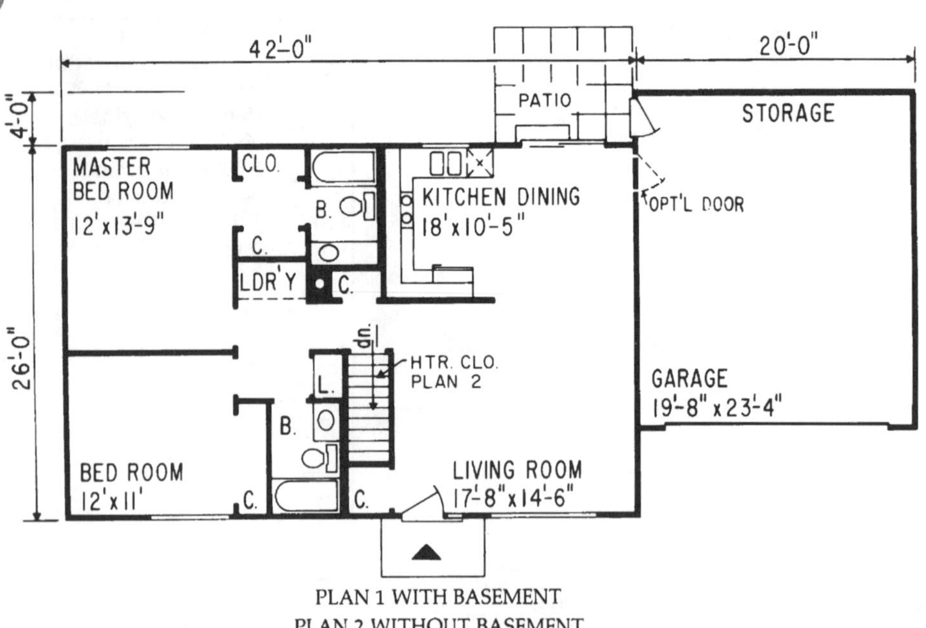
42'-0"
20'-0"
4'-0"
26'-0"
PATIO
STORAGE
MASTER BED ROOM 12'x13'-9"
CLO.
B.
C.
LDR'Y
C.
KITCHEN DINING 18'x10'-5"
OPT'L DOOR
dn.
HTR. CLO. PLAN 2
L.
B.
GARAGE 19'-8" x 23'-4"
BED ROOM 12'x11'
C.
C.
LIVING ROOM 17'-8" x 14'-6"

PLAN 1 WITH BASEMENT
PLAN 2 WITHOUT BASEMENT

Shake Cottage

Features

- Shake siding combined with vertical panel siding offers an attractive and cost-effective exterior.
- Entry into large living room.
- U-shaped kitchen with dining room.
- Access to patio from dining room.
- Master bedroom with walk-through closet and full bath.
- Second bedroom also features full bath.
- Optional attached two-car garage

Total Living Area **1,092 sq. ft.**

PRICE CODE: A

PLAN NP LEISURE TIME

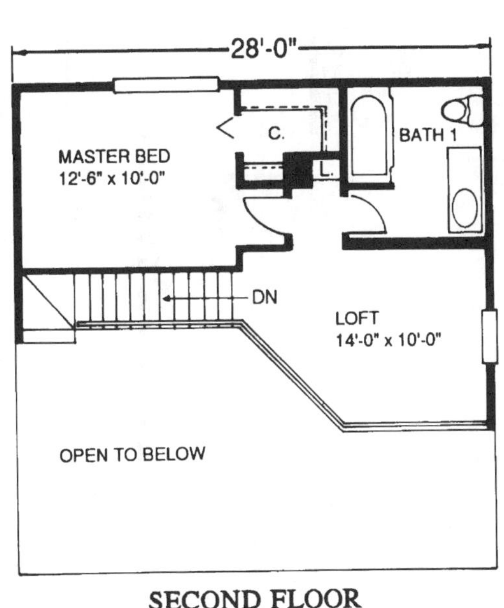

28'-0"
MASTER BED
12'-6" x 10'-0"
C.
BATH 1
L.
DN
LOFT
14'-0" x 10'-0"
OPEN TO BELOW

SECOND FLOOR

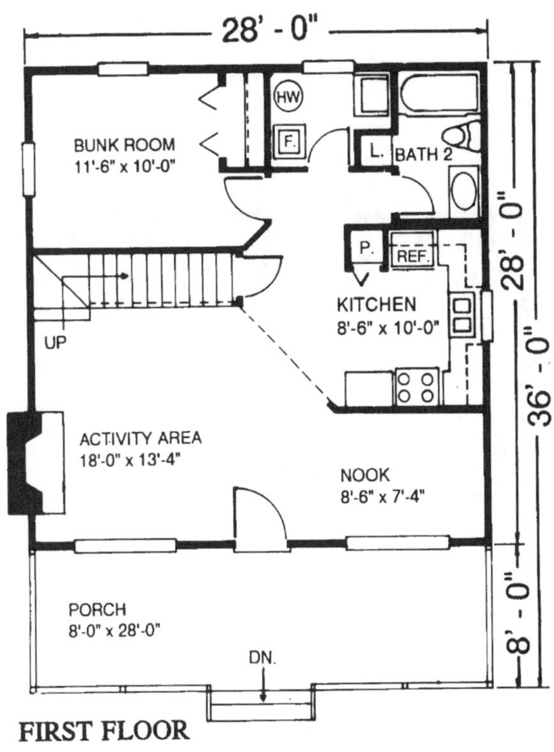

28' - 0"
BUNK ROOM
11'-6" x 10'-0"
HW
F.
L.
BATH 2
P.
REF.
KITCHEN
8'-6" x 10'-0"
UP
ACTIVITY AREA
18'-0" x 13'-4"
NOOK
8'-6" x 7'-4"
PORCH
8'-0" x 28'-0"
DN.
28' - 0"
36' - 0"
8' - 0"

FIRST FLOOR

First Floor	784 sq. ft.
Second Floor	416 sq. ft.
Total Living Area	1,200 sq. ft.

PRICE CODE: A

PLAN NP ASPEN

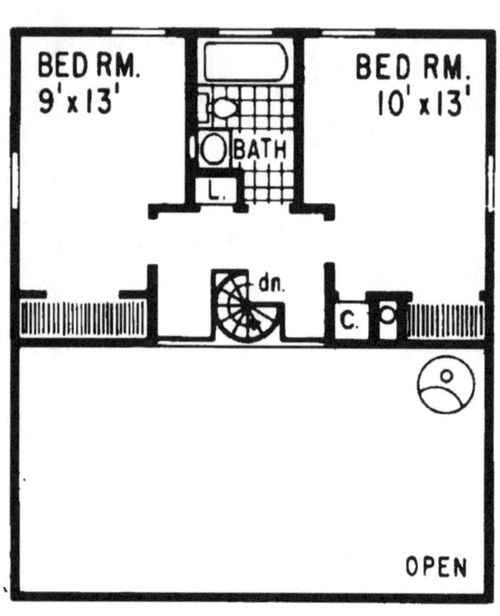
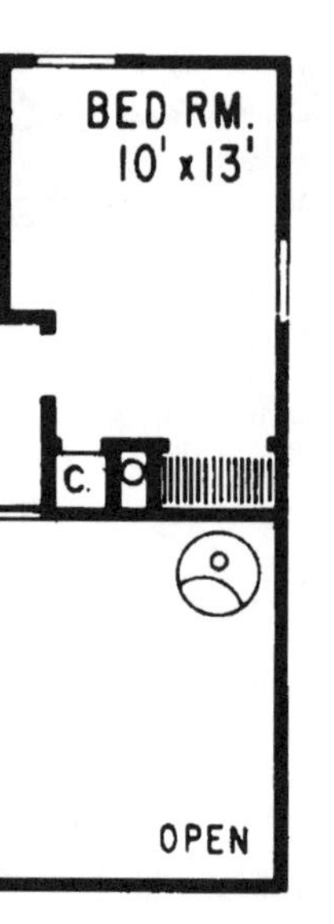
BED RM.
9'x13'
BATH
L.
BED RM.
10'x13'
dn.
C.
OPEN

SECOND FLOOR

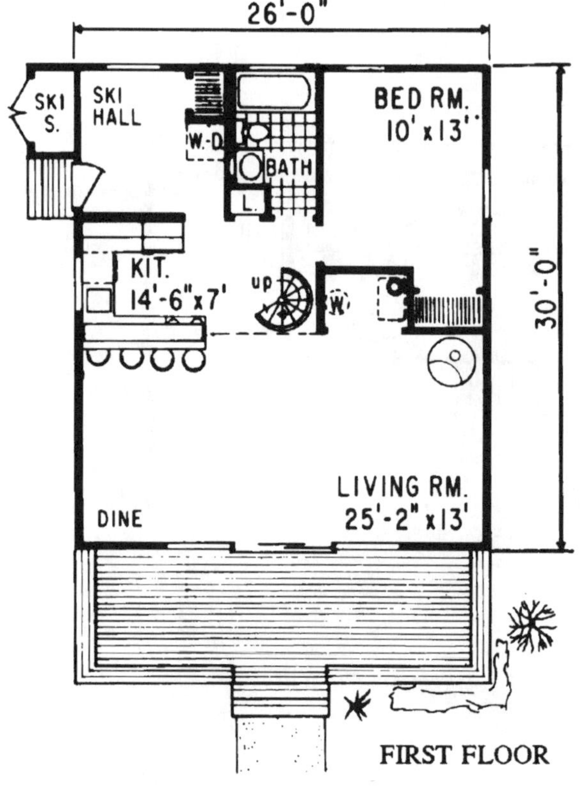
26'-0"
SKI S.
SKI HALL
W.-D.
BATH
L.
BED RM.
10'x13'
KIT.
14'-6"x7'
up
W.
30'-0"
LIVING RM.
25'-2"x13'
DINE

FIRST FLOOR

First Floor	780 sq. ft.
Second Floor	429 sq. ft.
Total Living Area	1,209 sq. ft.

PRICE CODE: A

PLAN NPHILL

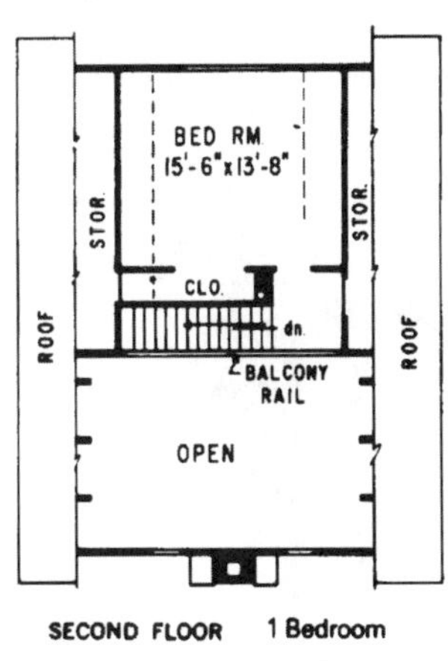

BED RM
15'-6" x 13'-8"
STOR.
STOR.
CLO.
dn.
ROOF
ROOF
BALCONY RAIL
OPEN

SECOND FLOOR 1 Bedroom

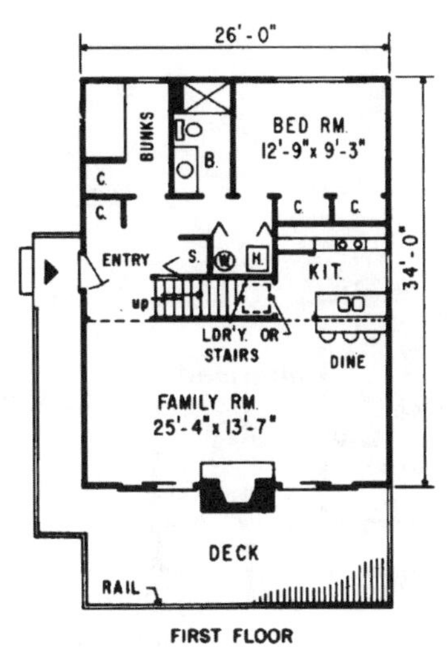

26'-0"
34'-0"
BUNKS
B.
BED RM.
12'-9" x 9'-3"
C.
C.
C.
C.
ENTRY
S.
W
H.
KIT.
up
LDR'Y. OR STAIRS
DINE
FAMILY RM.
25'-4" x 13'-7"
DECK
RAIL

FIRST FLOOR

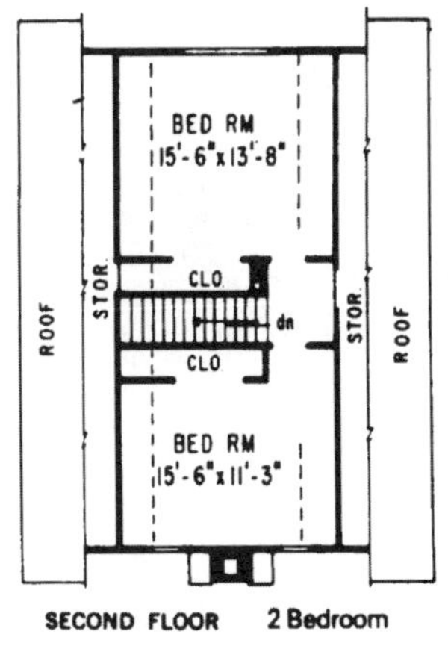

BED RM
15'-6" x 13'-8"
CLO.
dn
CLO
STOR.
STOR.
ROOF
ROOF
BED RM
15'-6" x 11'-3"

SECOND FLOOR 2 Bedroom

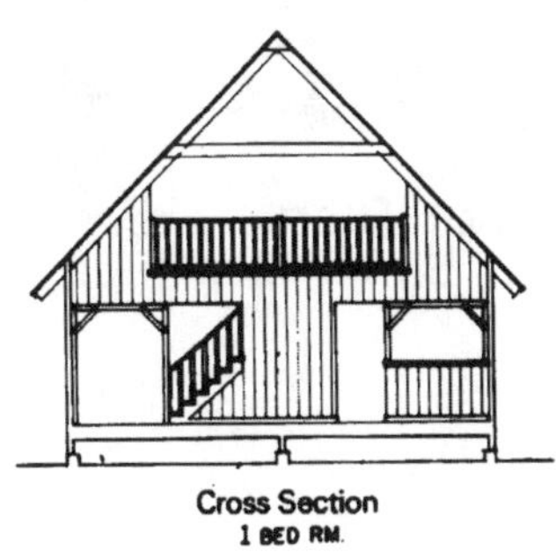

Cross Section
1 BED RM.

Total Living Area 1,211 sq. ft.

PRICE CODE: A

PLAN FD8103

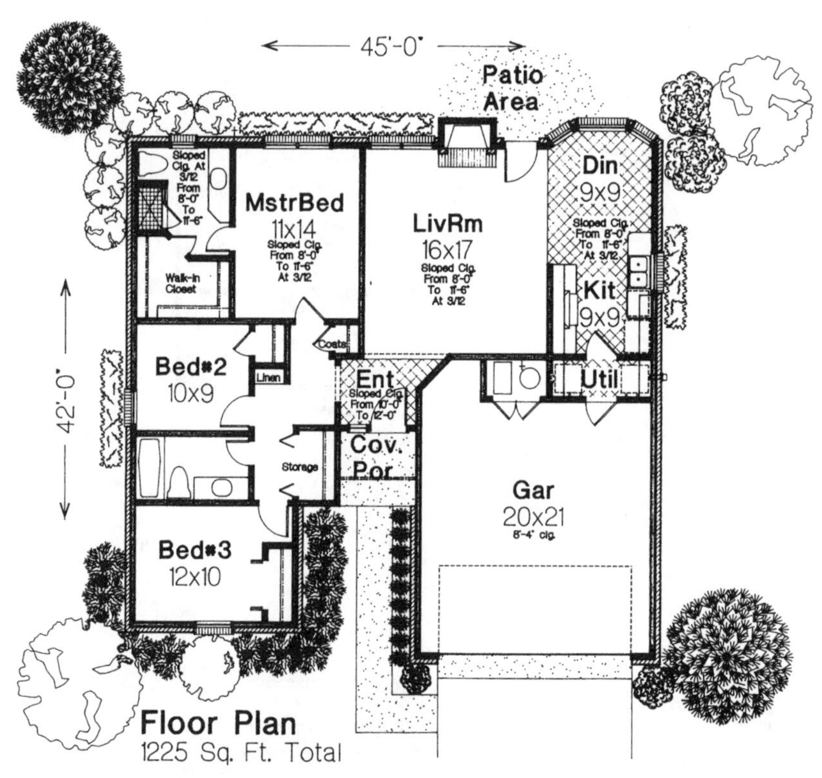
45'-0"
42'-0"
Patio Area
Sloped Clg. At 3/12 From 8'-0" To 11'-6"
MstrBed
11x14
Sloped Clg. From 8'-0" To 11'-6" At 3/12
Walk-In Closet
LivRm
16x17
Sloped Clg. From 8'-0" To 11'-6" At 3/12
Din
9x9
Sloped Clg. From 8'-0" To 11'-6" At 3/12
Kit
9x9
Coats
Bed#2
10x9
Linen
Ent
Sloped Clg. From 10'-0" To 12'-0"
Util
Storage
Cov. Por
Gar
20x21
8'-4" clg.
Bed#3
12x10
Floor Plan
1225 Sq. Ft. Total

Total Living Area 1,225 sq. ft.

PRICE CODE: A

CUSTOMIZE IT!

ORDER TOLL FREE 1-800-533-4350 24-HOUR FAX ORDERING 1-800-344-4293

PLAN NP KINGSPORT

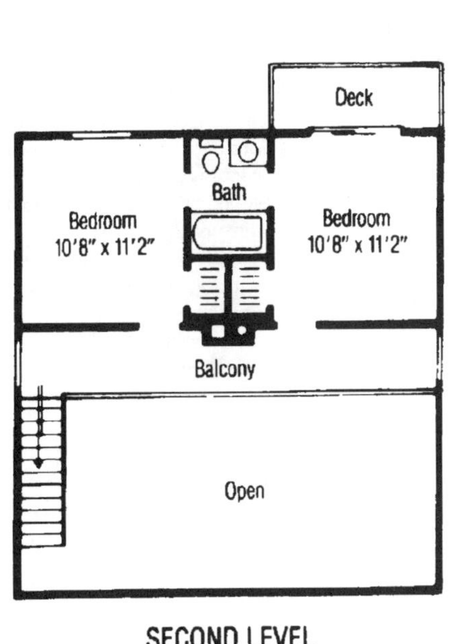
Deck
Bath
Bedroom
10'8" x 11'2"
Bedroom
10'8" x 11'2"
Balcony
Open

SECOND LEVEL

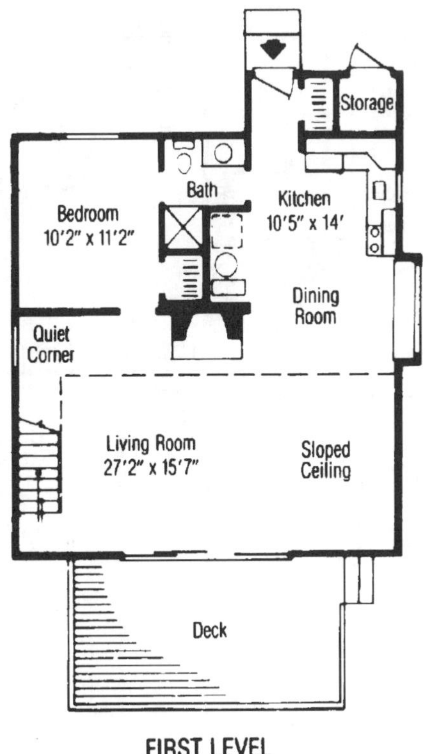
Storage
Bath
Kitchen
10'5" x 14'
Bedroom
10'2" x 11'2"
Dining
Room
Quiet
Corner
Living Room
27'2" x 15'7"
Sloped
Ceiling
Deck

FIRST LEVEL

First Floor	811 sq. ft.
Second Floor	488 sq. ft.
Total Living Area	1,299 sq. ft.

PRICE CODE: A

PLAN DB2761

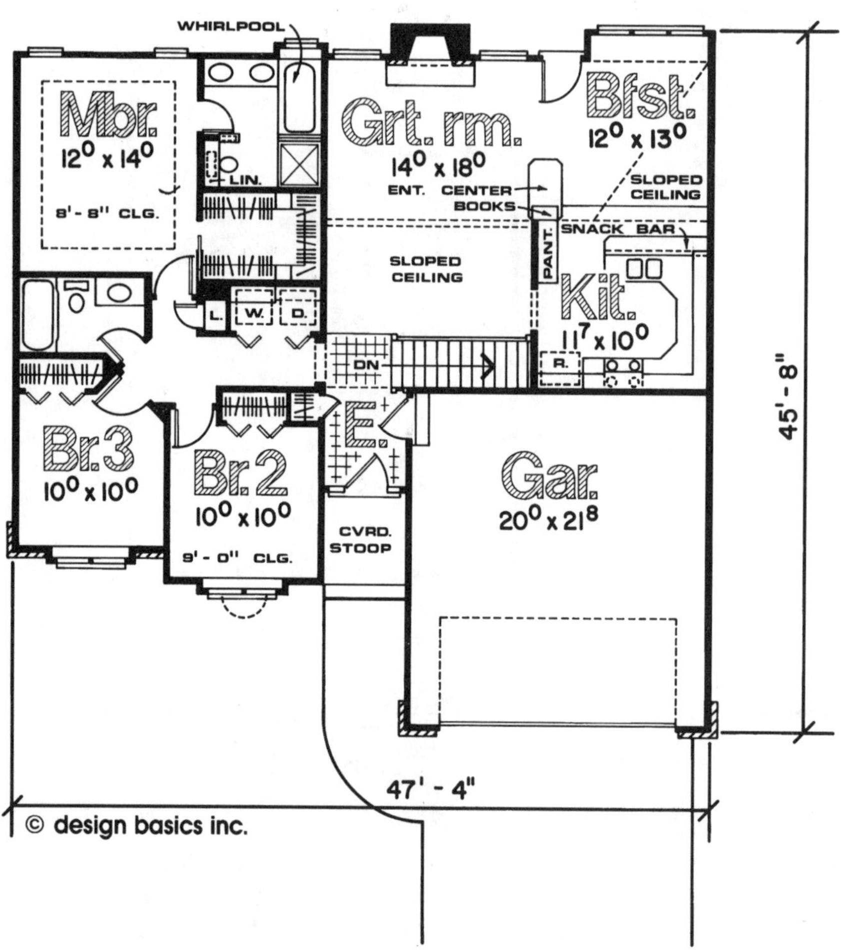

WHIRLPOOL
Mbr.
12⁰ x 14⁰
LIN.
8'-8" CLG.
Grt. rm.
14⁰ x 18⁰
ENT. CENTER
BOOKS
Bfst.
12⁰ x 13⁰
SLOPED CEILING
SNACK BAR
PANT.
SLOPED CEILING
Kit.
11⁷ x 10⁰
R.
L.
W.
D.
DN
E.
Br.3
10⁰ x 10⁰
Br.2
10⁰ x 10⁰
9'-0" CLG.
CVRD. STOOP
Gar.
20⁰ x 21⁸
45'-8"
47'-4"
© design basics inc.

40

Features

- Offering basement or alternate slab foundation, this home is the epitome of economy and efficiency.
- Sloped ceiling, and fireplace flanked by large windows expands the great room.
- Kitchen is exceptionally well planned featuring large pantry, 2 lazy Susans and snack bar serving the dinette.
- Strategically located TV cabinet/ entertainment center with lazy Susan affords viewing from great room, dinette or kitchen.
- Master suite features large walk-in closet and deluxe bath area with dual lavs and glass panel separating shower and whirlpool.

Total Living Area **1,341 sq. ft.**

PRICE CODE: C

PLAN FD6953

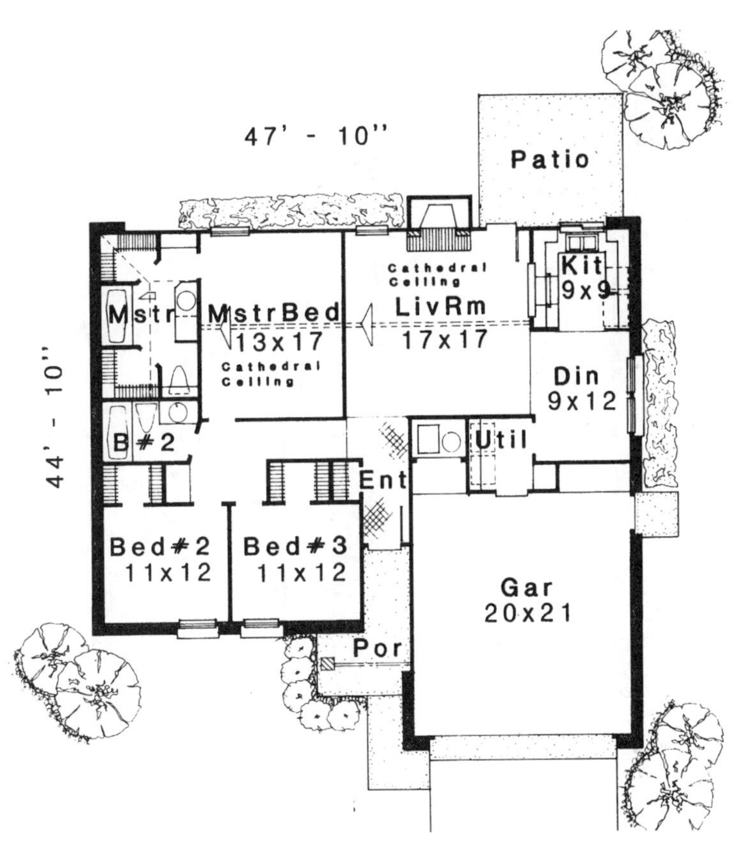
47' - 10"
44' - 10"
Patio
Cathedral Ceiling
LivRm
17x17
Kit
9x9
Mstr
MstrBed
13x17
Cathedral Ceiling
Din
9x12
B#2
Util
Ent
Bed#2
11x12
Bed#3
11x12
Gar
20x21
Por

41

Total Living Area 1,345 sq. ft.

PRICE CODE: B

PLAN MN1353

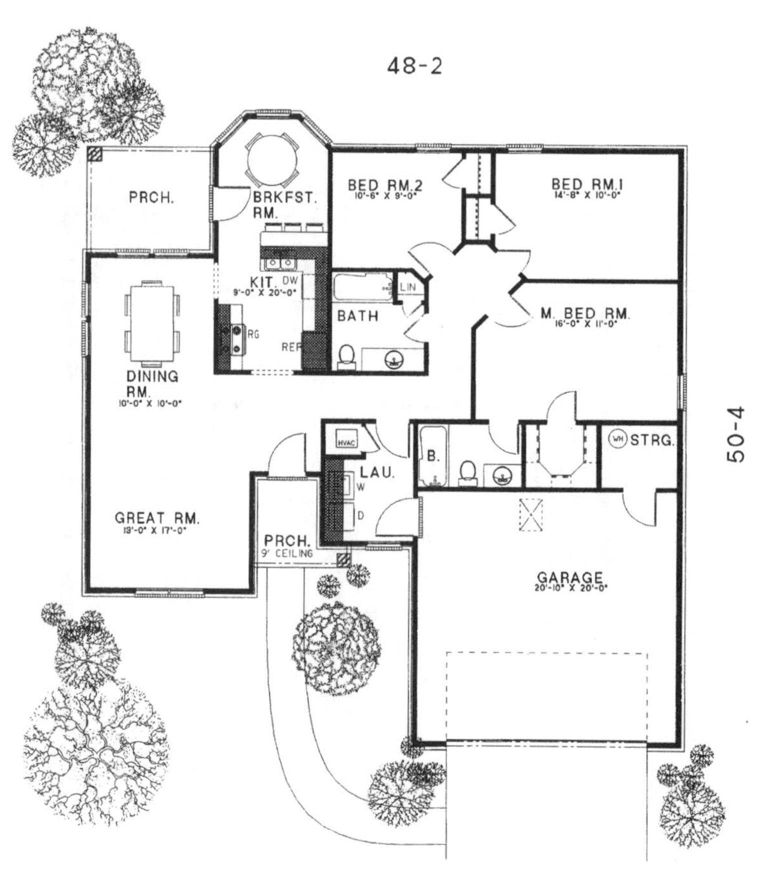
48-2
50-4
PRCH.
BRKFST. RM.
BED RM.2
10'-6" X 9'-0"
BED RM.1
14'-8" X 10'-0"
KIT.
9'-0" X 20'-0"
DW
LIN
BATH
M. BED RM.
16'-0" X 11'-0"
RG
REF
DINING RM.
10'-0" X 10'-0"
HVAC
LAU.
W
D
B.
WH
STRG.
GREAT RM.
13'-0" X 17'-0"
PRCH.
9' CEILING
GARAGE
20'-10" X 20'-0"

Total Living Area **1,353 sq. ft.**

PRICE CODE: B

PLAN NP WOODRIDGE

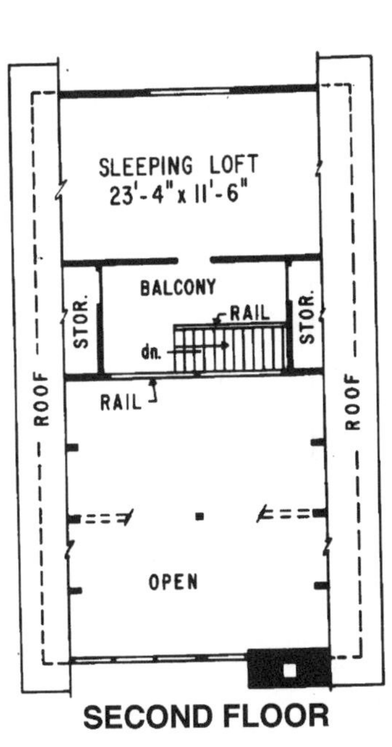
SLEEPING LOFT
23'-4" x 11'-6"
BALCONY
RAIL
STOR.
STOR.
dn.
RAIL
ROOF
ROOF
OPEN

SECOND FLOOR

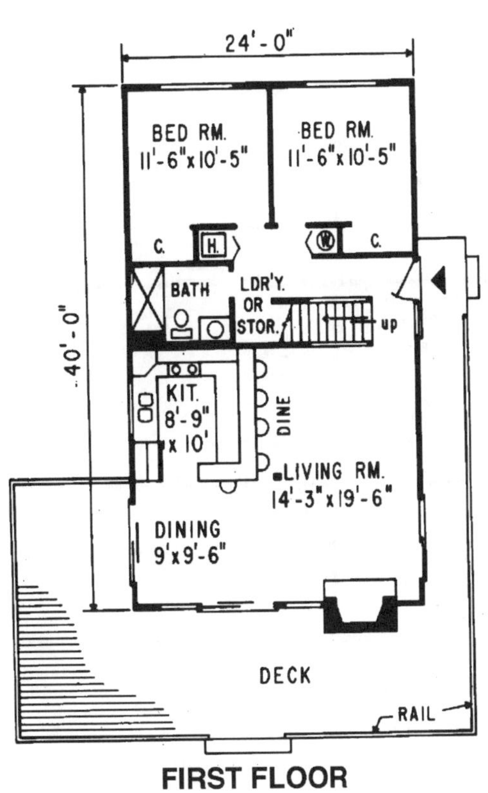
24'-0"
40'-0"
BED RM.
11'-6" x 10'-5"
BED RM.
11'-6" x 10'-5"
C.
H.
W
C.
BATH
LDR'Y. OR STOR.
up
KIT.
8'-9" x 10'
DINE
LIVING RM.
14'-3" x 19'-6"
DINING
9' x 9'-6"
DECK
RAIL

FIRST FLOOR

First Floor	960 sq. ft.
Second Floor	394 sq. ft.
Total Living Area	1,354 sq. ft.

PRICE CODE: B

PLAN NPES103

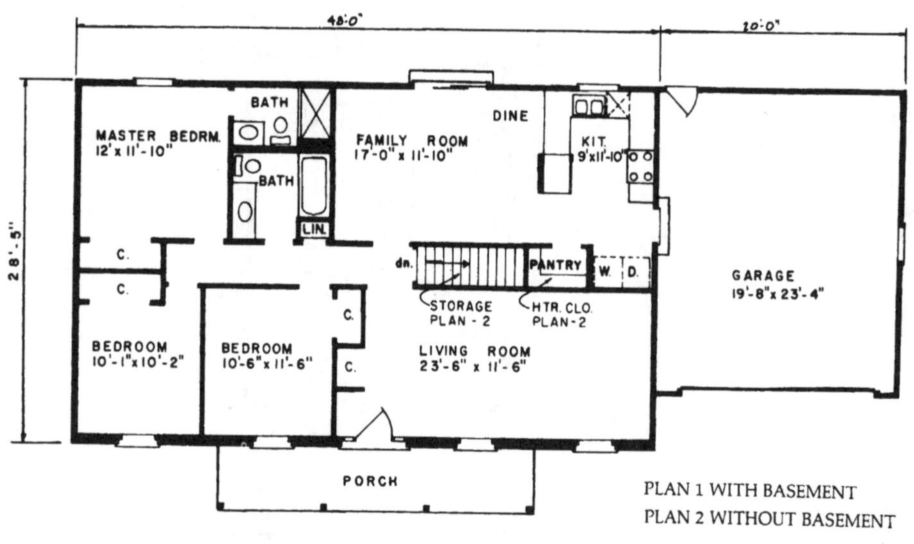

48'-0"
20'-0"
28'-5"
MASTER BEDRM.
12' x 11'-10"
BATH
BATH
LIN.
FAMILY ROOM
17'-0" x 11'-10"
DINE
KIT.
9'x11'-10"
C.
C.
C.
C.
dn.
PANTRY
W.
D.
STORAGE
PLAN - 2
HTR. CLO.
PLAN-2
GARAGE
19'-8" x 23'-4"
BEDROOM
10'-1" x 10'-2"
BEDROOM
10'-6" x 11'-6"
LIVING ROOM
23'-6" x 11'-6"
PORCH

PLAN 1 WITH BASEMENT
PLAN 2 WITHOUT BASEMENT

Features

- The look of an estate home with an affordable price tag! The U-shaped kitchen has an adjacent dining area and family room.
- Three bedrooms are clustered in the left wing.
- The master bedroom features a private bath while the other two bedrooms share a full bath.
- Truss roof construction allows you to adjust for varying roof loads.

Total Living Area **1,364 sq. ft.**

PRICE CODE: B

PLAN NP1329

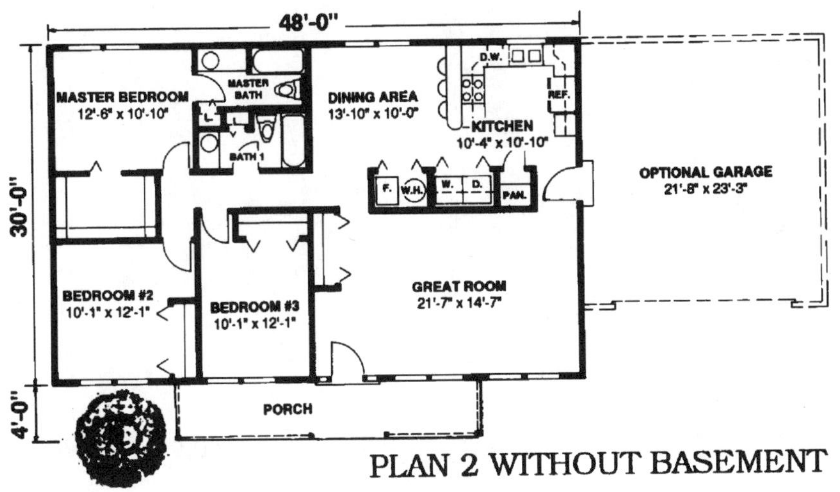

48'-0"
30'-0"
4'-0"
MASTER BEDROOM
12'-6" x 10'-10"
MASTER BATH
BATH 1
DINING AREA
13'-10" x 10'-0"
D.W.
REF.
KITCHEN
10'-4" x 10'-10"
F.
W.H.
W.
D.
PAN.
OPTIONAL GARAGE
21'-8" x 23'-3"
BEDROOM #2
10'-1" x 12'-1"
BEDROOM #3
10'-1" x 12'-1"
GREAT ROOM
21'-7" x 14'-7"
PORCH

PLAN 2 WITHOUT BASEMENT

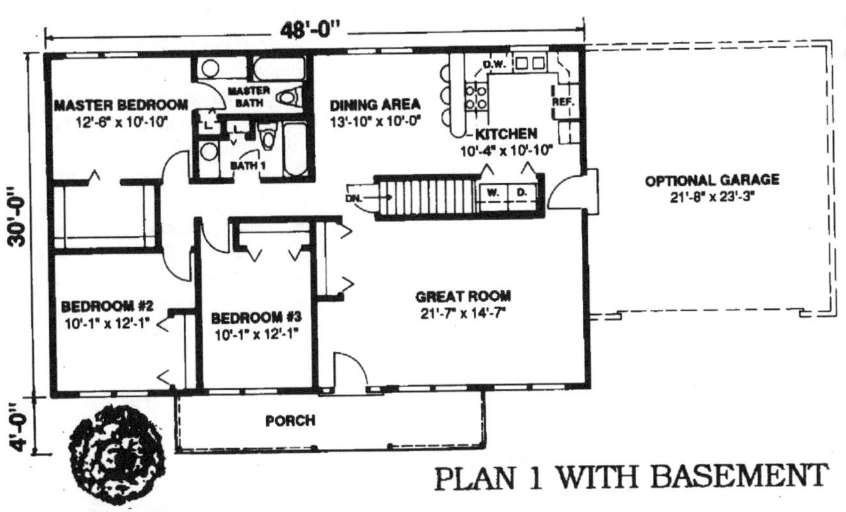

48'-0"
30'-0"
4'-0"
MASTER BEDROOM
12'-6" x 10'-10"
MASTER BATH
BATH 1
DINING AREA
13'-10" x 10'-0"
D.W.
REF.
KITCHEN
10'-4" x 10'-10"
DN.
W.
D.
OPTIONAL GARAGE
21'-8" x 23'-3"
BEDROOM #2
10'-1" x 12'-1"
BEDROOM #3
10'-1" x 12'-1"
GREAT ROOM
21'-7" x 14'-7"
PORCH

PLAN 1 WITH BASEMENT

Country Sprite

Features

- This home is an excellent choice for the first-time home buyer.
- Optional garage and optional front porch allow you to expand as your budget allows.
- U-shaped kitchen and dining area at rear of home.
- Master bedroom with private bath.
- Two additional bedrooms share one full bath.

Total Living Area 1,364 sq. ft.

PRICE CODE: B

PLAN NP1336

MALOU

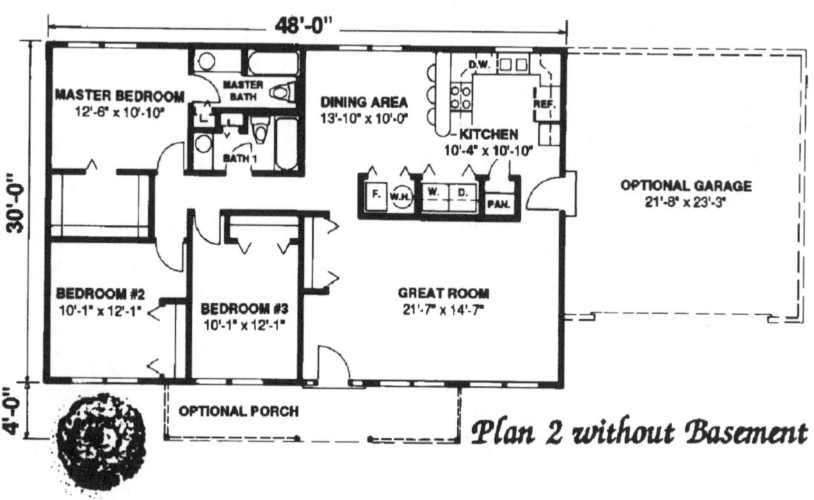
48'-0"
MASTER BEDROOM
12'-6" x 10'-10"
MASTER BATH
BATH 1
DINING AREA
13'-10" x 10'-0"
D.W.
REF.
KITCHEN
10'-4" x 10'-10"
F.
W.H.
W.
D.
PAN.
OPTIONAL GARAGE
21'-8" x 23'-3"
30'-0"
BEDROOM #2
10'-1" x 12'-1"
BEDROOM #3
10'-1" x 12'-1"
GREAT ROOM
21'-7" x 14'-7"
4'-0"
OPTIONAL PORCH

Plan 2 without Basement

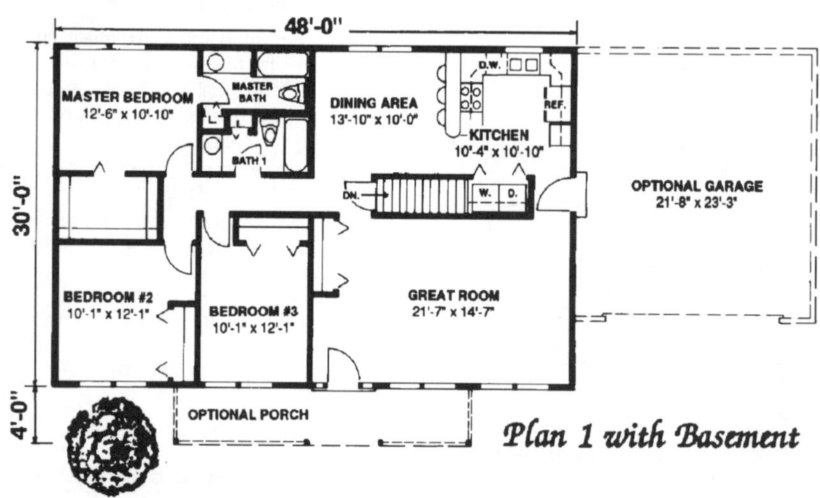
48'-0"
MASTER BEDROOM
12'-6" x 10'-10"
MASTER BATH
BATH 1
DINING AREA
13'-10" x 10'-0"
D.W.
REF.
KITCHEN
10'-4" x 10'-10"
DN.
W.
D.
OPTIONAL GARAGE
21'-8" x 23'-3"
30'-0"
BEDROOM #2
10'-1" x 12'-1"
BEDROOM #3
10'-1" x 12'-1"
GREAT ROOM
21'-7" x 14'-7"
4'-0"
OPTIONAL PORCH

Plan 1 with Basement

Country Bower

Features

- Excellent choice for first-time home buyer.
- Optional garage and optional front porch let you add to your home as your budget allows.
- Enter through the large great room in the right wing.
- U- shaped kitchen with dining area located at the rear.
- Two bedrooms share a full bath.
- Master bedroom with large walk-in closet and full bath.

Total Living Area 1,364 sq. ft.

PRICE CODE: B

PLAN DB3010

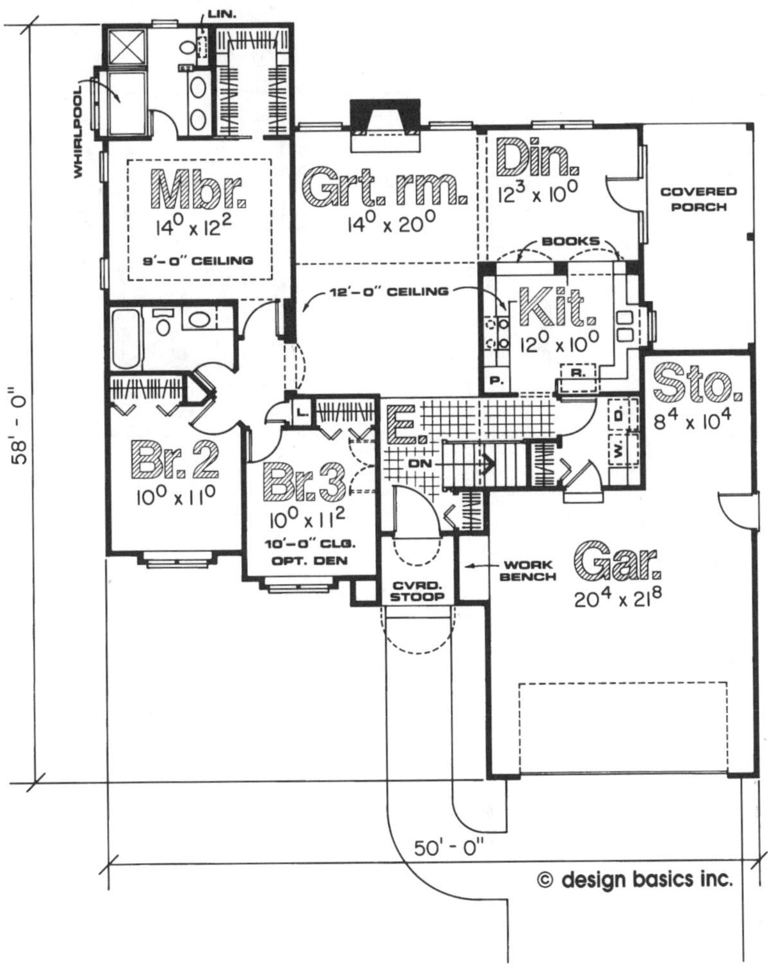

LIN.
WHIRLPOOL
Mbr.
14⁰ x 12²
9'-0" CEILING
Grt. rm.
14⁰ x 20⁰
Din.
12³ x 10⁰
COVERED PORCH
BOOKS
12'-0" CEILING
Kit.
12⁰ x 10⁰
P.
R.
Sto.
8⁴ x 10⁴
D.
W.
L.
E.
DN
Br. 2
10⁰ x 11⁰
Br. 3
10⁰ x 11²
10'-0" CLG.
OPT. DEN
WORK BENCH
Gar.
20⁴ x 21⁸
CVRD. STOOP
58' - 0"
50' - 0"
© design basics inc.

Features

- Small ranch home makes grand statement with prominent entry.
- 12-foot-tall ceiling integrates great room, semi-formal dining room and kitchen.
- Arched openings to kitchen with built-in bookcases provide dramatic backdrop for dining area.
- Efficient kitchen features 2 lazy Susans, plant shelf above upper cabinets and an airy window.
- Hall bath serves secondary bedrooms, with bedroom #3 easily optioned to a den.
- Master suite features a boxed 9-foot-high ceiling, whirlpool bath and walk-in closet.
- Space for work bench and sizeable storage area in garage.

Total Living Area 1,422 sq. ft.

PRICE CODE: C

PLAN NP1117

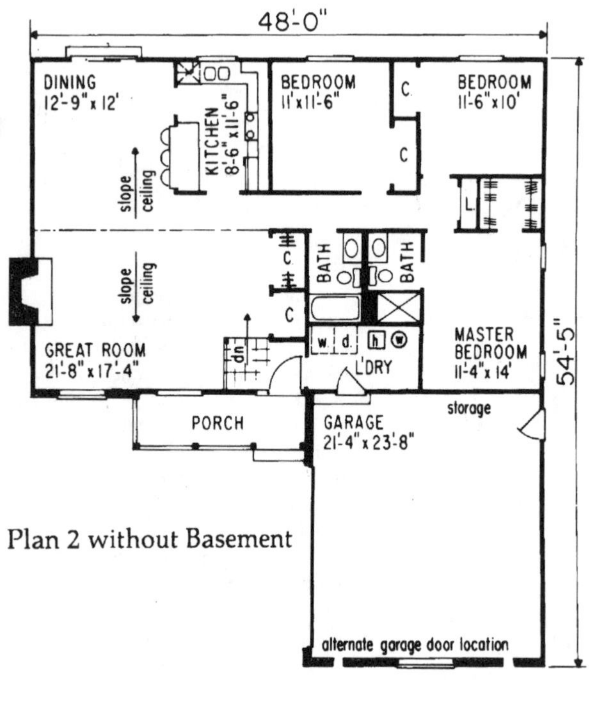
48'-0"
DINING
12'-9" x 12'
KITCHEN
8'-6" x 11'-6"
BEDROOM
11' x 11'-6"
C
BEDROOM
11'-6" x 10'
C
slope ceiling
slope ceiling
L
C
C
BATH
BATH
w d
h
GREAT ROOM
21'-8" x 17'-4"
dn
L'DRY
MASTER
BEDROOM
11'-4" x 14'
54'-5"
PORCH
GARAGE
21'-4" x 23'-8"
storage
alternate garage door location

Plan 2 without Basement

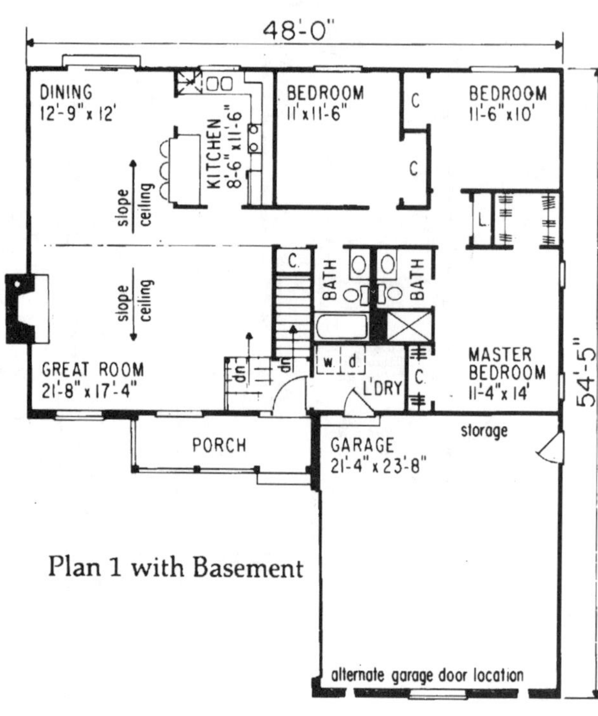
48'-0"
DINING
12'-9" x 12'
KITCHEN
8'-6" x 11'-6"
BEDROOM
11' x 11'-6"
C
BEDROOM
11'-6" x 10'
C
slope ceiling
slope ceiling
L
C.
BATH
BATH
GREAT ROOM
21'-8" x 17'-4"
dn
dn
w d
L'DRY
C
MASTER
BEDROOM
11'-4" x 14'
54'-5"
PORCH
GARAGE
21'-4" x 23'-8"
storage
alternate garage door location

Plan 1 with Basement

Harrow Wood Lodge

Features

- Colonial ranch design offers many amenities.
- Small porch gives a cozy welcome feeling to front entrance.
- Sunken great room with sloped ceiling features fireplace.
- Back-to-back full baths serve the three bedrooms.
- Kitchen with breakfast island adjoins dining room.

Total Living Area **1,440 sq. ft.**

PRICE CODE: B

PLAN NP1429

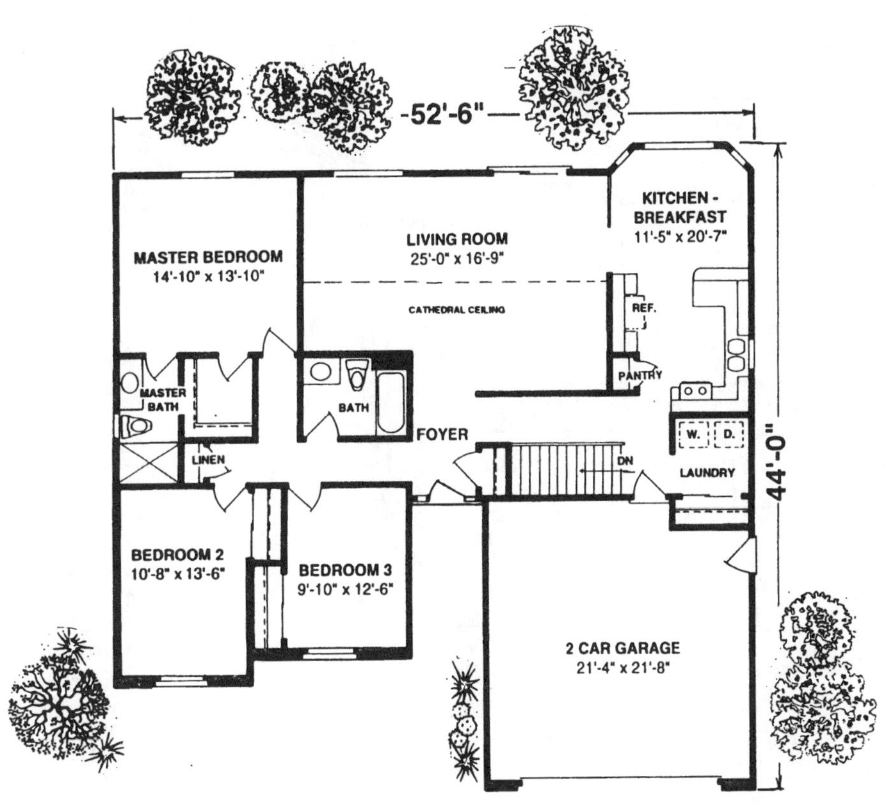

52'-6"
44'-0"
KITCHEN - BREAKFAST
11'-5" x 20'-7"
LIVING ROOM
25'-0" x 16'-9"
CATHEDRAL CEILING
MASTER BEDROOM
14'-10" x 13'-10"
REF.
PANTRY
MASTER BATH
BATH
FOYER
W.
D.
LINEN
DN
LAUNDRY
BEDROOM 2
10'-8" x 13'-6"
BEDROOM 3
9'-10" x 12'-6"
2 CAR GARAGE
21'-4" x 21'-8"

Total Living Area 1,500 sq. ft.

PRICE CODE: B

PLAN NP1276

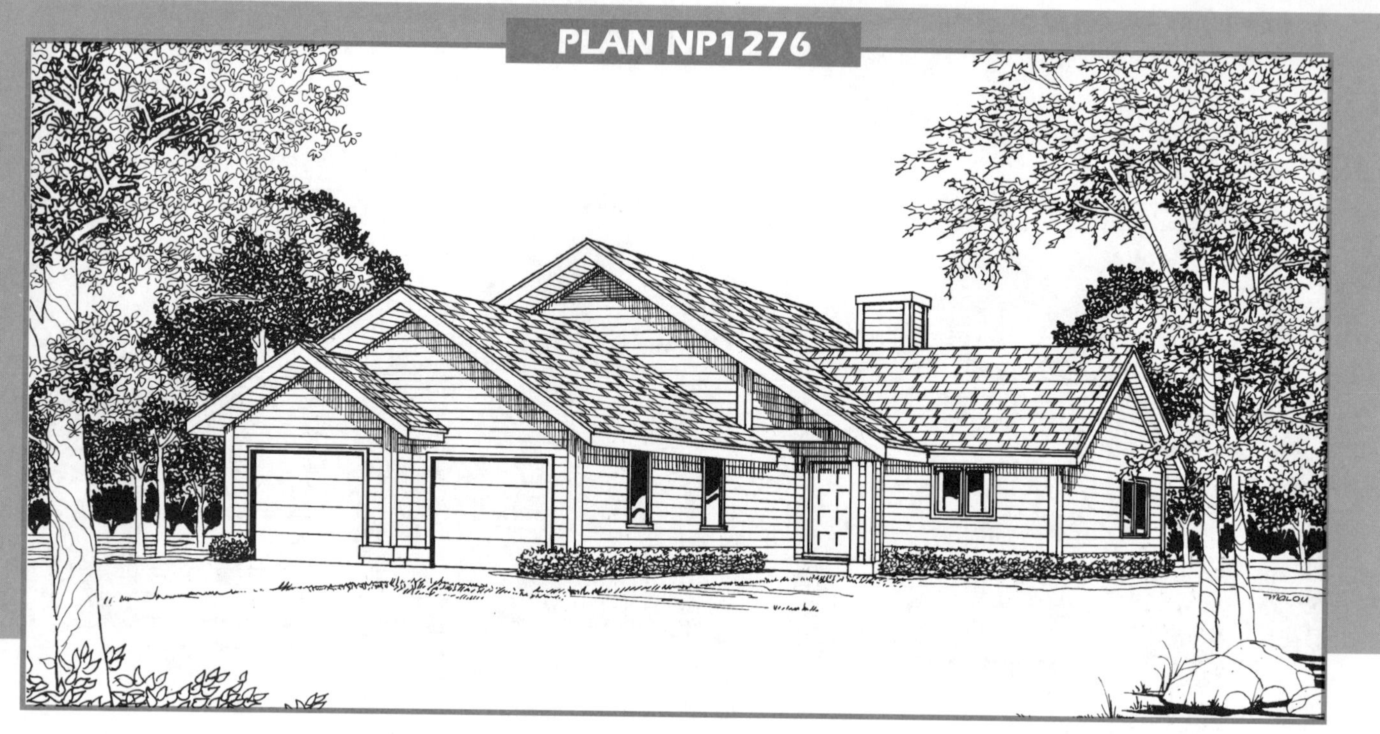

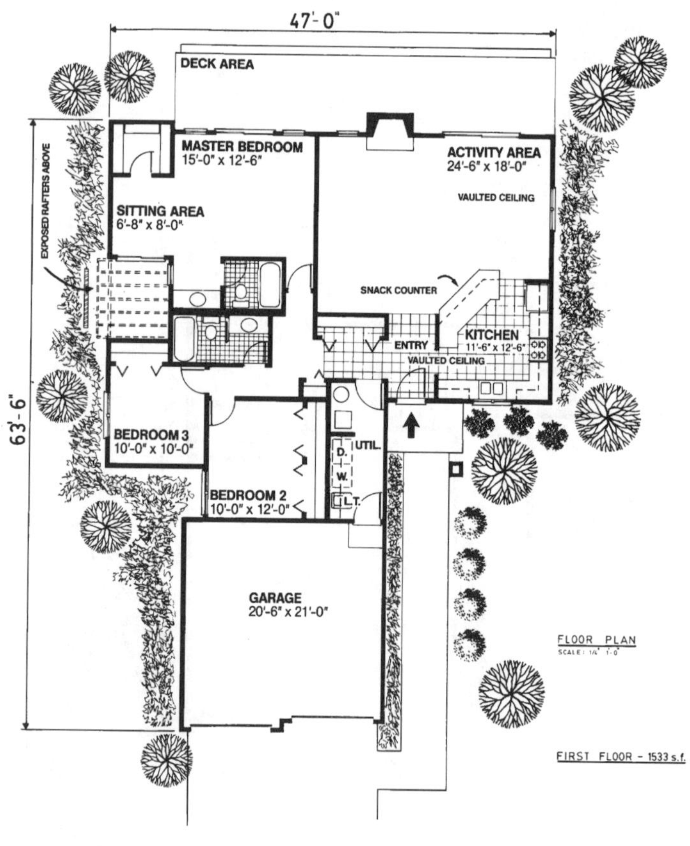
47'-0"
DECK AREA
MASTER BEDROOM
15'-0" x 12'-6"
ACTIVITY AREA
24'-6" x 18'-0"
VAULTED CEILING
SITTING AREA
6'-8" x 8'-0"
EXPOSED RAFTERS ABOVE
SNACK COUNTER
ENTRY
KITCHEN
11'-6" x 12'-6"
VAULTED CEILING
63'-6"
BEDROOM 3
10'-0" x 10'-0"
UTIL.
D.
W.
BEDROOM 2
10'-0" x 12'-0"
GARAGE
20'-6" x 21'-0"
FLOOR PLAN
FIRST FLOOR - 1533 s.f.

Features

- Multiple gabled roofs with dramatic overhangs add to the exterior charm of this three bedroom contemporary home.
- The interior is cozy, with plenty of features for folks who love outdoor living indoors.
- There's a private deck outside the master bedroom sitting area .
- Sloped ceilings add a sense of the great outdoors to the large activity area.
- The activity room also enjoys its own fireplace and snack bar and shares access to the backyard with the master bedroom.

Total Living Area **1,533 sq. ft.**

PRICE CODE: B

PLAN NP1220

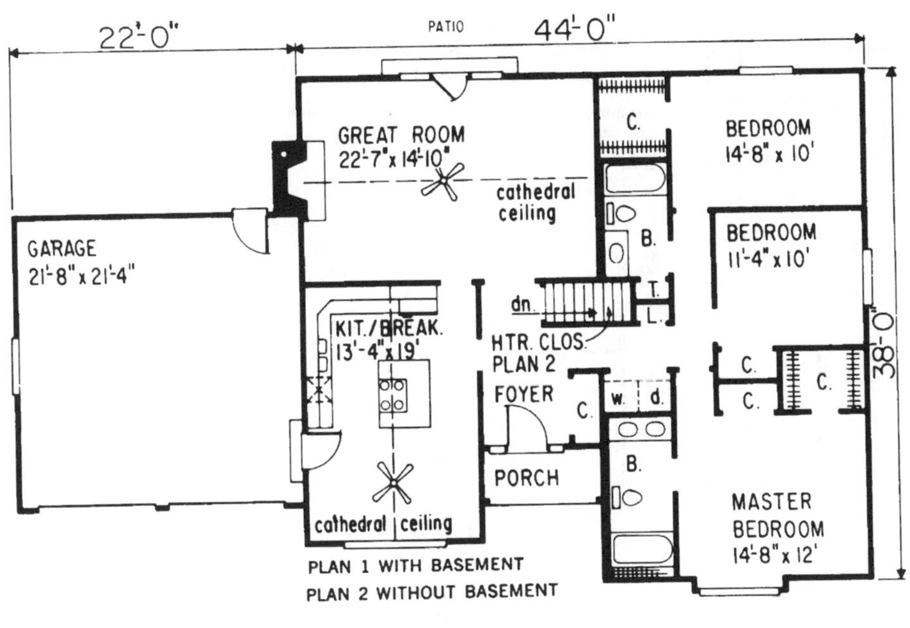
22'-0"
PATIO
44'-0"
GREAT ROOM
22'-7" x 14'-10"
cathedral ceiling
C.
BEDROOM
14'-8" x 10'
B.
BEDROOM
11'-4" x 10'
GARAGE
21'-8" x 21'-4"
dn.
T.
L.
KIT./BREAK.
13'-4" x 19'
HTR. CLOS.
PLAN 2
FOYER
C.
w.
d.
C.
C.
C.
38'-0"
PORCH
B.
MASTER
BEDROOM
14'-8" x 12'
cathedral ceiling
PLAN 1 WITH BASEMENT
PLAN 2 WITHOUT BASEMENT

Lighted Charm

Features

- Porch entrance into foyer leads to an impressive dining area with full window with half-circle window above.
- Kitchen/breakfast room features a center island and cathedral ceiling.
- Great room with cathedral ceiling and exposed beams accessible from foyer.
- Master bedroom includes full bath and walk-in closet.
- Two additional bedrooms share a full bath.

Total Living Area **1,540 sq. ft.**

PRICE CODE: B

PLAN VL1558

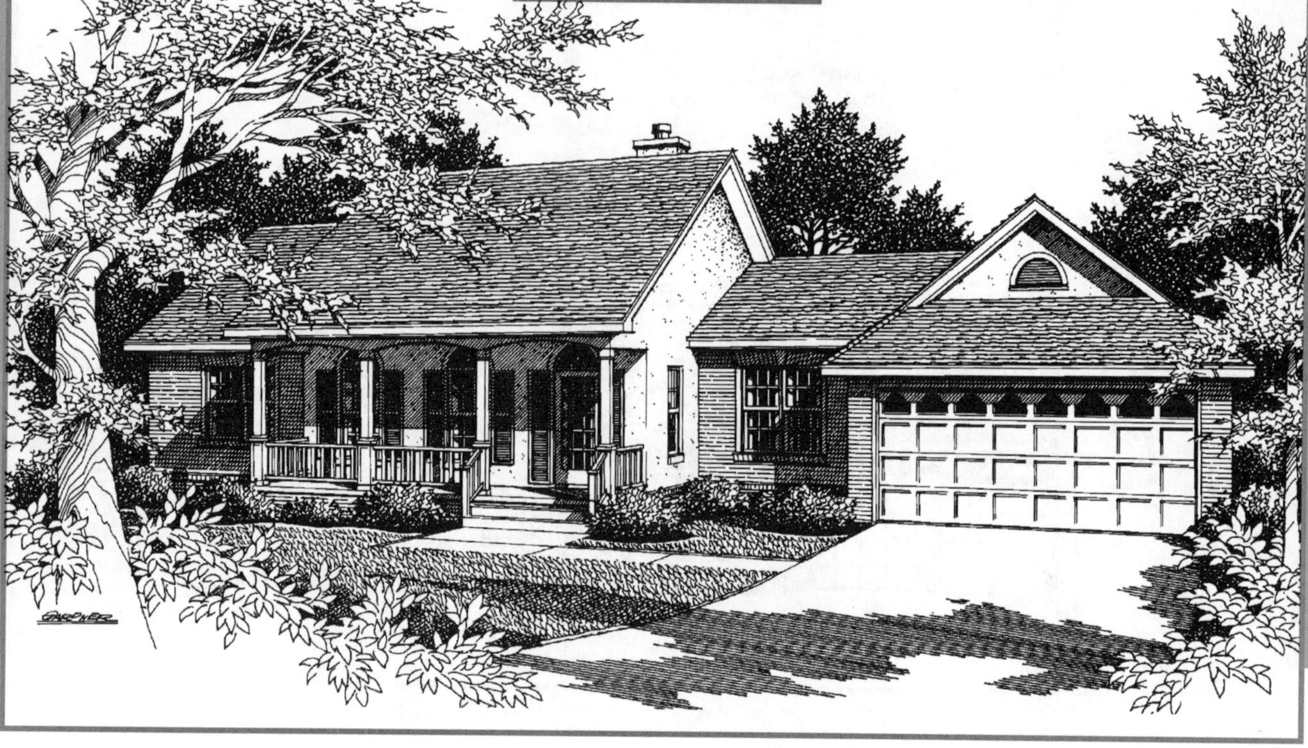

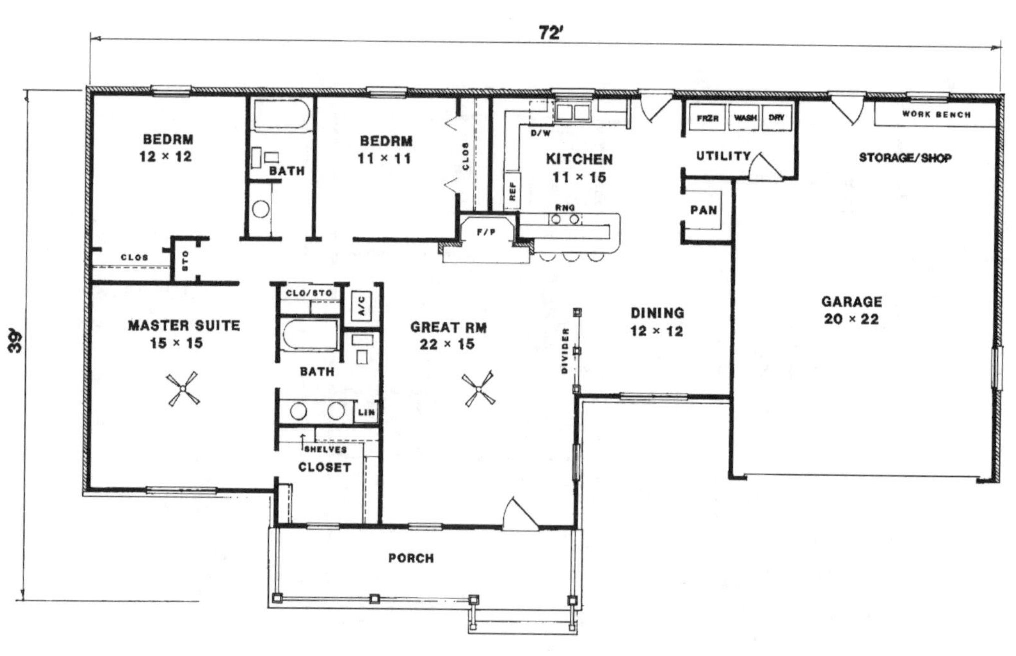
72'
39'
BEDRM
12 × 12
BATH
BEDRM
11 × 11
CLOS
D/W
KITCHEN
11 × 15
REF
RNG
F/P
FRZR
WASH
DRY
UTILITY
PAN
WORK BENCH
STORAGE/SHOP
CLOS
STO
CLO/STO
A/C
MASTER SUITE
15 × 15
BATH
LIN
SHELVES
CLOSET
GREAT RM
22 × 15
DIVIDER
DINING
12 × 12
GARAGE
20 × 22
PORCH

Total Living Area 1,558 sq. ft.

PRICE CODE: B

PLAN DB2526

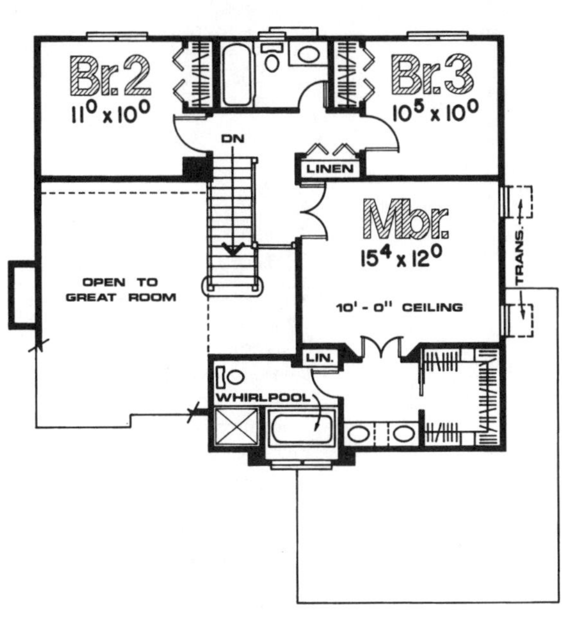

Br. 2
11⁰ x 10⁰
Br. 3
10⁵ x 10⁰
DN
LINEN
Mbr.
15⁴ x 12⁰
TRANS.
OPEN TO
GREAT ROOM
10' - 0" CEILING
LIN.
WHIRLPOOL

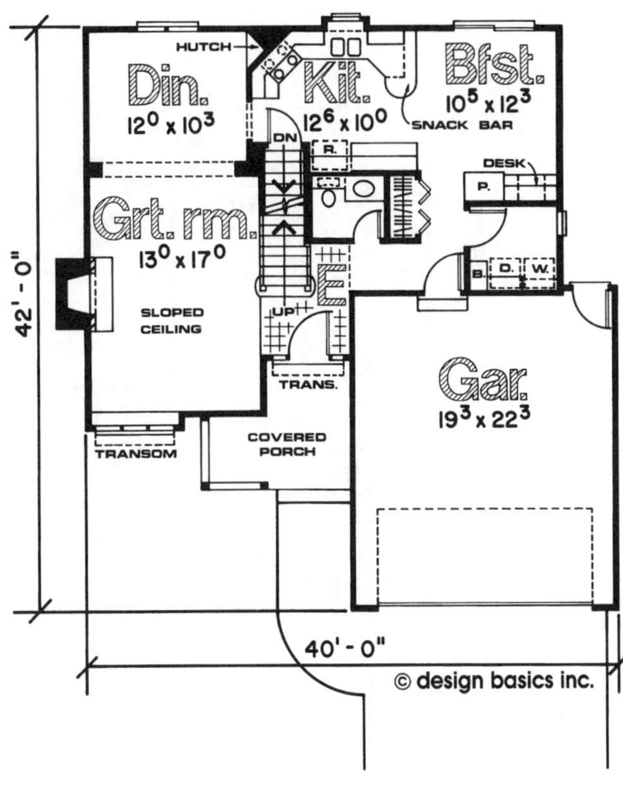

HUTCH
Din.
12⁰ x 10³
Kit.
12⁶ x 10⁰
Bfst.
10⁵ x 12³
SNACK BAR
DN
R.
DESK
P.
Grt. rm.
13⁰ x 17⁰
SLOPED
CEILING
B.
D.
W.
UP
TRANS.
Gar.
19³ x 22³
TRANSOM
COVERED
PORCH
42' - 0"
40' - 0"
© design basics inc.

Features

- Gabled roof, brick accents and covered front porch combine to present striking elevation.
- Ceiling slopes from 9 foot to 16'-10", plus raised hearth fireplace of great room makes dramatic presentation.
- Formal dining room features built-in hutch.
- Efficient kitchen with snack bar serves dinette, which has planning desk and large pantry.
- Laundry area has window, broom closet and hanging rod.
- French doors access master suite with 10-foot-high ceiling, and second set of French doors lead to private dressing area with dual lavs.
- Natural light floods master bath above whirlpool tub.

First Floor	845 sq. ft.
Second Floor	760 sq. ft.
Total Living Area	1,605 sq. ft.

PRICE CODE: C

PLAN SH1690-1620

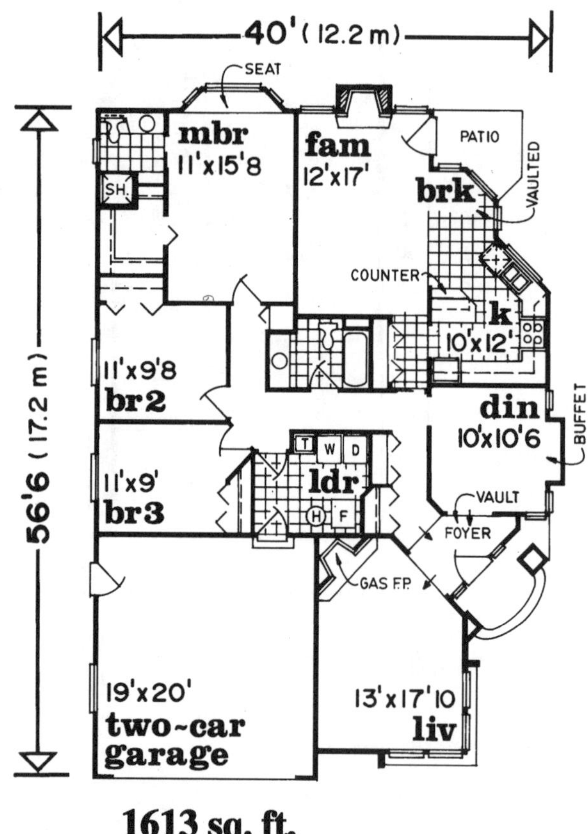

40' (12.2 m)
56'6 (17.2 m)
SEAT
mbr
11'x15'8
SH
fam
12'x17'
PATIO
VAULTED
brk
COUNTER
k
10'x12'
11'x9'8
br2
din
10'x10'6
BUFFET
11'x9'
br3
T W D
ldr
H F
VAULT
FOYER
GAS F.P.
19'x20'
two-car
garage
13'x17'10
liv

1613 sq. ft.

Features

- Tall arched entry introduces a three bedroom design well suited for a corner lot.
- Raised foyer spills into the sunken living with corner positioned fireplace.
- Archway leads from the foyer to the dining room.
- Island kitchen, with abundant counter space and pantry, serves a carrousel breakfast bay.
- Large family room is open to the kitchen and breakfast room.
- Master bedroom offers a window seat, walk-in closet and ensuite with shower.
- Two additional bedrooms share a main bathroom with soaking tub.

Total Living Area **1,613 sq. ft.**

PRICE CODE: B

PLAN FD7099

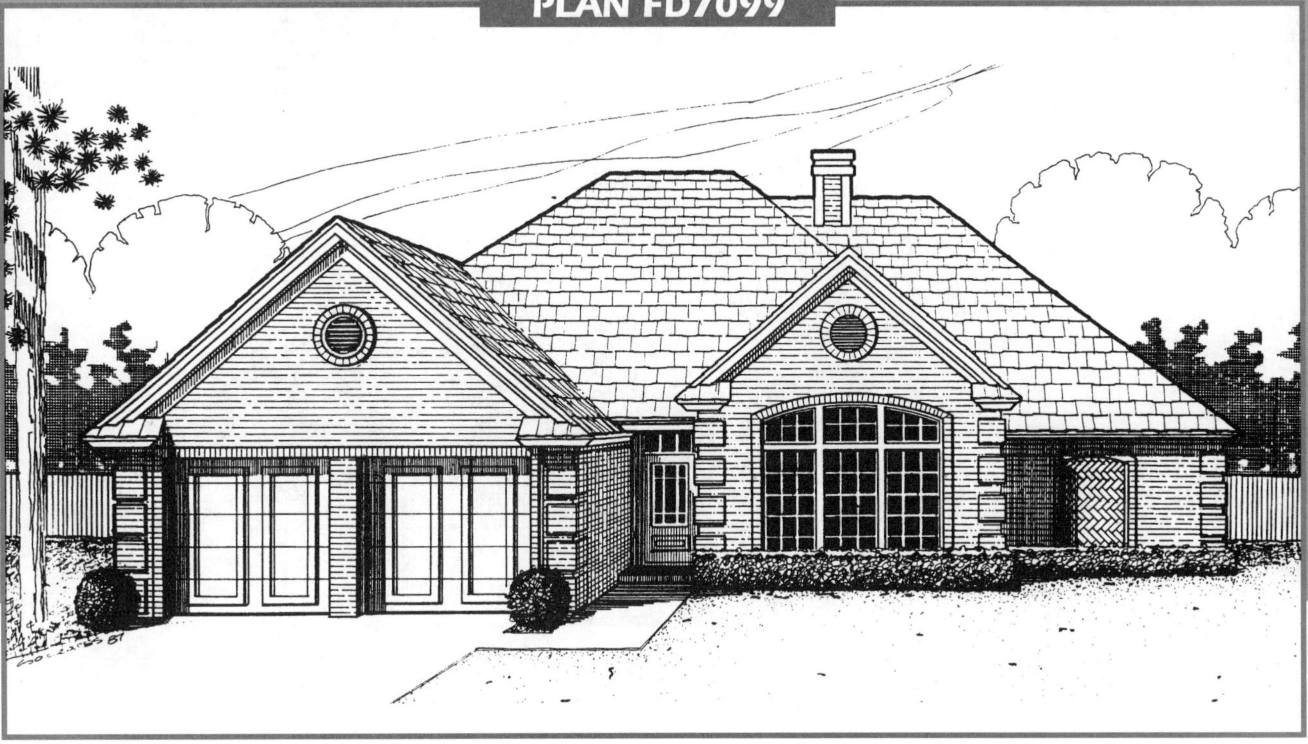

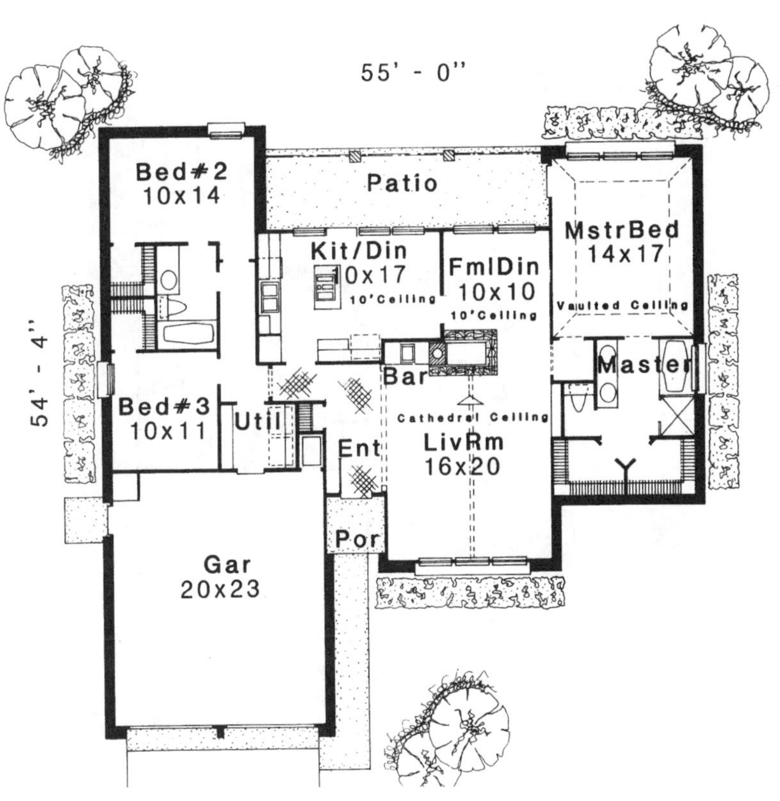

55' - 0"
54' - 4"
Bed#2
10x14
Patio
MstrBed
14x17
Kit/Din
10x17
10'Ceiling
FmlDin
10x10
10'Ceiling
Vaulted Ceiling
Master
Bar
Bed#3
10x11
Util
Cathedral Ceiling
LivRm
16x20
Ent
Por
Gar
20x23

Total Living Area 1,624 sq. ft.

PRICE CODE: B

PLAN MN1687

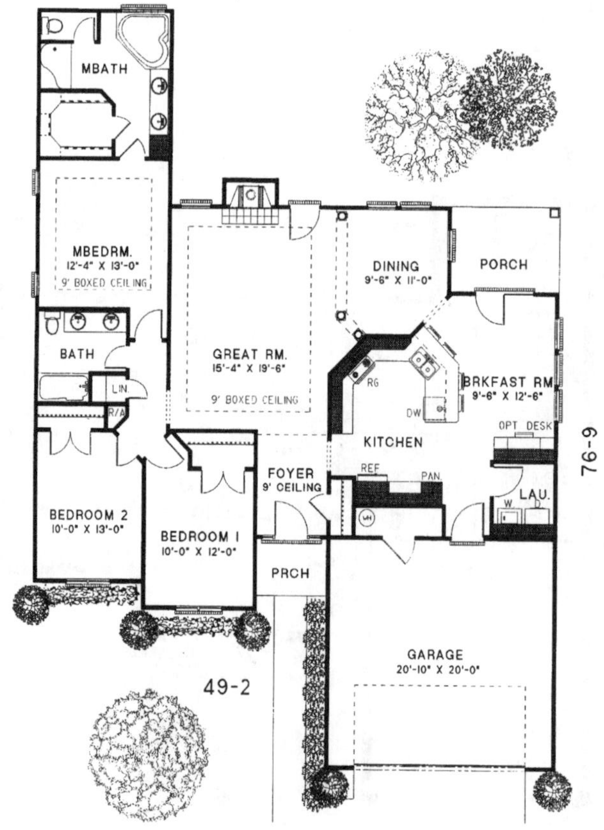
MBATH
MBEDRM.
12'-4" X 13'-0"
9' BOXED CEILING
BATH
LIN
R/A
BEDROOM 2
10'-0" X 13'-0"
BEDROOM 1
10'-0" X 12'-0"
GREAT RM.
15'-4" X 19'-6"
9' BOXED CEILING
DINING
9'-6" X 11'-0"
PORCH
BRKFAST RM
9'-6" X 12'-6"
OPT. DESK
KITCHEN
RG
DW
REF
PAN
FOYER
9' CEILING
LAU.
W
D
PRCH
GARAGE
20'-10" X 20'-0"
49-2
76-9

Total Living Area **1,687 sq. ft.**

PRICE CODE: B

PLAN DB3097

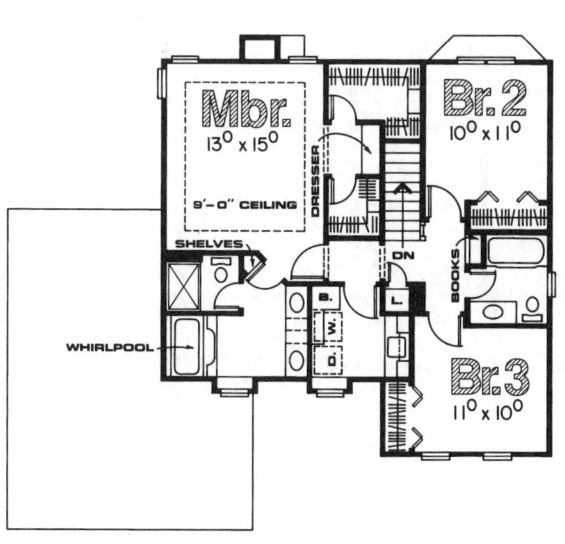

Mbr.
13⁰ x 15⁰
9'-0" CEILING
DRESSER
SHELVES
WHIRLPOOL
Br. 2
10⁰ x 11⁰
DN
BOOKS
B.
W.
D.
L.
Br. 3
11⁰ x 10⁰

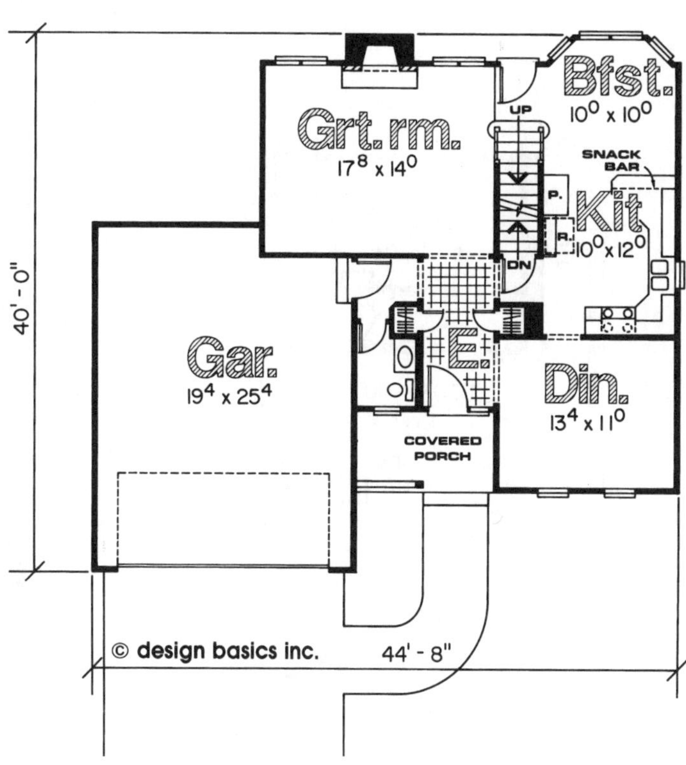

Grt. rm.
17⁸ x 14⁰
UP
Bfst.
10⁰ x 10⁰
SNACK BAR
P.
R.
Kit.
10⁰ x 12⁰
DN
40' - 0"
Gar.
19⁴ x 25⁴
E.
Din.
13⁴ x 11⁰
COVERED PORCH
© design basics inc.
44' - 8"

Features

- Traditional elevation combines aesthetics and economy.
- Symmetrical coat closets and cased openings frame view to great room and entry.
- Versatile dining room has parlor option.
- Bayed dinette with back yard access and staircase to second level.
- Deluxe laundry room and built-in bookcase provide ample amenities to fantastic upper level.
- Luxurious master suite contains built-in dresser between his and her walk-in closets.
- Roomy compartmented dressing area with whirlpool.
- Extra storage in deep garage.

First Floor	852 sq. ft.
Second Floor	893 sq. ft.
Total Living Area	1,745 sq. ft.

PRICE CODE: C

PLAN NP LAKEPOINT

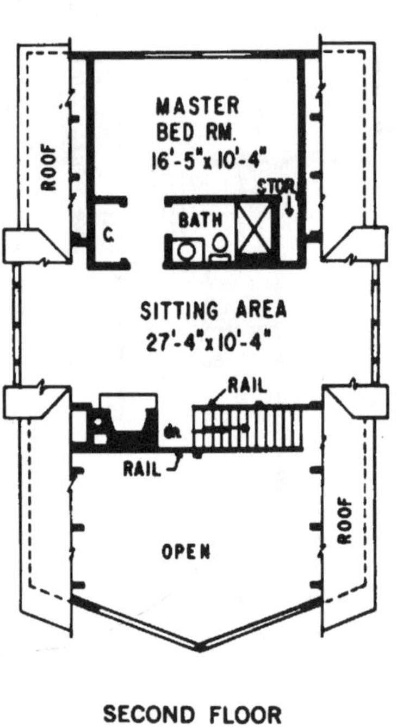
MASTER
BED RM.
16'-5"x 10'-4"
STOR
BATH
C.
ROOF
SITTING AREA
27'-4"x 10'-4"
RAIL
RAIL
OPEN
ROOF

SECOND FLOOR

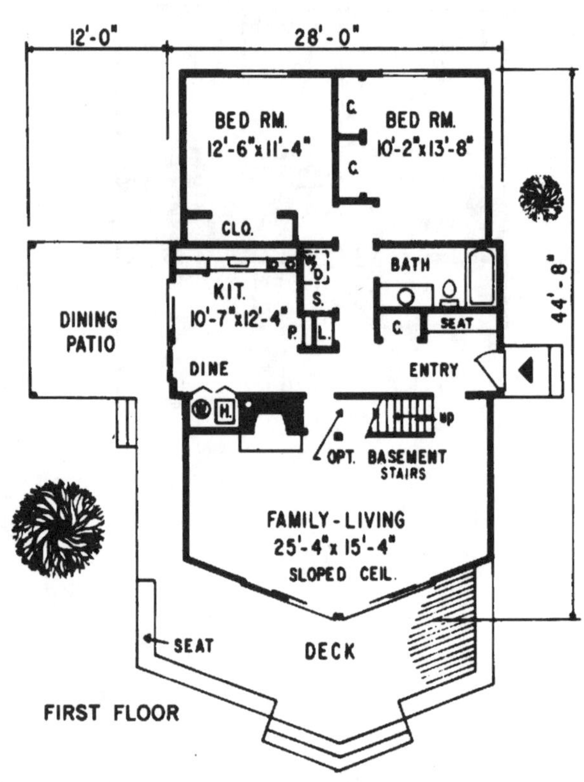
12'-0"
28'-0"
BED RM.
12'-6"x 11'-4"
BED RM.
10'-2"x 13'-8"
C.
C.
C.
CLO.
BATH
KIT.
10'-7"x 12'-4"
S.
P.
L.
C.
SEAT
DINING
PATIO
DINE
ENTRY
H.
UP
OPT. BASEMENT
STAIRS
44'-8"
FAMILY-LIVING
25'-4"x 15'-4"
SLOPED CEIL.
SEAT
DECK

FIRST FLOOR

First Floor	1,126 sq. ft.
Second Floor	624 sq. ft.
Total Living Area	1,750 sq. ft.

PRICE CODE: B

PLAN SH91-1749

Exterior view of Rear Elevation

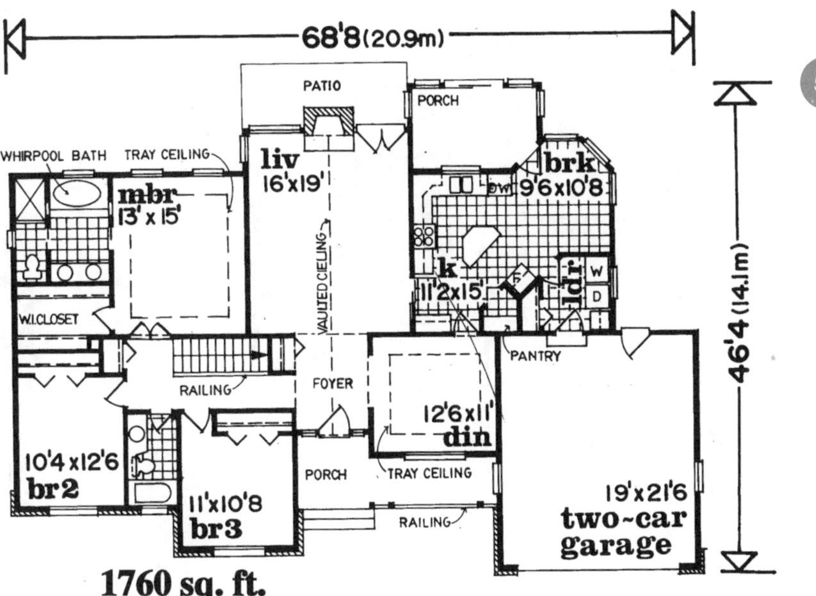
68'8 (20.9m)
46'4 (14.1m)
PATIO
PORCH
WHIRLPOOL BATH
TRAY CEILING
liv
16'x19'
brk
9'6x10'8
DW
mbr
13' x 15'
VAULTED CEILING
k
11'2x15'
ldr
W
D
W.I.CLOSET
PANTRY
RAILING
FOYER
12'6x11'
din
10'4x12'6
br2
PORCH
TRAY CEILING
11'x10'8
br3
RAILING
19'x21'6
two-car
garage

1760 sq. ft.

Features

- Covered, railed porch provides a weather-protected entry and introduces the vaulted foyer.
- Vaulted ceiling, extending from the foyer through to the living room, increases the sense of spaciousness.
- Floor plan is designed for a home with a view to the rear of the lot.
- Tray ceiling adds distinction and creates a formal atmosphere for the dining room.
- Open-plan kitchen includes a walk-in pantry, centre preparation island and breakfast bay.
- Windows surrounding the sunroom capture the sun's heat and warm this area.
- Master bedroom boasts a tray ceiling, walk-in closet and lavish ensuite with twin vanity, whirlpool spa and private plan shower.

Total Living Area: **1,760 sq. ft.**

PRICE CODE: B

PLAN DB2594

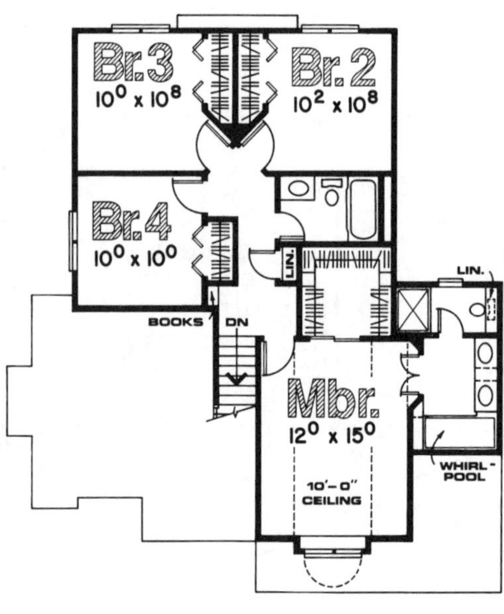
Br.3
10⁰ x 10⁸
Br.2
10² x 10⁸
Br.4
10⁰ x 10⁰
LIN.
LIN.
BOOKS
DN
Mbr.
12⁰ x 15⁰
10'-0" CEILING
WHIRL-POOL

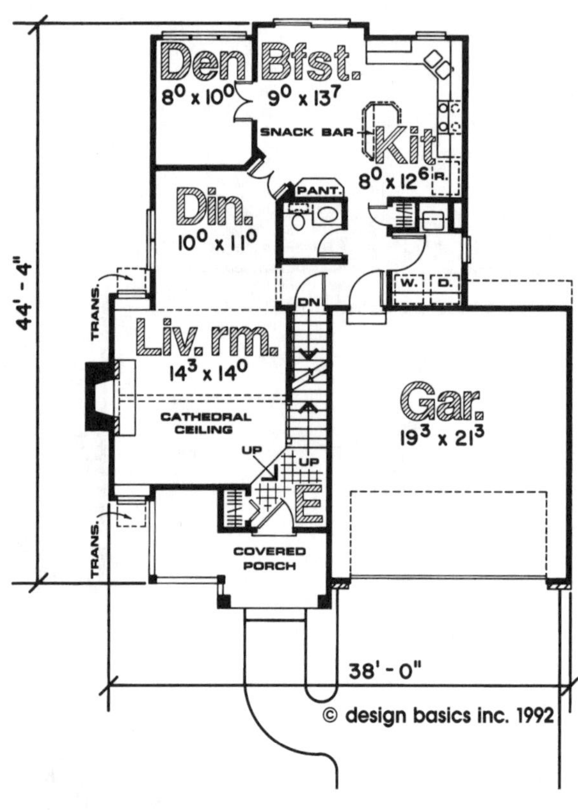
Den
8⁰ x 10⁰
Bfst.
9⁰ x 13⁷
SNACK BAR
Kit
8⁰ x 12⁶
R.
PANT.
Din.
10⁰ x 11⁰
W.
D.
DN
TRANS.
Liv. rm.
14³ x 14⁰
CATHEDRAL CEILING
UP
UP
E
Gar.
19³ x 21³
44' - 4"
TRANS.
COVERED PORCH
38' - 0"
© design basics inc. 1992

Features

- This simple but charming design presents a well-balanced elevation for narrow lots.
- From entry, step down into volume living room open to formal dining area for expanded entertaining flexibility.
- Double doors access formal dining room from kitchen.
- Open kitchen/dinette features large pantry, center island with snack bar and corner sink.
- Private den may be converted to sunroom.
- Laundry room conveniently located off dinette.
- Master suite includes volume ceilings, walk-in closet, dual lavs and whirlpool tub.

First Floor	869 sq. ft.
Second Floor	895 sq. ft.
Total Living Area	1,764 sq. ft.

PRICE CODE: C

PLAN MN1764

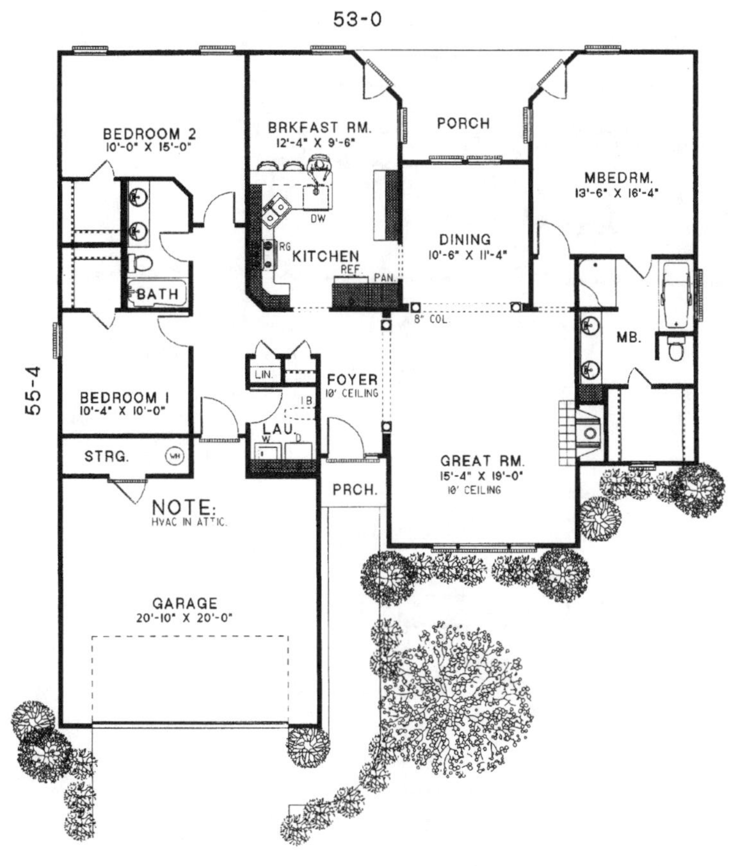

53-0
55-4
BEDROOM 2
10'-0" X 15'-0"
BRKFAST RM.
12'-4" X 9'-6"
PORCH
MBEDRM.
13'-6" X 16'-4"
DW
RG
KITCHEN
REF
PAN
DINING
10'-6" X 11'-4"
BATH
8" COL
MB.
LIN.
FOYER
10' CEILING
BEDROOM 1
10'-4" X 10'-0"
LAU.
STRG.
WH
GREAT RM.
15'-4" X 19'-0"
10' CEILING
PRCH.
NOTE:
HVAC IN ATTIC.
GARAGE
20'-10" X 20'-0"

Total Living Area 1,764 sq. ft.

PRICE CODE: B

PLAN NP1321

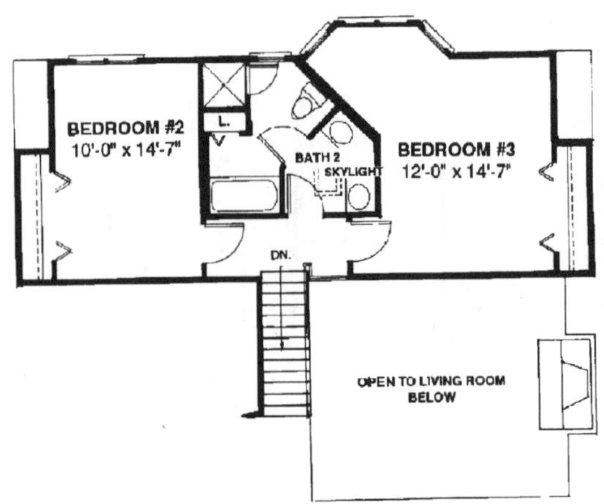
BEDROOM #2
10'-0" x 14'-7"
L.
BATH 2
SKYLIGHT
BEDROOM #3
12'-0" x 14'-7"
DN.
OPEN TO LIVING ROOM
BELOW

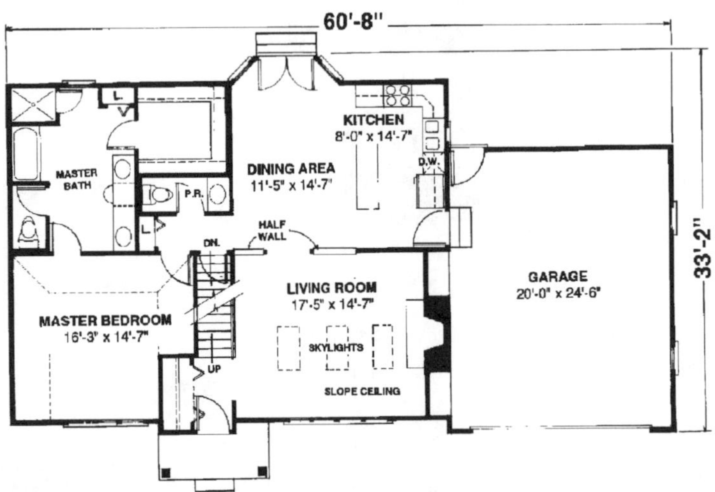
60'-8"
33'-2"
L
MASTER
BATH
P.R.
L
KITCHEN
8'-0" x 14'-7"
D.W.
DINING AREA
11'-5" x 14'-7'
HALF
WALL
DN.
LIVING ROOM
17'-5" x 14'-7"
SKYLIGHTS
SLOPE CEILING
UP
MASTER BEDROOM
16'-3" x 14'-7"
GARAGE
20'-0" x 24'-6"

Lillibrook Cottage

Features

- Compact design with contemporary amenities.
- Appealing gable roof design.
- Columned entry porch adds to the attractiveness of this home.
- Entry porch leads directly into sky lighted living room with fireplace.
- Dining room at rear features French doors and L-shaped kitchen.
- Left wing includes large master bedroom with deluxe master bath and walk-in closet.
- Upstairs, two additional bedrooms share a uniquely designed bath.

First Floor	1,220 sq. ft.
Second Floor	630 sq. ft.
Total Living Area	1,850 sq. ft.

PRICE CODE: B

PLAN DB2281

63

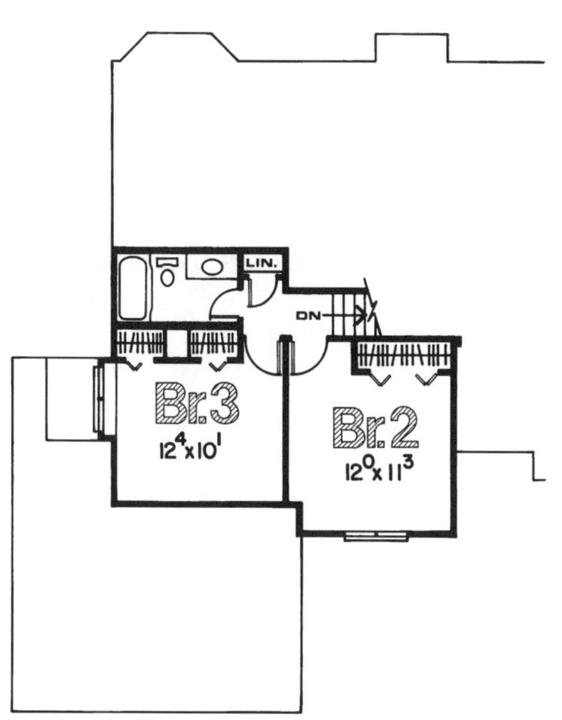

LIN.
DN
Br.3
12^{4}x10^{1}
Br.2
12^{0}x11^{3}

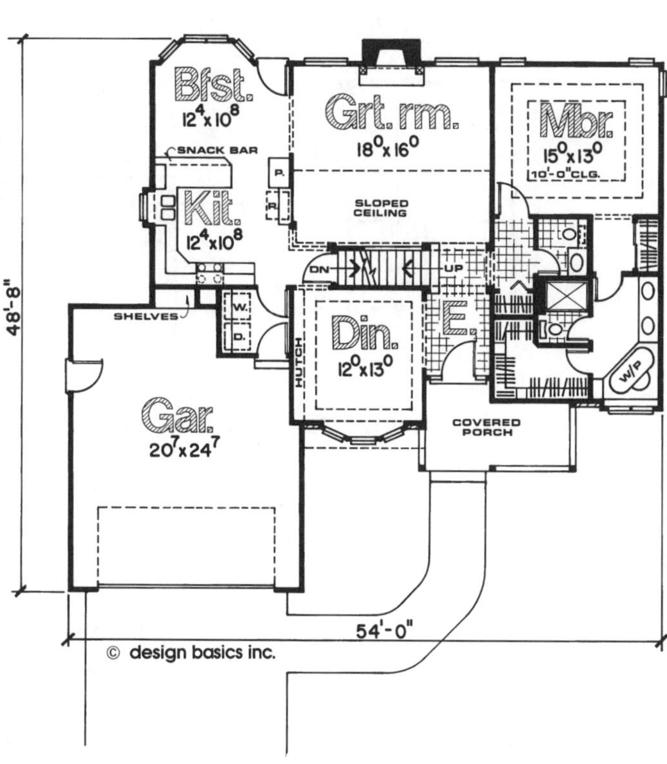

Bfst.
12^{4}x10^{8}
SNACK BAR
Grt. rm.
18^{0}x16^{0}
Mbr.
15^{0}x13^{0}
10'-0" CLG.
P.
Kit.
12^{4}x10^{8}
SLOPED CEILING
DN
UP
SHELVES
W.
D.
HUTCH
Din.
12^{0}x13^{0}
E.
W/P
Gar.
20^{7}x24^{7}
COVERED PORCH
48'-8"
54'-0"
© design basics inc.

Features

- Inviting covered porch.
- Elegant bayed window in formal dining room off entry.
- Beautiful fireplace with windows showcased in large great room.
- Bright bayed dinette.
- Kitchen with window above sink, pantry and snack bar.
- Utility entrance through garage.
- Additional storage in garage.
- Master suite features tiered ceiling,corner windows and luxurious dressing area with double lav vanity, 2 closets and corner whirlpool under windows.
- Convenient hall bath services secondary bedrooms.

First Floor	1,348 sq. ft.
Second Floor	430 sq. ft.
Total Living Area	1,778 sq. ft.

PRICE CODE: C

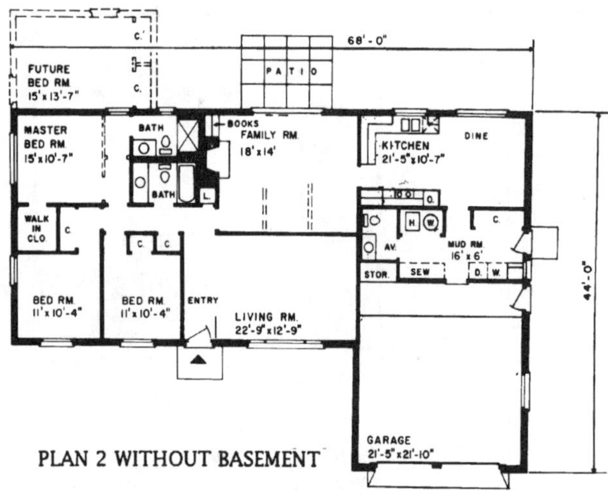

PLAN 2 WITHOUT BASEMENT

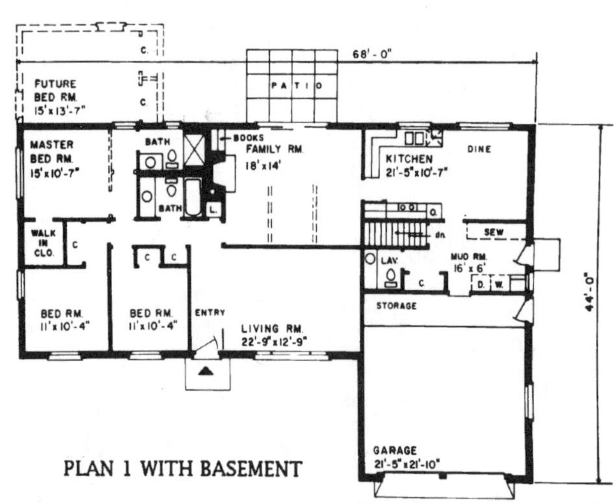

PLAN 1 WITH BASEMENT

Brick Ranch

Features

- Brick exudes a warm atmosphere in this attractive and spacious ranch.
- Formal entryway leads into large living room.
- Family room with fireplace opens to patio.
- Includes two bedrooms and a full bath, plus a master bedroom with walk-in closet and private bath with shower.
- Designed for practicality, kitchen/dining area are adjacent to the mud room/lavatory area that opens to the garage.
- Designed to allow additional bedroom, if future expansion is desired.
- Future fourth bedroom, 266 square feet.

Total Living Area 1,778 sq. ft.

PRICE CODE: B

PLAN DB3090

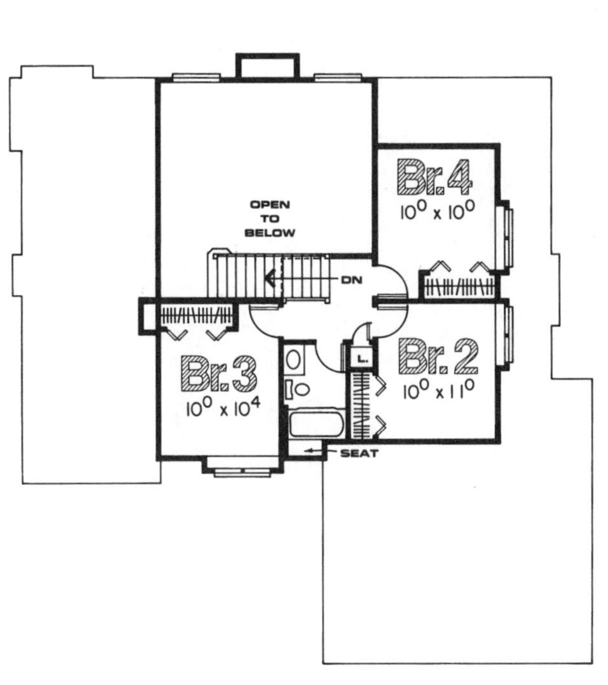

OPEN TO BELOW
Br. 4
10^0 x 10^0
DN
Br. 3
10^0 x 10^4
L.
Br. 2
10^0 x 11^0
SEAT

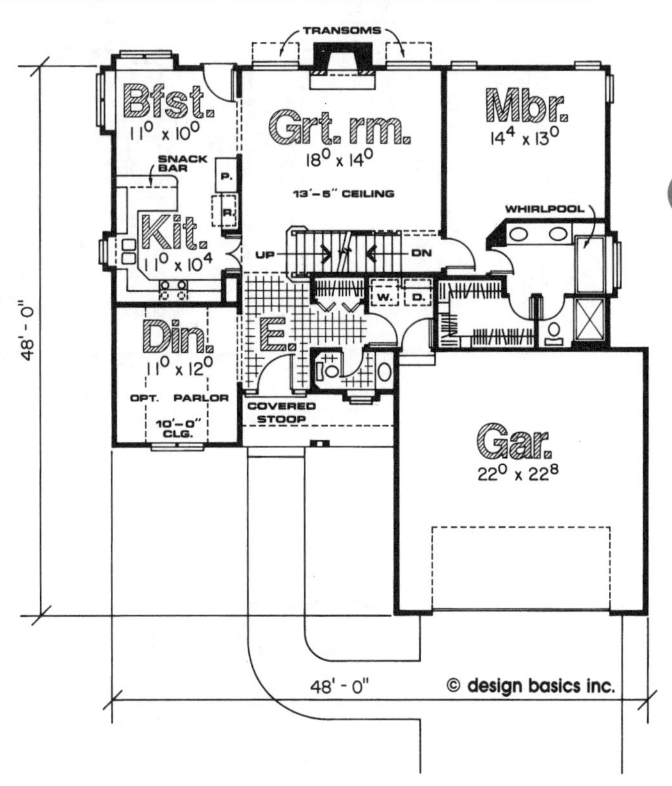

TRANSOMS
Bfst.
11^0 x 10^0
SNACK BAR
P.
R.
Grt. rm.
18^0 x 14^0
13'-5" CEILING
Mbr.
14^4 x 13^0
WHIRLPOOL
Kit.
11^0 x 10^4
UP
DN
W.
D.
Din.
11^0 x 12^0
OPT. PARLOR
10'-0" CLG.
E.
COVERED STOOP
Gar.
22^0 x 22^8
48' - 0"
48' - 0"
© design basics inc.

Features

- Versatile dining room off entry has 10-foot volume ceiling and parlor option.
- French doors at base of stairs create an elegant passage to peninsula kitchen with snack bar.
- Corner boxed windows create sunny and inviting breakfast area.
- Volume ceiling allows staircase to overlook great room.
- Secluded master suite features dual lavs, whirlpool bath and generous walk-in closet.
- Upstairs, 3 secondary bedrooms share hall bath with seat at tub.

First Floor	**1,265 sq. ft.**
Second Floor	**518 sq. ft.**
Total Living Area	**1,783 sq. ft.**

PRICE CODE: C

PLAN NP1173

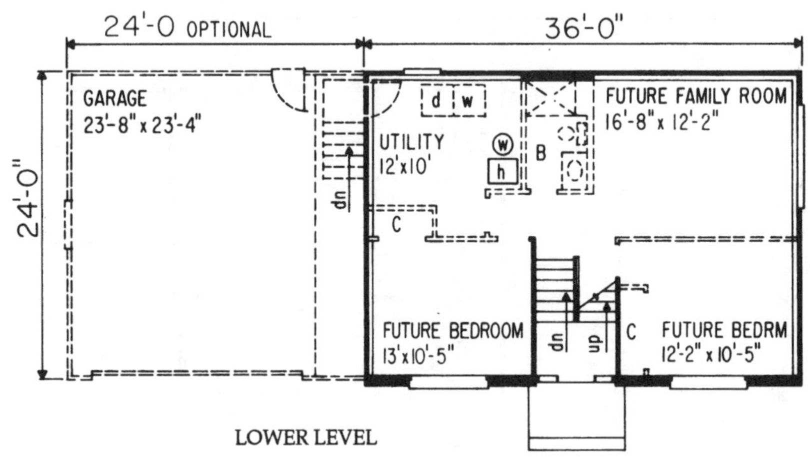
24'-0 OPTIONAL
36'-0"
24'-0"
GARAGE
23'-8" x 23'-4"
UTILITY
12'x10'
FUTURE FAMILY ROOM
16'-8" x 12'-2"
FUTURE BEDROOM
13'x10'-5"
FUTURE BEDRM
12'-2" x 10'-5"

LOWER LEVEL

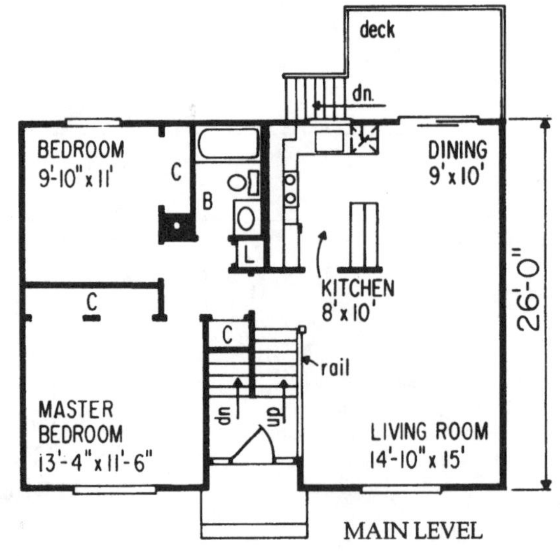
deck
BEDROOM
9'-10" x 11'
DINING
9'x10'
KITCHEN
8'x10'
rail
MASTER
BEDROOM
13'-4" x 11'-6"
LIVING ROOM
14'-10" x 15'
26'-0"

MAIN LEVEL

Expansion Bi-Level

Features

- This is the perfect home for those willing to add to their dream home.
- Main floor can be built with future expansion possible in lower level.
- Combined living and dining areas are located on the right.
- Master bedroom and second bedroom occupy the left side.

First Floor	**923 sq. ft.**
Second Floor	**876 sq. ft.**
Total Living Area	**1,799 sq. ft.**

PRICE CODE: B

PLAN JA5219

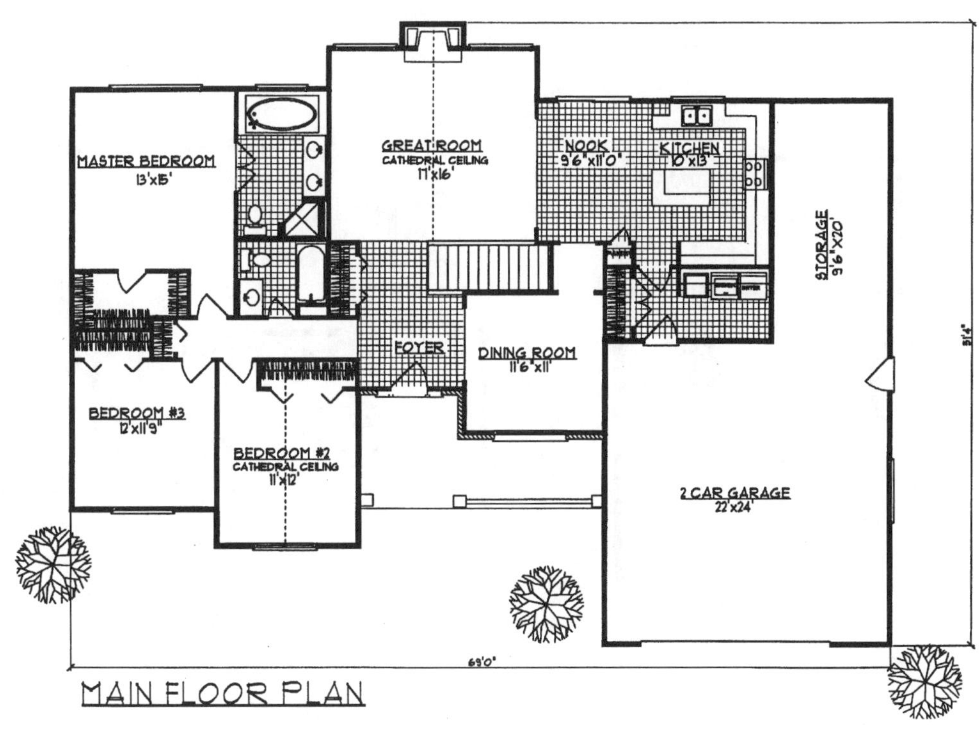

MASTER BEDROOM
13'x15'
GREAT ROOM
CATHEDRAL CEILING
17'x16'
NOOK
9'6"x11'0"
KITCHEN
10'x13'
STORAGE
9'6"X20'
FOYER
DINING ROOM
11'6"x11'
BEDROOM #3
12'x11'9"
BEDROOM #2
CATHEDRAL CEILING
11'x12'
2 CAR GARAGE
22'x24'
51'4"
69'0"
MAIN FLOOR PLAN

Total Living Area 1,802 sq. ft.

PRICE CODE: B

PLAN AM2138

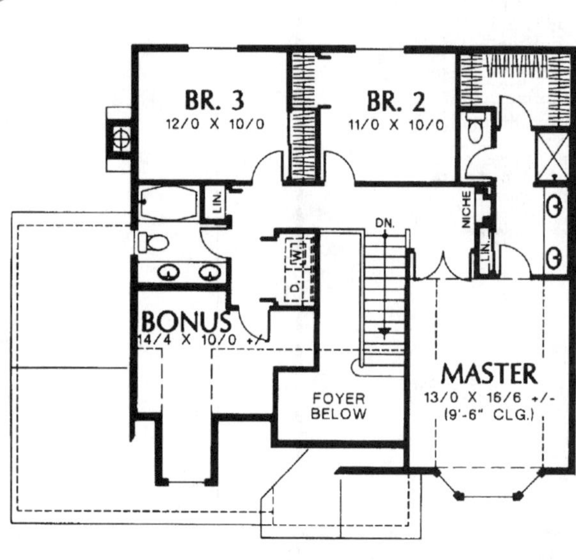
BR. 3
12/0 X 10/0
BR. 2
11/0 X 10/0
LIN.
DN.
NICHE
LIN.
D. W.
BONUS
14/4 X 10/0 +/-
FOYER
BELOW
MASTER
13/0 X 16/6 +/-
(9'-6" CLG.)

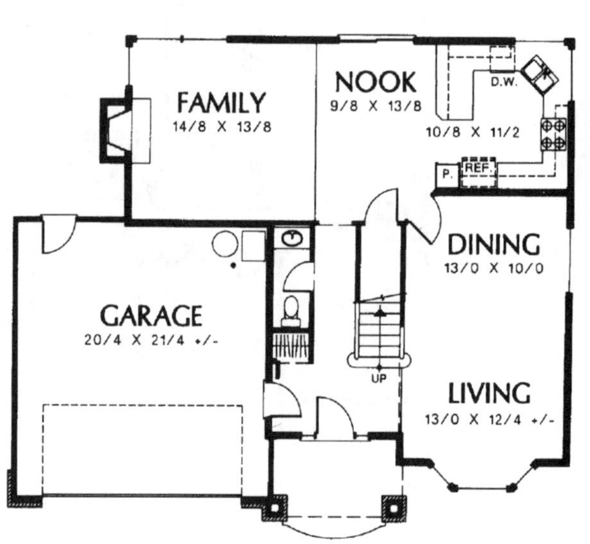
45'
37'
FAMILY
14/8 X 13/8
NOOK
9/8 X 13/8
D.W.
10/8 X 11/2
P.
REF.
DINING
13/0 X 10/0
GARAGE
20/4 X 21/4 +/-
UP
LIVING
13/0 X 12/4 +/-

First Floor	972 sq. ft.
Second Floor	843 sq. ft.
Total Living Area	1,815 sq. ft.
Bonus Room	+180 sq. ft.

PRICE CODE: B

PLAN MN1817

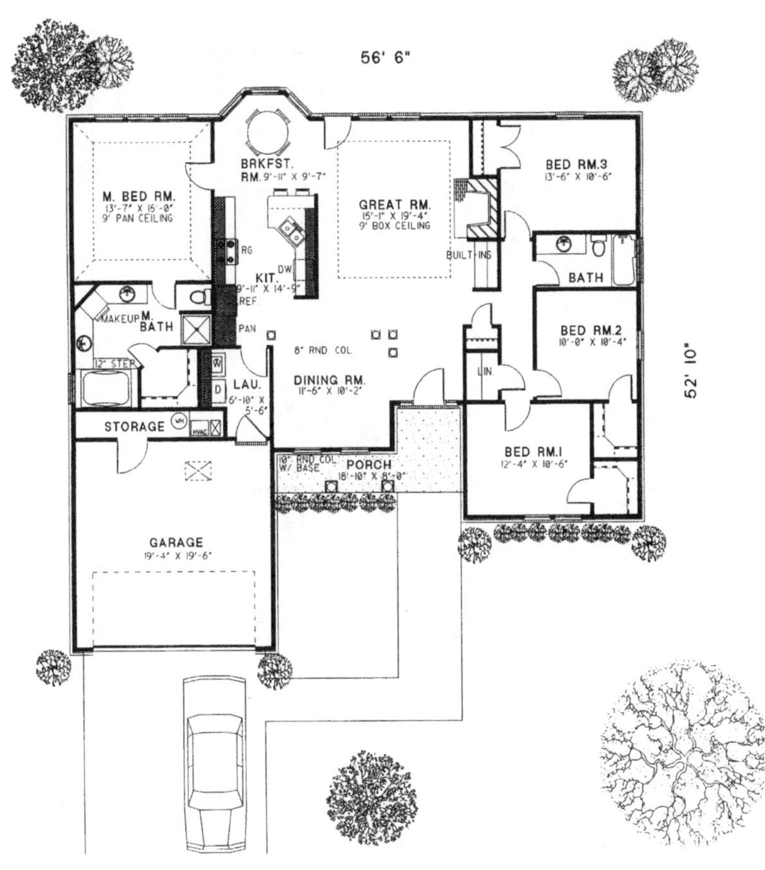
56' 6"
52' 10"
M. BED RM.
13'-7" X 15'-0"
9' PAN CEILING
BRKFST. RM. 9'-11" X 9'-7"
GREAT RM.
15'-1" X 19'-4"
9' BOX CEILING
BED RM.3
13'-6" X 10'-6"
BUILT-INS
BATH
KIT.
9'-11" X 14'-9"
RG
DW
REF
PAN
MAKEUP
M. BATH
12" STEP
8" RND COL
DINING RM.
11'-6" X 10'-2"
BED RM.2
10'-0" X 10'-4"
LIN.
LAU.
6'-10" X 5'-6"
W
D
STORAGE
WH
HVAC
10" RND COL W/ BASE
PORCH
18'-10" X 8'-0"
BED RM.1
12'-4" X 10'-6"
GARAGE
19'-4" X 19'-6"

Total Living Area **1,817 sq. ft.**

PRICE CODE: B

PLAN NP1396

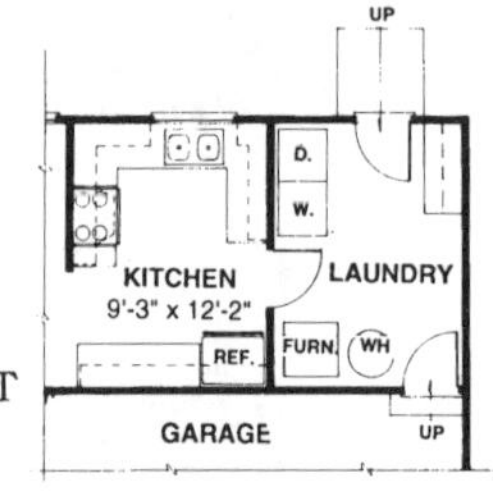
UP
D.
W.
KITCHEN
9'-3" x 12'-2"
LAUNDRY
REF.
FURN.
WH
GARAGE
UP

PLAN 2 WITHOUT BASEMENT

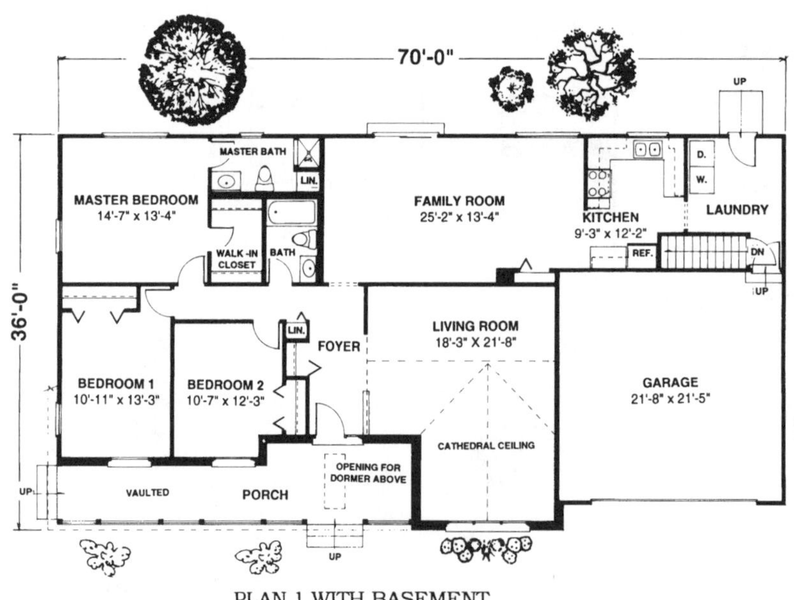
70'-0"
36'-0"
MASTER BATH
LIN.
MASTER BEDROOM
14'-7" x 13'-4"
WALK-IN CLOSET
BATH
FAMILY ROOM
25'-2" x 13'-4"
KITCHEN
9'-3" x 12'-2"
REF.
D.
W.
LAUNDRY
UP
DN
UP
LIVING ROOM
18'-3" X 21'-8"
LIN.
FOYER
BEDROOM 1
10'-11" x 13'-3"
BEDROOM 2
10'-7" x 12'-3"
CATHEDRAL CEILING
GARAGE
21'-8" x 21'-5"
OPENING FOR DORMER ABOVE
UP
VAULTED
PORCH
UP

PLAN 1 WITH BASEMENT

Sunny Bower

Features

- Stunning design elements on exterior of this home make it a stand- out.
- Vaulted roof on wide front porch and unique porch dormer greet the eye.
- Porch entrance leads to ample foyer with entry closet.
- Step-down leads to large, cathedral-ceiling living room on the right.
- The left wing contains the master bedroom with master bath and walk-in closet.
- Two additional bedrooms share a full bath.

Total Living Area **1,820 sq. ft.**

PRICE CODE: B

PLAN DB1752

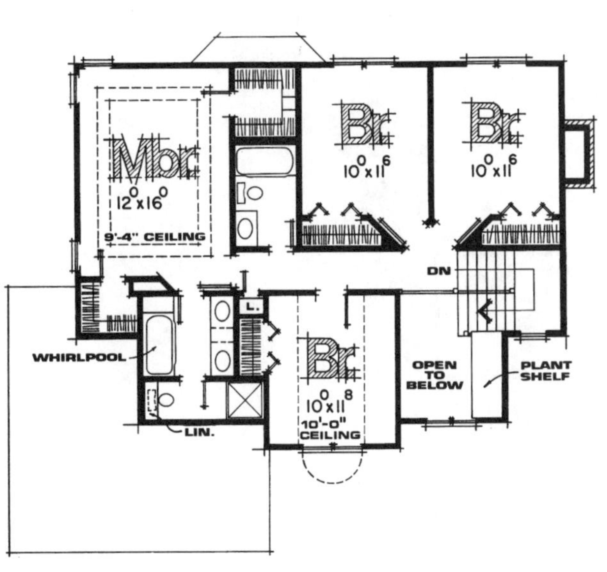
Mbr.
12^{0}x16^{0}
9'-4" CEILING
Br.
10^{0}x11^{6}
Br.
10^{0}x11^{6}
DN
WHIRLPOOL
L.
LIN.
Br.
10^{0}x11^{8}
10'-0" CEILING
OPEN TO BELOW
PLANT SHELF

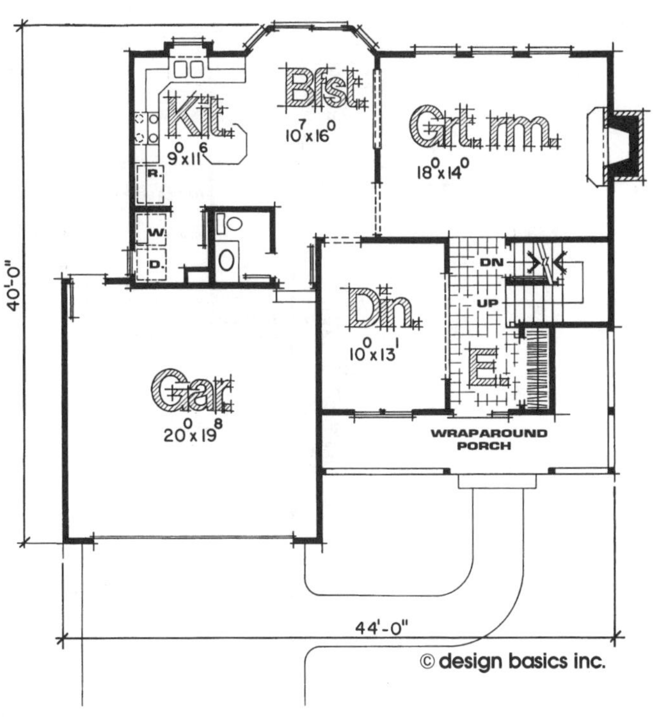
Kit.
9^{0}x11^{6}
Bfst.
10^{7}x16^{0}
Grt. rm.
18^{0}x14^{0}
R.
W.
D.
DN
UP
Din.
10^{0}x13^{1}
E.
Gar.
20^{0}x19^{8}
WRAPAROUND PORCH
40'-0"
44'-0"
© design basics inc.

Features

- 2-story entry with large coat closet and plant shelf above.
- Strategically located staircase.
- Great room with many windows.
- Island kitchen with boxed window over sink.
- Large bayed dinette.
- Convenient powder bath location.
- Main floor laundry.
- Volume ceiling and arched window in front bedroom.
- Pleasant secondary bedrooms with interesting angles.
- Large master suite with his and her walk-in closets, corner windows and bath area featuring double vanity and whirlpool bath.

First Floor	919 sq. ft.
Second Floor	927 sq. ft.
Total Living Area	1,846 sq. ft.

PRICE CODE: C

PLAN NP1255

MALOU

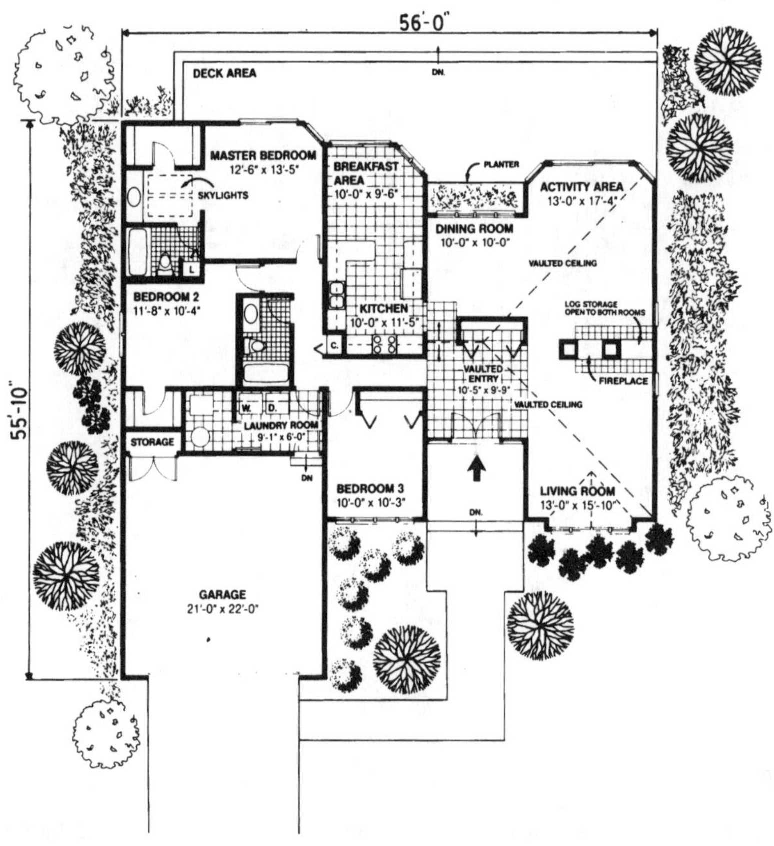
56'-0"
55'-10"
DECK AREA
DN.
MASTER BEDROOM
12'-6" x 13'-5"
SKYLIGHTS
L
BREAKFAST AREA
10'-0" x 9'-6"
PLANTER
ACTIVITY AREA
13'-0" x 17'-4"
DINING ROOM
10'-0" x 10'-0"
VAULTED CEILING
BEDROOM 2
11'-8" x 10'-4"
KITCHEN
10'-0" x 11'-5"
C.
LOG STORAGE OPEN TO BOTH ROOMS
FIREPLACE
VAULTED ENTRY
10'-5" x 9'-9"
VAULTED CEILING
W.
D.
LAUNDRY ROOM
9'-1" x 6'-0"
STORAGE
DN
BEDROOM 3
10'-0" x 10'-3"
DN.
LIVING ROOM
13'-0" x 15'-10"
GARAGE
21'-0" x 22'-0"

Total Living Area 1,850 sq. ft.

PRICE CODE: B

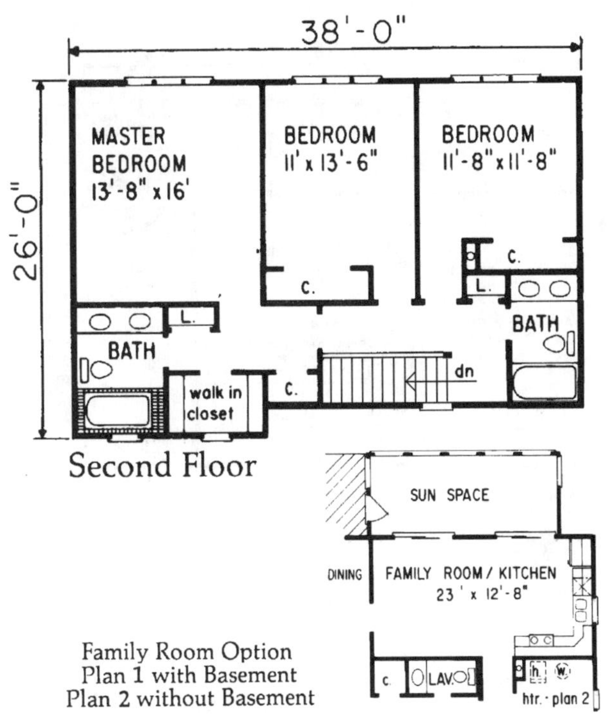
38'-0"
26'-0"
MASTER BEDROOM 13'-8" x 16'
BEDROOM 11' x 13'-6"
BEDROOM 11'-8" x 11'-8"
C.
C.
L.
L.
BATH
BATH
walk in closet
C.
dn
SUN SPACE
DINING
FAMILY ROOM / KITCHEN 23' x 12'-8"
c.
LAV.
h.
W.
htr. - plan 2

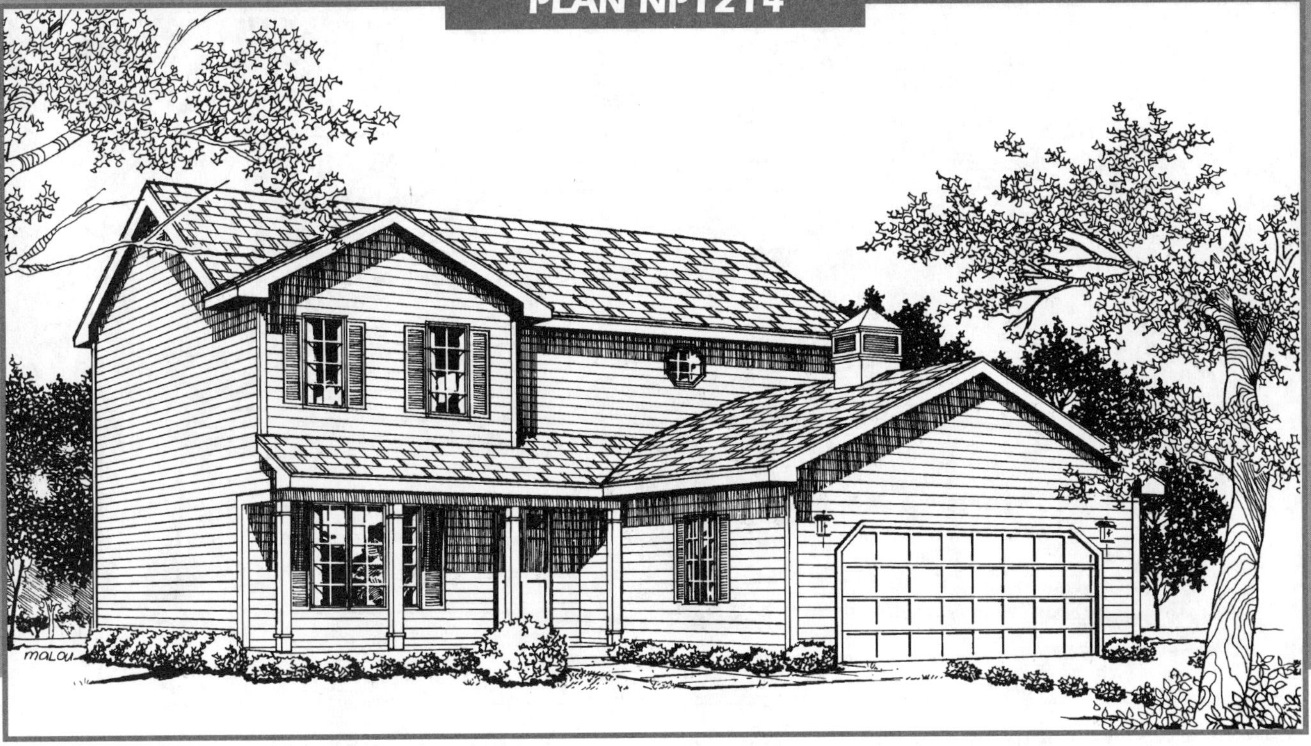

Second Floor

Family Room Option
Plan 1 with Basement
Plan 2 without Basement

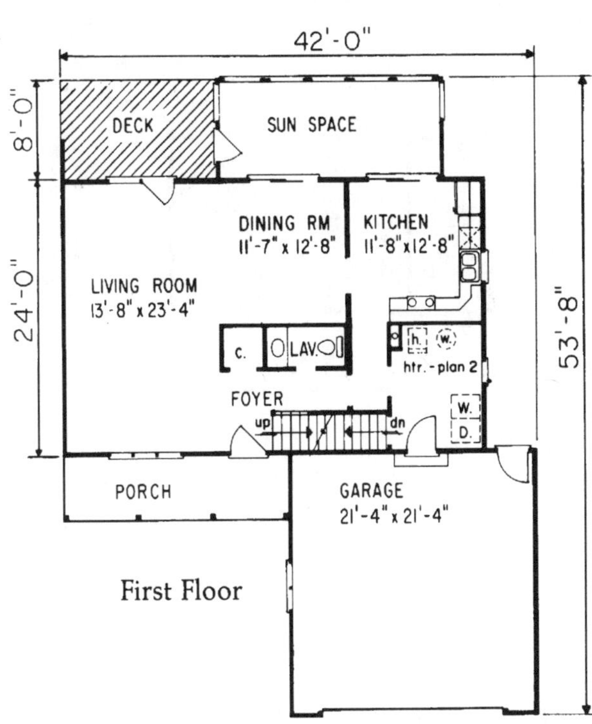
42'-0"
8'-0"
24'-0"
53'-8"
DECK
SUN SPACE
DINING RM 11'-7" x 12'-8"
KITCHEN 11'-8" x 12'-8"
LIVING ROOM 13'-8" x 23'-4"
c.
LAV.
h.
W.
htr. - plan 2
FOYER
up
dn
W.
D.
PORCH
GARAGE 21'-4" x 21'-4"

First Floor

Stylish Colonial Haven

Features

- Foyer opens to large L-shaped living room/ dining room.
- Two sliding glass doors provide access to rear sun space from the dining room and L-shaped kitchen.
- Access the rear deck from either the sun room or living room.
- Second floor features a master bedroom with walk-in closet and full bath with double vanity.
- Bedrooms upstairs are served by a full bath with double vanity. Sun space,160 square feet.

First Floor	**912 sq. ft.**
Second Floor	**940 sq. ft.**
Sun Space	**160 sq. ft.**
Total Living Area	**2,012 sq. ft.**

PRICE CODE: B

PLAN NP1335

74

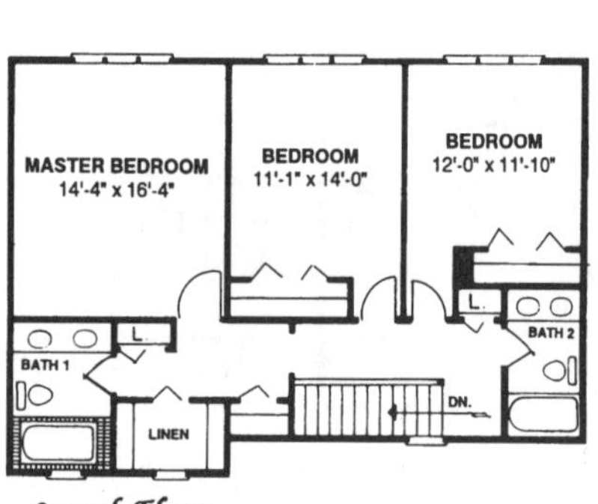
MASTER BEDROOM
14'-4" x 16'-4"
BEDROOM
11'-1" x 14'-0"
BEDROOM
12'-0" x 11'-10"
BATH 1
BATH 2
L.
LINEN
DN.

Second Floor

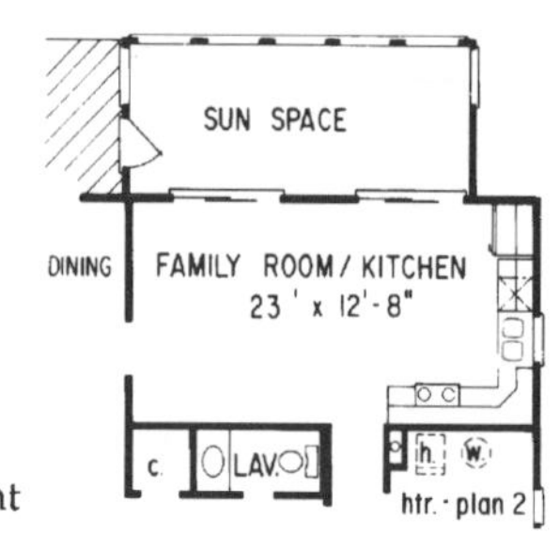
SUN SPACE
DINING
FAMILY ROOM / KITCHEN
23' x 12'-8"
C.
LAV.
h.
W.
htr. - plan 2

Family Room Option
Plan 1 with Basement
Plan 2 without Basement

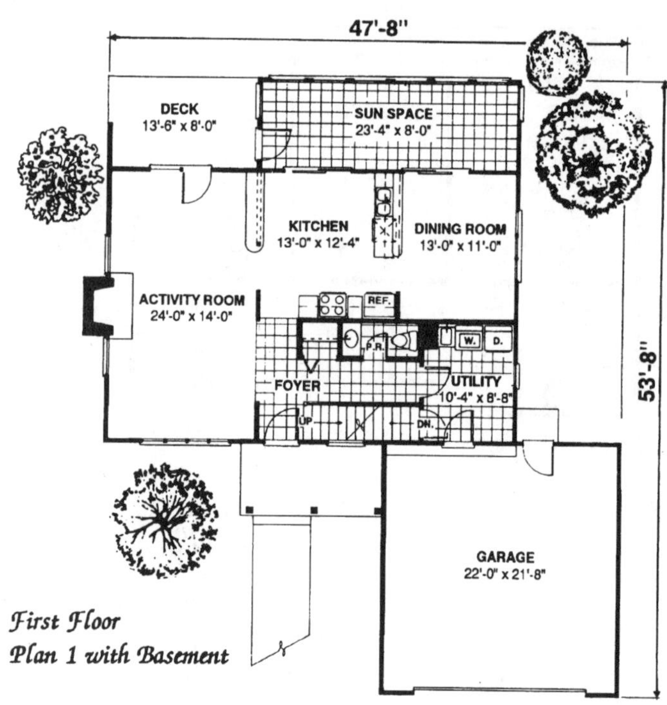
47'-8"
DECK
13'-6" x 8'-0"
SUN SPACE
23'-4" x 8'-0"
KITCHEN
13'-0" x 12'-4"
DINING ROOM
13'-0" x 11'-0"
ACTIVITY ROOM
24'-0" x 14'-0"
REF.
P.R.
W.
D.
FOYER
UTILITY
10'-4" x 8'-8"
UP
DN.
GARAGE
22'-0" x 21'-8"
53'-8"

First Floor
Plan 1 with Basement

Sunshine Manor

Features

- Traditional Colonial design with special, contemporary touches.
- Tiled entry foyer opens to staircase and large activity room with fireplace.
- Powder room, entry closet, and utility area conveniently located near entrance.
- Tiled sun space room has sliding door access to both the kitchen and dining room.
- Upstairs features three comfortable bedrooms and two full baths.
- Sun space, 160 square feet.

First Floor	912 sq. ft.
Second Floor	940 sq. ft.
Sun Space	192 sq. ft.
Total Living Area	2,044 sq. ft.

PRICE CODE: B

PLAN NPT109

MOLOU

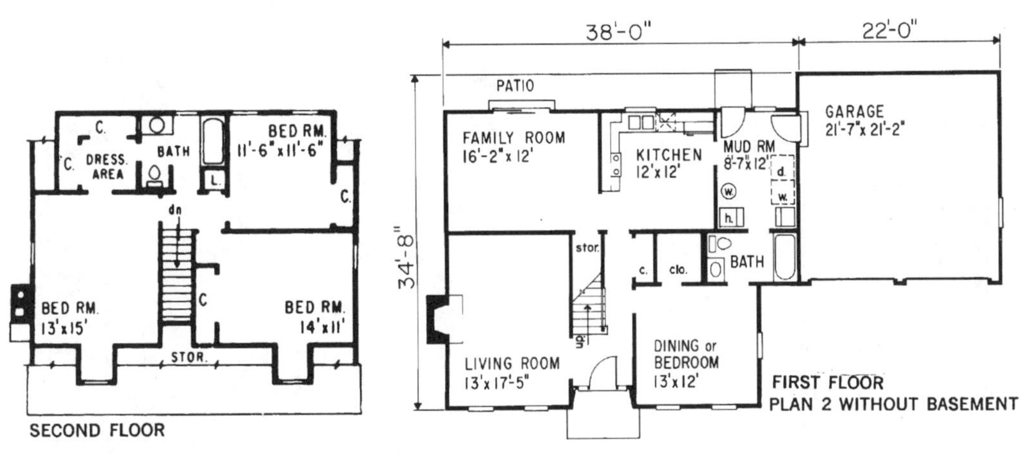
38'-0"
22'-0"
34'-8"
PATIO
FAMILY ROOM
16'-2"x 12'
KITCHEN
12'x12'
MUD RM
8'-7"x12'
GARAGE
21'-7"x 21'-2"
BATH
stor.
c.
clo.
LIVING ROOM
13'x17'-5"
DINING or
BEDROOM
13'x12'
FIRST FLOOR
PLAN 2 WITHOUT BASEMENT
C.
BATH
BED RM.
11'-6"x11'-6"
DRESS.
AREA
dn
BED RM.
13'x15'
BED RM.
14'x11'
STOR.
SECOND FLOOR

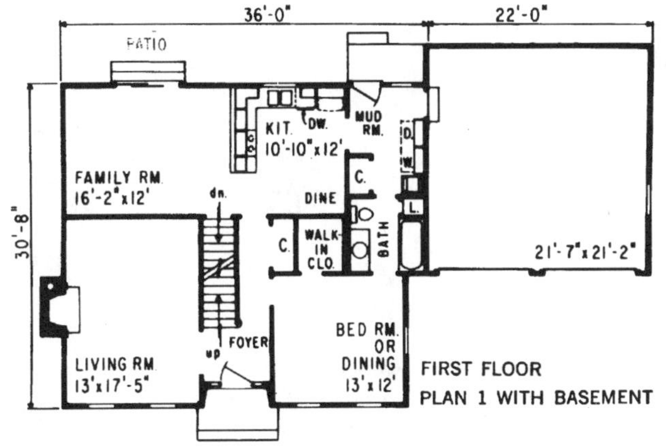
36'-0"
22'-0"
30'-8"
PATIO
KIT.
10'-10"x12'
DW.
MUD RM.
FAMILY RM
16'-2"x12'
dn.
DINE
WALK-IN CLO.
BATH
21'-7"x21'-2"
FOYER
up
LIVING RM
13'x17'-5"
BED RM. OR DINING
13'x12'
FIRST FLOOR
PLAN 1 WITH BASEMENT

First Floor	1,068 sq. ft.
Second Floor	804 sq. ft.
Total Living Area	1,872 sq. ft.

PLEASE SPECIFY PLAN 1 OR 2 WHEN ORDERING BLUEPRINT PLAN

PRICE CODE: B

PLAN NP1270

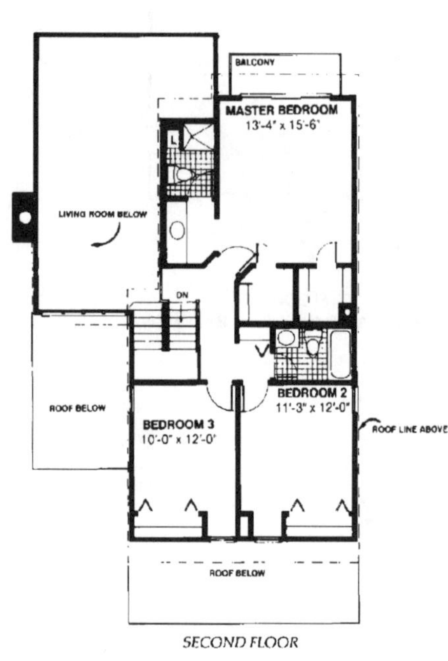

BALCONY
MASTER BEDROOM
13'-4" x 15'-6"
LIVING ROOM BELOW
DN
ROOF BELOW
BEDROOM 3
10'-0" x 12'-0"
BEDROOM 2
11'-3" x 12'-0"
ROOF LINE ABOVE
ROOF BELOW

SECOND FLOOR

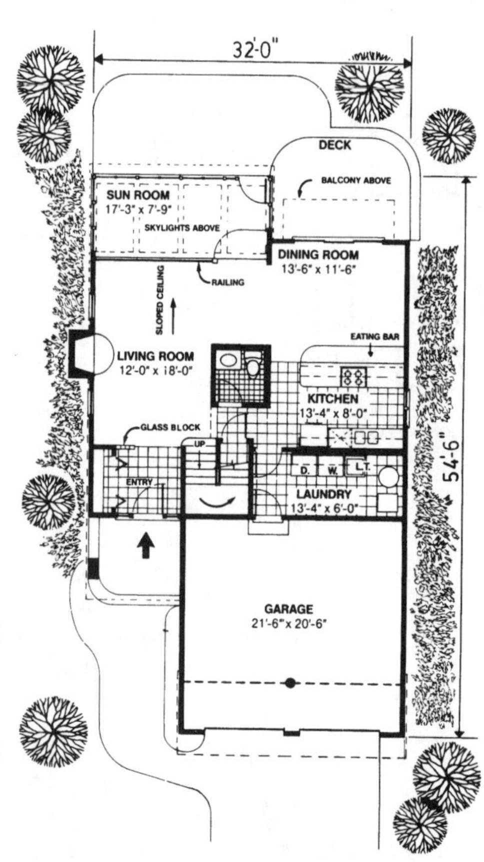

32'-0"
DECK
BALCONY ABOVE
SUN ROOM
17'-3" x 7'-9"
SKYLIGHTS ABOVE
DINING ROOM
13'-6" x 11'-6"
RAILING
SLOPED CEILING
EATING BAR
LIVING ROOM
12'-0" x 18'-0"
KITCHEN
13'-4" x 8'-0"
GLASS BLOCK
UP
ENTRY
LAUNDRY
13'-4" x 6'-0"
54'-6"
GARAGE
21'-6" x 20'-6"

Hidden Treasures

Features

- Perfect for a narrow lot.
- Spacious, comfortable design.
- Sloped ceilings crown entry and living room.
- Dining room adjoins kitchen with breakfast bar.
- Sunken sun room with skylights is delightful retreat or perfect for entertaining.
- Optional multi- level wooden deck can be accessed either from sun room or dining room.
- Two bedrooms with bath and master bedroom with private bath upstairs.
- Balcony off master bedroom overlooks living room.

First Floor	**896 sq. ft.**
Second Floor	**977 sq. ft.**
Total Living Area	**1,873 sq. ft.**

PRICE CODE: B

PLAN JA5299

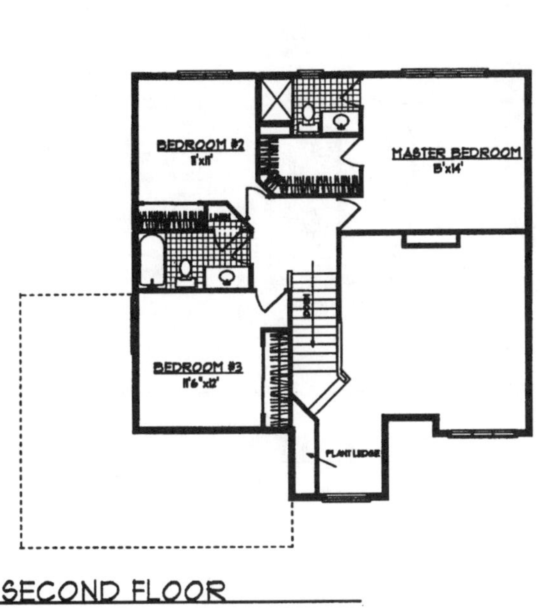
BEDROOM #2
MASTER BEDROOM
BEDROOM #3
PLANT LEDGE
SECOND FLOOR

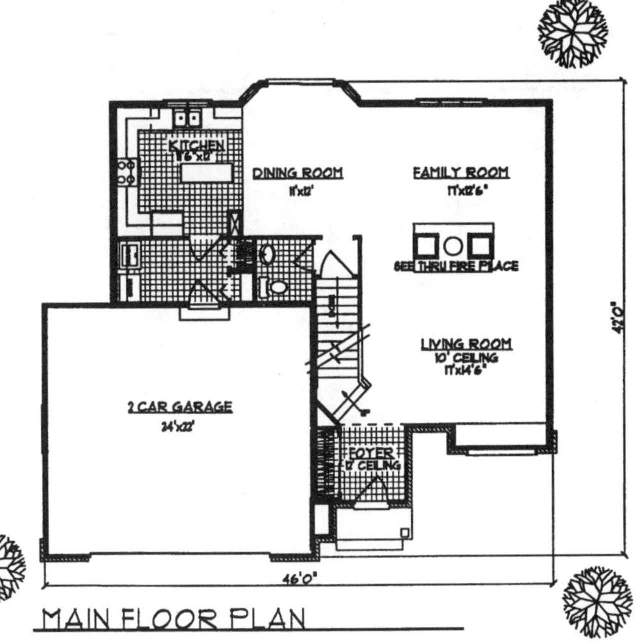
KITCHEN
DINING ROOM
11'x12'
FAMILY ROOM
17'x12'6"
SEE THRU FIRE PLACE
LIVING ROOM
10' CEILING
17'x14'6"
2 CAR GARAGE
24'x22'
FOYER
12' CEILING
42'0"
46'0"
MAIN FLOOR PLAN

First Floor	1,080 sq. ft.
Second Floor	794 sq. ft.
Total Living Area	1,874 sq. ft.

PRICE CODE: B

PLAN DB746

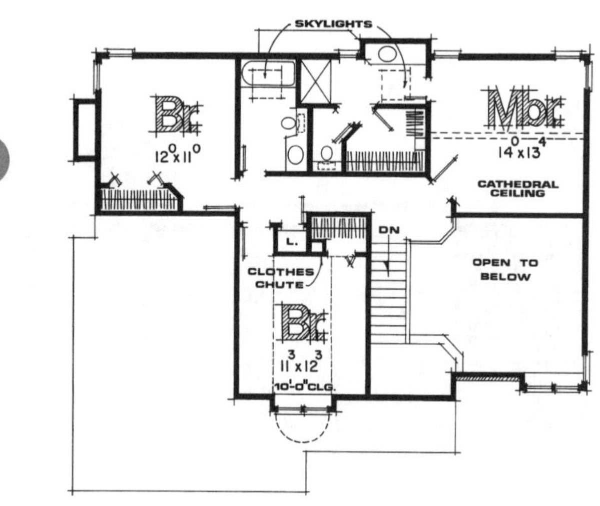
SKYLIGHTS
Br.
12⁰x11⁰
Mbr.
14⁰x13⁴
CATHEDRAL CEILING
DN
L.
CLOTHES CHUTE
OPEN TO BELOW
Br.
11³x12³
10'-0" CLG.

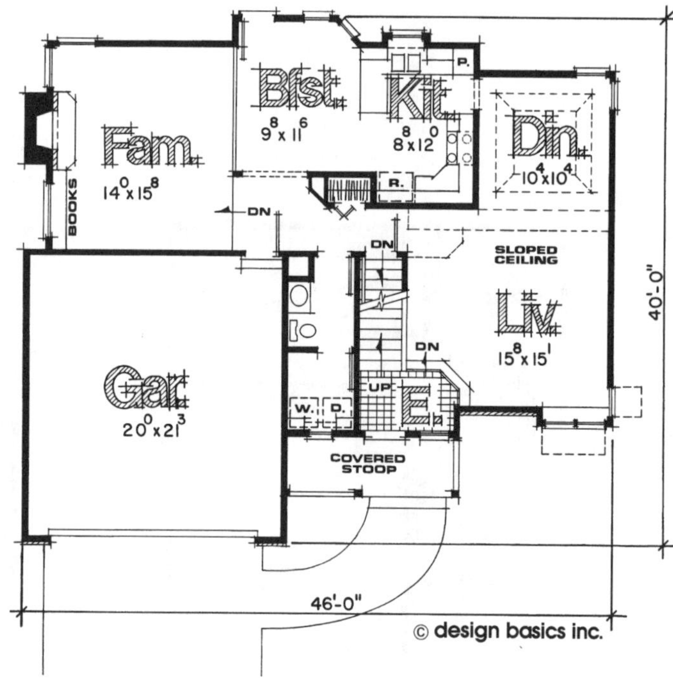
Bfst.
9⁸x11⁶
Kit.
8⁸x12⁰
P.
Fam.
14⁰x15⁸
BOOKS
Din.
10⁴x10⁴
R.
DN
SLOPED CEILING
Liv.
15⁸x15¹
Gar.
20⁰x21³
W.
D.
UP
E.
COVERED STOOP
40'-0"
46'-0"
© design basics inc.

Features

- Covered front porch.
- Step-down from entry into volume living room open to formal dining room with vaulted ceiling.
- Window in compartmented main-floor laundry area.
- Awning window centers above bookcase in family room with fireplace.
- Well-planned kitchen with lazy Susan, pantry and many cabinets is open to breakfast area.
- Cathedral ceiling in master bedroom.
- Skylit dressing area and compartmented stool in master bath, plus walk-in closet.
- Volume ceiling in front bedroom with beautiful arched window.

First Floor	1,042 sq. ft.
Second Floor	833 sq. ft.
Total Living Area	1,875 sq. ft.

PRICE CODE: C

PLAN AM2130B

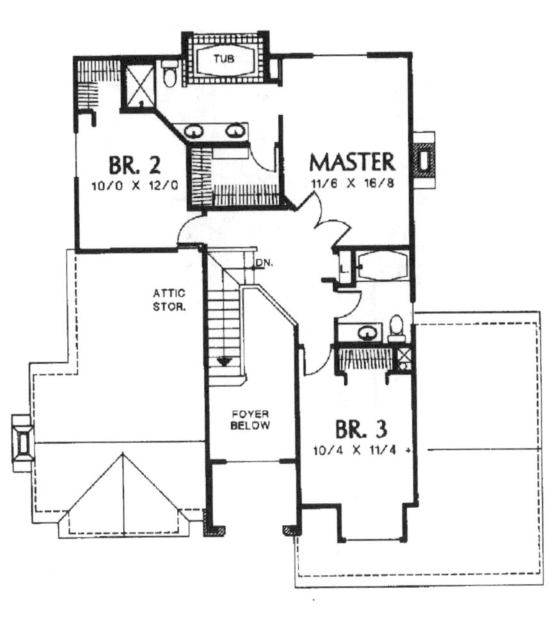

TUB
BR. 2
10/0 X 12/0
MASTER
11/6 X 16/8
DN.
ATTIC STOR.
FOYER BELOW
BR. 3
10/4 X 11/4

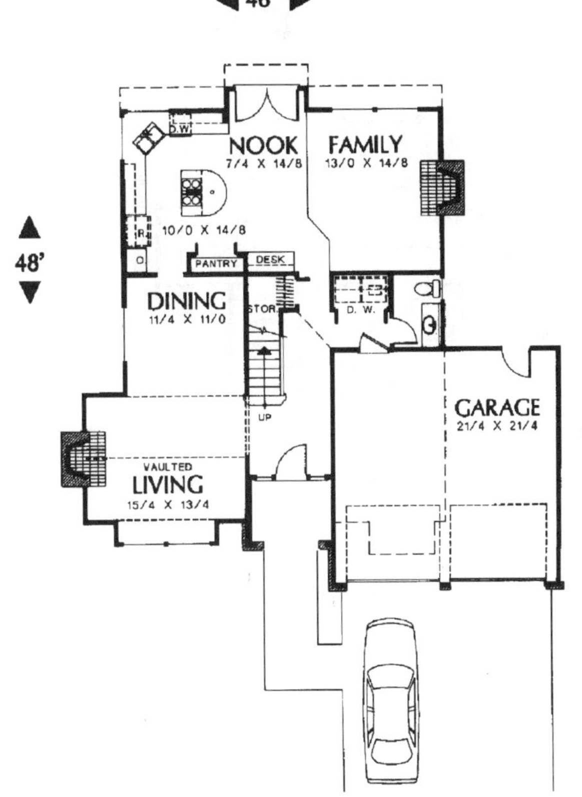

46'
48'
D.W.
NOOK
7/4 X 14/8
FAMILY
13/0 X 14/8
10/0 X 14/8
PANTRY
DESK
DINING
11/4 X 11/0
STOR.
D. W.
GARAGE
21/4 X 21/4
UP
VAULTED
LIVING
15/4 X 13/4

First Floor	1,062 sq. ft.
Second Floor	838 sq. ft.
Total Living Area	1,900 sq. ft.

PRICE CODE: B

PLAN DB1867

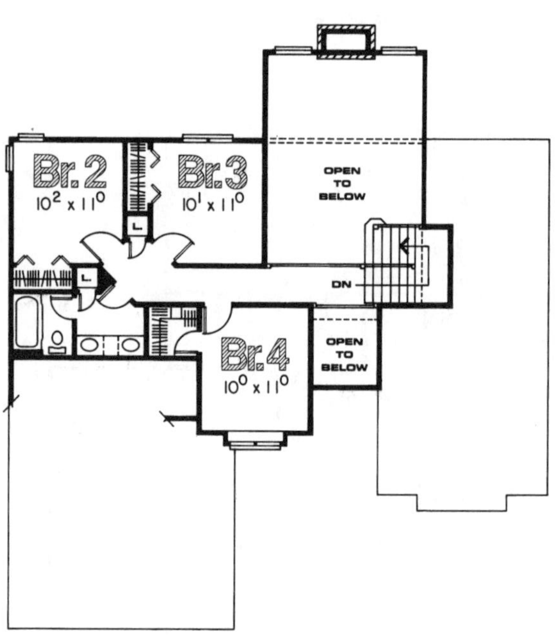

Br. 2
10^2 x 11^0
Br. 3
10^1 x 11^0
OPEN TO BELOW
DN
Br. 4
10^0 x 11^0
OPEN TO BELOW

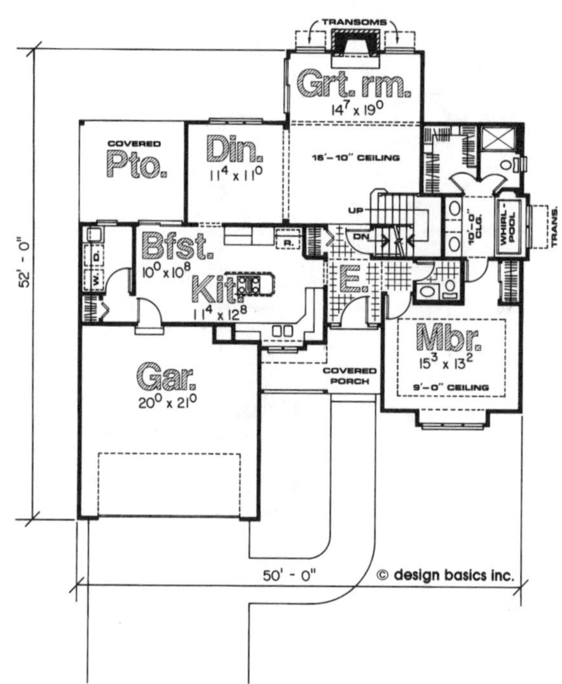

TRANSOMS
Grt. rm.
14^7 x 19^0
COVERED
Pto.
Din.
11^4 x 11^0
16'-10" CEILING
UP
DN
Bfst.
10^0 x 10^8
Kit.
11^4 x 12^8
E.
WHIRL-POOL
TRANS.
Mbr.
15^3 x 13^2
9'-0" CEILING
Gar.
20^0 x 21^0
COVERED PORCH
52' - 0"
50' - 0"
© design basics inc.

Features

- Sleek lines coupled with impressive detailing enhance elevation.
- Entry opens into volume great room with fireplace flanked by cheerful windows.
- Dining room off great room offers entertaining options.
- Kitchen and breakfast area has cooktop in island and access to covered patio.
- Bridge overlook on second level.
- Secondary bedrooms share compartmented bath with dual lavs.
- Master bedroom secluded on first level includes decorative ceiling and bright boxed window.
- Luxurious master bath has two closets, separate wet and dry areas, dual lavs and whirlpool tub.

First Floor	**1,302 sq. ft.**
Second Floor	**599 sq. ft.**
Total Living Area	**1,901 sq. ft.**

PRICE CODE: C

PLAN DB1727

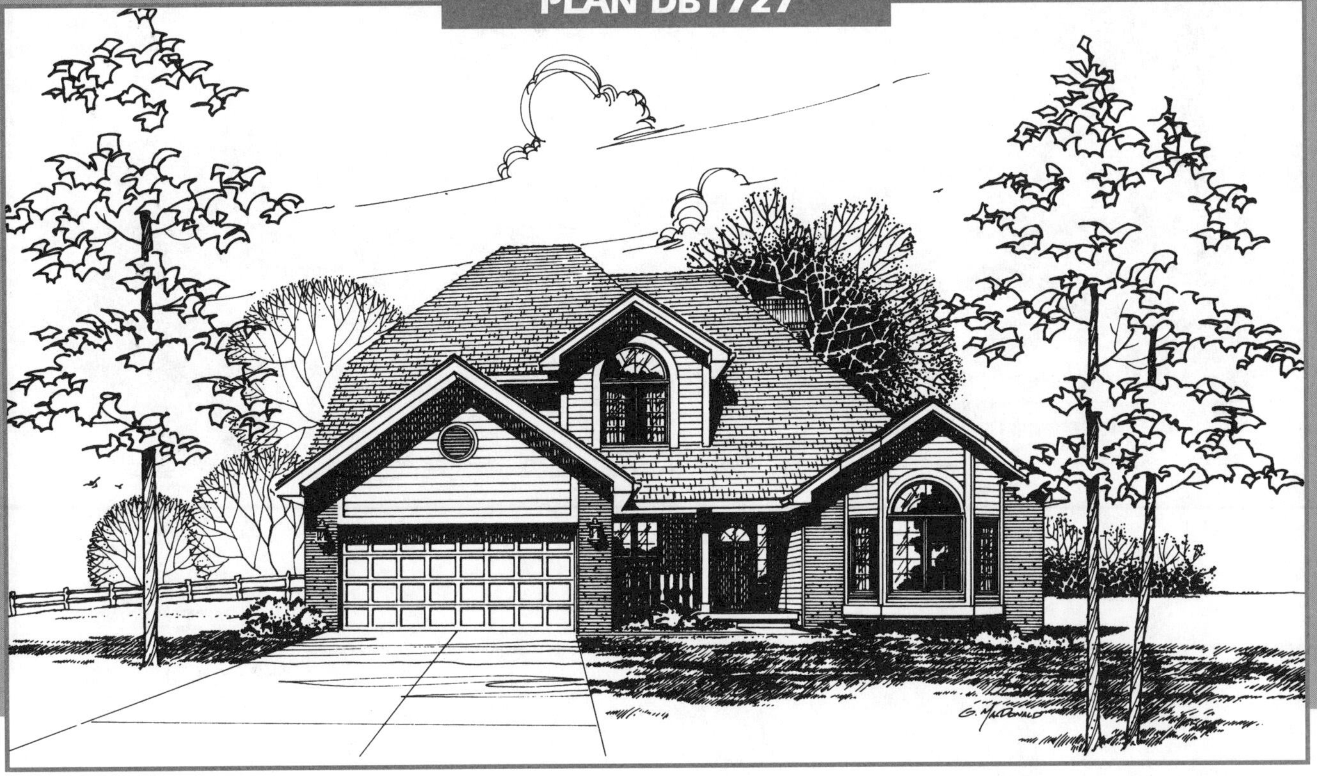

81

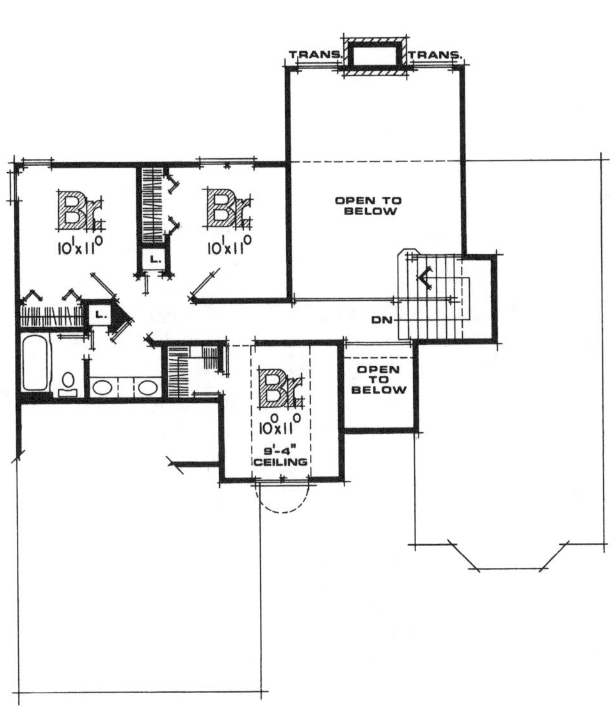
TRANS.
TRANS.
Br.
10'x11⁰
Br.
10'x11⁰
OPEN TO BELOW
L.
L.
DN
Br.
10⁰x11⁰
9'-4" CEILING
OPEN TO BELOW

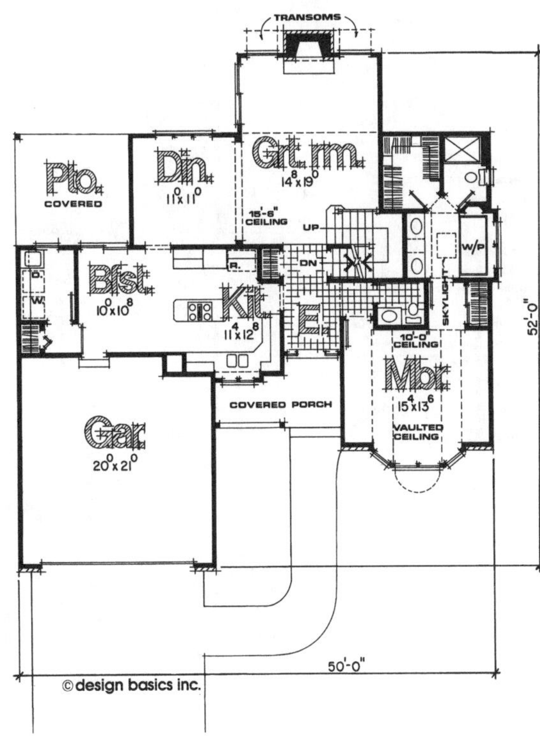
TRANSOMS
Pto.
COVERED
Din.
11⁰x11⁰
Grt.rm.
14⁸x19⁰
15'-8" CEILING
UP
DN
Brfst.
10⁰x10⁸
Kit.
11⁴x12⁸
E.
W/P
SKYLIGHT
10'-0" CEILING
Mbr.
15⁴x13⁶
VAULTED CEILING
COVERED PORCH
Gar.
20⁰x21⁰
52'-0"
50'-0"
©design basics inc.

Features

- Volume hard-surfaced entry with coat closet.
- Volume ceiling in great room with fireplace flanked by windows.
- Dining room open to great room for expanded entertaining.
- Island kitchen adjoins breakfast area with access to covered patio.
- Laundry room with sink, closet and window to the back.
- Upstairs landing overlooks entry and great room below.
- Master bedroom with volume ceiling and arched bayed window adjoins luxury skylit dressing/bath area with whirlpool, walk-in closet and plant shelf.
- Secondary bedrooms share generous compartmented bath

First Floor	1,306 sq. ft.
Second Floor	599 sq. ft.
Total Living Area	1,905 sq. ft.

PRICE CODE: C

PLAN NP1271

MALOU

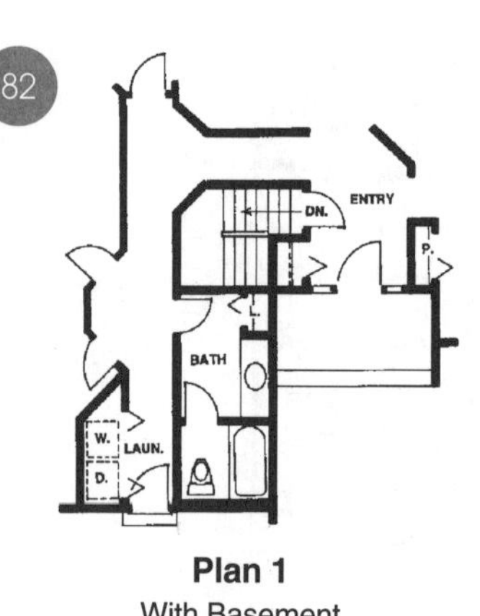

DN.
ENTRY
P.
BATH
W.
LAUN.
D.

Plan 1
With Basement

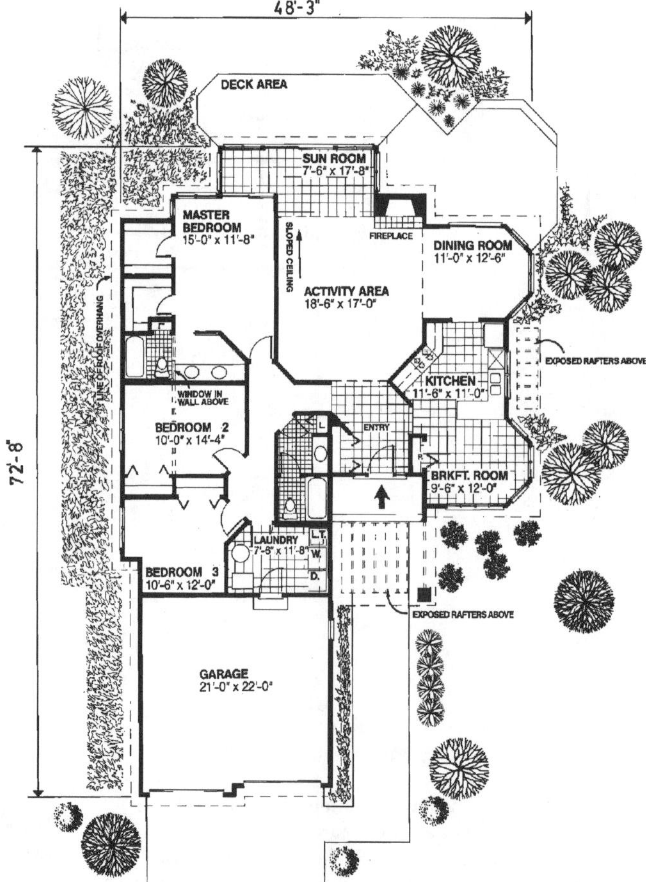

48'-3"
DECK AREA
SUN ROOM
7'-6" x 17'-8"
MASTER BEDROOM
15'-0" x 11'-8"
SLOPED CEILING
FIREPLACE
DINING ROOM
11'-0" x 12'-6"
ACTIVITY AREA
18'-6" x 17'-0"
EXPOSED RAFTERS ABOVE
KITCHEN
11'-6" x 11'-0"
WINDOW IN WALL ABOVE
BEDROOM 2
10'-0" x 14'-4"
ENTRY
BRKFT. ROOM
9'-6" x 12'-0"
72'-8"
LAUNDRY
7'-6" x 11'-8"
BEDROOM 3
10'-6" x 12'-0"
EXPOSED RAFTERS ABOVE
GARAGE
21'-0" x 22'-0"

Arboure Wood

Features

- Exposed entry rafters, wide overhanging gable roof lines, and vertical windows combine to make this home smartly elegant.
- Activity area with fireplace opens to dining room.
- Sun room off activity area leads to deck.
- Laundry room conveniently located in bedroom wing of home.
- Two bedrooms share a full bath.
- Additional master bedroom suite features access to the sun room plus a deluxe master bath with clerestory window and large closets.

Total Living Area **1,907 sq. ft.**

PRICE CODE: B

PLAN NP1355

BEDROOM
12'-0" x 12'-0"
BATH
LAUNDRY AREA
MASTER BATH
LINEN
DN.
BEDROOM
12'-0" x 13'-0"
OPEN BELOW
MASTER BEDROOM
19'-0" x 14'-0"

SECOND FLOOR

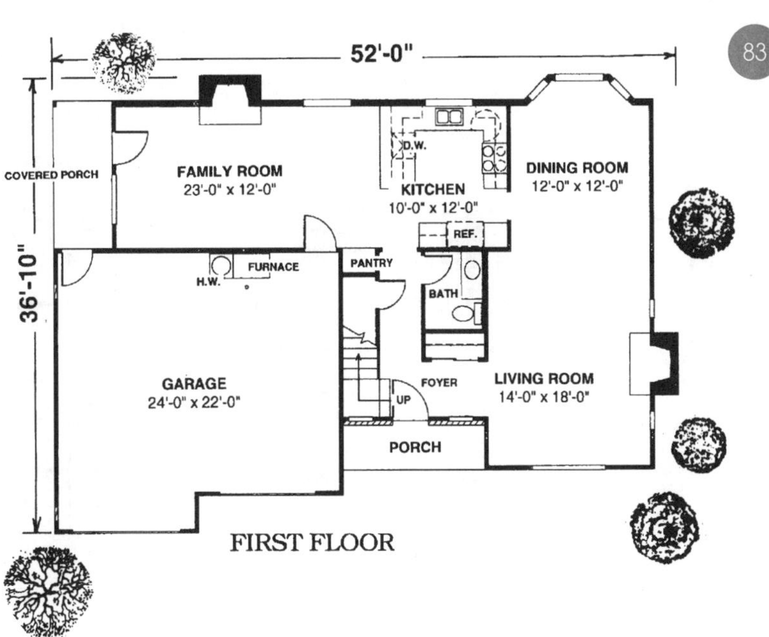
52'-0"
36'-10"
COVERED PORCH
FAMILY ROOM
23'-0" x 12'-0"
D.W.
KITCHEN
10'-0" x 12'-0"
DINING ROOM
12'-0" x 12'-0"
REF.
PANTRY
FURNACE
H.W.
BATH
GARAGE
24'-0" x 22'-0"
FOYER
UP
LIVING ROOM
14'-0" x 18'-0"
PORCH

FIRST FLOOR

First Floor	984 sq. ft.
Second Floor	943 sq. ft.
Total Living Area	1,927 sq. ft.

PRICE CODE: B

PLAN NP1100

84

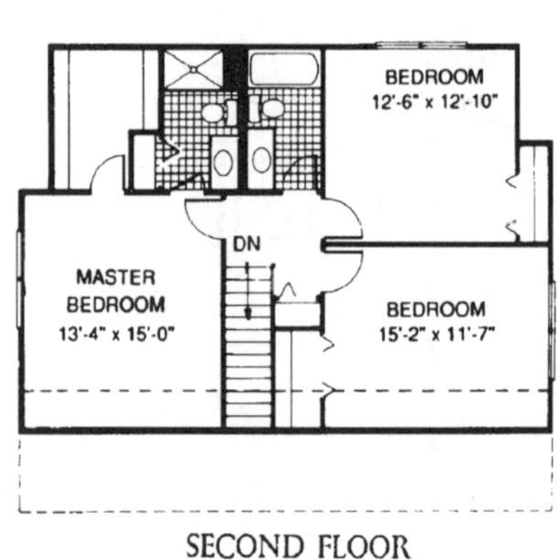

BEDROOM
12'-6" x 12'-10"
DN
MASTER BEDROOM
13'-4" x 15'-0"
BEDROOM
15'-2" x 11'-7"

SECOND FLOOR

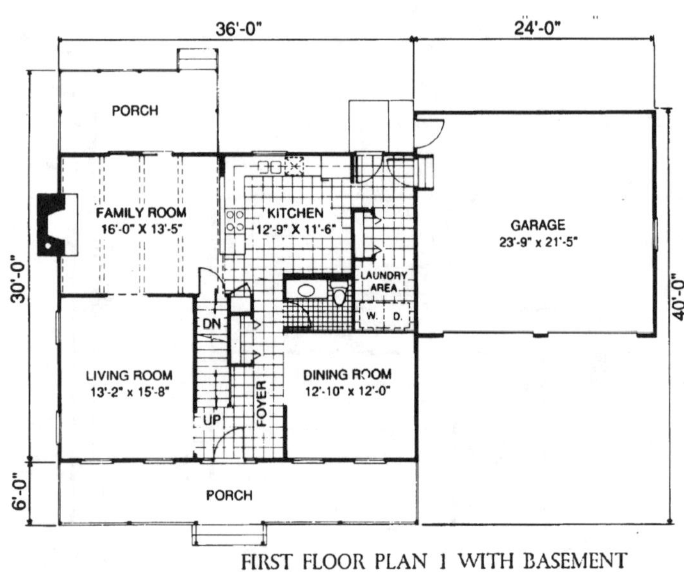

36'-0"
24'-0"
PORCH
FAMILY ROOM
16'-0" X 13'-5"
KITCHEN
12'-9" X 11'-6"
GARAGE
23'-9" x 21'-5"
30'-0"
40'-0"
LAUNDRY AREA
W.
D.
DN
LIVING ROOM
13'-2" x 15'-8"
FOYER
DINING ROOM
12'-10" x 12'-0"
UP
6'-0"
PORCH

FIRST FLOOR PLAN 1 WITH BASEMENT

Down-Home Delight

Features

- Nothing could be sweeter than to view this home as yours.
- Beautiful, front-spanning porch exudes warmth.
- Living room and dining room flank the entrance hall.
- Cozy family room features beamed ceiling and fireplace.
- L-shaped kitchen roomy enough for small dining table.
- Upstairs, master bedroom has generous walk-in closet and private bath.
- Two additional upstairs bedrooms are served by full bath.

First Floor	**1,080 sq. ft.**
Second Floor	**868 sq. ft.**
Total Living Area	**1,948 sq. ft.**

PRICE CODE: B

PLAN DB2719

G. MacDONALD

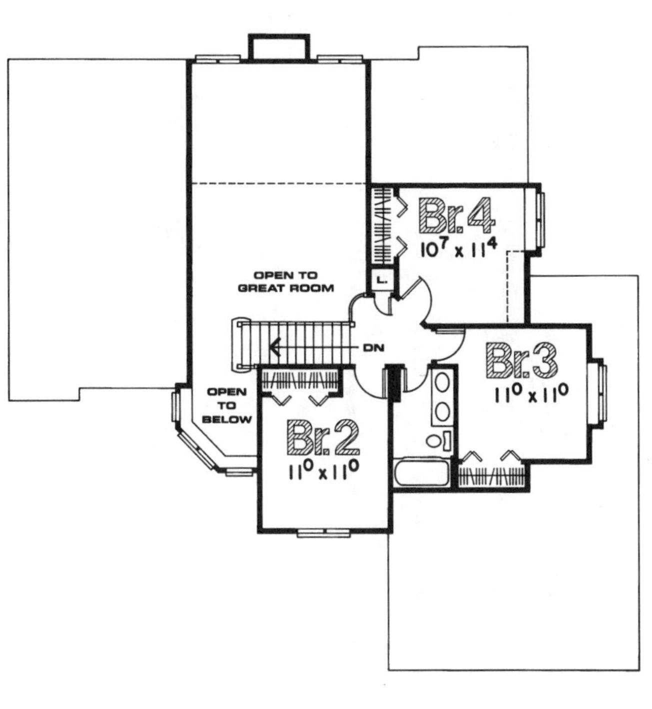

Br. 4
10⁷ x 11⁴
OPEN TO GREAT ROOM
L.
DN
Br. 3
11⁰ x 11⁰
OPEN TO BELOW
Br. 2
11⁰ x 11⁰

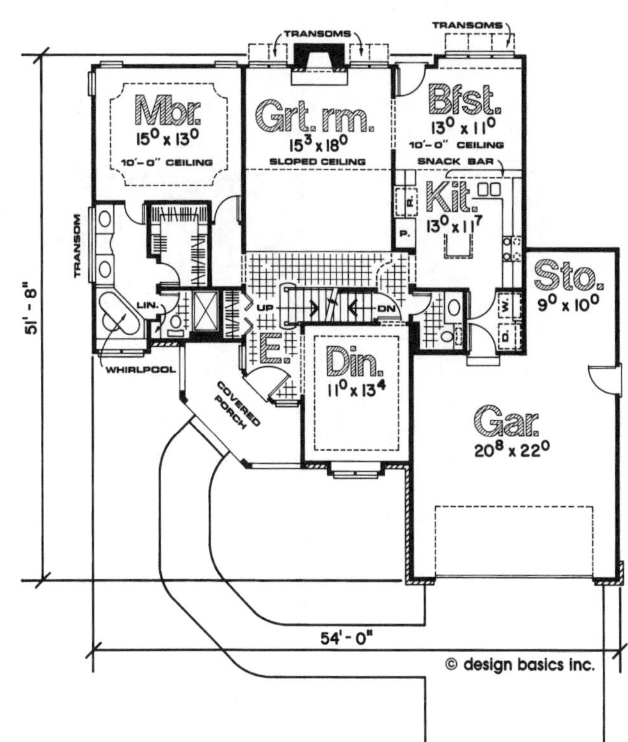

TRANSOMS
TRANSOMS
Mbr.
15⁰ x 13⁰
10'-0" CEILING
Grt. rm.
15³ x 18⁰
SLOPED CEILING
Bfst.
13⁰ x 11⁰
10'-0" CEILING
SNACK BAR
Kit.
13⁰ x 11⁷
TRANSOM
51'-8"
Sto.
9⁰ x 10⁰
LIN.
UP
DN
WHIRLPOOL
E.
Din.
11⁰ x 13⁴
COVERED PORCH
Gar.
20⁸ x 22⁰
54'-0"
© design basics inc.

PLAN FD7110

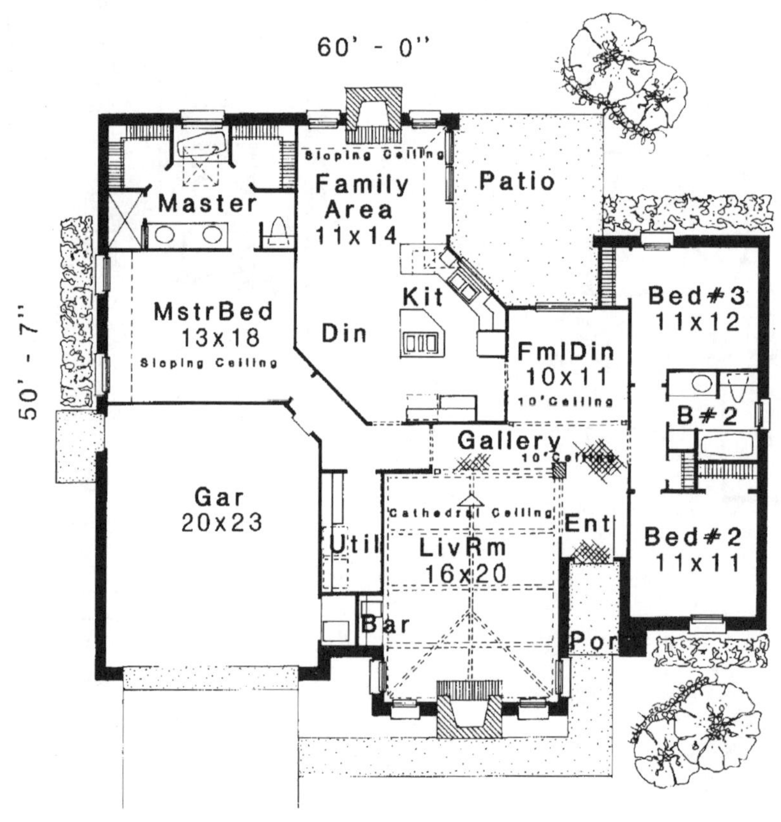
60' - 0"
50' - 7"
Master
Sloping Ceiling
Family Area 11x14
Patio
MstrBed 13x18
Sloping Ceiling
Kit
Din
Bed#3 11x12
FmlDin 10x11
10'Ceiling
B#2
Gallery
10'Ceiling
Gar 20x23
Cathedral Ceiling
Ent
Util
LivRm 16x20
Bed#2 11x11
Bar
Por

Total Living Area 1,980 sq. ft.

PRICE CODE: B

PLAN DB2619

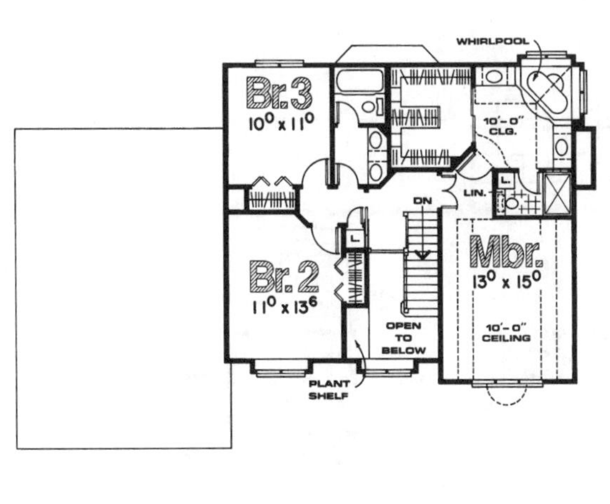
WHIRLPOOL
Br. 3
$10^{0} \times 11^{0}$
10'-0" CLG.
LIN.
DN
L
Mbr.
$13^{0} \times 15^{0}$
Br. 2
$11^{0} \times 13^{6}$
OPEN TO BELOW
10'-0" CEILING
PLANT SHELF

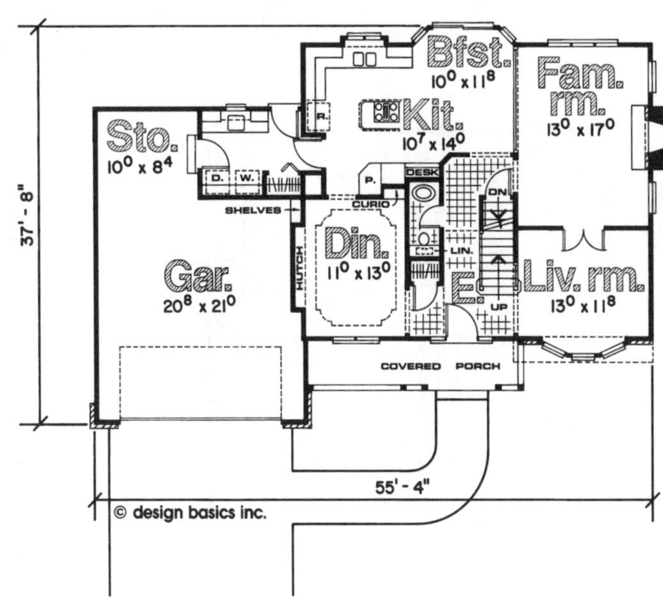
Bfst.
$10^{0} \times 11^{8}$
Fam. rm.
$13^{0} \times 17^{0}$
Sto.
$10^{0} \times 8^{4}$
Kit.
$10^{7} \times 14^{0}$
R.
D.
W.
P.
DESK
SHELVES
CURIO
HUTCH
Din.
$11^{0} \times 13^{0}$
Gar.
$20^{8} \times 21^{0}$
LIN.
DN
UP
E.
Liv. rm.
$13^{0} \times 11^{8}$
COVERED PORCH
37' - 8"
55' - 4"
© design basics inc.

Features

- Distinctive design personality is complemented by large covered porch with wood railing.
- Living room is distinguished by warmth of bayed window and French doors leading to family room.
- Built-in curio cabinet adds interest to formal dining room.
- Large laundry room provides practical and desirable access from garage, outdoors and kitchen.
- Well-appointed kitchen with island cook top is planned to save you steps.
- Secondary bedrooms share comparmented hall bath.

First Floor	1,093 sq. ft.
Second Floor	905 sq. ft.
Total Living Area	1,998 sq. ft.

PRICE CODE: C

PLAN NPT145

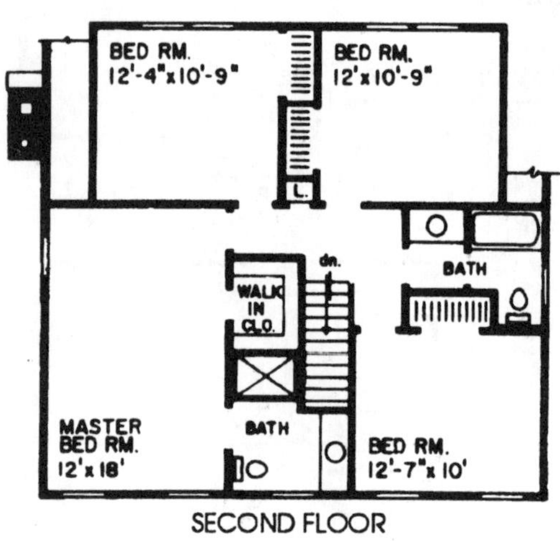
BED RM.
12'-4"x10'-9"
BED RM.
12'x10'-9"
L.
WALK IN CLO.
dn.
BATH
MASTER BED RM.
12'x18'
BATH
BED RM.
12'-7"x10'
SECOND FLOOR

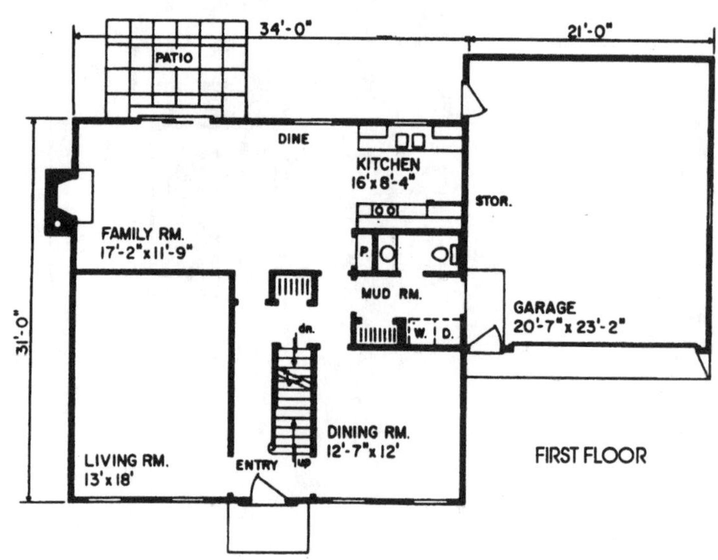
34'-0"
21'-0"
PATIO
DINE
KITCHEN
16'x8'-4"
STOR.
FAMILY RM.
17'-2"x11'-9"
P.
MUD RM.
W. D.
GARAGE
20'-7"x23'-2"
31'-0"
dn.
DINING RM.
12'-7"x12'
LIVING RM.
13'x18'
ENTRY
up
FIRST FLOOR

Westward

Features

- Salt-box design reminds us of our heritage while modern comforts surround in this beautiful home.
- Well-defined activity area in this home includes U-shaped kitchen with open dining/family room with fireplace.
- Formal living room and formal dining room occupy the front of the home.
- Upstairs, the master bedroom features walk-in closet and full bath.
- Three additional upstairs bedrooms share a full bath.

First Floor	1,054 sq. ft.
Second Floor	953 sq. ft.
Total Living Area	2,007 sq. ft.

PRICE CODE: B

PLAN FD7627-L

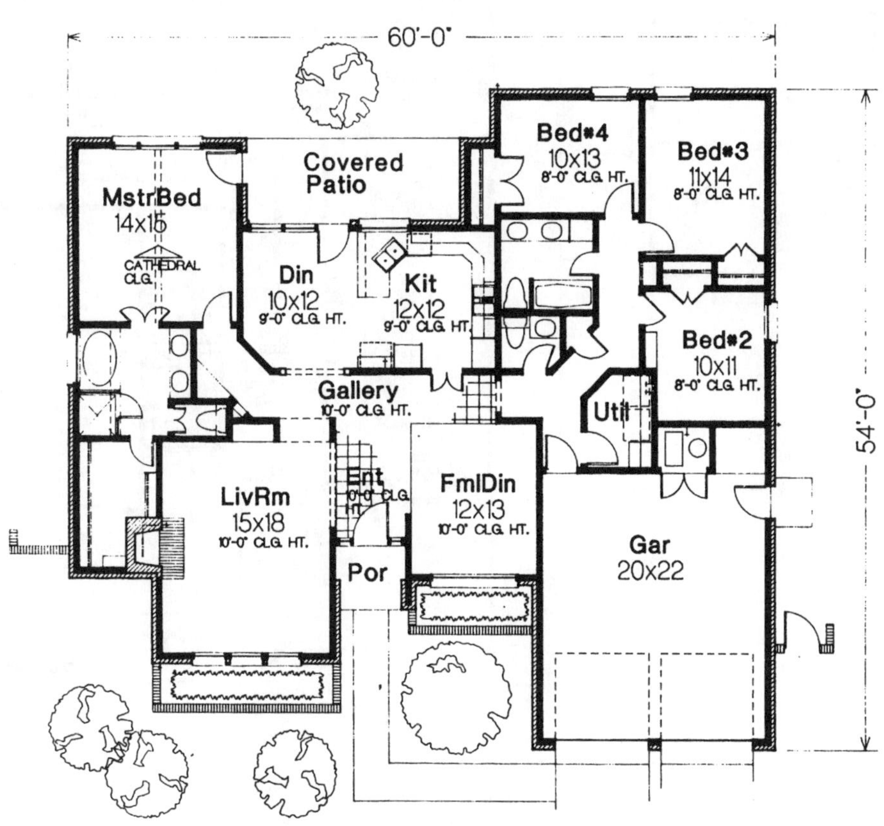
60'-0"
54'-0"
Covered Patio
MstrBed
14x15
CATHEDRAL CLG.
Bed#4
10x13
8'-0" CLG. HT.
Bed#3
11x14
8'-0" CLG. HT.
Din
10x12
9'-0" CLG. HT.
Kit
12x12
9'-0" CLG. HT.
Bed#2
10x11
8'-0" CLG. HT.
Gallery
10'-0" CLG. HT.
Util
LivRm
15x18
10'-0" CLG. HT.
Ent
FmlDin
12x13
10'-0" CLG. HT.
Gar
20x22
Por

89

Total Living Area 2,030 sq. ft.

PRICE CODE: B

PLAN DB1769

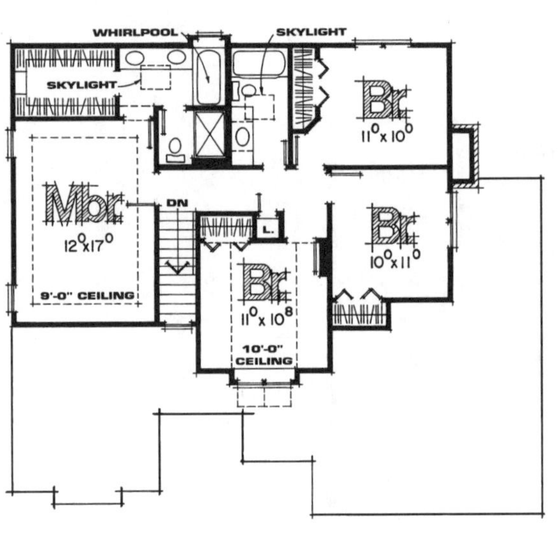
WHIRLPOOL
SKYLIGHT
SKYLIGHT
Br.
11⁰x 10⁰
Mbr.
12⁰x17⁰
9'-0" CEILING
DN
L.
Br.
10⁰x 11⁰
Br.
11⁰x 10⁸
10'-0" CEILING

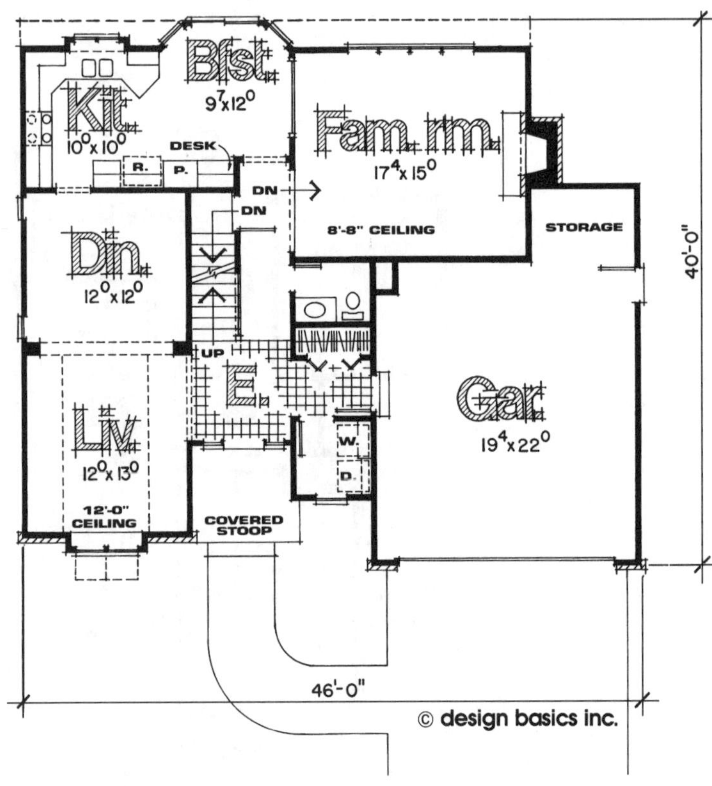
Bfst.
9⁷x12⁰
Kit.
10⁰x 10⁰
DESK
R.
P.
Fam. rm.
17⁴x 15⁰
DN
DN
8'-8" CEILING
STORAGE
40'-0"
Din.
12⁰x 12⁰
UP
E.
Liv.
12⁰x 13⁰
12'-0" CEILING
W.
D.
Gar.
19⁴x 22⁰
COVERED STOOP
46'-0"
© design basics inc.

Features

- Large hall coat closet and nearby laundry room convenient to garage entrance into home.
- Volume living room opens to large dining room for entertaining.
- Efficient kitchen with pantry and planning desk open to bayed dinette.
- Sunken family room, private from entry, has fireplace and many windows.
- Extra storage space in garage.
- Secondary bedrooms segregated for privacy share skylit hall bath.
- Large master bedroom with elaborate skylit master bath includes walk-in closet, double vanity and compartmented stool and shower.

First Floor	1,081 sq. ft.
Second Floor	950 sq. ft.
Total Living Area	2,031 sq. ft.

PRICE CODE: C

PLAN FD8047-L

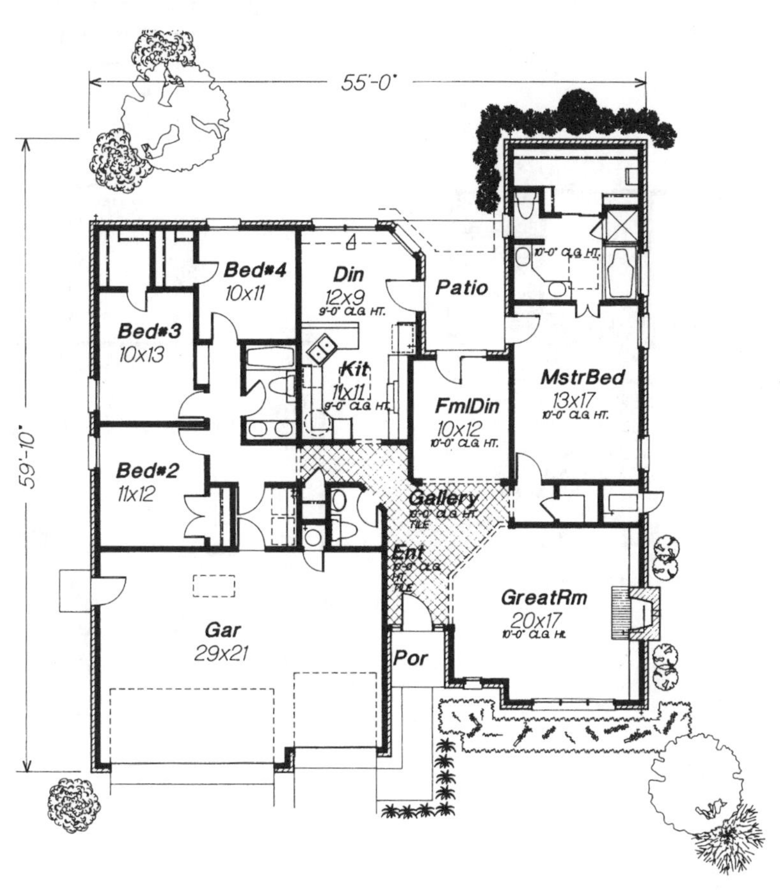

55'-0"
59'-10"
Bed#4
10x11
Din
12x9
9'-0" CLG. HT.
Patio
Bed#3
10x13
Kit
11x11
9'-0" CLG. HT.
MstrBed
13x17
10'-0" CLG. HT.
FmlDin
10x12
10'-0" CLG. HT.
Bed#2
11x12
Gallery
10'-0" CLG. HT.
TILE
Ent
GreatRm
20x17
10'-0" CLG. Ht.
Gar
29x21
Por

Total Living Area 2,038 sq. ft.

PRICE CODE: B

CUSTOMIZE IT!

ORDER TOLL FREE 1-800-533-4350 24-HOUR FAX ORDERING 1-800-344-4293

PLAN AM2212

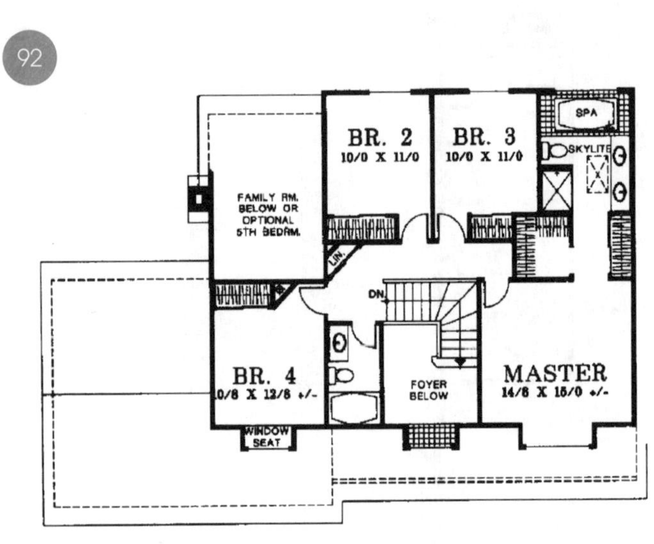
FAMILY RM. BELOW OR OPTIONAL 5TH BEDRM.
BR. 2
10/0 X 11/0
BR. 3
10/0 X 11/0
SPA
SKYLITE
LIN.
DN
BR. 4
10/8 X 12/8 +/-
FOYER BELOW
MASTER
14/6 X 15/0 +/-
WINDOW SEAT

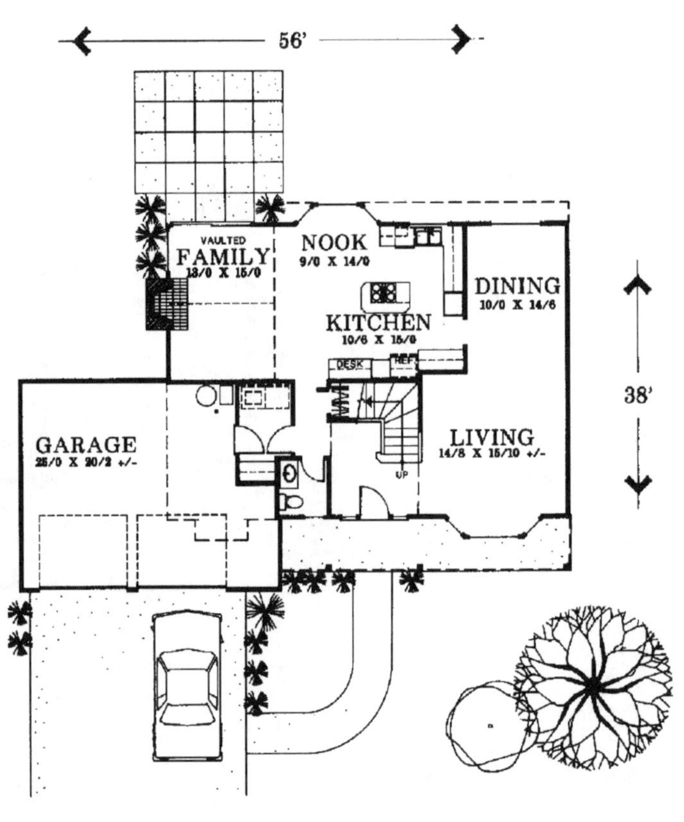
56'
VAULTED
FAMILY
13/0 X 15/0
NOOK
9/0 X 14/0
DINING
10/0 X 14/6
KITCHEN
10/6 X 15/0
DESK
REF
38'
GARAGE
25/0 X 20/2 +/-
LIVING
14/8 X 15/10 +/-
UP

First Floor	1,105 sq. ft.
Second Floor	950 sq. ft.
Total Living Area	2,055 sq. ft.

PRICE CODE: B

PLAN FD7999

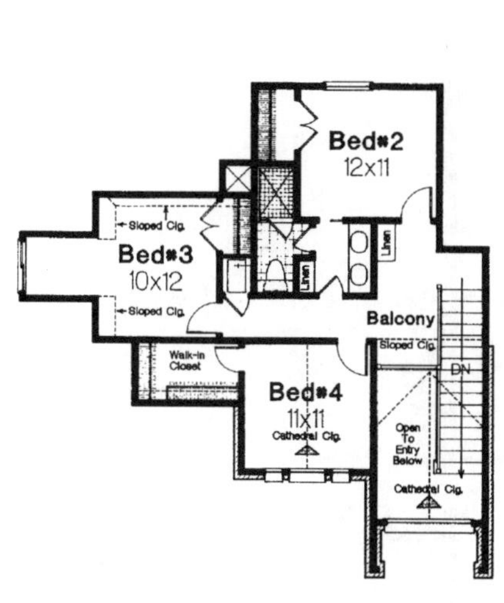
Bed#2
12x11
Bed#3
10x12
Sloped Clg.
Sloped Clg.
Linen
Balcony
Sloped Clg.
DN
Walk-in Closet
Bed#4
11x11
Cathedral Clg.
Open To Entry Below
Cathedral Clg.

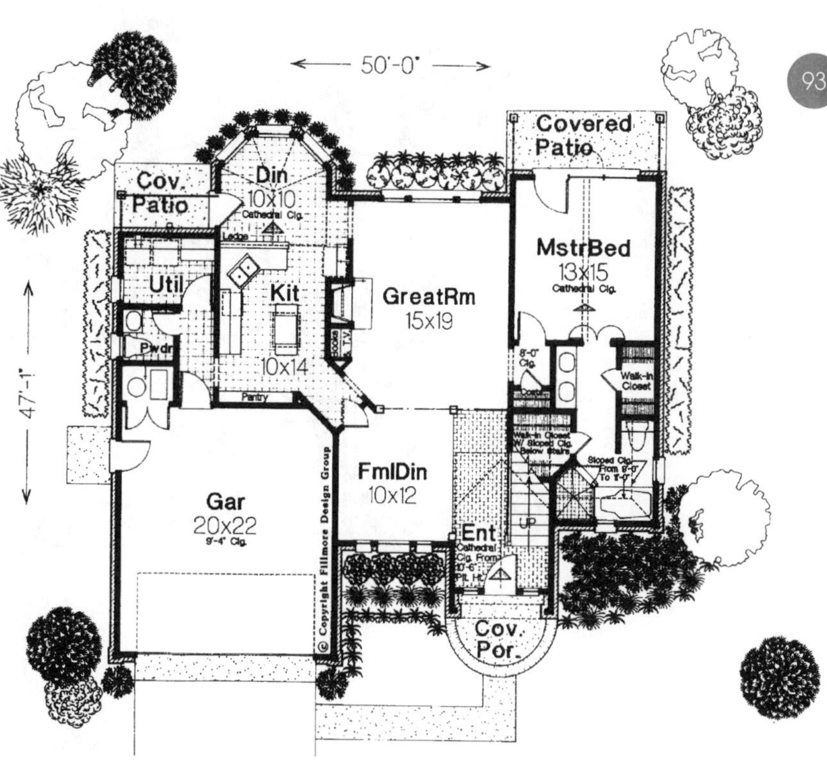
50'-0"
Covered Patio
Cov. Patio
Din
10x10
Cathedral Clg.
MstrBed
13x15
Cathedral Clg.
Util
Kit
10x14
GreatRm
15x19
Pwdr
Pantry
Walk-in Closet
47'-1"
Gar
20x22
9'-4" Clg.
© Copyright Fillmore Design Group
FmlDin
10x12
Ent
UP
Cov. Por.

First Floor	1,359 sq. ft.
Second Floor	697 sq. ft.
Total Living Area	2,056 sq. ft.

PRICE CODE: B

PLAN FD8166-L

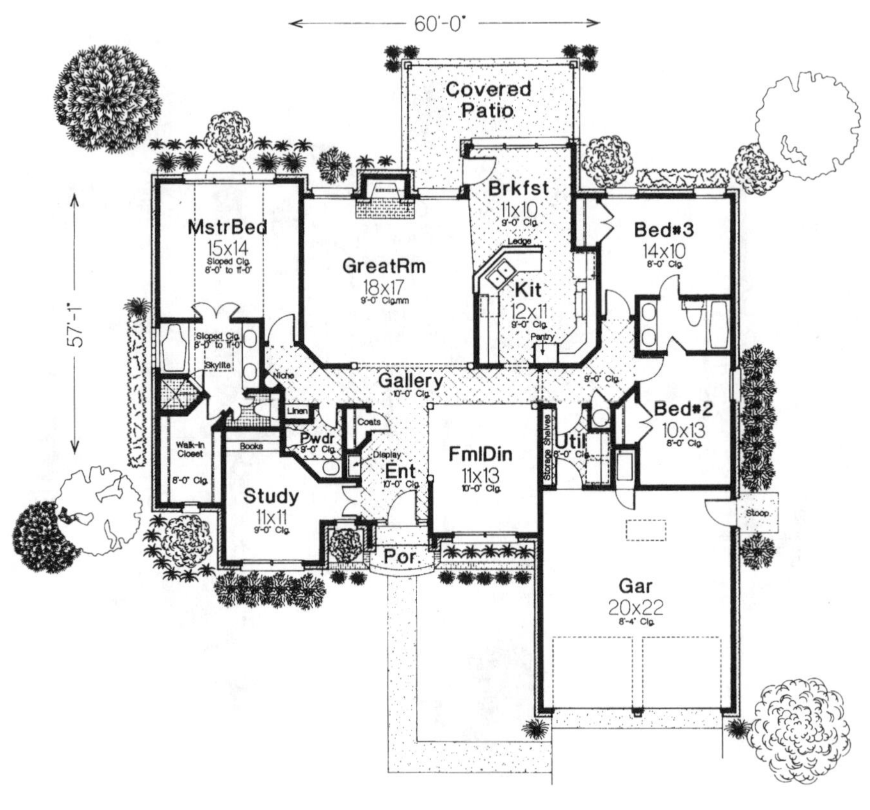

60'-0"
57'-1"
Covered Patio
Brkfst
11x10
MstrBed
15x14
GreatRm
18x17
Kit
12x11
Bed#3
14x10
Gallery
Bed#2
10x13
Pwdr
Ent
FmlDin
11x13
Util
Study
11x11
Por.
Gar
20x22

Total Living Area **2,061 sq. ft.**

PRICE CODE: B

PLAN FD7965-LB

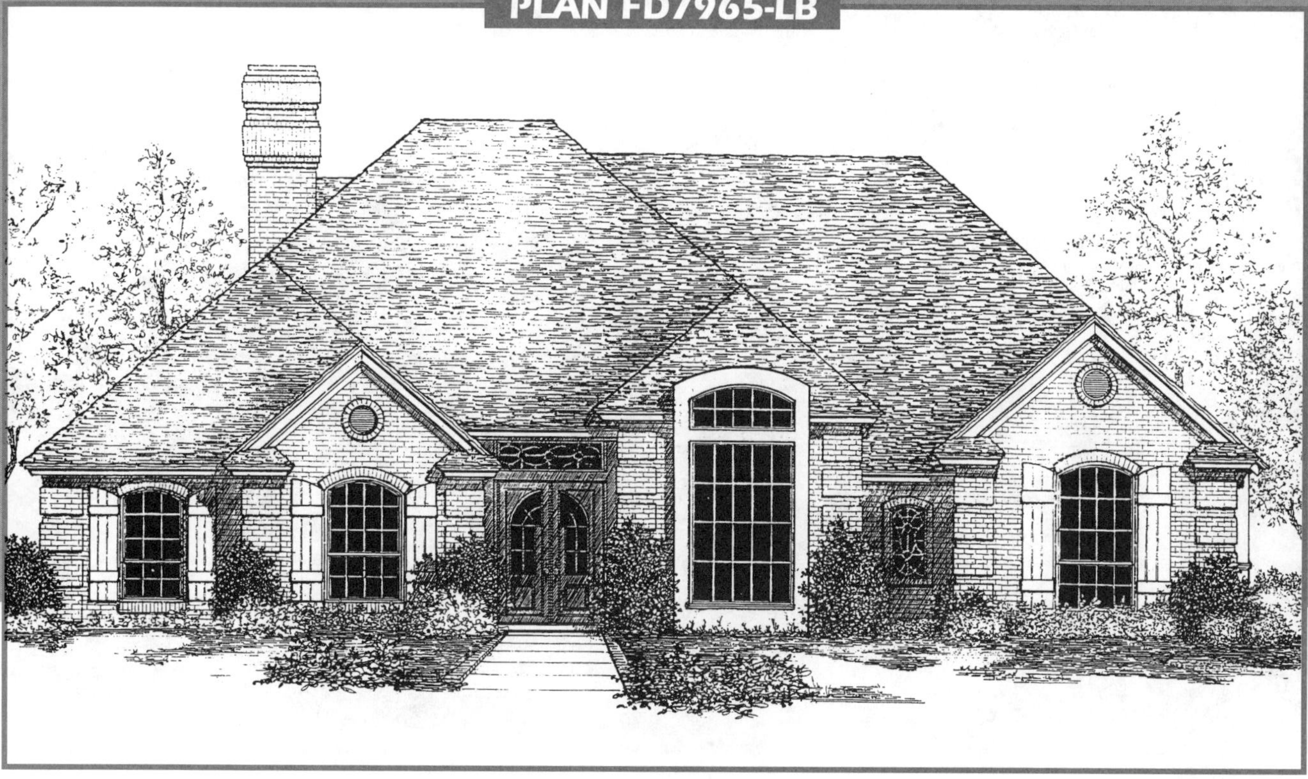

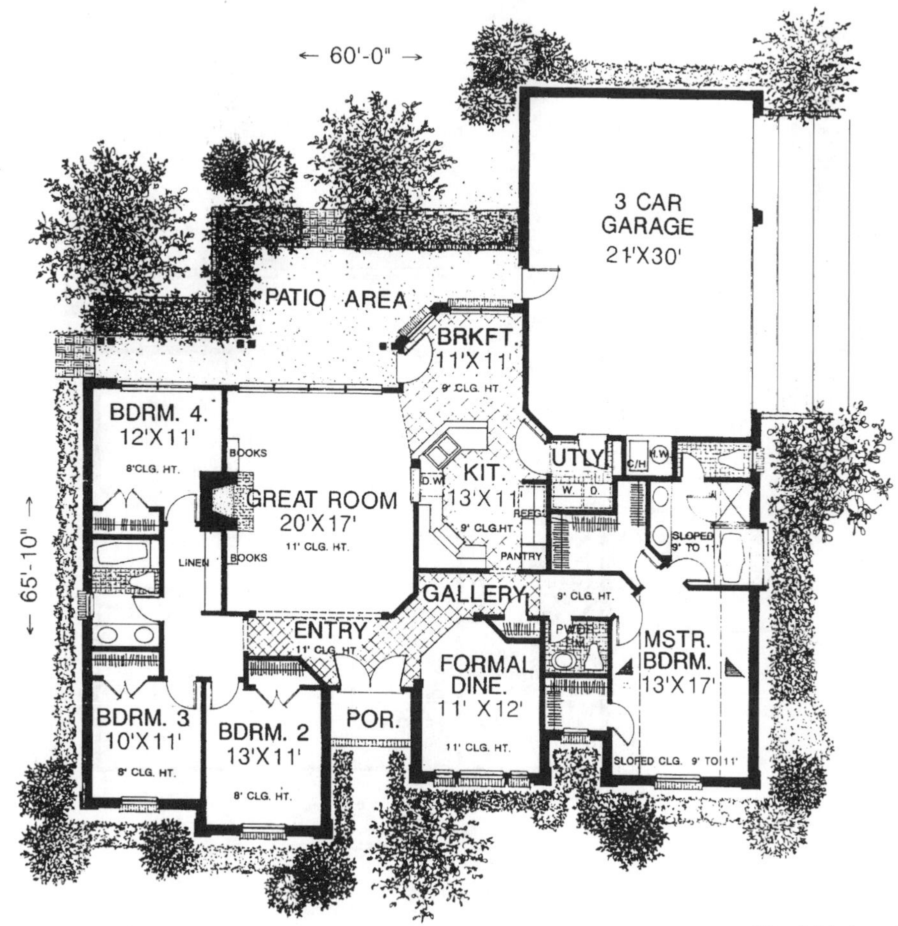

60'-0"
65'-10"
3 CAR GARAGE
21'X30'
PATIO AREA
BRKFT.
11'X11'
9' CLG. HT.
BDRM. 4.
12'X11'
8' CLG. HT.
BOOKS
GREAT ROOM
20'X17'
11' CLG. HT.
BOOKS
LINEN
UTLY
W.
D.
C/H
H.W.
KIT.
13'X11'
D.W.
9' CLG.HT.
REFG.
PANTRY
SLOPED
9' TO 11'
GALLERY
9' CLG. HT.
ENTRY
11' CLG. HT.
PWDR.
MSTR.
BDRM.
13'X17'
FORMAL
DINE.
11' X12'
11' CLG. HT.
POR.
BDRM. 3
10'X11'
8' CLG. HT.
BDRM. 2
13'X11'
8' CLG. HT.
SLOPED CLG. 9' TO 11'

Total Living Area 2,065 sq. ft.

PRICE CODE: B

CUSTOMIZE IT!

PLAN VL2069

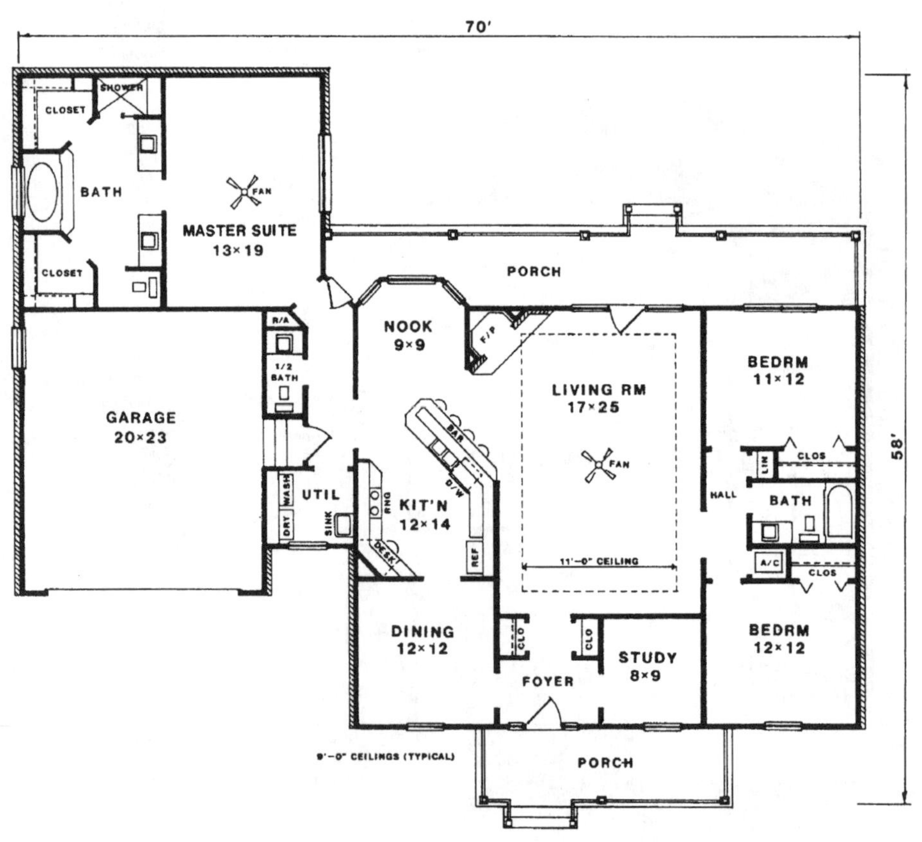

70'
58'
CLOSET
SHOWER
BATH
MASTER SUITE 13×19
FAN
CLOSET
PORCH
NOOK 9×9
F/P
LIVING RM 17×25
FAN
BEDRM 11×12
R/A
1/2 BATH
GARAGE 20×23
BAR
D/W
LIN
CLOS
BATH
HALL
UTIL
WASH
DRY
SINK
RNG
KIT'N 12×14
DESK
REF
11'-0" CEILING
A/C
CLOS
DINING 12×12
CLO
CLO
STUDY 8×9
FOYER
BEDRM 12×12
9'-0" CEILINGS (TYPICAL)
PORCH

Total Living Area 2,069 sq. ft.

PRICE CODE: B

PLAN JA5129

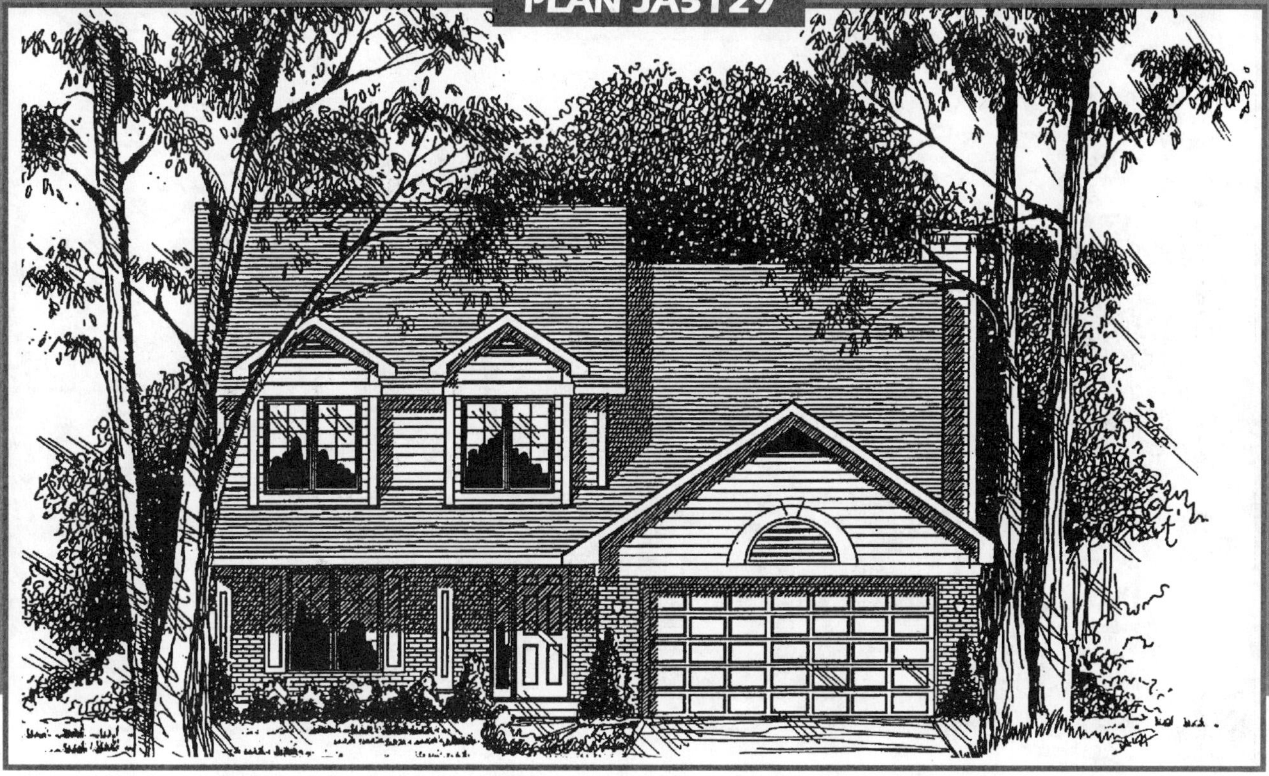

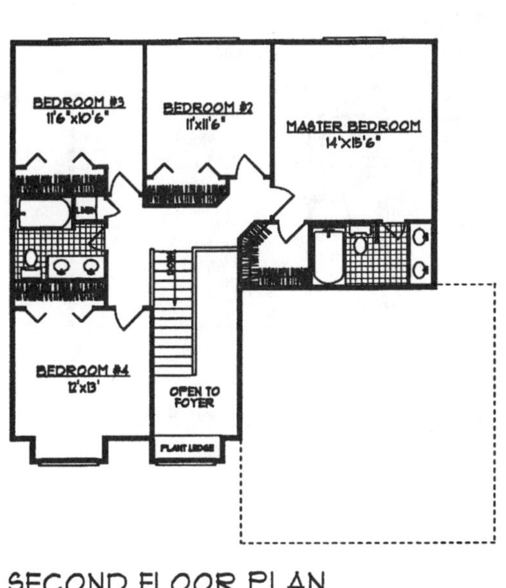

BEDROOM #3
11'6"x10'6"
BEDROOM #2
11'x11'6"
MASTER BEDROOM
14'x15'6"
BEDROOM #4
12'x13'
OPEN TO FOYER
PLANT LEDGE

SECOND FLOOR PLAN

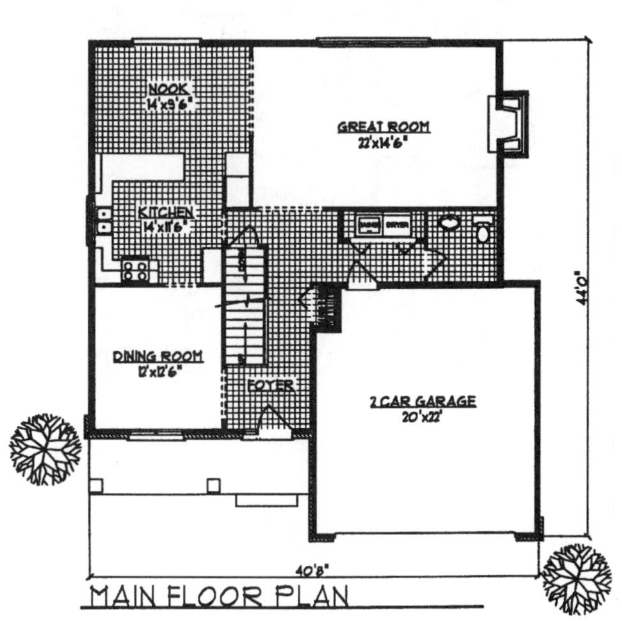

NOOK
14'x9'6"
GREAT ROOM
22'x14'6"
KITCHEN
14'x11'6"
DINING ROOM
12'x12'6"
FOYER
2 CAR GARAGE
20'x22'
44'0"
40'8"

MAIN FLOOR PLAN

First Floor	1,102 sq. ft.
Second Floor	971 sq. ft.
Total Living Area	2,073 sq. ft.

PRICE CODE: B

PLAN DB1870

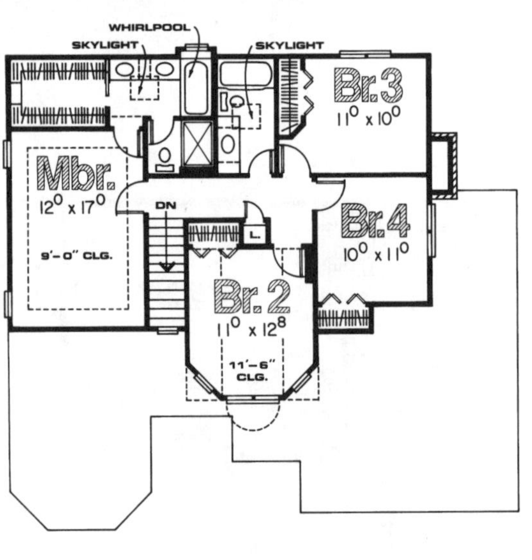
WHIRLPOOL
SKYLIGHT
SKYLIGHT
Br.3
11^{0} x 10^{0}
Mbr.
12^{0} x 17^{0}
9'-0" CLG.
DN
Br.4
10^{0} x 11^{0}
L.
Br.2
11^{0} x 12^{8}
11'-6" CLG.

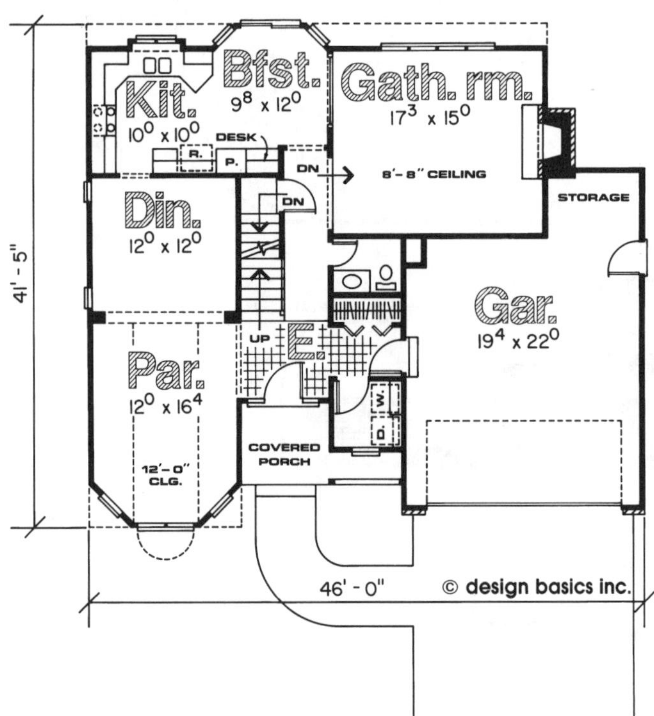
Kit.
10^{0} x 10^{0}
Bfst.
9^{8} x 12^{0}
Gath. rm.
17^{3} x 15^{0}
DESK
R.
P.
DN
8'-8" CEILING
STORAGE
Din.
12^{0} x 12^{0}
DN
41' - 5"
UP
E.
Gar.
19^{4} x 22^{0}
Par.
12^{0} x 16^{4}
12'-0" CLG.
W.
D.
COVERED PORCH
46' - 0"
© design basics inc.

Features

- Charming porch and arched windows of elevation allude to elegance within.
- Parlor with large bayed window and sloped ceiling harks back to simpler life.
- Formal dining area open to parlor invites entertaining with ease from kitchen.
- Bright kitchen and bayed breakfast area features wrapping counters, pantry and desk.
- Step down into expansive gathering room with fireplace and abundant windows.
- Indulging master bedroom with skylit dressing area, dual lavs, whirlpool tub and large walk-in closet.

First Floor	1,113 sq. ft.
Second Floor	965 sq. ft.
Total Living Area	2,078 sq. ft.

PRICE CODE: C

CUSTOMIZE IT!

ORDER TOLL FREE 1-800-533-4350 24-HOUR FAX ORDERING 1-800-344-4293

PLAN DB2217

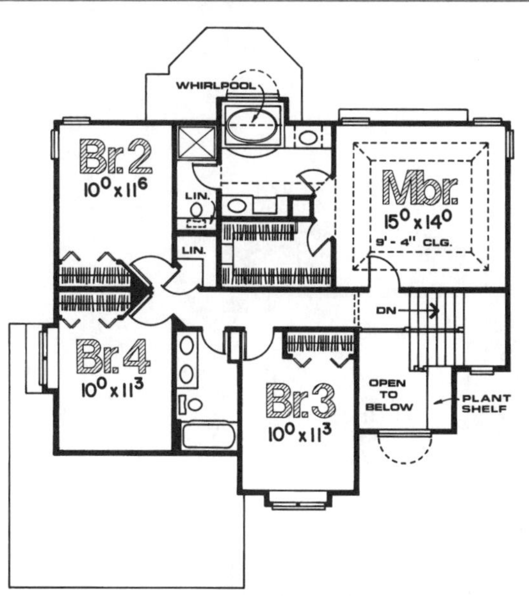

WHIRLPOOL
Br.2
$10^{0} \times 11^{6}$
LIN.
Mbr.
$15^{0} \times 14^{0}$
9' - 4" CLG.
LIN.
DN
Br.4
$10^{0} \times 11^{3}$
Br.3
$10^{0} \times 11^{3}$
OPEN TO BELOW
PLANT SHELF

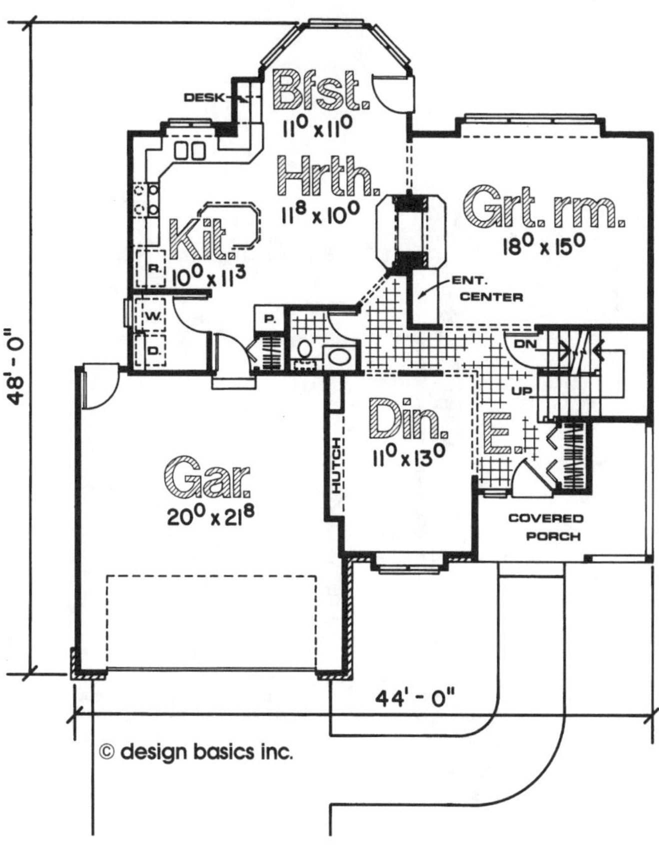

DESK
Bfst.
$11^{0} \times 11^{0}$
Hrth.
$11^{8} \times 10^{0}$
Kit.
$10^{0} \times 11^{3}$
R.
W.
D.
P.
Grt. rm.
$18^{0} \times 15^{0}$
ENT. CENTER
DN
UP
Din.
$11^{0} \times 13^{0}$
HUTCH
E.
Gar.
$20^{0} \times 21^{8}$
COVERED PORCH
48' - 0"
44' - 0"
© design basics inc.

Features

- 2-story entry open to interesting staircase and formal dining room with boxed window and hutch space.
- Great room with large windows, entertainment center and see-thru fireplace.
- Hearth room takes advantage of see-thru fireplace.
- Island counter, desk and pantry in kitchen open to bayed dinette.
- Vaulted ceiling and unique angle into walk-in closet and dressing area make this a special master suite.
- Irresistible oval whirlpool under arched window and his and her vanities in master bath/dressing area.

First Floor	1,062 sq. ft.
Second Floor	1,023 sq. ft.
Total Living Area	2,085 sq. ft.

PRICE CODE: C

PLAN FD8162-L

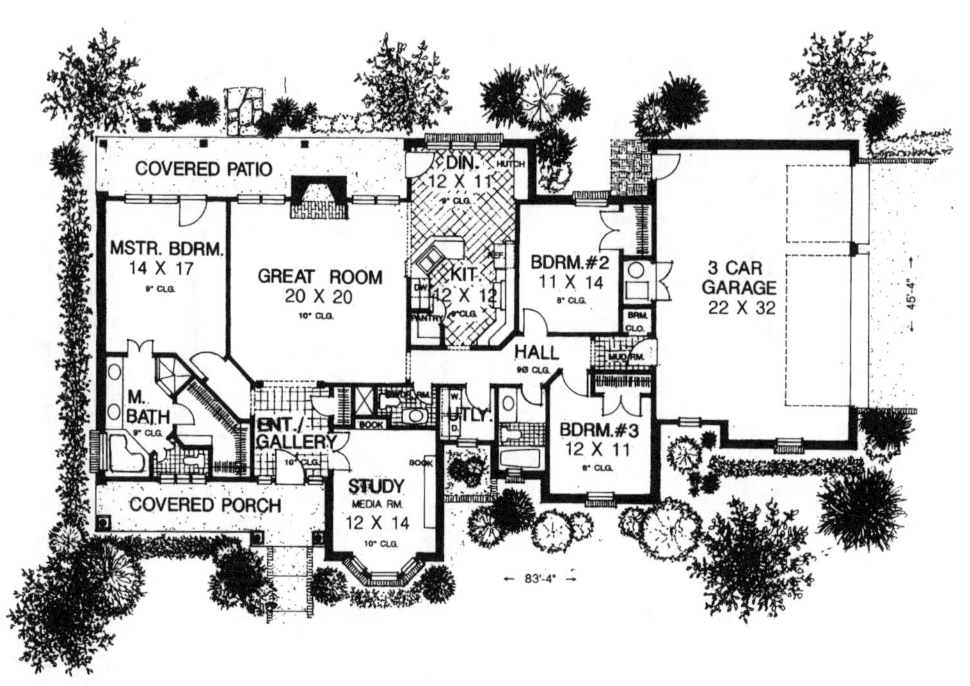
COVERED PATIO
DIN.
12 X 11
9" CLG.
HUTCH
MSTR. BDRM.
14 X 17
9" CLG.
GREAT ROOM
20 X 20
10" CLG.
KIT.
12 X 12
PANTRY
BDRM.#2
11 X 14
8" CLG.
3 CAR
GARAGE
22 X 32
45'-4"
HALL
M.
BATH
9" CLG.
ENT./
GALLERY
10" CLG.
BOOK
STUDY
MEDIA RM.
12 X 14
10" CLG.
UTLY.
BDRM.#3
12 X 11
8" CLG.
COVERED PORCH
83'-4"

Total Living Area 2,086 sq. ft.

PRICE CODE: B

PLAN NP1266

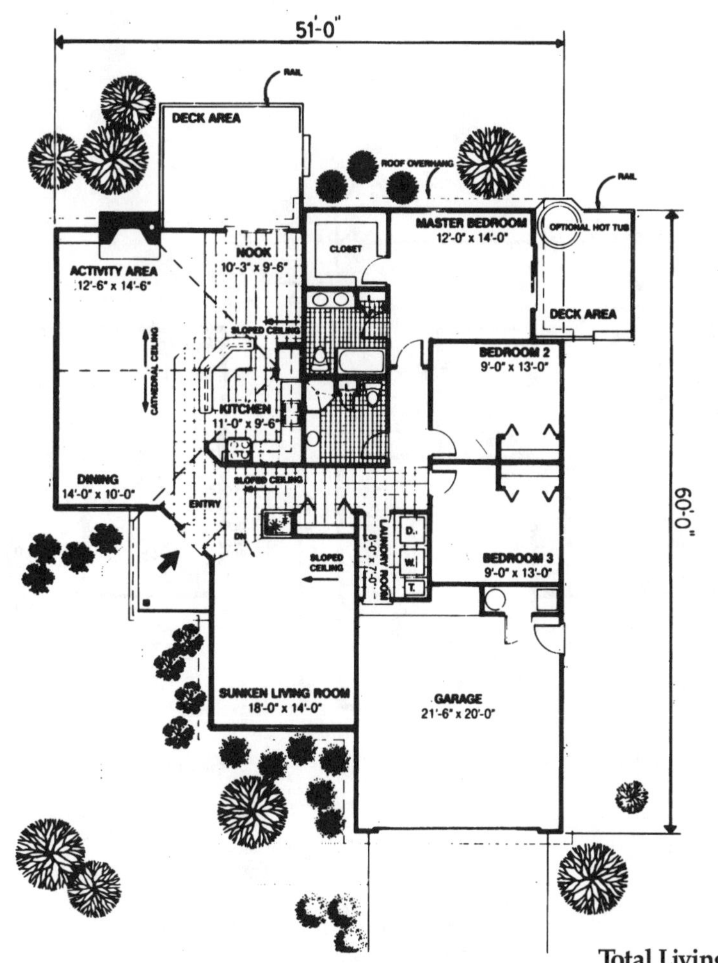

51'-0"
60'-0"
RAIL
DECK AREA
ROOF OVERHANG
OPTIONAL HOT TUB
MASTER BEDROOM
12'-0" x 14'-0"
CLOSET
NOOK
10'-3" x 9'-6"
ACTIVITY AREA
12'-6" x 14'-6"
CATHEDRAL CEILING
SLOPED CEILING
KITCHEN
11'-0" x 9'-6"
BEDROOM 2
9'-0" x 13'-0"
DINING
14'-0" x 10'-0"
ENTRY
LAUNDRY ROOM
BEDROOM 3
9'-0" x 13'-0"
SUNKEN LIVING ROOM
18'-0" x 14'-0"
GARAGE
21'-6" x 20'-0"

Total Living Area 2,086 sq. ft.

PRICE CODE: B

PLAN SH1189-2073

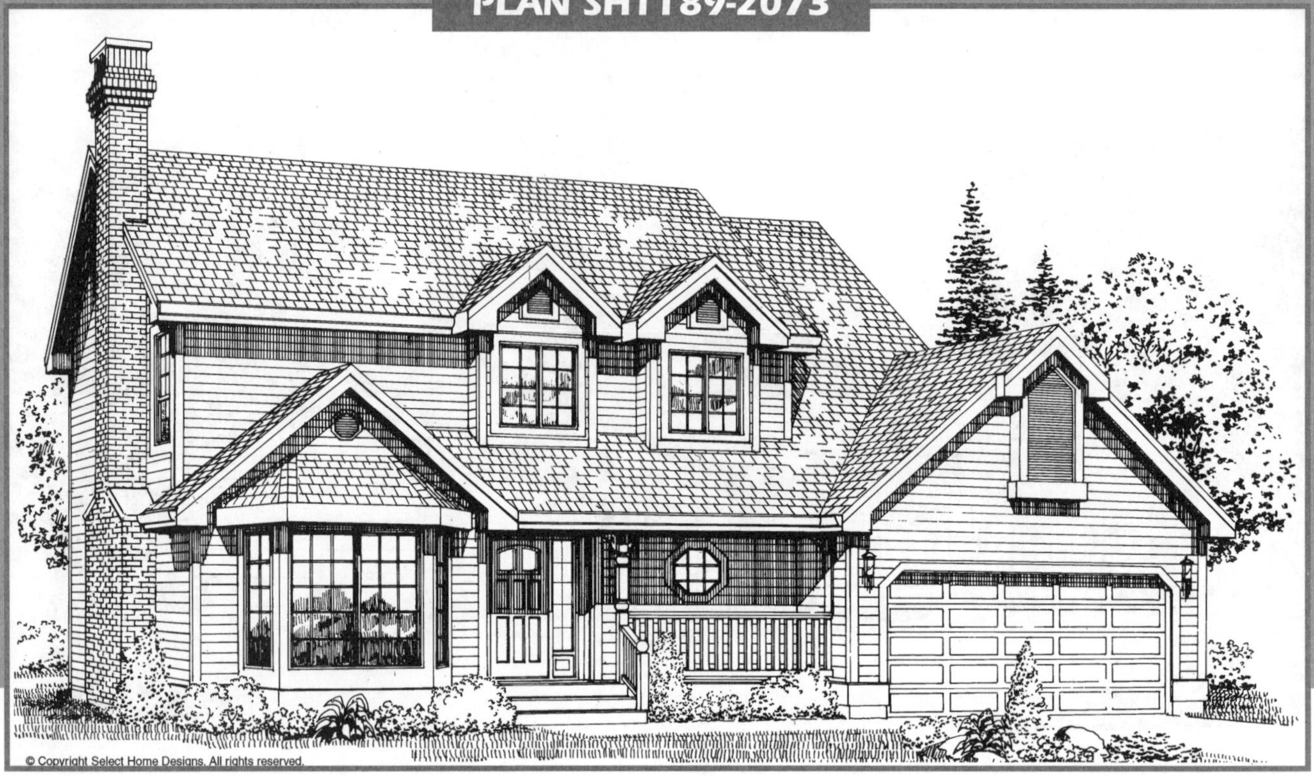

102

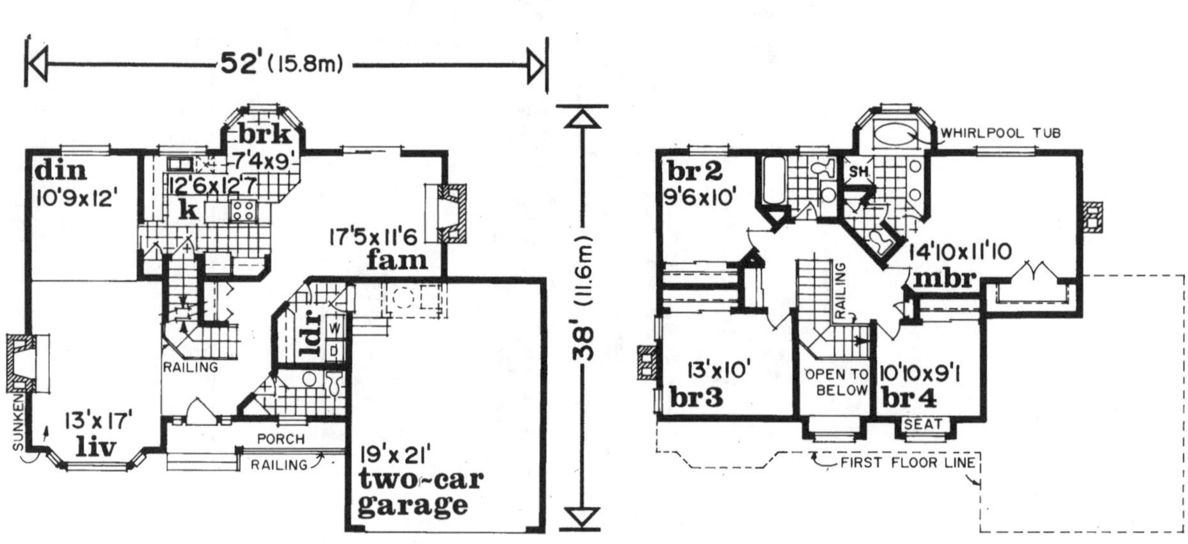

52' (15.8m)
38' (11.6m)
brk
7'4x9'
din
10'9x12'
12'6x12'7
k
17'5x11'6
fam
ldr
W
D
RAILING
SUNKEN
13'x17'
liv
PORCH
RAILING
19'x21'
two-car
garage
WHIRLPOOL TUB
br 2
9'6x10'
SH
14'10x11'10
mbr
RAILING
13'x10'
br3
OPEN TO
BELOW
10'10x9'1
br 4
SEAT
FIRST FLOOR LINE

First Level 1062 square feet

Second Level 1026 square feet

Features

- Dormer window brightens foyer and open staircase.
- Sunken living room boasts bay window and masonry fireplace.
- Kitchen, with centre cooking island, is open to breakfast bay and family room.
- Family room has masonry fireplace and sliding glass walk-through to patio.
- Master bedroom features walk-in closet and lavish ensuite.
- Ensuite features spa, tucked in windowed-bay, twin vanity and shower.

Total Living Area **2,088 sq. ft.**

PRICE CODE: B

PLAN DB1179

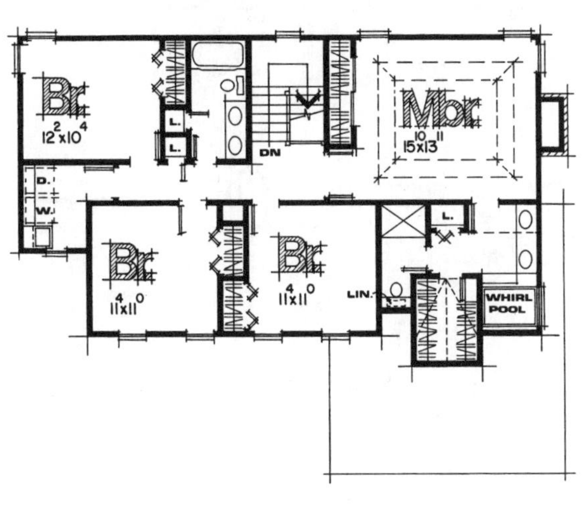

Br.
12²x10⁴
Mbr.
15¹⁰x13¹¹
DN
D.
W.
Br.
11⁴x11⁰
Br.
11⁴x11⁰
L.
LIN.
WHIRL POOL

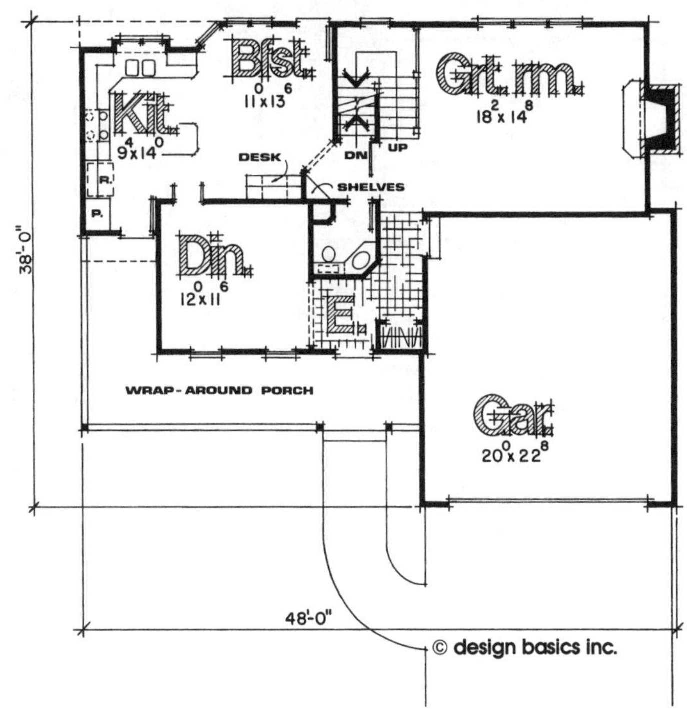

Bfst.
11⁰x13⁶
Grt. rm.
18²x14⁸
Kit.
9⁴x14⁰
DESK
DN
UP
SHELVES
R.
P.
Din.
12⁰x11⁶
E.
WRAP-AROUND PORCH
Gar.
20⁰x22⁸
38'-0"
48'-0"
© design basics inc.

Features

- Main level footage optimized and second level footage maximized.
- Private door onto spacious wrap-around porch from kitchen.
- Large kitchen includes pantry, island counter, roll-top desk and lazy Susan.
- Convenient main floor powder bath.
- Great room opens to staircase at the rear brightened with window on landing.
- Double doors to large master bedroom.
- Deluxe master bath area with whirlpool, transom windows and sloped ceiling.
- Laundry room with soaking sink on same level as bedrooms.
- 3 linen closets on second level .
- Secondary bedrooms share centrally located bath with double vanity.

First Floor	927 sq. ft.
Second Floor	1,163 sq. ft.
Total Living Area	2,090 sq. ft.

PRICE CODE: C

PLAN DB2638

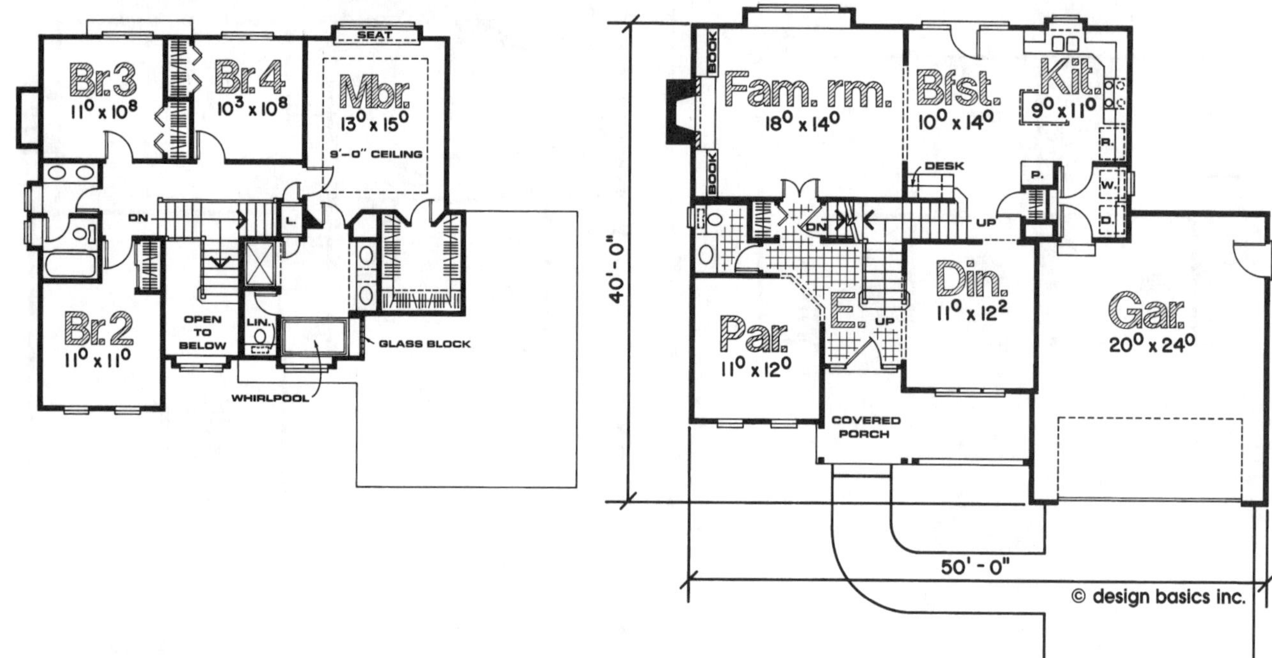

Br.3
11^{0} x 10^{8}
Br.4
10^{3} x 10^{8}
SEAT
Mbr.
13^{0} x 15^{0}
9'-0" CEILING
DN
L
Br.2
11^{0} x 11^{0}
OPEN TO BELOW
LIN.
GLASS BLOCK
WHIRLPOOL
40'-0"
BOOK
Fam. rm.
18^{0} x 14^{0}
BOOK
Bfst.
10^{0} x 14^{0}
Kit.
9^{0} x 11^{0}
R.
DESK
P.
W.
D.
DN
UP
E.
UP
Din.
11^{0} x 12^{2}
Par.
11^{0} x 12^{0}
Gar.
20^{0} x 24^{0}
COVERED PORCH
50'-0"
© design basics inc.

Features

- Covered porch invites you into this country style home.
- Handsome bookcases frame fireplace in spacious family room.
- Double doors off entry provide family room added privacy.
- Kitchen features island, lazy Susan and easy access to walk-in laundry.
- Master bedroom features boxed ceiling and separate entries into walk-in closet and master bath.
- Upstairs, hall bath is compartmentalized, allowing maximum usage for today's busy families.

First Floor	1,082 sq. ft.
Second Floor	1,021 sq. ft.
Total Living Area	2,103 sq. ft.

PRICE CODE: C

PLAN AM2239N

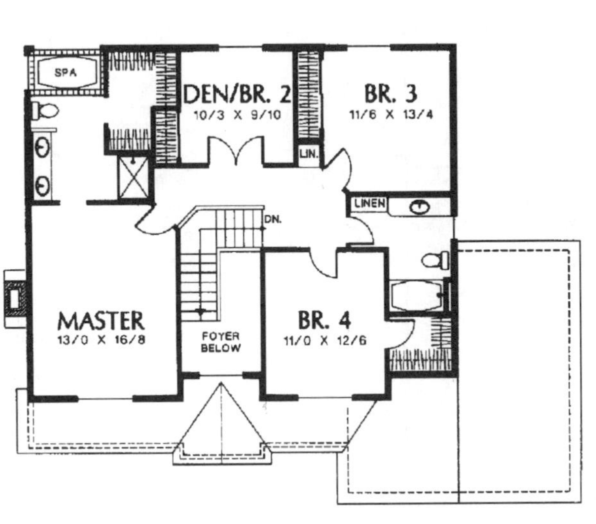

SPA
DEN/BR. 2
10/3 X 9/10
BR. 3
11/6 X 13/4
LIN.
LINEN
DN.
MASTER
13/0 X 16/8
FOYER
BELOW
BR. 4
11/0 X 12/6

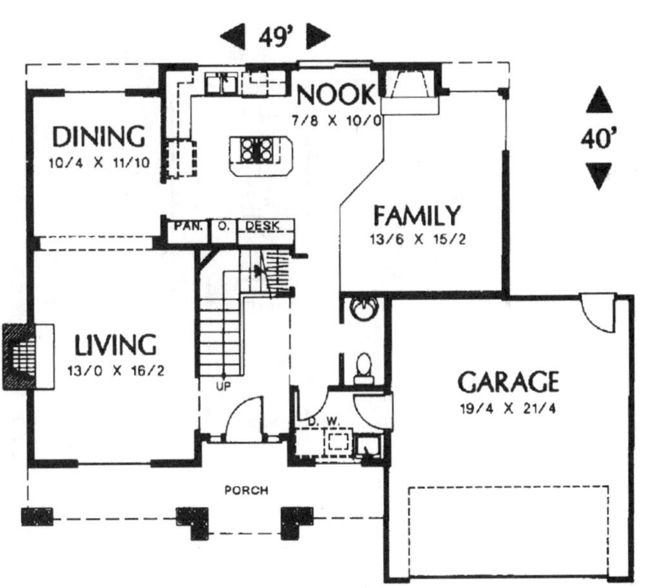

49'
40'
NOOK
7/8 X 10/0
DINING
10/4 X 11/10
FAMILY
13/6 X 15/2
PAN.
O.
DESK
LIVING
13/0 X 16/2
UP
GARAGE
19/4 X 21/4
D.W.
PORCH

First Floor	1,032 sq. ft.
Second Floor	1,075 sq. ft.
Total Living Area	2,107 sq. ft.

PRICE CODE: B

PLAN MN2107

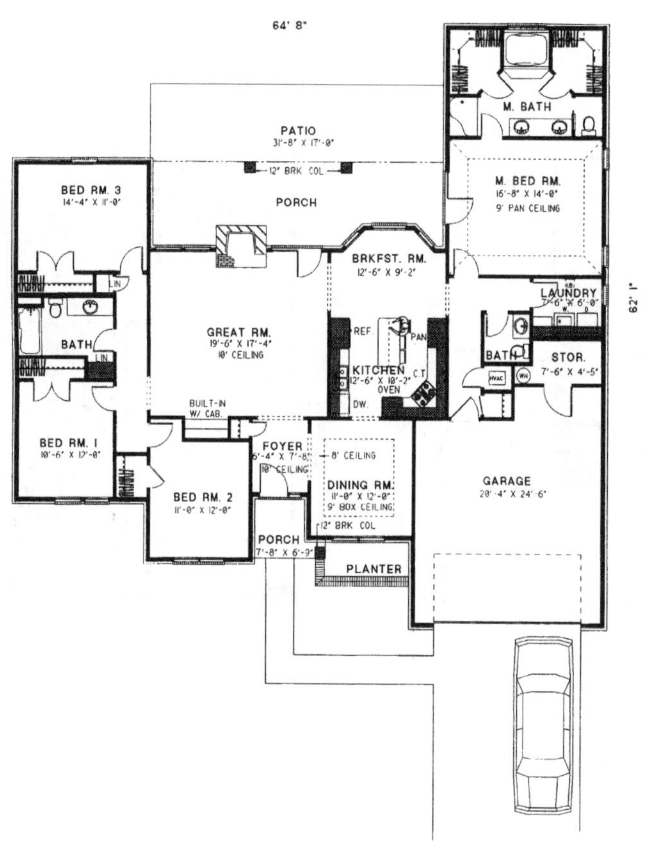

64' 8"
62' 1"
M. BATH
PATIO
31'-8" X 17'-0"
12" BRK COL
PORCH
BED RM. 3
14'-4" X 11'-0"
M. BED RM.
16'-8" X 14'-0"
9' PAN CEILING
BRKFST. RM.
12'-6" X 9'-2"
LIN
LAUNDRY
GREAT RM.
19'-6" X 17'-4"
10' CEILING
REF
PAN
BATH
LIN
KITCHEN
12'-6" X 10'-2"
C.T.
OVEN
BATH
STOR.
7'-6" X 4'-5"
HVAC
WH
DW.
BUILT-IN
W/ CAB.
BED RM. 1
10'-6" X 12'-0"
FOYER
6'-4" X 7'-8"
10' CEILING
8' CEILING
DINING RM.
11'-0" X 12'-0"
9' BOX CEILING
GARAGE
20'-4" X 24'-6"
BED RM. 2
11'-0" X 12'-0"
12" BRK COL
PORCH
7'-8" X 6'-9"
PLANTER

Total Living Area **2,107 sq. ft.**

PRICE CODE: B

PLAN NP1311

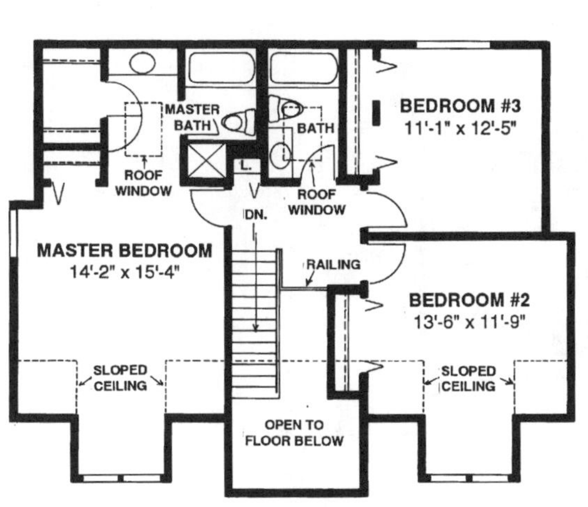
MASTER BATH
BATH
ROOF WINDOW
ROOF WINDOW
L.
DN.
BEDROOM #3
11'-1" x 12'-5"
MASTER BEDROOM
14'-2" x 15'-4"
RAILING
BEDROOM #2
13'-6" x 11'-9"
SLOPED CEILING
SLOPED CEILING
OPEN TO FLOOR BELOW

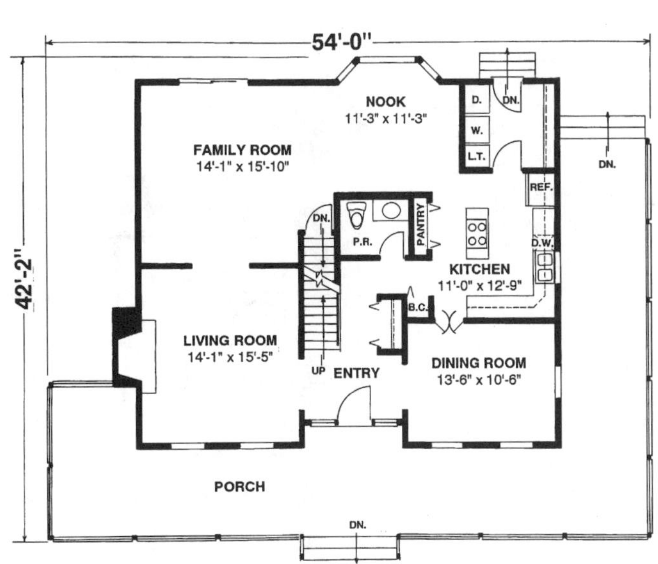
54'-0"
42'-2"
NOOK
11'-3" x 11'-3"
D.
W.
L.T.
DN.
DN.
FAMILY ROOM
14'-1" x 15'-10"
REF.
DN.
P.R.
PANTRY
D.W.
KITCHEN
11'-0" x 12'-9"
B.C.
LIVING ROOM
14'-1" x 15'-5"
UP
ENTRY
DINING ROOM
13'-6" x 10'-6"
PORCH
DN.

Stately Country

Features

- Combine country comfort with stately simplicity in this home.
- Wide, wrap-around porch brackets the front and right side of this home.
- At the left, a large living room with fireplace leads to a family room and bay-windowed nook.
- At right, a dining room is accessed from the large kitchen with centrally located cooking island and built-in pantry by swinging, saloon-style doors.
- Upstairs, master bedroom includes a dressing area with roof window, walk-in closet, and full bath.

First Floor	1,216 sq. ft.
Second Floor	896 sq. ft.
Total Living Area	2,112 sq. ft.

PRICE CODE: B

PLAN FD8028A

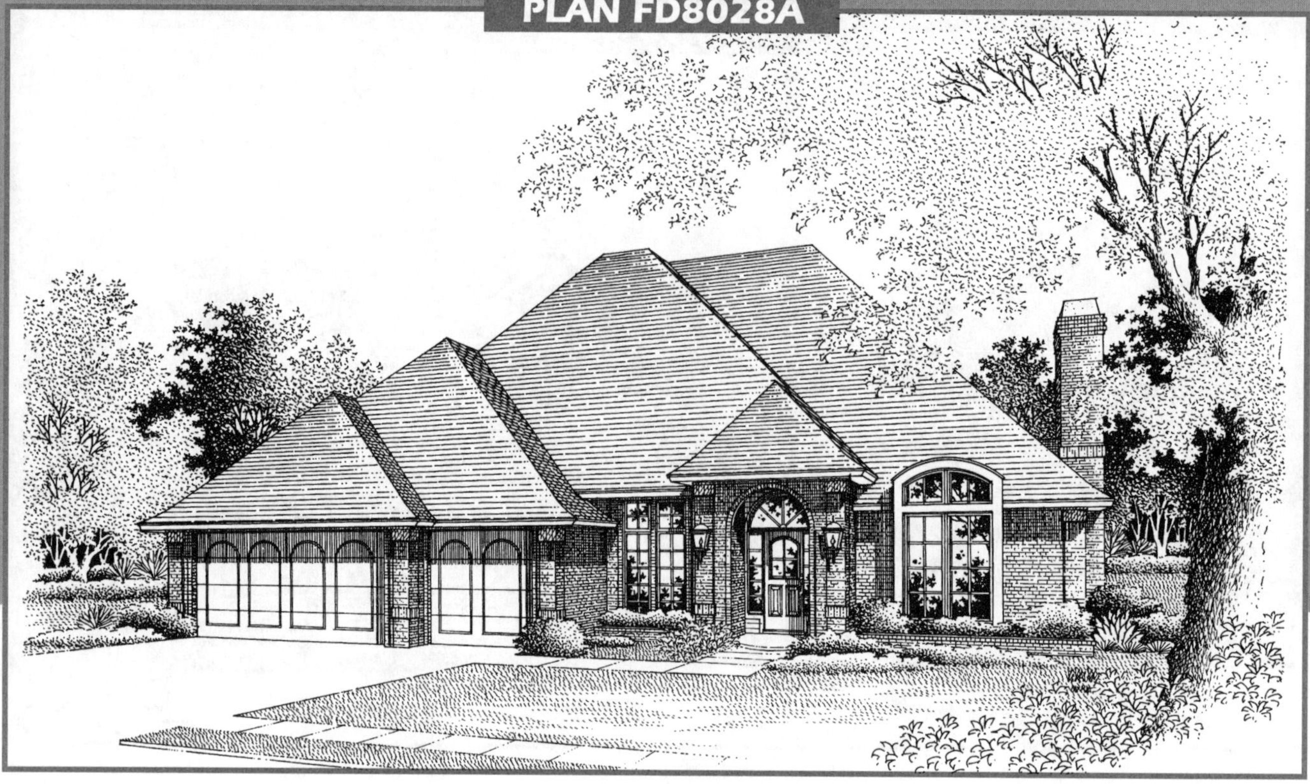

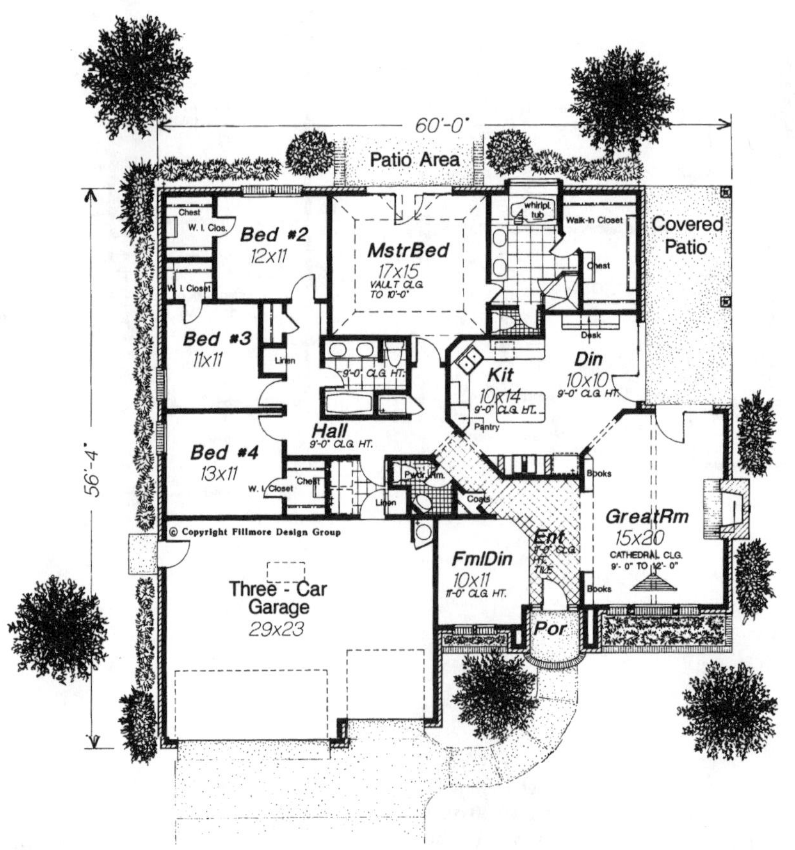

60'-0"
Patio Area
Covered Patio
Bed #2
12x11
MstrBed
17x15
VAULT CLG. TO 10'-0"
Walk-in Closet
Bed #3
11x11
Kit
10x14
9'-0" CLG. HT.
Din
10x10
9'-0" CLG. HT.
Hall
9'-0" CLG. HT.
Bed #4
13x11
GreatRm
15x20
CATHEDRAL CLG.
9'-0" TO 12'-0"
Ent
FmlDin
10x11
11'-0" CLG. HT.
Por
Three - Car Garage
29x23
56'-4"
© Copyright Fillmore Design Group

Total Living Area **2,118 sq. ft.**

PRICE CODE: B

PLAN FD8028B

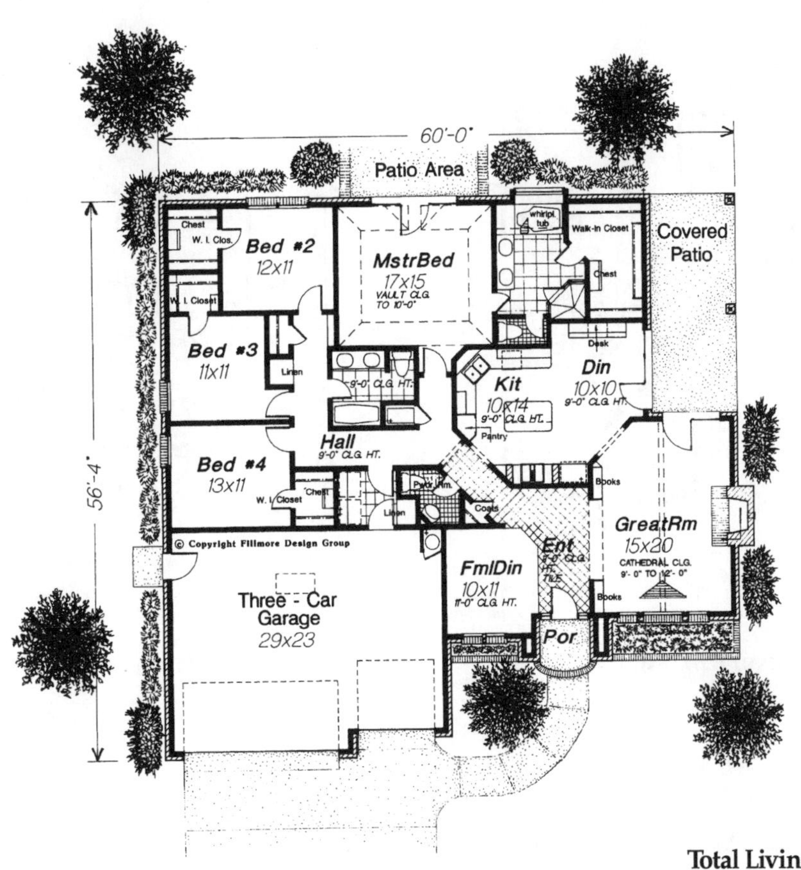

60'-0"
Patio Area
Covered Patio
Bed #2
12x11
MstrBed
17x15
VAULT CLG. TO 10'-0"
Walk-In Closet
Bed #3
11x11
Linen
Kit
10x14
9'-0" CLG. HT.
Pantry
Din
10x10
9'-0" CLG. HT.
Desk
Hall
9'-0" CLG. HT.
Bed #4
13x11
W. I. Closet
Books
GreatRm
15x20
CATHEDRAL CLG.
9'-0" TO 12'-0"
Coats
Ent
FmlDin
10x11
11'-0" CLG. HT.
Por
56'-4"
© Copyright Fillmore Design Group
Three - Car Garage
29x23

Total Living Area 2,118 sq. ft.

PRICE CODE: B

CUSTOMIZE IT!

ORDER TOLL FREE 1-800-533-4350 24-HOUR FAX ORDERING 1-800-344-4293

PLAN SH90-2173

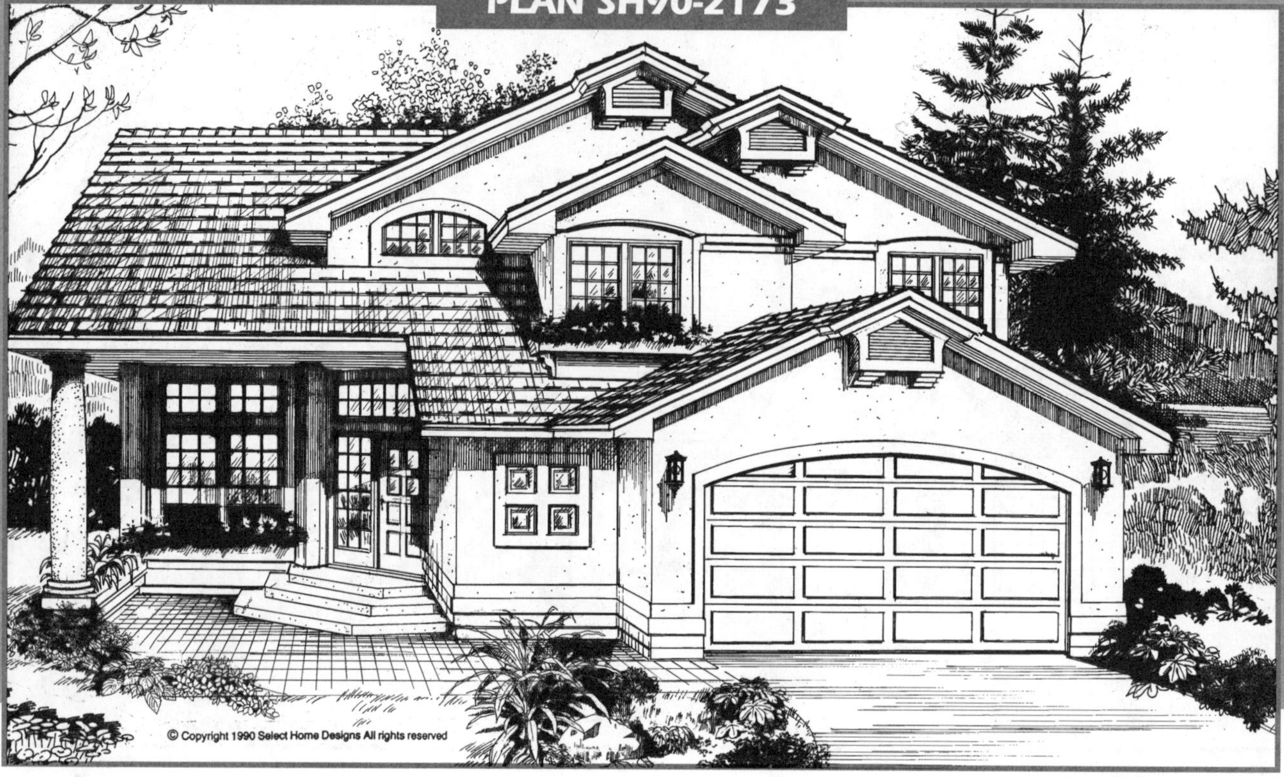

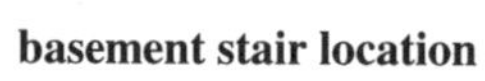
basement stair location

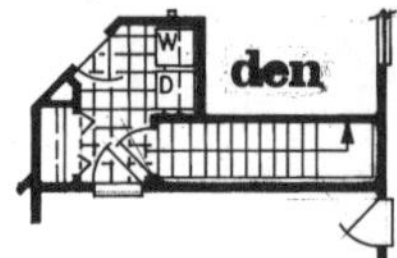
den

110

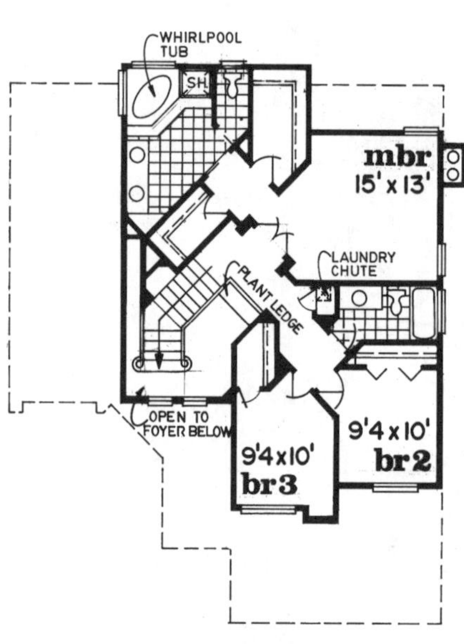
WHIRLPOOL TUB
SH
mbr
15' x 13'
LAUNDRY CHUTE
PLANT LEDGE
OPEN TO FOYER BELOW
9'4 x 10'
br3
9'4 x 10'
br2

second level 921 sq. ft.

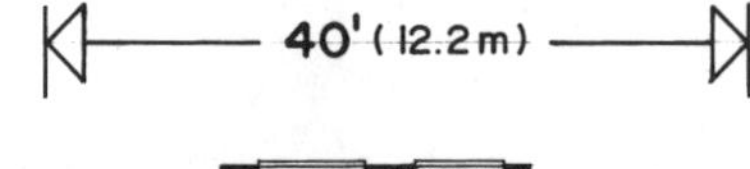
40' (12.2m)

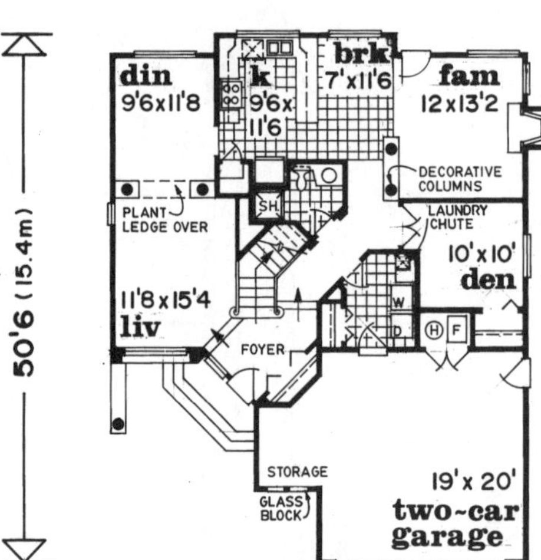
50'6 (15.4m)
din
9'6 x 11'8
k
9'6 x 11'6
brk
7' x 11'6
fam
12 x 13'2
DECORATIVE COLUMNS
PLANT LEDGE OVER
SH
LAUNDRY CHUTE
10' x 10'
den
11'8 x 15'4
liv
FOYER
W
D
H
F
STORAGE
GLASS BLOCK
19' x 20'
two-car garage

first level 1199 sq. ft.

Features

- Tall multipaned window walls accentuate the two storey entry and the high ceiling in the living room.
- Pair of decorative columns, with planter ledge over, provides visual separation of the living and dining room.
- U-plan shaped kitchen, with walk-in pantry and abundant counter space, serves the breakfast area.
- Laundry chute from the second level eases household chores.
- Master bedroom boasts his and hers walk-in closets and ensuite with raised spa.
- Plan includes a basement and crawlspace foundation.

Total Living Area: 2,120 sq. ft.

PRICE CODE: B

PLAN FD8023

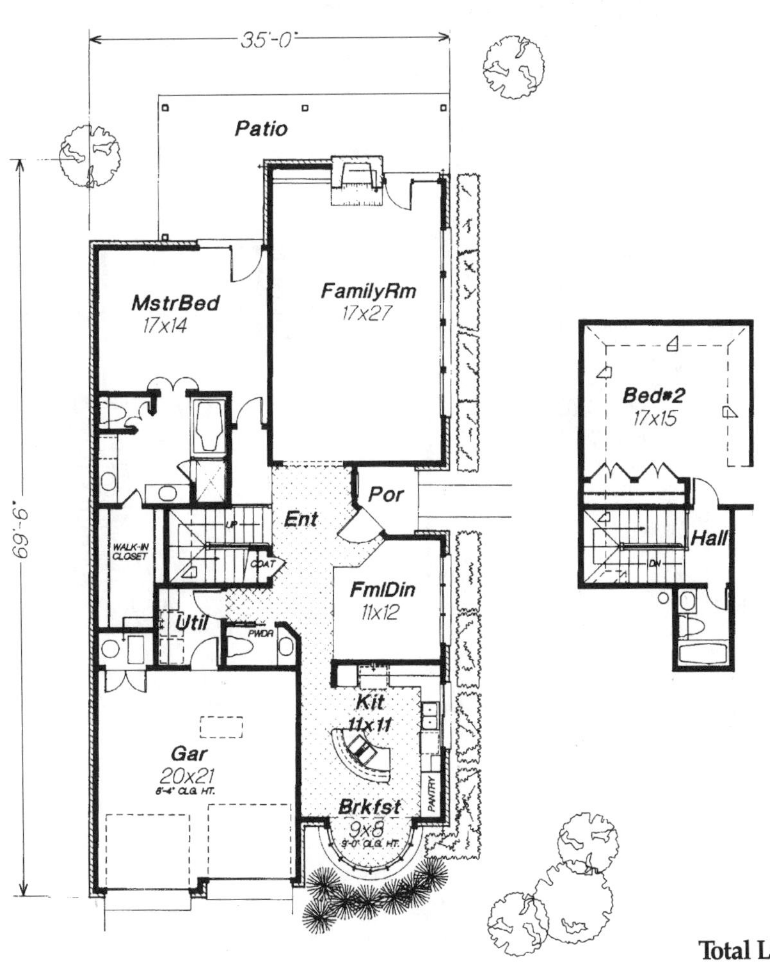
35'-0"
Patio
MstrBed
17x14
FamilyRm
17x27
WALK-IN CLOSET
Ent
Por
COAT
Util
PWDR
FmlDin
11x12
Kit
11x11
Gar
20x21
8'-4" CLG. HT.
Brkfst
9x8
9'-0" CLG. HT.
PANTRY
69'-6"
Bed#2
17x15
Hall
DN

111

Total Living Area 2,124 sq. ft.

PRICE CODE: B

CUSTOMIZE IT!

ORDER TOLL FREE 1-800-533-4350 24-HOUR FAX ORDERING 1-800-344-4293

PLAN JA5409

112

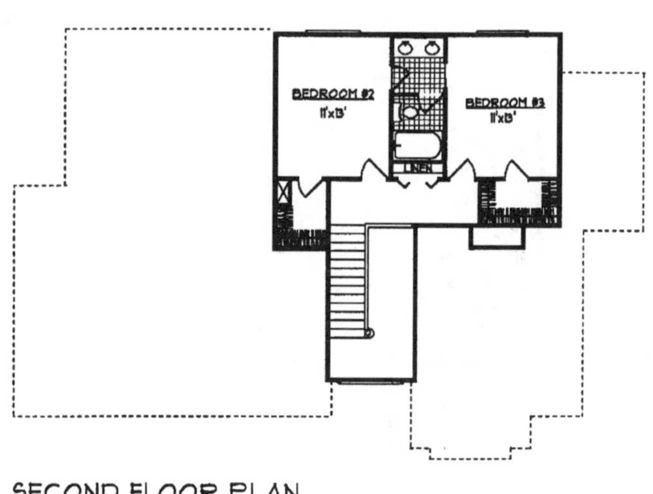
BEDROOM #2
11'x13'
BEDROOM #3
11'x13'
LINEN

SECOND FLOOR PLAN

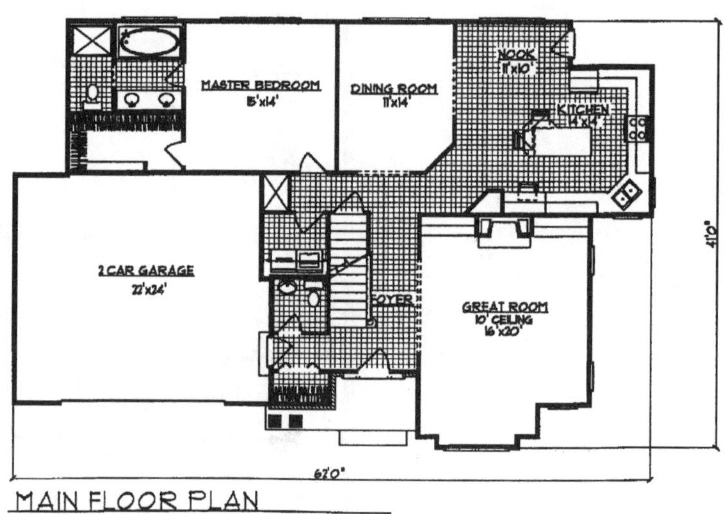
MASTER BEDROOM
15'x14'
DINING ROOM
11'x14'
NOOK
11'x10'
KITCHEN
2 CAR GARAGE
22'x24'
FOYER
GREAT ROOM
10' CEILING
16'x20'
41'0"
67'0"

MAIN FLOOR PLAN

First Floor	1,565 sq. ft.
Second Floor	563 sq. ft.
Total Living Area	2,128 sq. ft.

PRICE CODE: B

PLAN DB2618

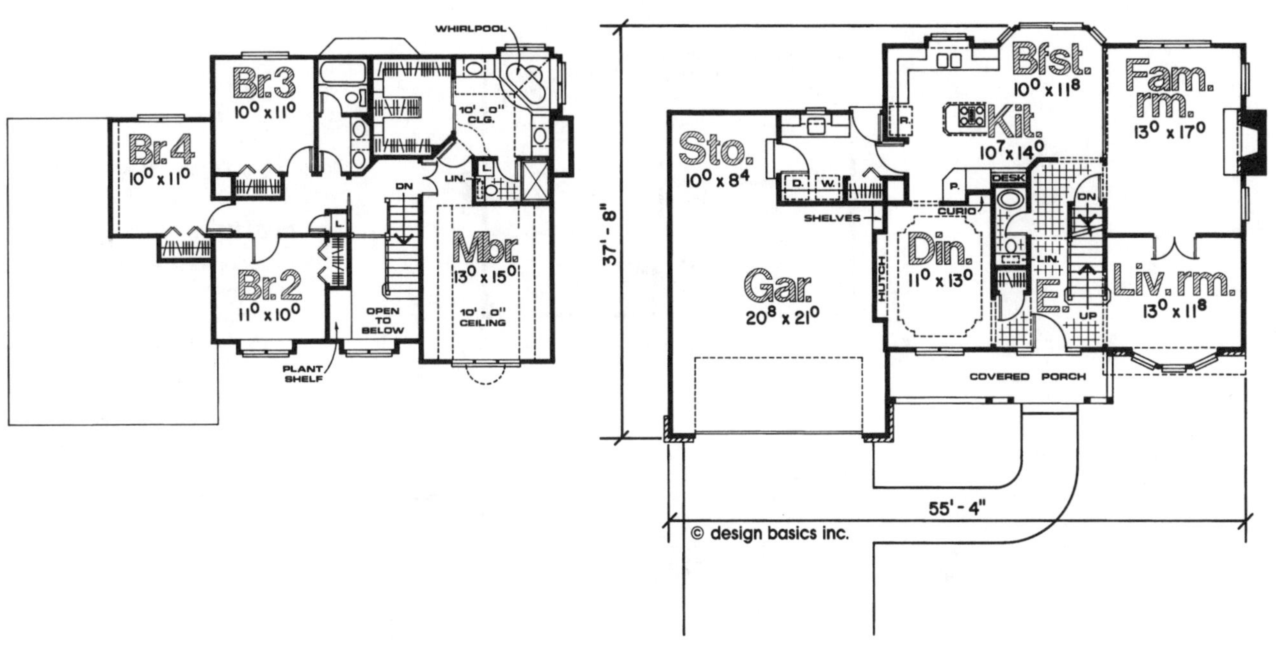

WHIRLPOOL
Br.3
10^0 x 11^0
Br.4
10^0 x 11^0
10' - 0" CLG.
LIN.
DN
Mbr.
13^0 x 15^0
10' - 0" CEILING
Br.2
11^0 x 10^0
OPEN TO BELOW
PLANT SHELF
37' - 8"
Bfst.
10^0 x 11^8
Fam. rm.
13^0 x 17^0
Kit.
10^7 x 14^0
Sto.
10^0 x 8^4
D. W.
P.
DESK
SHELVES
CURIO
HUTCH
Din.
11^0 x 13^0
LIN.
DN
UP
E.
Liv. rm.
13^0 x 11^8
Gar.
20^8 x 21^0
COVERED PORCH
55' - 4"
© design basics inc.

113

Features

- Beautifully proportioned design is complemented by large covered porch framed with wood railing.
- Living room is enhanced by warmth of a bayed window and double French doors opening to family room.
- Spacious dining room is accented by built-in curio cabinet.
- Efficient kitchen is just steps away from dinette and dining room.
- Laundry room is conveniently accessible from kitchen, garage and directly outside.
- Storage space abounds in garage area.
- Double doors open to luxurious master bedroom with distinctive vaulted ceiling.

First Floor	**1,093 sq. ft.**
Second Floor	**1,038 sq. ft.**
Total Living Area	**2,131 sq. ft.**

PRICE CODE: C

PLAN NPT124

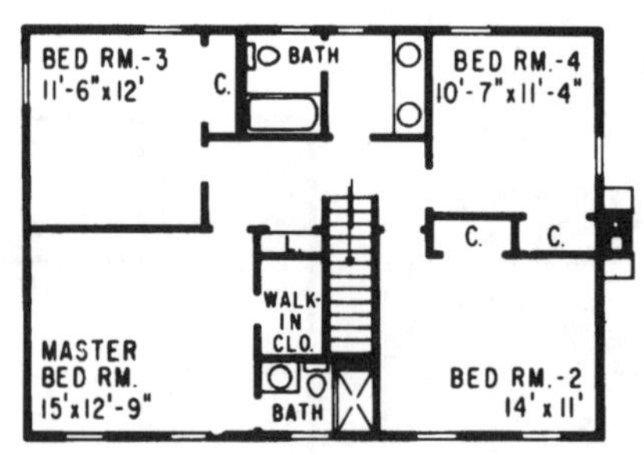
BED RM.-3
11'-6"x12'
C.
BATH
BED RM.-4
10'-7"x11'-4"
C.
C.
WALK-IN CLO.
MASTER
BED RM.
15'x12'-9"
BATH
BED RM.-2
14'x11'

Second Floor

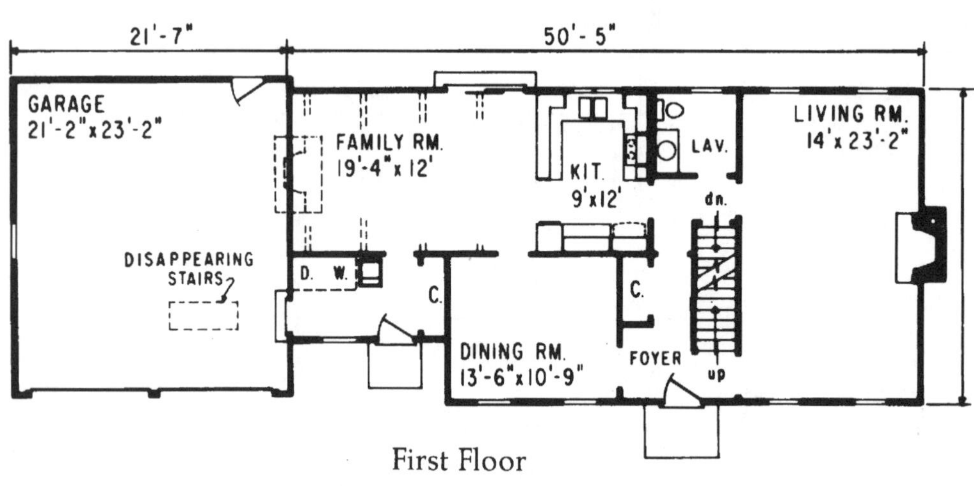
21'-7"
50'-5"
GARAGE
21'-2"x23'-2"
FAMILY RM.
19'-4"x12'
KIT.
9'x12'
LAV.
LIVING RM.
14'x23'-2"
dn.
DISAPPEARING
STAIRS
D. W.
C.
C.
DINING RM.
13'-6"x10'-9"
FOYER
up

First Floor

Bryrewood Deluxe

Features

- Graciousness and convenient living are the themes of this Early American home.
- Designed for a family with children.
- Entry hall leads to U-shaped kitchen.
- Long, exposed beam family room with optional fireplace includes access to backyard.
- Living room with fireplace occupies the right side of the home.
- Second-floor master bedroom includes private bath and walk-in closet.
- Three additional bedrooms upstairs share a large bath with double-vanity.
- Garage loft, reached by disappearing stairs, adds extra space for hobby or play room

First Floor	**1,149 sq. ft.**
Second Floor	**988 sq. ft.**
Total Living Area	**2,137 sq. ft.**

PRICE CODE: B

PLAN NP1284

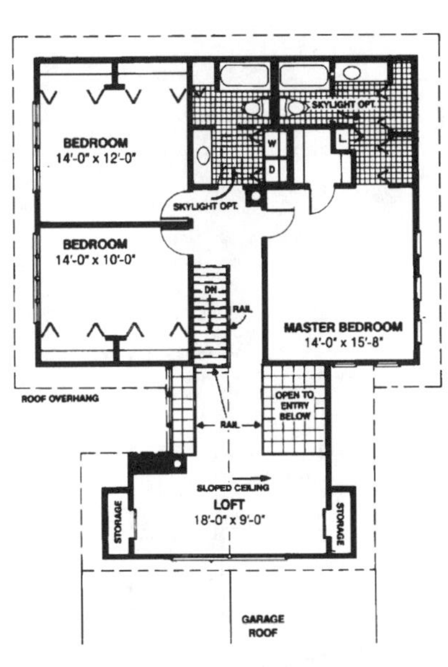
BEDROOM
14'-0" x 12'-0"
BEDROOM
14'-0" x 10'-0"
SKYLIGHT OPT.
SKYLIGHT OPT.
MASTER BEDROOM
14'-0" x 15'-8"
RAIL
ROOF OVERHANG
OPEN TO ENTRY BELOW
SLOPED CEILING
LOFT
18'-0" x 9'-0"
STORAGE
STORAGE
GARAGE ROOF

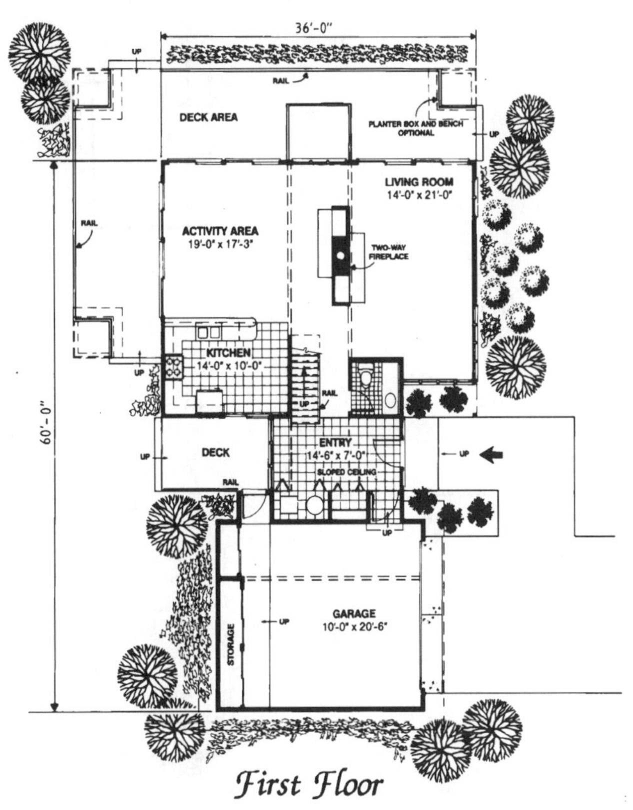
36'-0"
DECK AREA
PLANTER BOX AND BENCH OPTIONAL
ACTIVITY AREA
19'-0" x 17'-3"
LIVING ROOM
14'-0" x 21'-0"
TWO-WAY FIREPLACE
KITCHEN
14'-0" x 10'-0"
60'-0"
DECK
ENTRY
14'-6" x 7'-0"
SLOPED CEILING
GARAGE
10'-0" x 20'-6"
STORAGE
First Floor

Lofty Ideals

Features

- This two-story home features a front-facing loft and balcony for extra appeal.
- Large, tiled entryway leads to living room and activity room, which share a two-way fireplace.
- Three optional deck areas with planters extend the living/entertaining possibilities.
- Skylights brighten both the compartmented hall bath and master bath.
- Second- floor master bedroom features include sloped ceilings and walk-in closet.
- Loft, 230 square feet.

First Floor	1,129 sq. ft.
Second Floor	1,008 sq. ft.
Loft	230 sq. ft.
Total Living Area	2,367 sq. ft.

PRICE CODE: C

PLAN NP1128

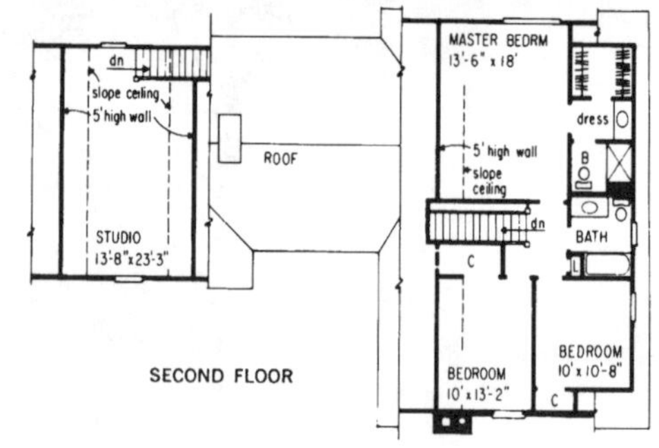

MASTER BEDRM
13'-6" x 18'
dress
B
5' high wall
slope ceiling
dn
BATH
C
BEDROOM
10' x 10'-8"
BEDROOM
10' x 13'-2"
C
ROOF
dn
slope ceiling
5' high wall
STUDIO
13'-8" x 23'-3"

SECOND FLOOR

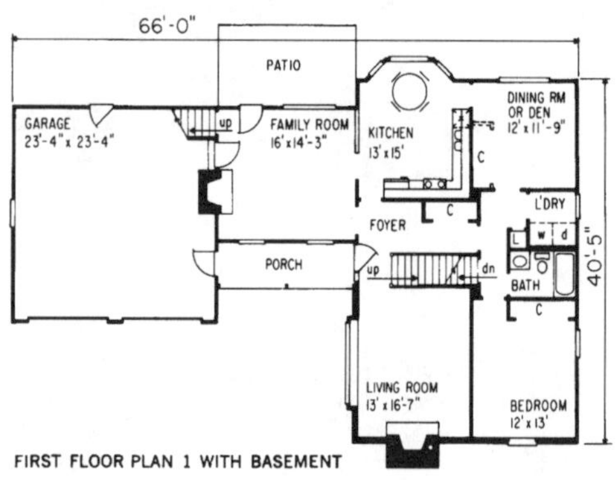

66'-0"
PATIO
GARAGE
23'-4" x 23'-4"
up
FAMILY ROOM
16' x 14'-3"
KITCHEN
13' x 15'
DINING RM
OR DEN
12' x 11'-9"
C
L'DRY
FOYER
PORCH
up
dn
BATH
C
40'-5"
LIVING ROOM
13' x 16'-7"
BEDROOM
12' x 13'

FIRST FLOOR PLAN 1 WITH BASEMENT

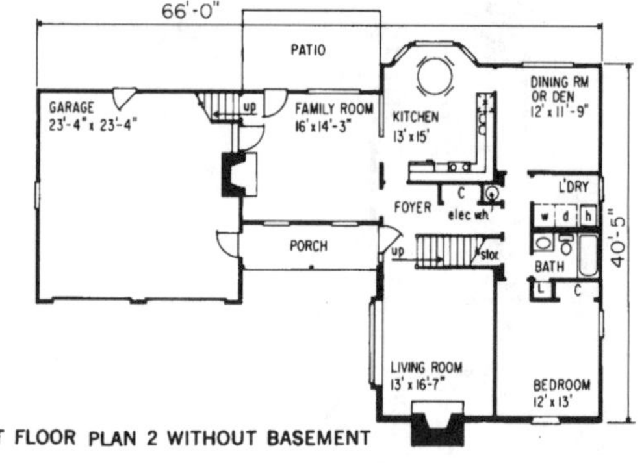

66'-0"
PATIO
GARAGE
23'-4" x 23'-4"
up
FAMILY ROOM
16' x 14'-3"
KITCHEN
13' x 15'
DINING RM
OR DEN
12' x 11'-9"
L'DRY
FOYER
elec wh
PORCH
up
stor
BATH
C
40'-5"
LIVING ROOM
13' x 16'-7"
BEDROOM
12' x 13'

FIRST FLOOR PLAN 2 WITHOUT BASEMENT

Features

- Wrap-around styling of this 1-1/2 story colonial looks cozy, offers plenty of space.
- L-shaped kitchen with bay-window eating area leads to dining room or den.
- Living room includes a fireplace.
- One bedroom downstairs with full bath for guests.
- Upstairs is the master bedroom with dressing area and private bath and two additional bedrooms with a full bath.
- Large studio area over garage with slope ceiling offers many possibilities.
- Studio, 344 square feet

First Floor	**1,322 sq. ft.**
Second Floor	**833 sq. ft.**
Total Living Area	**2,155 sq. ft.**

PRICE CODE: B

PLAN NP1263

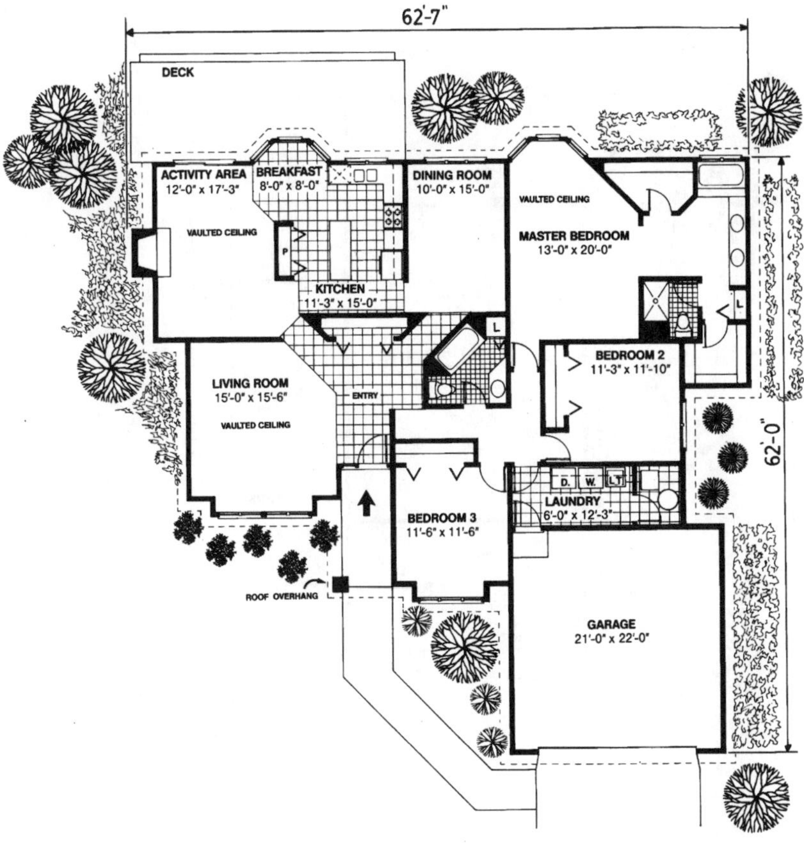

62'-7"
DECK
ACTIVITY AREA
12'-0" x 17'-3"
VAULTED CEILING
BREAKFAST
8'-0" x 8'-0"
DINING ROOM
10'-0" x 15'-0"
VAULTED CEILING
MASTER BEDROOM
13'-0" x 20'-0"
KITCHEN
11'-3" x 15'-0"
LIVING ROOM
15'-0" x 15'-6"
VAULTED CEILING
ENTRY
BEDROOM 2
11'-3" x 11'-10"
62'-0"
LAUNDRY
6'-0" x 12'-3"
BEDROOM 3
11'-6" x 11'-6"
ROOF OVERHANG
GARAGE
21'-0" x 22'-0"

Vaulted Villa

Features

- Unique roof angles make this an eye-catching design.
- Foyer entrance angles to access living room, activity area, and dining room.
- Vaulted ceilings featured in the living room and activity room.
- Activity room also includes fireplace.
- Kitchen with center island opens to breakfast bay area and dining room.
- Master bedroom with bay windows includes a raised-tub master bath and two walk-in closets.
- Two additional bedrooms share full bath.

Total Living Area 2,155 sq. ft.

PRICE CODE: B

PLAN VL2162

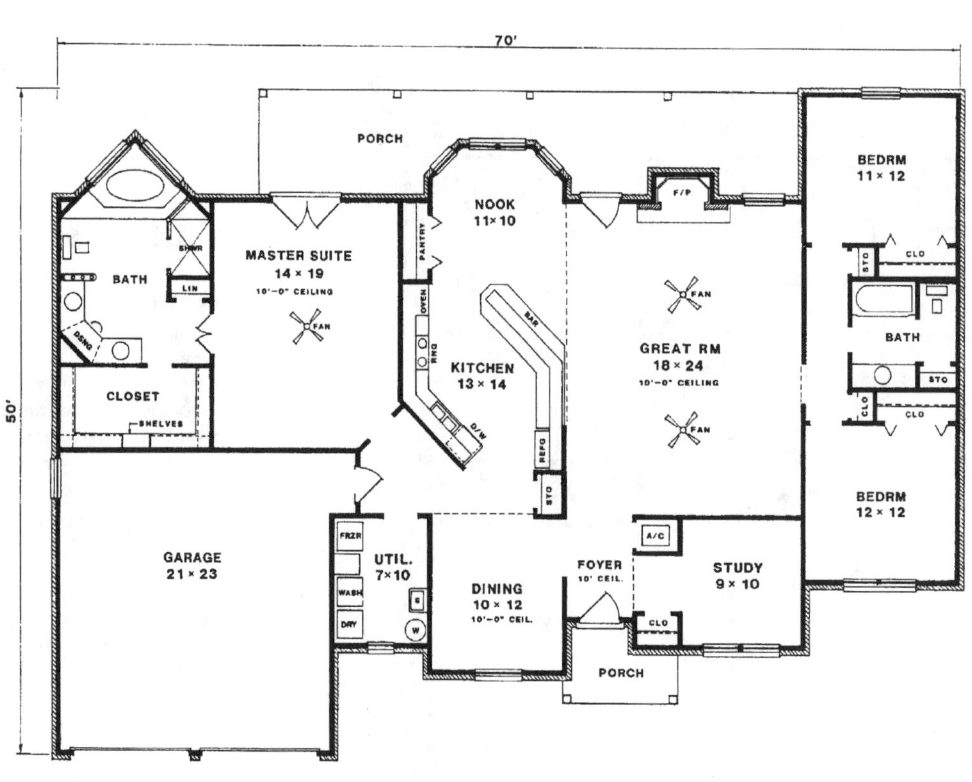

70'
50'
PORCH
NOOK
11×10
BEDRM
11 × 12
F/P
MASTER SUITE
14 × 19
10'-0" CEILING
FAN
BATH
SHWR
LIN
DRSG
PANTRY
OVEN
RNG
BAR
KITCHEN
13 × 14
D/W
REFG
STO
GREAT RM
18 × 24
10'-0" CEILING
FAN
STO
CLO
BATH
STO
CLO
CLO
BEDRM
12 × 12
CLOSET
SHELVES
GARAGE
21 × 23
FRZR
UTIL.
7×10
WASH
DRY
W
DINING
10 × 12
10'-0" CEIL.
FOYER
10' CEIL.
A/C
STUDY
9 × 10
CLO
PORCH

Total Living Area 2,162 sq. ft.

PRICE CODE: B

PLAN SH1989-2145

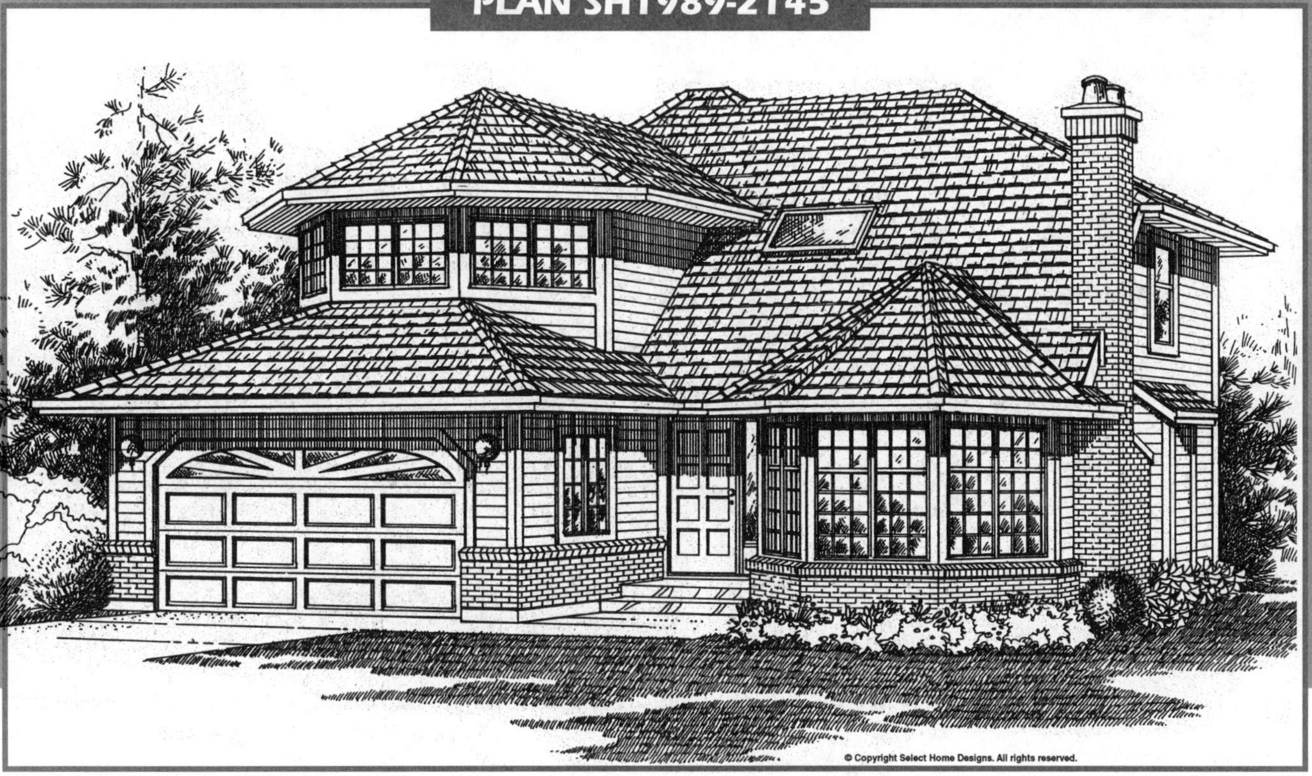

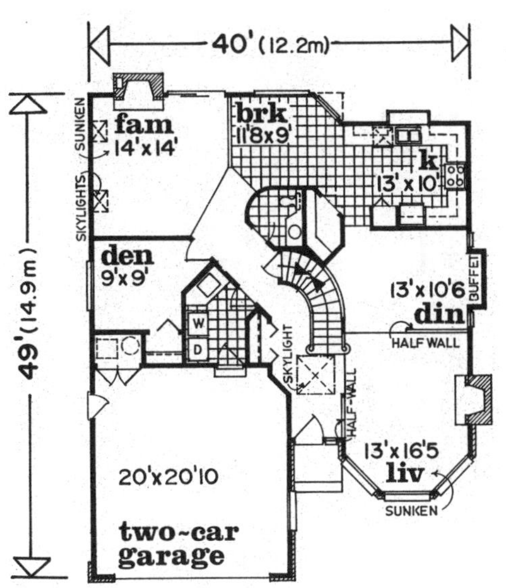
40' (12.2m)
49' (14.9m)
fam
14'x14'
SKYLIGHTS
SUNKEN
brk
11'8x9'
k
13'x10'
den
9'x9'
W
D
13'x10'6
din
BUFFET
HALF WALL
SKYLIGHT
HALF-WALL
20'x20'10
two-car
garage
13'x16'5
liv
SUNKEN

first level 1227 sq. ft.

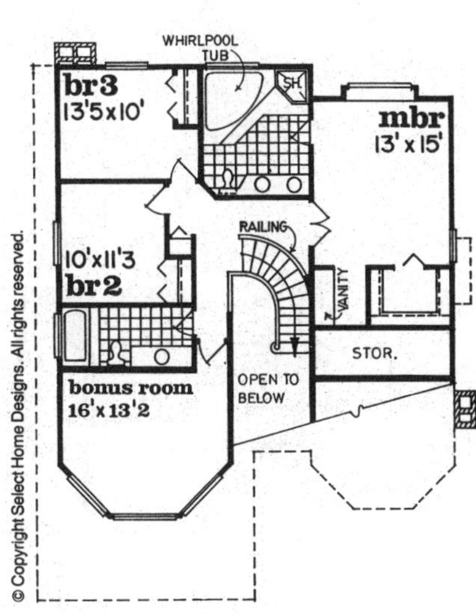
WHIRLPOOL
TUB
SH
br3
13'5x10'
mbr
13' x 15'
RAILING
10'x11'3
br2
VANITY
STOR.
bonus room
16'x13'2
OPEN TO
BELOW
© Copyright Select Home Designs. All rights reserved.

second level 938 sq. ft.

Features

- Sweeping curved staircase dominates skylit foyer.
- Sunken living room rests in windowed bay.
- Half wall separates dining room from living room.
- Kitchen, with walk-in pantry and breakfast room, overlooks sunken family room.
- Skylights and sliding glass doors brighten family room.
- Master bedroom features a walk-in closet and ensuite, with whirlpool spa, twin vanity and shower.
- Bonus room, with expansive windows, provides 212 additional square feet.

Total Living Area **2,165 sq. ft.**

PRICE CODE: B

PLAN NP1274

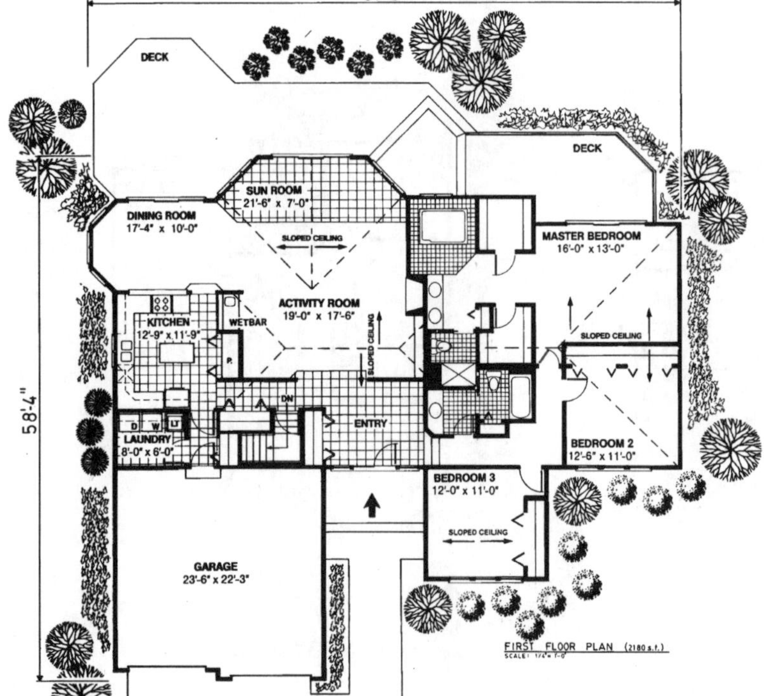
67'-8"
DECK
DECK
SUN ROOM
21'-6" x 7'-0"
DINING ROOM
17'-4" x 10'-0"
SLOPED CEILING
MASTER BEDROOM
16'-0" x 13'-0"
ACTIVITY ROOM
19'-0" x 17'-6"
KITCHEN
12'-9" x 11'-9"
WETBAR
SLOPED CEILING
SLOPED CEILING
ENTRY
LAUNDRY
8'-0" x 6'-0"
BEDROOM 2
12'-6" x 11'-0"
BEDROOM 3
12'-0" x 11'-0"
SLOPED CEILING
GARAGE
23'-6" x 22'-3"
58'-4"
FIRST FLOOR PLAN (2180 s.f.)

Total Living Area 2,180 sq. ft.

PRICE CODE: B

PLAN NP1418

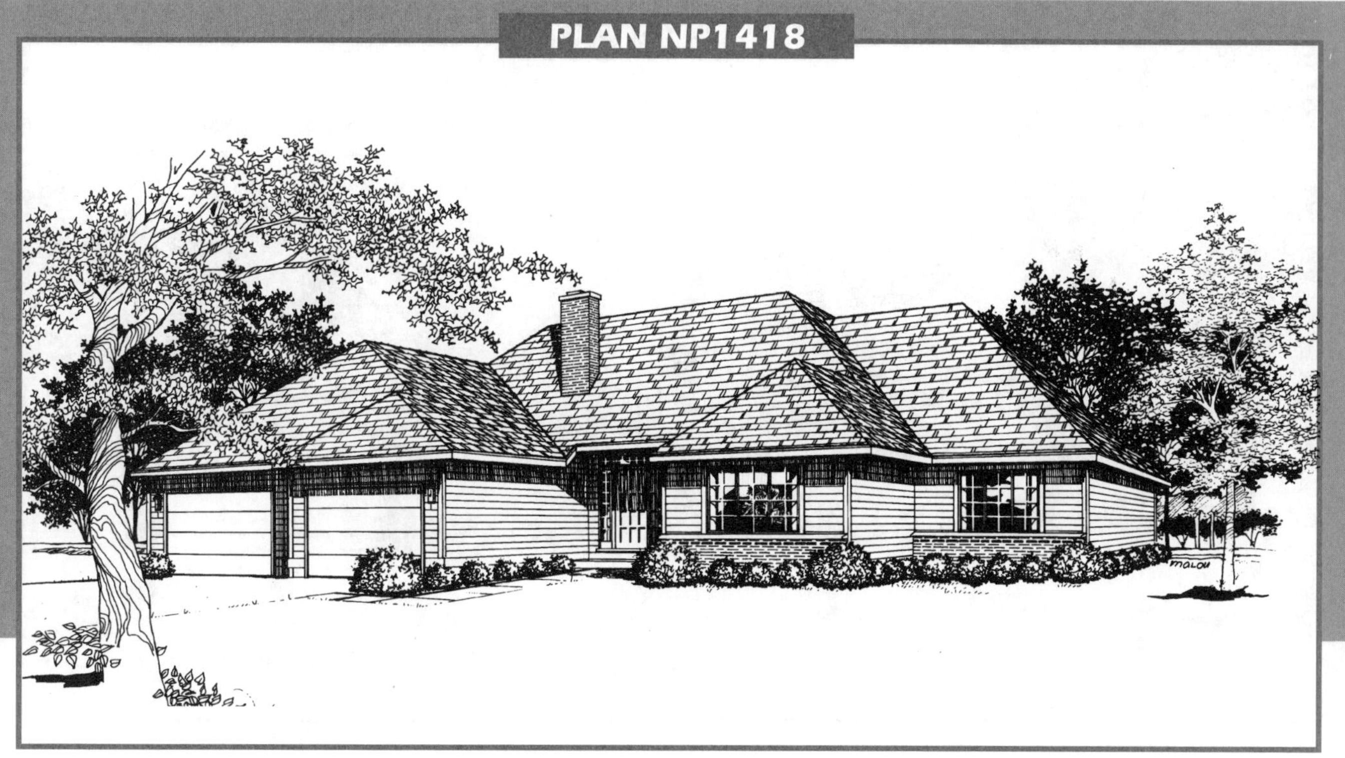

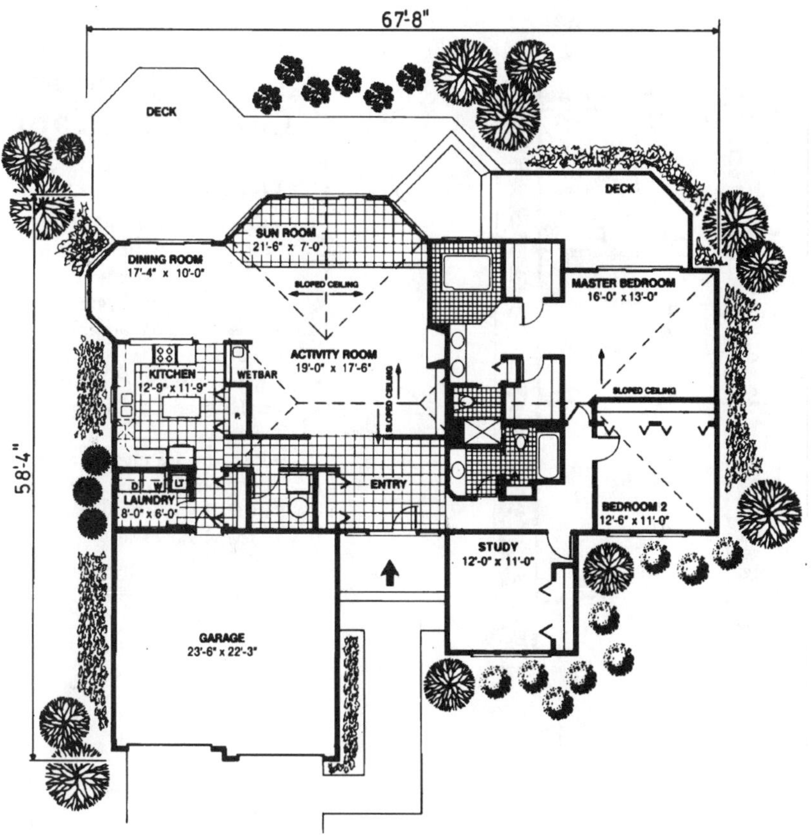

67'-8"
58'-4"
DECK
DECK
SUN ROOM 21'-6" x 7'-0"
DINING ROOM 17'-4" x 10'-0"
SLOPED CEILING
ACTIVITY ROOM 19'-0" x 17'-6"
SLOPED CEILING
MASTER BEDROOM 16'-0" x 13'-0"
SLOPED CEILING
KITCHEN 12'-9" x 11'-9"
WETBAR
ENTRY
LAUNDRY 8'-0" x 6'-0"
BEDROOM 2 12'-6" x 11'-0"
STUDY 12'-0" x 11'-0"
GARAGE 23'-6" x 22'-3"

Sunny Retreat

Features

- Pleasing roof line angles and well-windowed entry catch the eye in this one-story home.
- Large, cathedral-ceiling entry leads to sloped ceiling activity room , sunken sun room.
- Wet bar in activity room is open to kitchen, which features a snack bar and serve-through to dining room.
- Garage entrance to home leads to laundry room and lavatory.
- Right wing of home includes a master bedroom with dual, walk-in closets, raised Roman tub and compartmented shower.
- Second bedroom with access to full bath.
- Front-facing study with closet would make a perfect office.

Total Living Area **2,180 sq. ft.**

PRICE CODE: B

PLAN NP1260

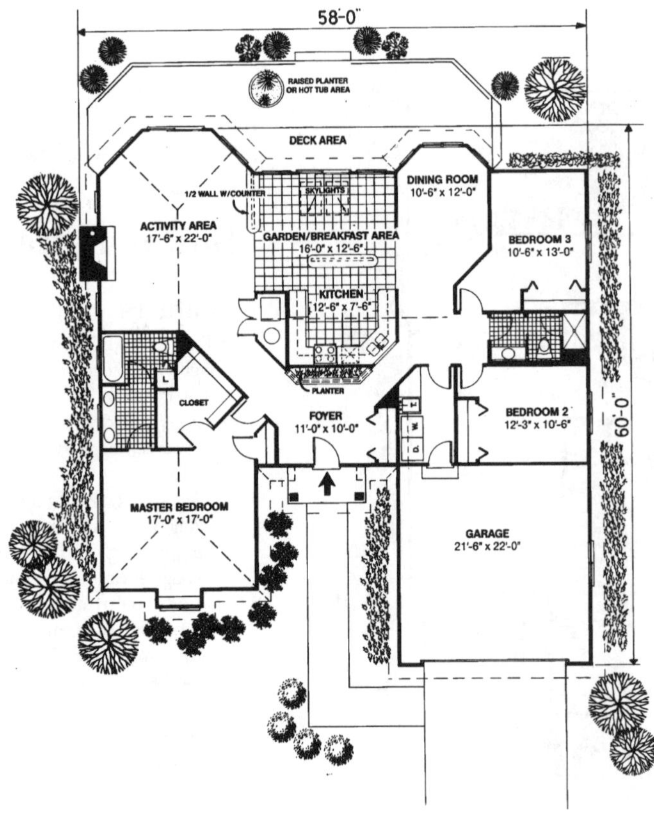
58'-0"
RAISED PLANTER OR HOT TUB AREA
DECK AREA
1/2 WALL W/COUNTER
SKYLIGHTS
ACTIVITY AREA
17'-6" x 22'-0"
GARDEN/BREAKFAST AREA
16'-0" x 12'-6"
DINING ROOM
10'-6" x 12'-0"
BEDROOM 3
10'-6" x 13'-0"
KITCHEN
12'-6" x 7'-6"
CLOSET
PLANTER
FOYER
11'-0" x 10'-0"
BEDROOM 2
12'-3" x 10'-6"
60'-0"
MASTER BEDROOM
17'-0" x 17'-0"
GARAGE
21'-6" x 22'-0"

Great Expectations

Features

- Comfort and good-looks are combined in this design for modern families.
- Perfect for those who love a sense of indoor/outdoor living.
- Enter pillared main entrance to the foyer with built-in planter.
- Right wing includes two bedrooms with full bath and laundry room with access to garage.
- Left wing features the enormous master bedroom with private bath and compartmented shower and water closet plus a cozy window seat.
- Rear of home features centrally located kitchen and garden/breakfast area with access to optional rear deck with raised planter or optional hot tub.

Total Living Area **2,190 sq. ft.**

PRICE CODE: B

PLAN DB1536

123

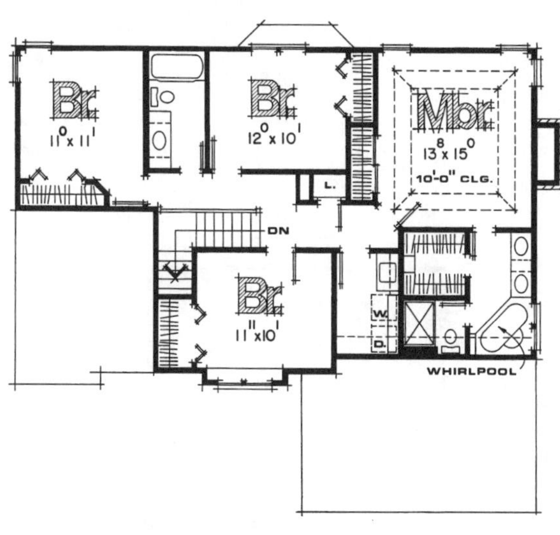
Br.
11^{0} x 11^{1}
Br.
12^{0} x 10^{1}
Mbr.
13^{8} x 15^{0}
10'-0" CLG.
L.
DN
Br.
11^{11} x 10^{1}
W.
D.
WHIRLPOOL

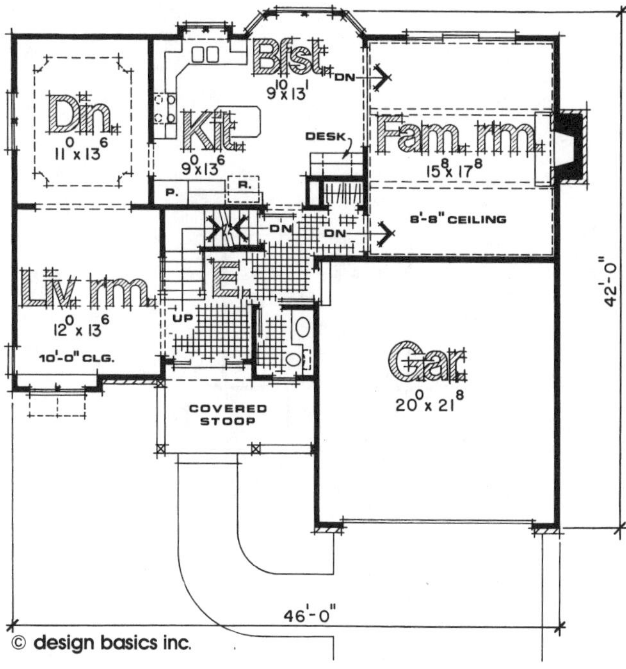
Bfst.
9^{10} x 13^{1}
DN
Din.
11^{0} x 13^{6}
Kit.
9^{0} x 13^{6}
DESK
Fam. rm.
15^{8} x 17^{8}
8'-8" CEILING
P.
R.
DN
DN
Liv. rm.
12^{0} x 13^{6}
10'-0" CLG.
E.
UP
Gar.
20^{0} x 21^{8}
COVERED STOOP
42'-0"
46'-0"
© design basics inc.

Features

- Simplified foundation.
- Volume living room opens to dining room with formal ceiling.
- Powder bath off entry.
- Planning desk and pantry in island kitchen.
- Bayed breakfast area open to family room.
- Step-down family room with beamed ceiling and raised hearth fireplace.
- Secondary bedrooms share hall bath.
- Efficient second level laundry.
- Large master bedroom with vaulted ceiling and corner windows.
- Luxurious master bath with window over corner whirlpool, walk-in closet, double vanity and compartmented stool and shower.

First Floor	1,098 sq. ft.
Second Floor	1,095 sq. ft.
Total Living Area	2,193 sq. ft.

PRICE CODE: C

PLAN AM2280

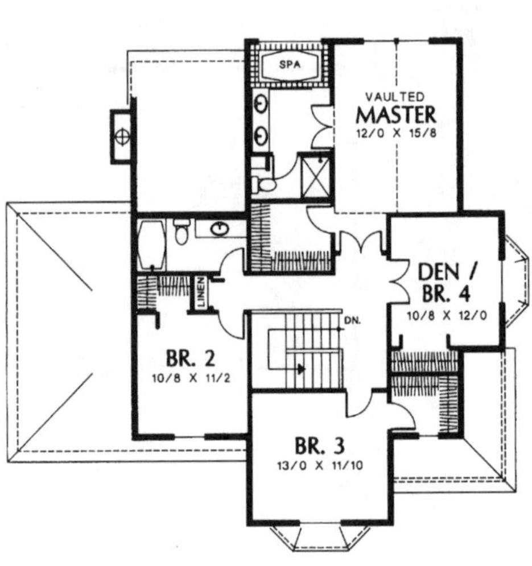

SPA
VAULTED
MASTER
12/0 X 15/8
LINEN
DN.
DEN / BR. 4
10/8 X 12/0
BR. 2
10/8 X 11/2
BR. 3
13/0 X 11/10

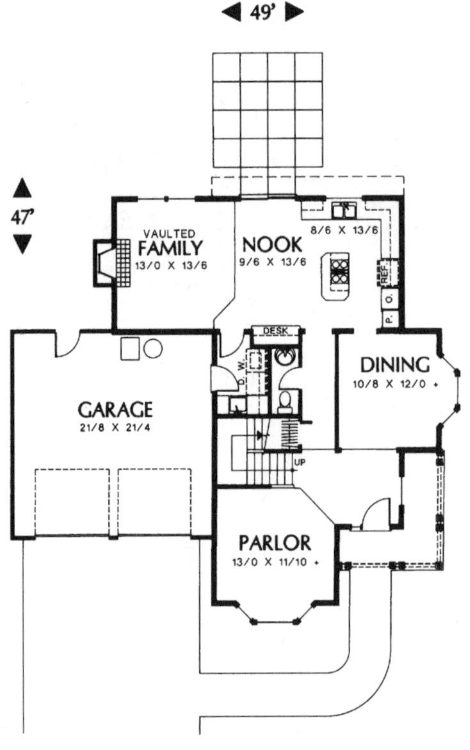

49'
47'
VAULTED
FAMILY
13/0 X 13/6
NOOK
9/6 X 13/6
8/6 X 13/6
REF.
P.
DESK
W.
D.
DINING
10/8 X 12/0 +
GARAGE
21/8 X 21/4
UP
PARLOR
13/0 X 11/10 +

First Floor	1,085 sq. ft.
Second Floor	1,110 sq. ft.
Total Living Area	2,195 sq. ft.

PRICE CODE: B

PLAN NP1077

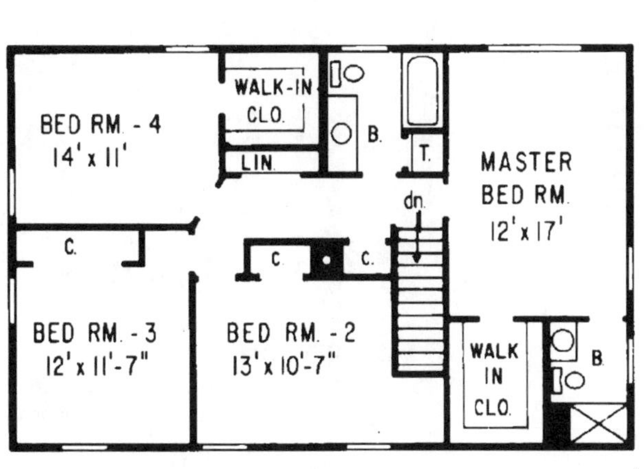

WALK-IN CLO.
BED RM. - 4
14' x 11'
B.
T.
LIN.
MASTER BED RM.
12' x 17'
dn.
C.
C.
C.
BED RM. - 3
12' x 11'-7"
BED RM. - 2
13' x 10'-7"
WALK IN CLO.
B

SECOND FLOOR

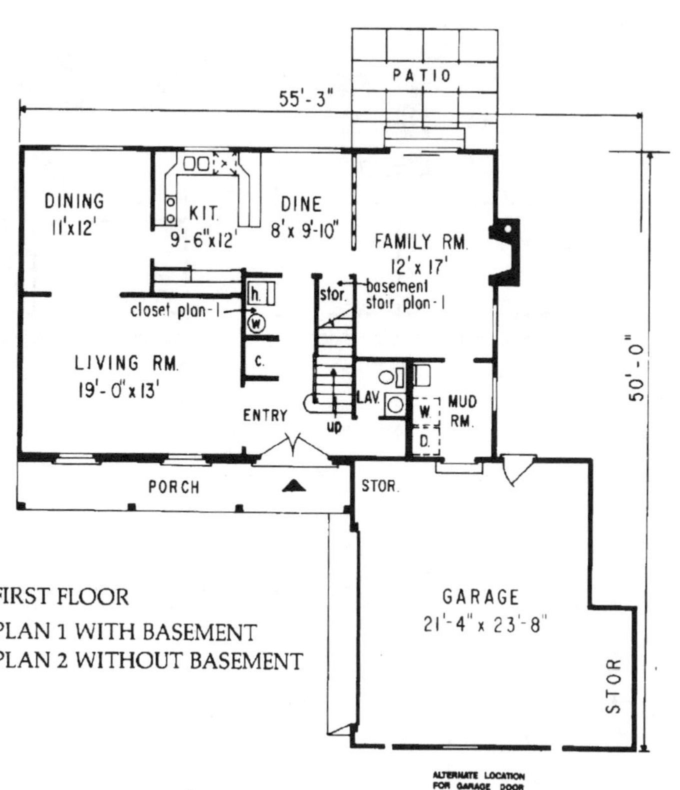

PATIO
55'-3"
DINING
11'x12'
KIT.
9'-6"x12'
DINE
8'x 9'-10"
FAMILY RM.
12' x 17'
stor.
basement stair plan-1
closet plan-1
h.
W
C.
LIVING RM.
19'-0" x 13'
ENTRY
up
LAV.
W
D.
MUD RM.
50'-0"
PORCH
STOR.
GARAGE
21'-4" x 23'-8"
STOR
ALTERNATE LOCATION FOR GARAGE DOOR

FIRST FLOOR
PLAN 1 WITH BASEMENT
PLAN 2 WITHOUT BASEMENT

First Floor	1,104 sq. ft.
Second Floor	1,092 sq. ft.
Total Living Area	2,196 sq. ft.

PRICE CODE: B

PLAN NP1134

126

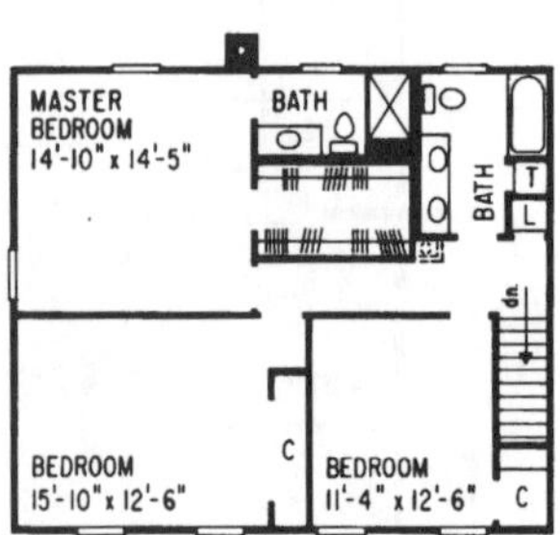
MASTER BEDROOM
14'-10" x 14'-5"
BATH
BATH
T
L
dn
BEDROOM
15'-10" x 12'-6"
C
BEDROOM
11'-4" x 12'-6"
C

SECOND FLOOR THREE BEDROOMS

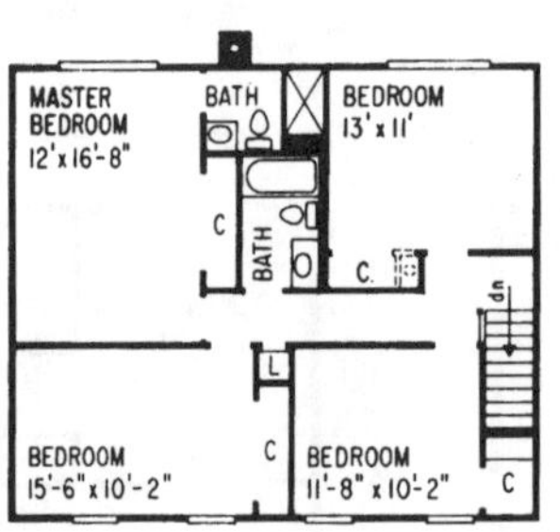
MASTER BEDROOM
12' x 16'-8"
BATH
BEDROOM
13' x 11'
C
BATH
C.
dn
L
BEDROOM
15'-6" x 10'-2"
C
BEDROOM
11'-8" x 10'-2"
C

SECOND FLOOR FOUR BEDROOMS

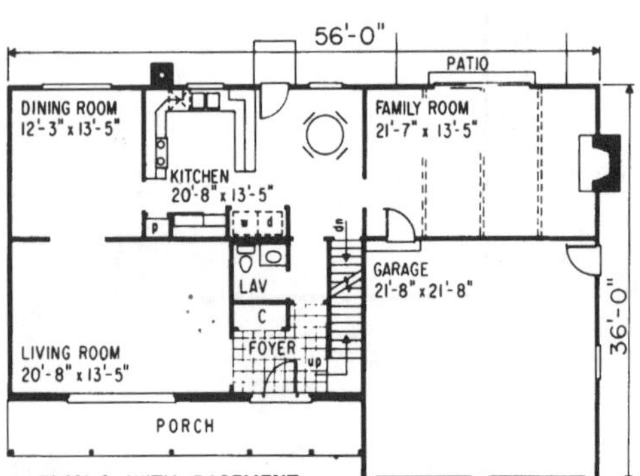
56'-0"
PATIO
DINING ROOM
12'-3" x 13'-5"
KITCHEN
20'-8" x 13'-5"
FAMILY ROOM
21'-7" x 13'-5"
LAV
C
GARAGE
21'-8" x 21'-8"
LIVING ROOM
20'-8" x 13'-5"
FOYER
up
dn
36'-0"
PORCH

PLAN 1 WITH BASEMENT

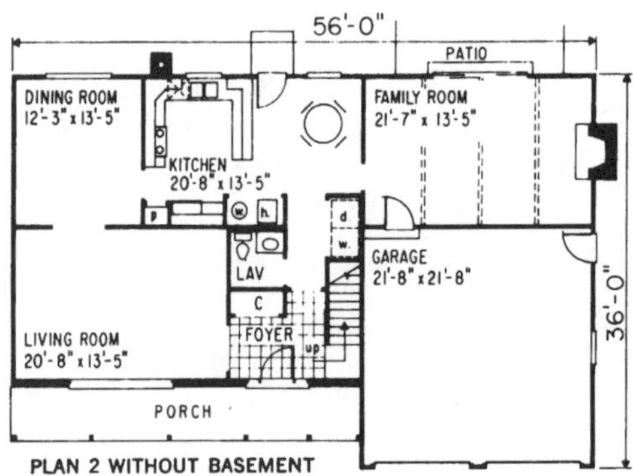
56'-0"
PATIO
DINING ROOM
12'-3" x 13'-5"
KITCHEN
20'-8" x 13'-5"
FAMILY ROOM
21'-7" x 13'-5"
LAV
C
GARAGE
21'-8" x 21'-8"
LIVING ROOM
20'-8" x 13'-5"
FOYER
up
36'-0"
PORCH

PLAN 2 WITHOUT BASEMENT

Classic Country

Features

- Enjoy the pleasures of front-porch sitting in this rustic-looking country home.
- Generously sized living room off foyer.
- Dining room adjacent to U-shaped kitchen with lunch counter and breakfast nook.
- Family room with beamed ceiling and fireplace.
- Second floor features a three- or four-bedroom option with two fulls baths.

First Floor	**1,260 sq. ft.**
Second Floor	**952 sq. ft.**
Total Living Area	**2,212 sq. ft.**

PRICE CODE: C

PLAN NPES114

127

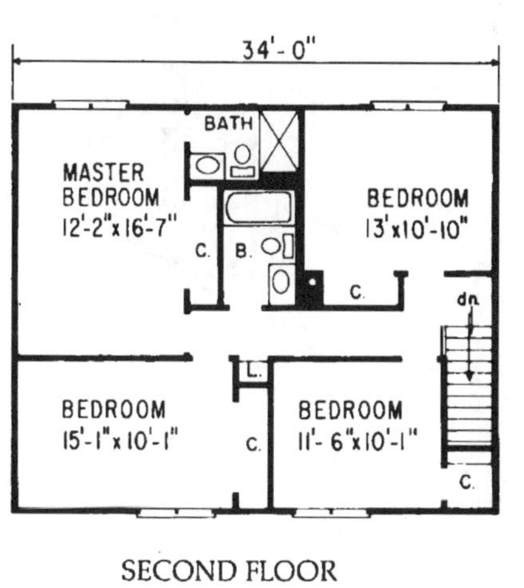
34'-0"
BATH
MASTER BEDROOM 12'-2"x16'-7"
BEDROOM 13'x10'-10"
C.
B.
C.
dn.
L.
BEDROOM 15'-1"x10'-1"
C.
BEDROOM 11'-6"x10'-1"
C.

SECOND FLOOR

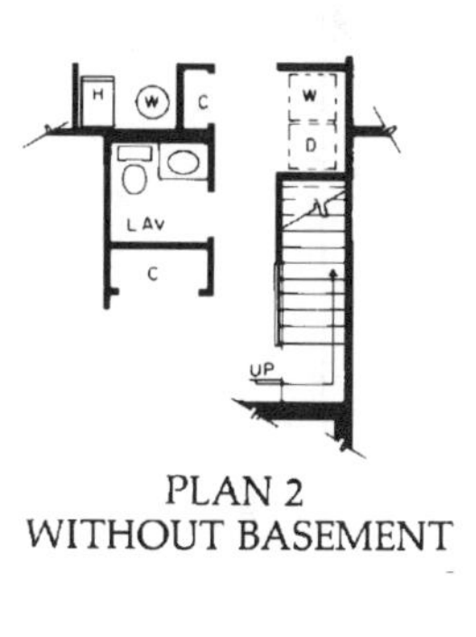
H
W
C
W
D
LAV
C
UP

PLAN 2
WITHOUT BASEMENT

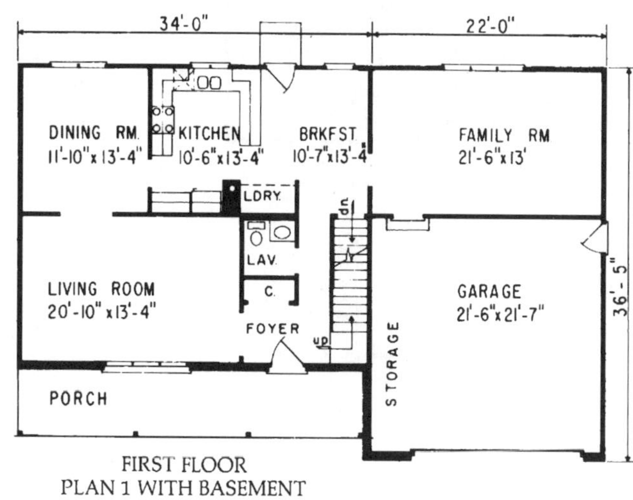
34'-0"
22'-0"
DINING RM. 11'-10"x13'-4"
KITCHEN 10'-6"x13'-4"
BRKFST. 10'-7"x13'-4
FAMILY RM 21'-6"x13'
LDRY.
dn.
LAV.
C.
LIVING ROOM 20'-10"x13'-4"
FOYER
up
GARAGE 21'-6"x21'-7"
36'-5"
STORAGE
PORCH

FIRST FLOOR
PLAN 1 WITH BASEMENT

Features

- This energy-saving design offers considerable total living area for the economy-minded homeowner.
- The covered front porch invites you to the front entry and entry foyer with the L-shaped living and dining room areas to your left.
- At the rear you'll discover a large U-shaped kitchen, breakfast nook, and family room area.
- Upstairs are four bedrooms served by two baths.

First Floor	**1,274 sq. ft.**
Second Floor	**952 sq. ft.**
Total Living Area	**2,226 sq. ft.**

PRICE CODE: C

CUSTOMIZE IT!

ORDER TOLL FREE 1-800-533-4350 **24-HOUR FAX ORDERING 1-800-344-4293**

PLAN DB2176

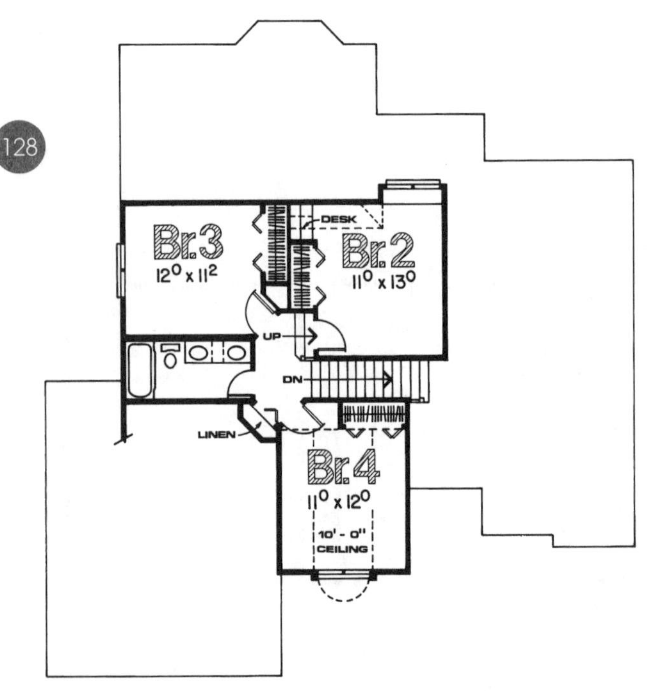

Br. 3
$12^0 \times 11^2$
Br. 2
$11^0 \times 13^0$
DESK
UP
DN
LINEN
Br. 4
$11^0 \times 12^0$
10' - 0" CEILING

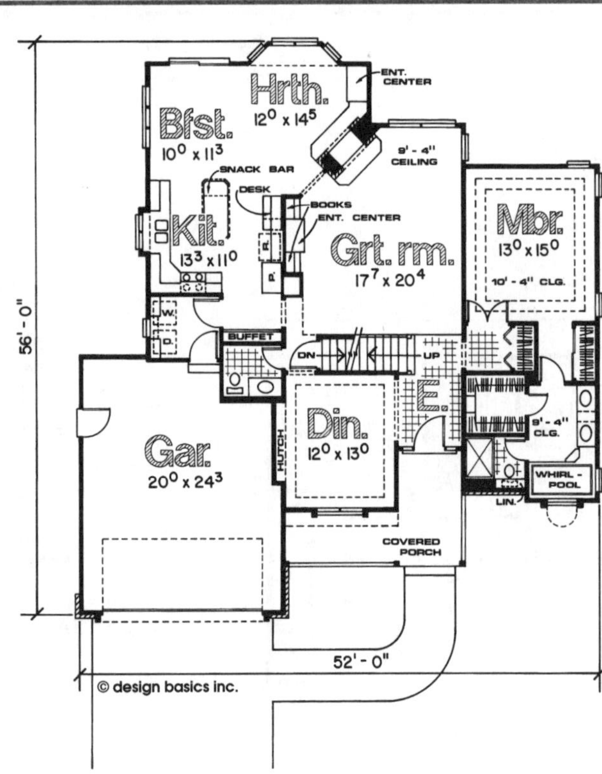

Hrth.
$12^0 \times 14^5$
ENT. CENTER
Bfst.
$10^0 \times 11^3$
9' - 4" CEILING
SNACK BAR
DESK
BOOKS
ENT. CENTER
Kit.
$13^3 \times 11^0$
Grt. rm.
$17^7 \times 20^4$
Mbr.
$13^0 \times 15^0$
10' - 4" CLG.
56' - 0"
BUFFET
DN
UP
E.
Din.
$12^0 \times 13^0$
HUTCH
Gar.
$20^0 \times 24^3$
9' - 4" CLG.
WHIRL - POOL
LIN.
COVERED PORCH
52' - 0"
© design basics inc.

Features

- Generous covered front porch.
- Great room features bookcases, entertainment center and angled see-thru fireplace.
- Island kitchen offers abundant amenities including built-in buffet serving counter for formal dining convenience.
- Hearth room with bayed window and entertainment center.
- Convenient utility entrance.
- Double doors into master bedroom with tiered ceiling.
- Master dressing area with whirlpool under arched window.
- Upstairs, bedroom #4 has beautiful arched window with volume ceiling.

First Floor	1,595 sq. ft.
Second Floor	641 sq. ft.
Total Living Area	2,236 sq. ft.

PRICE CODE: D

PLAN JA5539

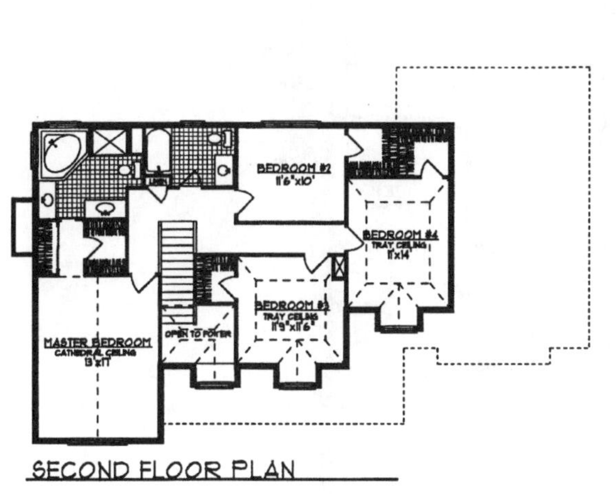
BEDROOM #2
11'6"x10'
BEDROOM #4
TRAY CEILING
11'x14'
BEDROOM #3
TRAY CEILING
11'9"x11'6"
OPEN TO FOYER
MASTER BEDROOM
CATHEDRAL CEILING
13'x17'

SECOND FLOOR PLAN

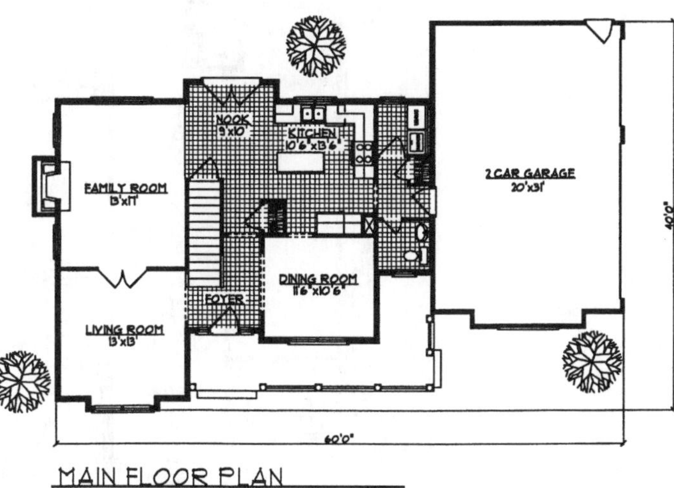
NOOK
9'x10'
KITCHEN
10'6"x13'6"
FAMILY ROOM
13'x17'
2 CAR GARAGE
20'x31'
40'0"
DINING ROOM
11'6"x10'6"
FOYER
LIVING ROOM
13'x13'
60'0"

MAIN FLOOR PLAN

First Floor	1,065 sq. ft.
Second Floor	1,171 sq. ft.
Total Living Area	2,236 sq. ft.

PRICE CODE: C

PLAN FD8096-LB

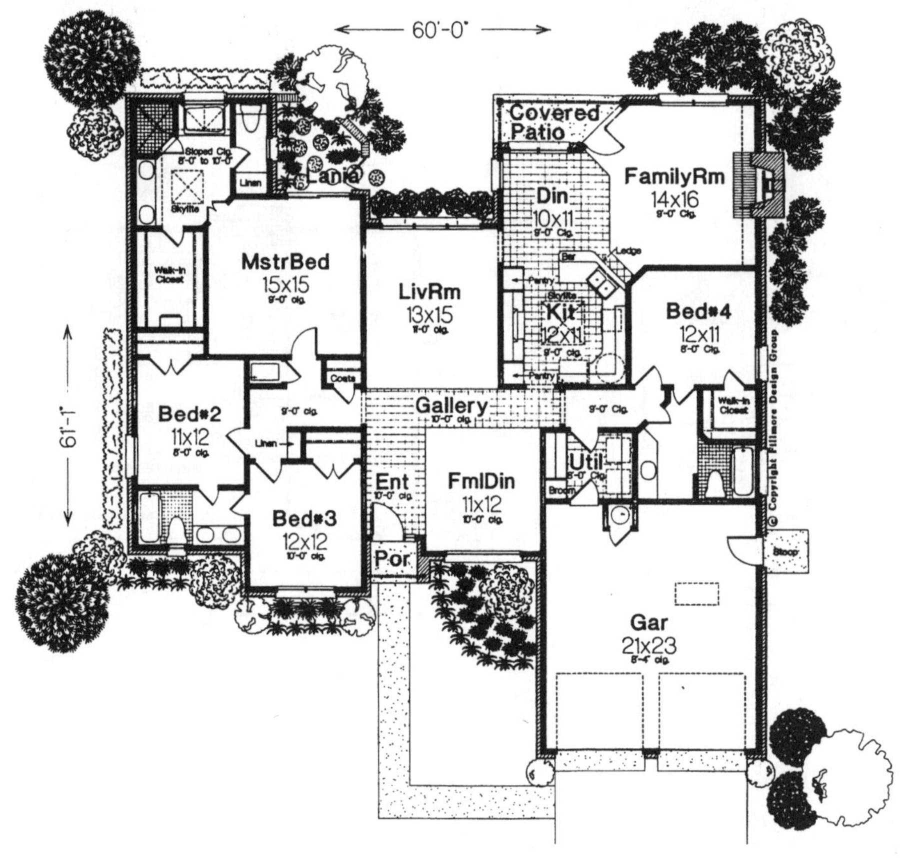

60'-0"
61'-1"
Covered Patio
FamilyRm
14x16
Din
10x11
Kit
12x11
Lanai
MstrBed
15x15
Walk-In Closet
Skylite
Linen
LivRm
13x15
Bed#4
12x11
Walk-in Closet
Gallery
Bed#2
11x12
Linen
Util
Ent
FmlDin
11x12
Bed#3
12x12
Por
Gar
21x23
Stoop
© Copyright Fillmore Design Group

Total Living Area 2,238 sq. ft.

PRICE CODE: C

CUSTOMIZE IT!

ORDER TOLL FREE 1-800-533-4350 24-HOUR FAX ORDERING 1-800-344-4293

PLAN NP1317

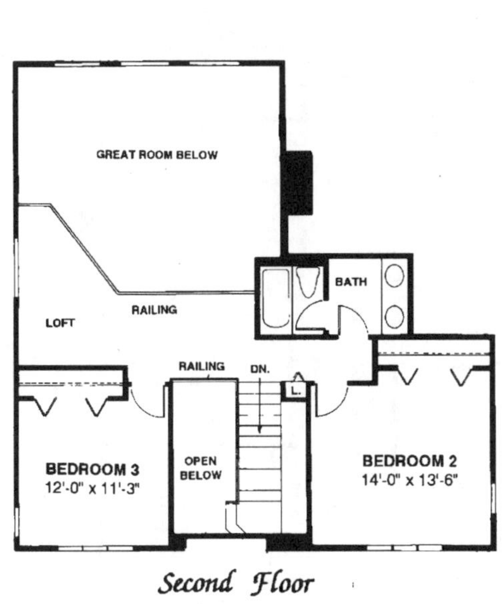

GREAT ROOM BELOW
LOFT
RAILING
BATH
RAILING
DN.
BEDROOM 3
12'-0" x 11'-3"
OPEN BELOW
BEDROOM 2
14'-0" x 13'-6"

Second Floor

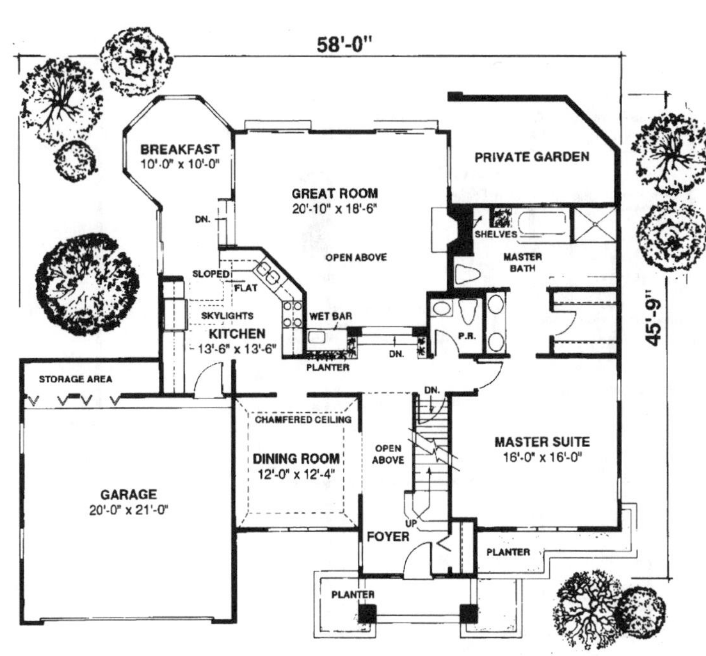

58'-0"
45'-9"
BREAKFAST
10'-0" x 10'-0"
GREAT ROOM
20'-10" x 18'-6"
OPEN ABOVE
PRIVATE GARDEN
SHELVES
MASTER BATH
DN.
SLOPED
FLAT
SKYLIGHTS
KITCHEN
13'-6" x 13'-6"
WET BAR
P.R.
DN.
PLANTER
STORAGE AREA
CHAMFERED CEILING
DINING ROOM
12'-0" x 12'-4"
OPEN ABOVE
DN.
MASTER SUITE
16'-0" x 16'-0"
GARAGE
20'-0" x 21'-0"
UP
FOYER
PLANTER
PLANTER

First Floor
Plan 1 with Basement

Sunny Stucco

Features

- Impressive stucco exterior and large windows makes this home a sun-worshipers haven.
- Front entrance features built-in planters on either side.
- Large open foyer is open above.
- Formal dining room has beautiful chamfered ceiling.
- Hall to kitchen includes built-in planter.
- Kitchen incorporates skylights and octagonal breakfast nook.
- First-floor master suite of impressive dimensions.
- Second-floor loft overlooks great room.

First Floor	1,599 sq. ft.
Second Floor	725 sq. ft.
Total Living Area	2,324 sq. ft.

PRICE CODE: C

PLAN NP1300

132

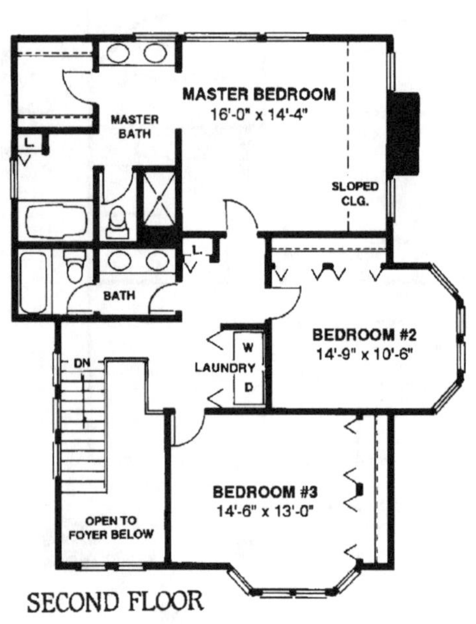
MASTER BEDROOM
16'-0" x 14'-4"
MASTER BATH
SLOPED CLG.
L
BATH
BEDROOM #2
14'-9" x 10'-6"
DN
W
LAUNDRY
D
BEDROOM #3
14'-6" x 13'-0"
OPEN TO FOYER BELOW
SECOND FLOOR

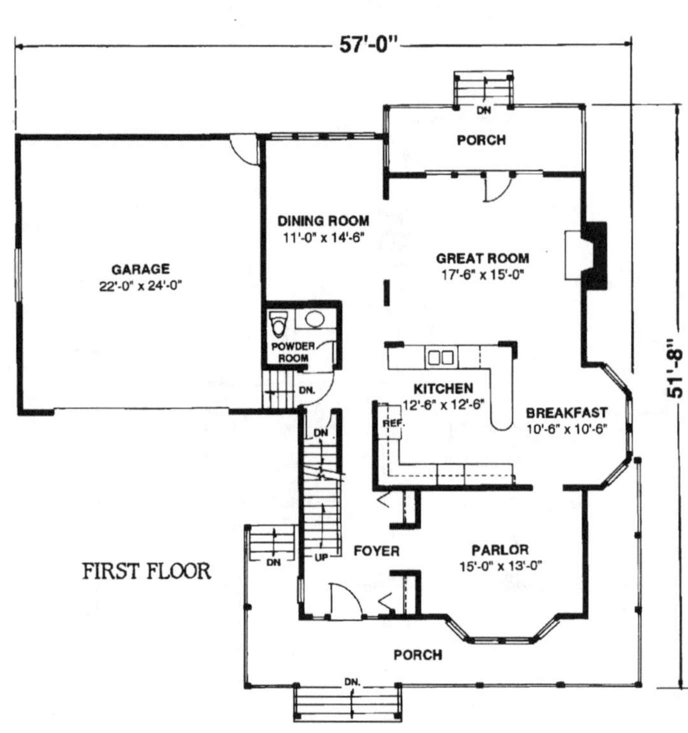
57'-0"
51'-8"
DN
PORCH
DINING ROOM
11'-0" x 14'-6"
GARAGE
22'-0" x 24'-0"
GREAT ROOM
17'-6" x 15'-0"
POWDER ROOM
DN.
KITCHEN
12'-6" x 12'-6"
REF.
BREAKFAST
10'-6" x 10'-6"
DN
UP
FOYER
PARLOR
15'-0" x 13'-0"
FIRST FLOOR
PORCH
DN.

Victorian Hideaway

Features

- Contemporary comfort lodges in this compact Victorian design.
- Front parlor with bay window recaptures the charm of yesteryear.
- Centrally located kitchen shares counter with bay-windowed breakfast nook.
- Upstairs, the master bedroom, with dual-vanity bath, private water closet and shower area, and walk-in closet occupies the rear of the home.
- Two additional bedrooms share a deluxe bath.
- An upstairs laundry room adds to the convenience.

First Floor	1,203 sq. ft.
Second Floor	1,050 sq. ft.
Total Living Area	2,253 sq. ft.

PRICE CODE: C

PLAN FD8109-L

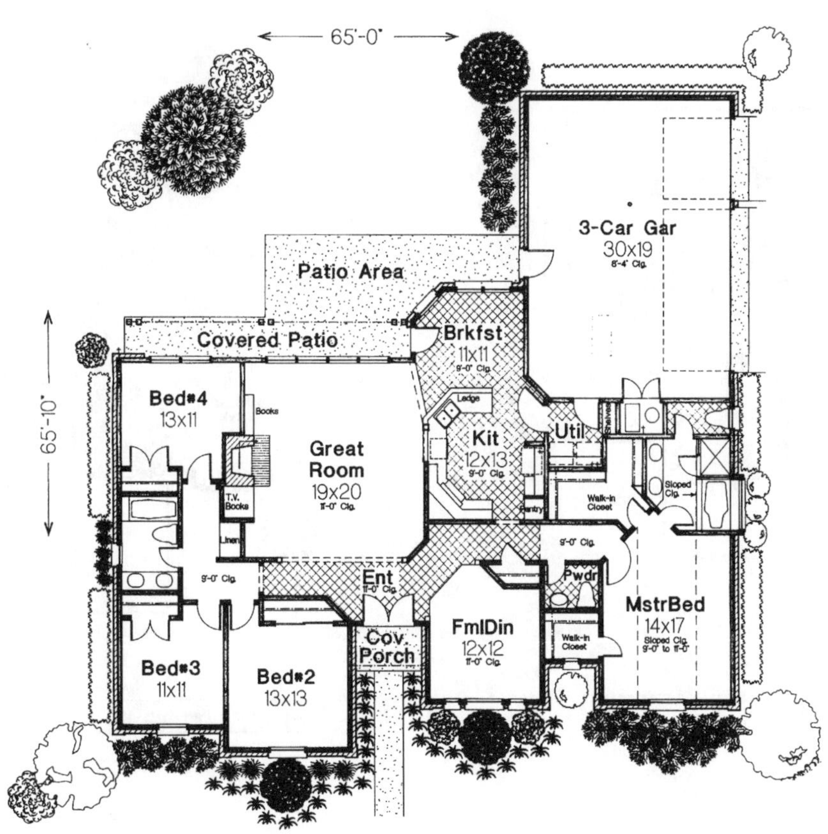

65'-0"
65'-10"
3-Car Gar
30x19
8'-4" Clg.
Patio Area
Covered Patio
Brkfst
11x11
9'-0" Clg.
Kit
12x13
9'-0" Clg.
Util
Bed#4
13x11
Great
Room
19x20
11'-0" Clg.
Walk-in
Closet
Sloped
Clg.
9'-0" Clg.
Pwdr
MstrBed
14x17
Sloped Clg.
9'-0" to 11'-0"
Ent
Cov.
Porch
FmlDin
12x12
11'-0" Clg.
Bed#3
11x11
Bed#2
13x13

Total Living Area 2,257 sq. ft.

PRICE CODE: C

CUSTOMIZE IT!

ORDER TOLL FREE 1•800•533•4350 24-HOUR FAX ORDERING 1•800•344•4293

PLAN JA5329

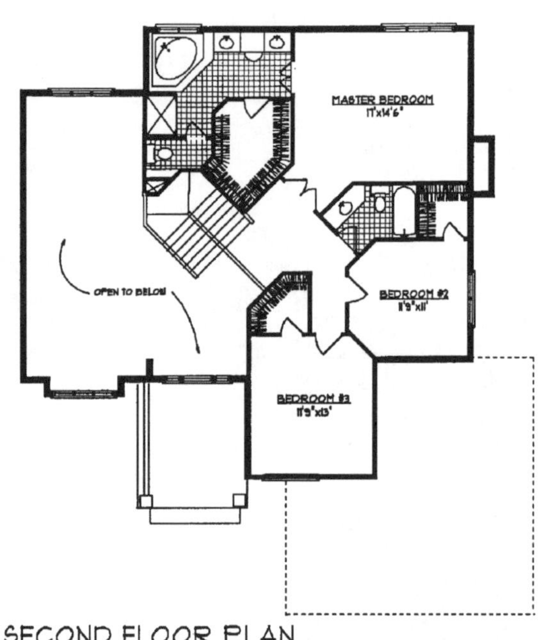
MASTER BEDROOM
17'x14'6"
OPEN TO BELOW
BEDROOM #2
11'9"x11'
BEDROOM #3
11'9"x13'
SECOND FLOOR PLAN

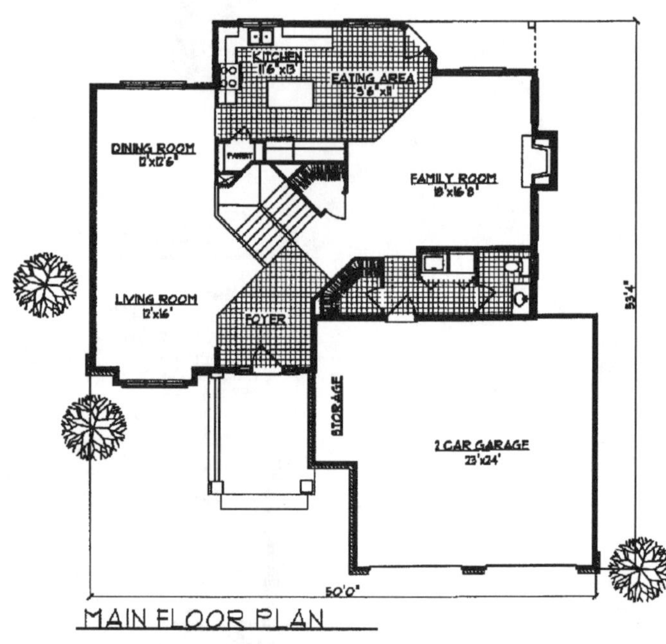
KITCHEN
11'6"x13'
EATING AREA
9'6"x11'
DINING ROOM
12'x12'6"
FAMILY ROOM
18'x16'8"
LIVING ROOM
12'x16'
FOYER
STORAGE
2 CAR GARAGE
23'x24'
53'4"
50'0"
MAIN FLOOR PLAN

First Floor	1,271 sq. ft.
Second Floor	991 sq. ft.
Total Living Area	2,262 sq. ft.

PRICE CODE: C

PLAN AM2239F

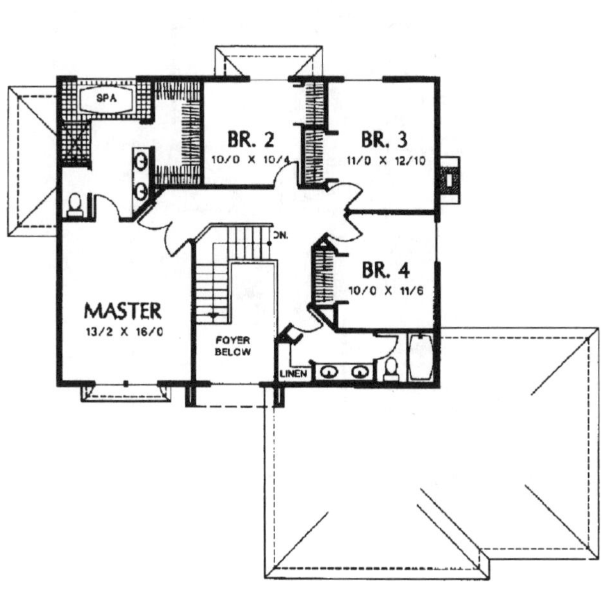
SPA
BR. 2
10/0 X 10/4
BR. 3
11/0 X 12/10
DN.
BR. 4
10/0 X 11/6
MASTER
13/2 X 16/0
FOYER
BELOW
LINEN

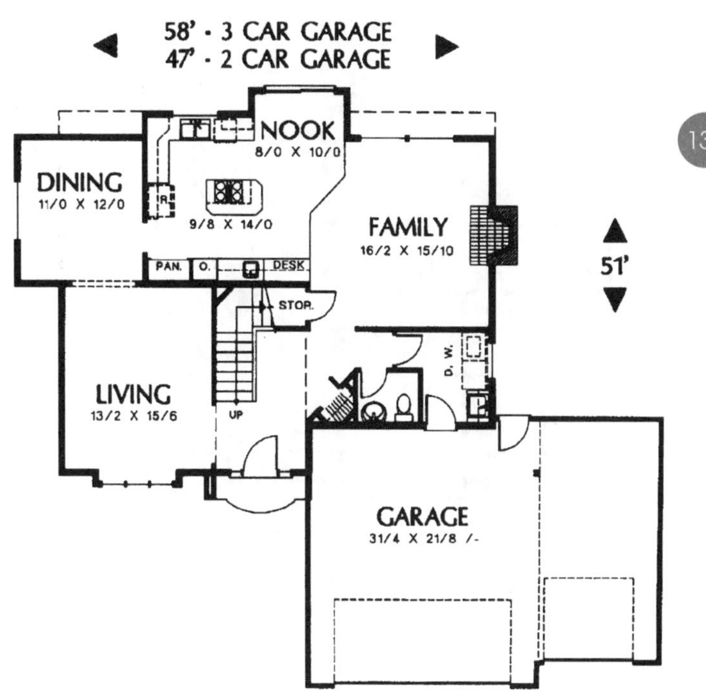
58' - 3 CAR GARAGE
47' - 2 CAR GARAGE
NOOK
8/0 X 10/0
DINING
11/0 X 12/0
R
9/8 X 14/0
FAMILY
16/2 X 15/10
51'
PAN.
O.
DESK
STOR.
LIVING
13/2 X 15/6
UP
D. W.
GARAGE
31/4 X 21/8 /-

135

First Floor	1,180 sq. ft.
Second Floor	1,084 sq. ft.
Total Living Area	2,264 sq. ft.

PRICE CODE: C

PLAN DB2408

136

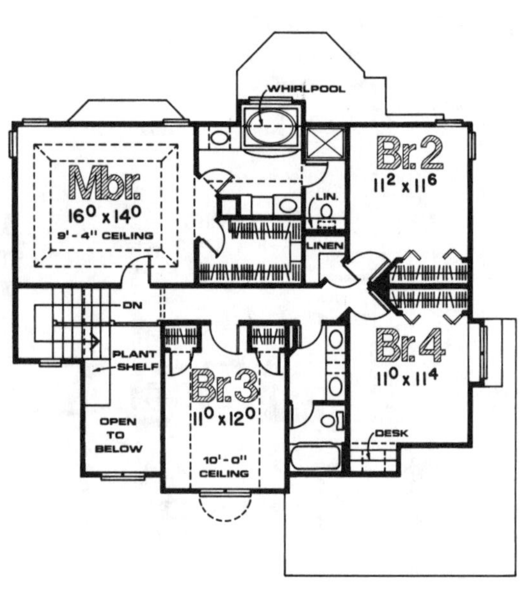

WHIRLPOOL
Mbr.
16^0 x 14^0
9'-4" CEILING
Br. 2
11^2 x 11^6
LIN.
LINEN
DN
PLANT SHELF
OPEN TO BELOW
Br. 3
11^0 x 12^0
10'-0" CEILING
Br. 4
11^0 x 11^4
DESK

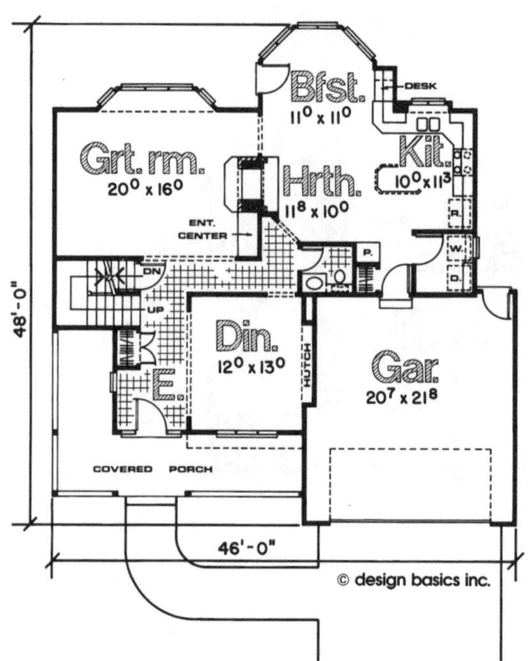

Bfst.
11^0 x 11^0
DESK
Grt. rm.
20^0 x 16^0
Kit.
10^0 x 11^3
Hrth.
11^8 x 10^0
ENT. CENTER
DN
UP
P.
W.
D.
R.
Din.
12^0 x 13^0
HUTCH
E.
Gar.
20^7 x 21^8
COVERED PORCH
48'-0"
46'-0"
© design basics inc.

Features

- Elevation enhanced by expansive covered porch.
- Spacious 2-story entry surveys formal dining room with hutch space.
- Entertainment center and see-thru fireplace highlight great room.
- Kitchen/breakfast/hearth room areas feature gazebo dining, wrapping counters and numerous amenities.
- Bedroom #3 features half round transom and volume ceiling,Bedroom #4 includes built-in desk.
- Convenient compartmented bath and large walk-in linen storage serves secondary bedrooms.
- Luxurious master suite with vaulted ceiling enjoys his/her vanities, walk-in closet and whirlpool.

First Floor	**1,150 sq. ft.**
Second Floor	**1,120 sq. ft.**
Total Living Area	**2,270 sq. ft.**

PRICE CODE: D

PLAN DB1771

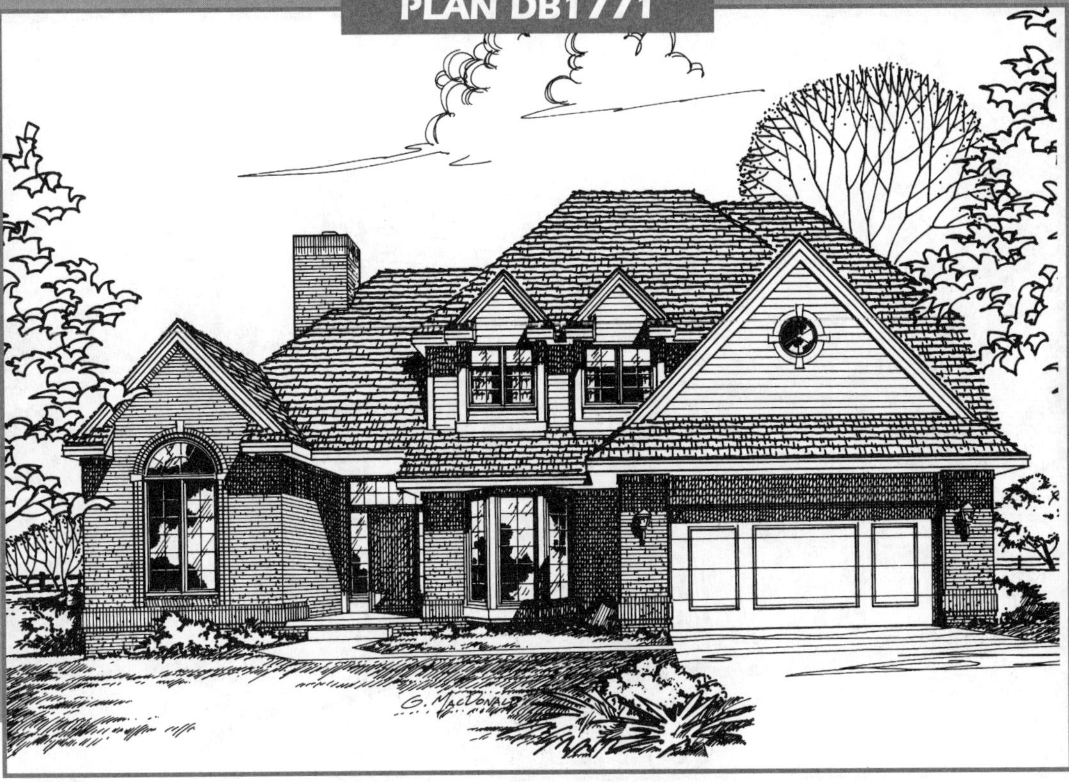

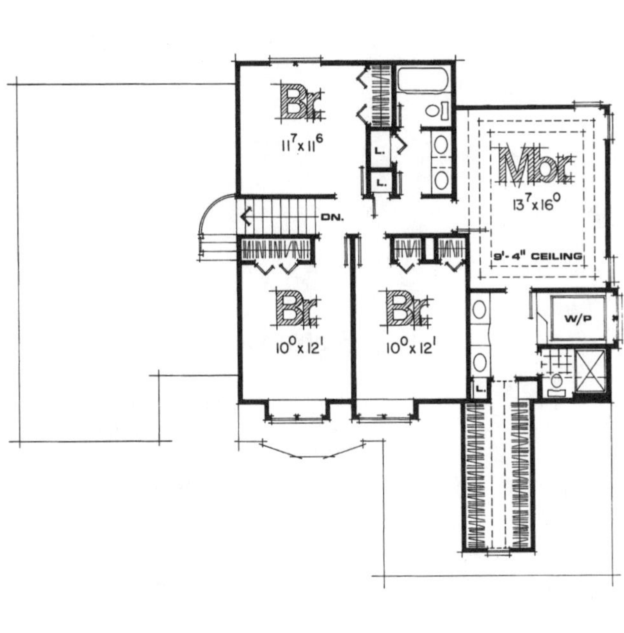

Br.
$11^{7} \times 11^{6}$
L.
L.
DN.
Mbr.
$13^{7} \times 16^{0}$
9'-4" CEILING
Br.
$10^{0} \times 12^{1}$
Br.
$10^{0} \times 12^{1}$
W/P

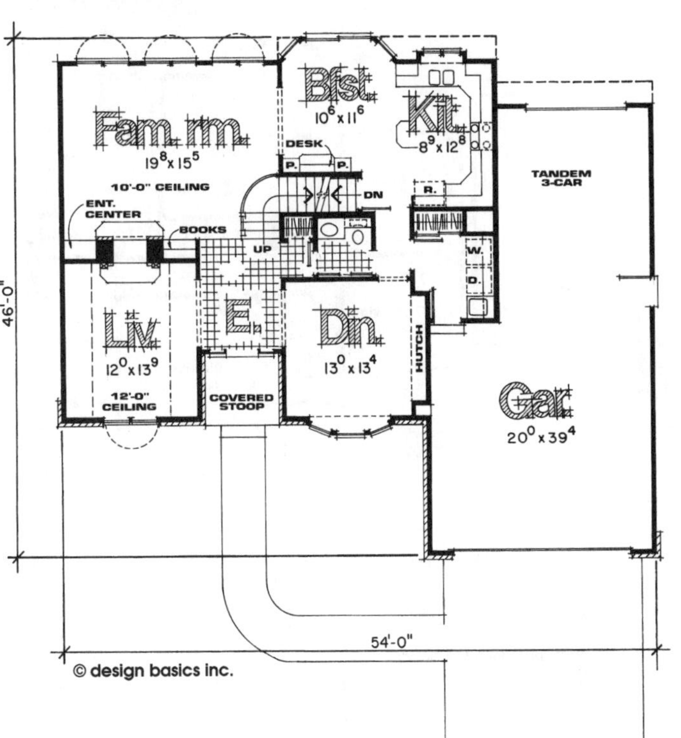

Bfst.
$10^{6} \times 11^{6}$
Kit.
$8^{9} \times 12^{8}$
Fam. rm.
$19^{8} \times 15^{5}$
10'-0" CEILING
DESK
P.
P.
DN
R.
TANDEM 3-CAR
ENT. CENTER
BOOKS
UP
W.
D.
Liv.
$12^{0} \times 13^{9}$
12'-0" CEILING
E.
Din.
$13^{0} \times 13^{4}$
HUTCH
COVERED STOOP
Gar.
$20^{0} \times 39^{4}$
46'-0"
54'-0"
© design basics inc.

Features

- Expansive entry views to arched transom windows in family room.
- Volume ceilings in entry, family room and living room .
- Bayed windows and hutch space in dining room.
- Powder bath located for dual access.
- See-thru fireplace serves both living room and family room.
- Island kitchen adjoins sunny dinette with built-in desk.
- Well-equipped laundry.
- Secondary bedrooms served by compartmented bath with double vanity and large linen closet.
- Tiered ceiling in large master bedroom.
- Master bath with 2-person whirlpool and huge walk-in closet.

First Floor	1,204 sq. ft.
Second Floor	1,075 sq. ft.
Total Living Area	2,279 sq. ft.

PRICE CODE: D

PLAN NP1308

MASTER BEDROOM
16'-6" x 12'-6"
MASTER BATH
OPEN TO FAMILY ROOM BELOW
BEDROOM #3
10'-0" x 10'-9"
BEDROOM #4
10'-0" x 10'-0"
BATH
L.
D.
W.
DN.
BEDROOM #2
12'-6" x 13'-6"
OPEN TO ENTRY BELOW

SECOND FLOOR

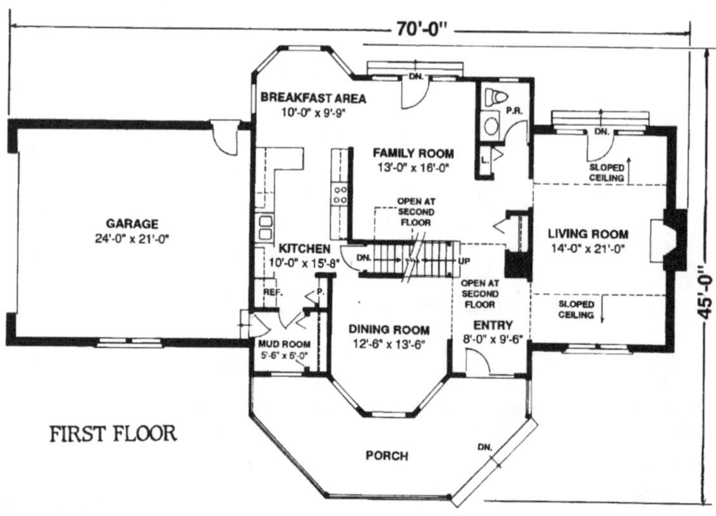
70'-0"
45'-0"
BREAKFAST AREA
10'-0" x 9'-9"
DN.
P.R.
FAMILY ROOM
13'-0" x 16'-0"
OPEN AT SECOND FLOOR
SLOPED CEILING
LIVING ROOM
14'-0" x 21'-0"
GARAGE
24'-0" x 21'-0"
KITCHEN
10'-0" x 15'-8"
UP
REF.
P.
OPEN AT SECOND FLOOR
MUD ROOM
5'-6" x 6'-0"
DINING ROOM
12'-6" x 13'-6"
ENTRY
8'-0" x 9'-6"
PORCH

FIRST FLOOR

Features

- Here's a beautiful Victorian with large living spaces for family activities and entertaining friends and family.
- Double entry doors lead into an open ceiling foyer with the formal dining room on the left and very spacious sloped ceiling living room with fireplace on the right.
- Upstairs you'll be pleased to find a large master bedroom served by double vanity master bath with linen closet, walk-in closet, and private water closet/shower area.
- Three other upstairs bedrooms share a full bath and laundry room.

First Floor	1,231 sq. ft.
Second Floor	1,049 sq. ft.
Total Living Area	2,280 sq. ft.

PRICE CODE: C

PLAN NP1209

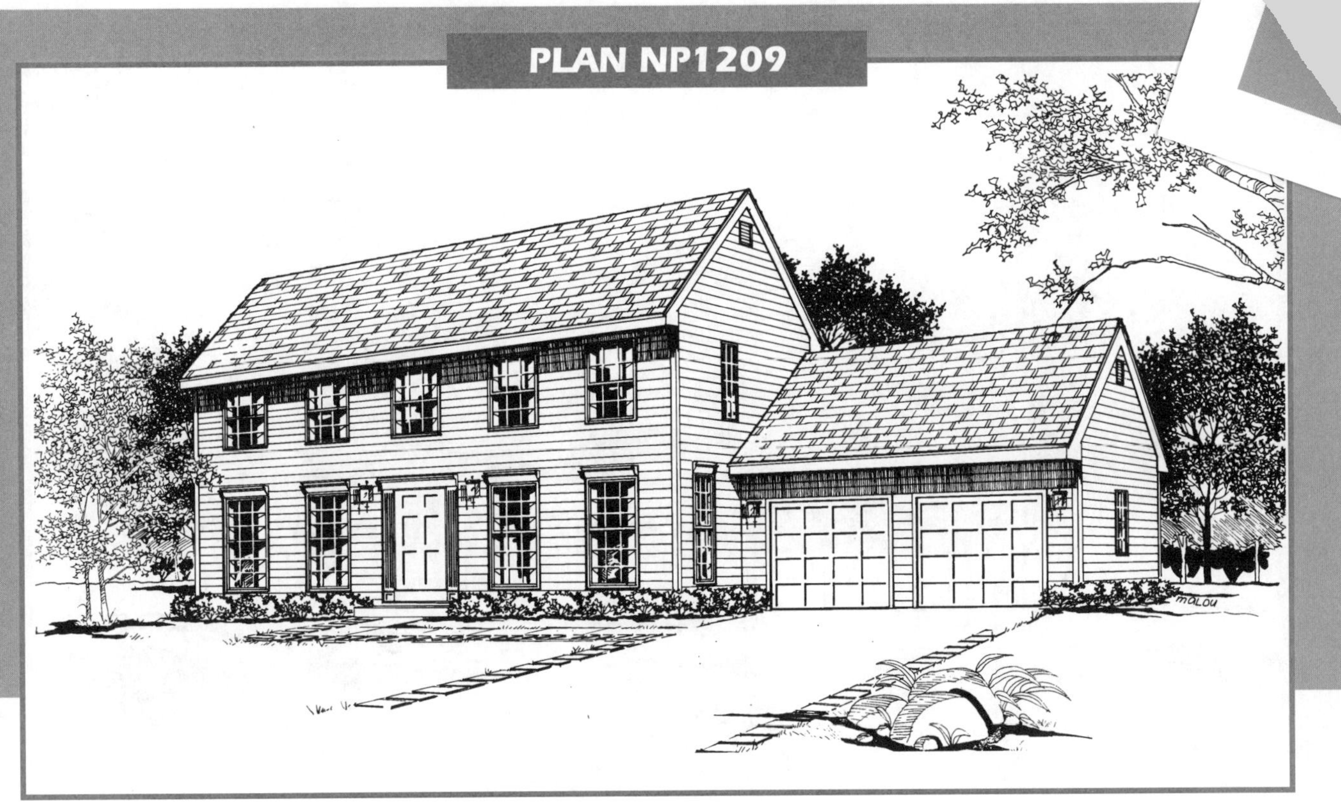

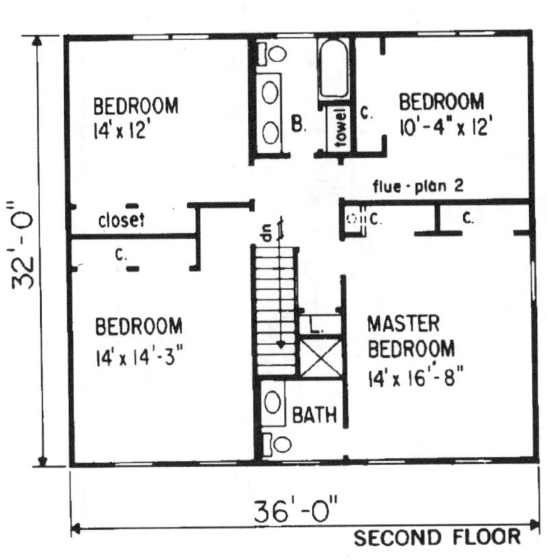
BEDROOM
14' x 12'
B.
towel
C.
BEDROOM
10'-4" x 12'
flue - plan 2
closet
C.
C.
C.
dn
BEDROOM
14' x 14'-3"
MASTER
BEDROOM
14' x 16'-8"
BATH
32'-0"
36'-0"
SECOND FLOOR

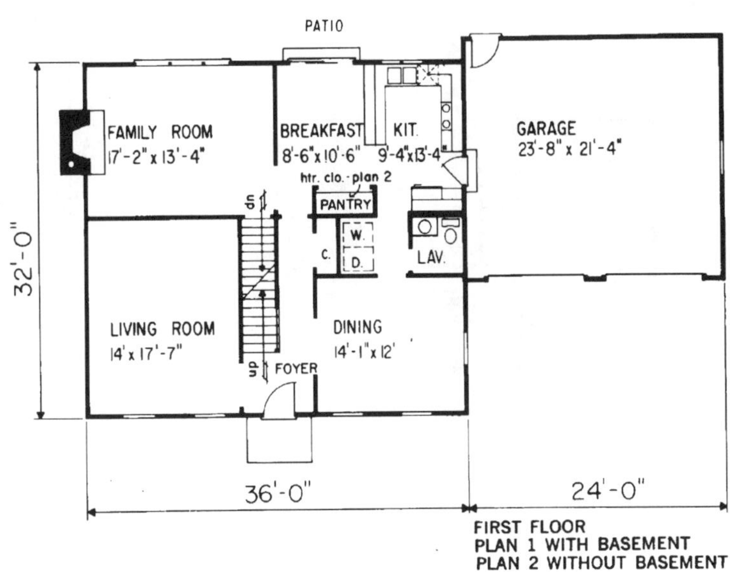
PATIO
FAMILY ROOM
17'-2" x 13'-4"
BREAKFAST
8'-6" x 10'-6"
KIT.
9'-4" x 13'-4"
GARAGE
23'-8" x 21'-4"
htr. clo. - plan 2
PANTRY
W.
D.
C.
LAV.
dn
LIVING ROOM
14' x 17'-7"
DINING
14'-1" x 12'
up
FOYER
32'-0"
36'-0"
24'-0"
FIRST FLOOR
PLAN 1 WITH BASEMENT
PLAN 2 WITHOUT BASEMENT

Traditional Colonial

Features

- Exterior view of this traditional Colonial exhibits double-hung windows and horizontal siding.
- Foyer opens to large living room for formal entertaining at the left and dining room at the right.
- Family room with fireplace occupies the rear of the first floor.
- U- shaped kitchen features a large pantry and breakfast area.
- Second- floor master bedroom includes full bath.
- Three additional bedrooms share a full bath with double vanity and linen closet.

First Floor	1,152 sq. ft.
Second Floor	1,152 sq. ft.
Total Living Area	2,304 sq. ft.

PRICE CODE: C

PLAN DB2836

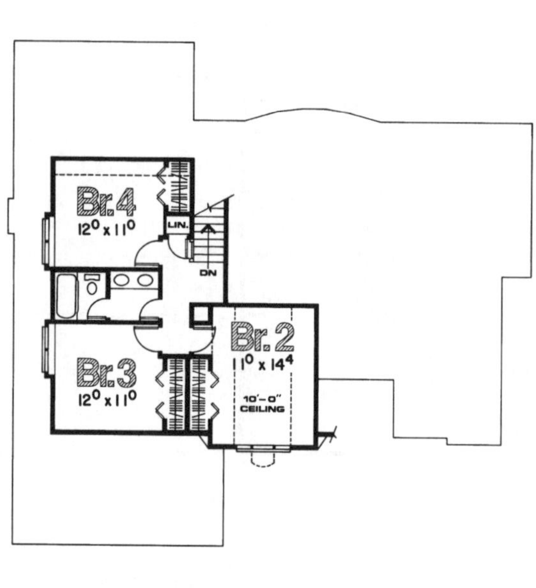
Br. 4
12⁰ x 11⁰
LIN.
DN
Br. 3
12⁰ x 11⁰
Br. 2
11⁰ x 14⁴
10'-0" CEILING

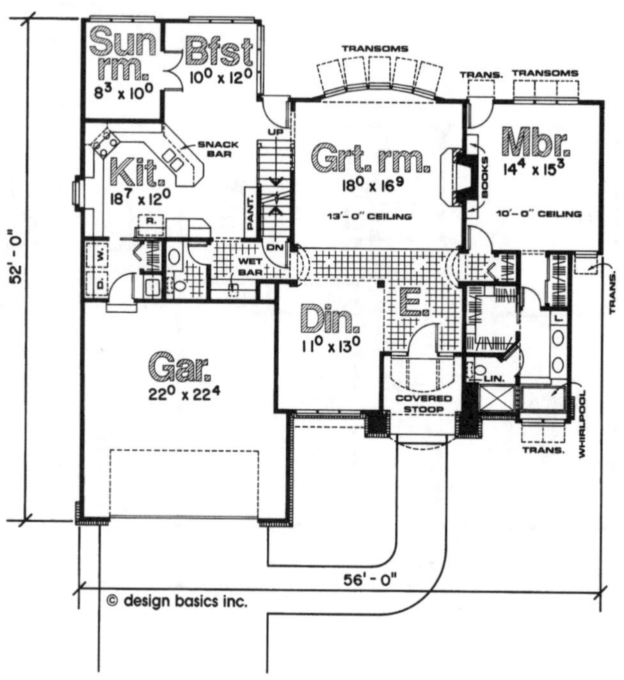
Sun rm.
8³ x 10⁰
Bfst
10⁰ x 12⁰
TRANSOMS
TRANS.
TRANSOMS
SNACK BAR
UP
Kit.
18⁷ x 12⁰
Grt. rm.
18⁰ x 16⁹
13'-0" CEILING
Mbr.
14⁴ x 15³
10'-0" CEILING
BOOKS
PANT.
DN
WET BAR
Din.
11⁰ x 13⁰
E.
Gar.
22⁰ x 22⁴
COVERED STOOP
LIN.
WHIRLPOOL
TRANS.
52'-0"
56'-0"
© design basics inc.

Features

- Brick accents and bright windows highlight this appealing front elevation.
- Entry provides wide, dramatic view of formal dining room and spacious great room.
- Extra-tall bowed window complements 13-foot ceiling in great room.
- French doors connect delightful sun room to kitchen/dinette area.
- Wet bar is conveniently placed to serve dining room and great room.
- Dramatic master suite with dual bookcases features deluxe bath, abundant windows, outdoor access. Staircase is conveniently located in back of home.

First Floor	1,654 sq. ft.
Second Floor	654 sq. ft.
Total Living Area	2,308 sq. ft.

PRICE CODE: D

CUSTOMIZE IT!

ORDER TOLL FREE 1■800■533■4350 24-HOUR FAX ORDERING 1■800■344■4293

PLAN AM2258D

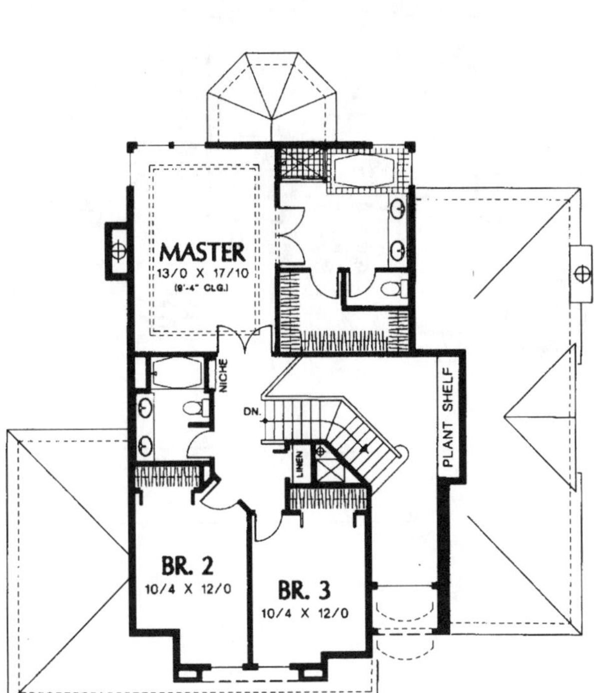

MASTER
13/0 X 17/10
(9'-4" CLG.)
NICHE
DN.
LINEN
PLANT SHELF
BR. 2
10/4 X 12/0
BR. 3
10/4 X 12/0

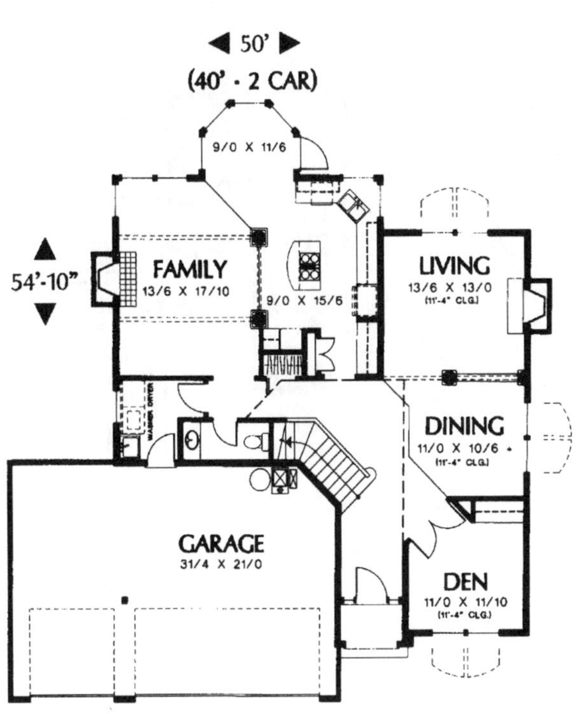

50'
(40' - 2 CAR)
54'-10"
9/0 X 11/6
FAMILY
13/6 X 17/10
9/0 X 15/6
LIVING
13/6 X 13/0
(11'-4" CLG.)
DINING
11/0 X 10/6
(11'-4" CLG.)
GARAGE
31/4 X 21/0
DEN
11/0 X 11/10
(11'-4" CLG.)

First Floor	1,322 sq. ft.
Second Floor	1,000 sq. ft.
Total Living Area	2,322 sq. ft.

PRICE CODE: C

PLAN DB1869

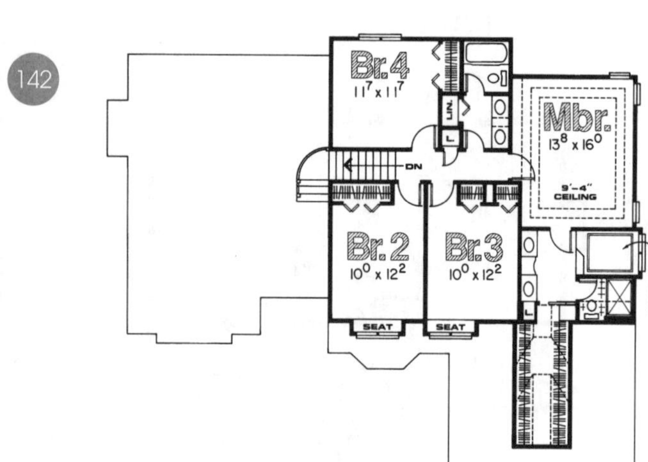
Br.4
11⁷ x 11⁷
LIN.
DN
Mbr.
13⁸ x 16⁰
9'-4" CEILING
Br.2
10⁰ x 12²
Br.3
10⁰ x 12²
WHIRLPOOL
SEAT
SEAT

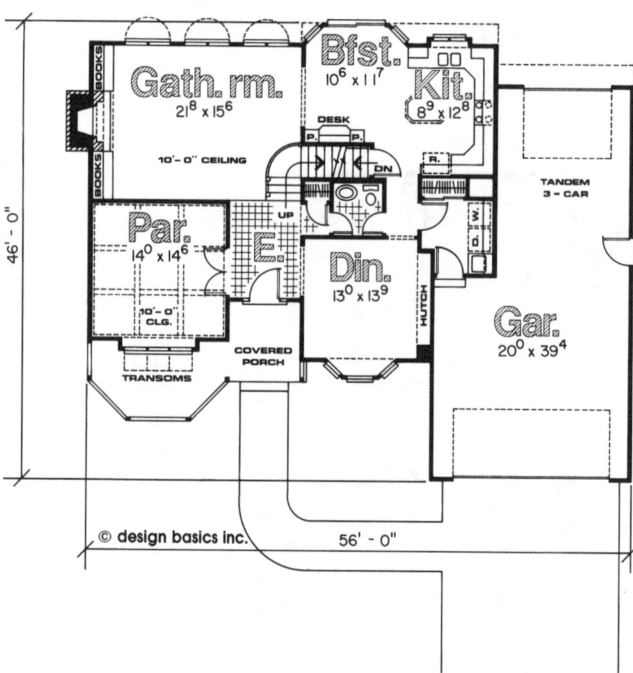
Gath. rm.
21⁸ x 15⁶
10'-0" CEILING
BOOKS
BOOKS
Bfst.
10⁶ x 11⁷
Kit.
8⁹ x 12⁸
DESK
DN
UP
R.
TANDEM 3-CAR
W.
D.
Par.
14⁰ x 14⁶
10'-0" CLG.
E.
Din.
13⁰ x 13⁹
HUTCH
Gar.
20⁰ x 39⁴
COVERED PORCH
TRANSOMS
46' - 0"
56' - 0"
© design basics inc.

Features

- Window detailing and gazebo porch highlight elevation.
- Dining room with hutch space and bayed window suits entertaining needs.
- Gathering room with three repeating arched windows, fireplace and two bookcases offers comfortable retreat.
- Island kitchen with bayed breakfast features two pantries, planning desk and wrapping counters.
- Stairway with curved landing leads to upstairs bedrooms, two with window seats.
- Impressive master suite enjoys tiered ceiling, massive closet and dressing area with dual lavs and whirlpool tub.

First Floor	**1,249 sq. ft.**
Second Floor	**1,075 sq. ft.**
Total Living Area	**2,324 sq. ft.**

PRICE CODE: D

PLAN DB2701

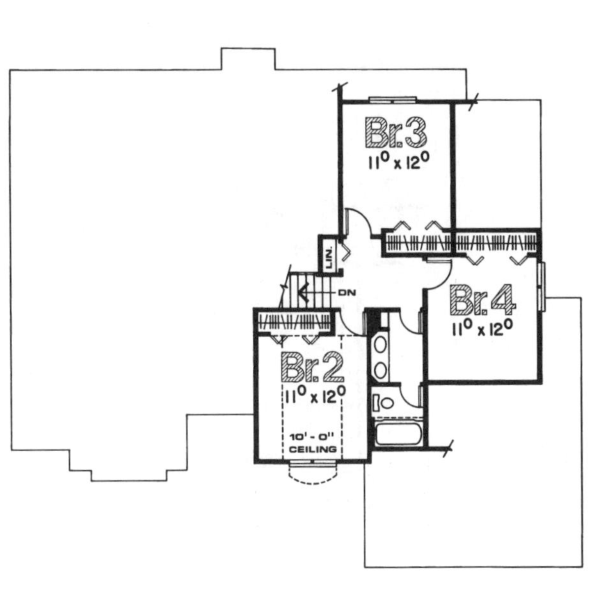
Br.3
11^0 x 12^0
LIN.
DN
Br.4
11^0 x 12^0
Br.2
11^0 x 12^0
10'-0" CEILING

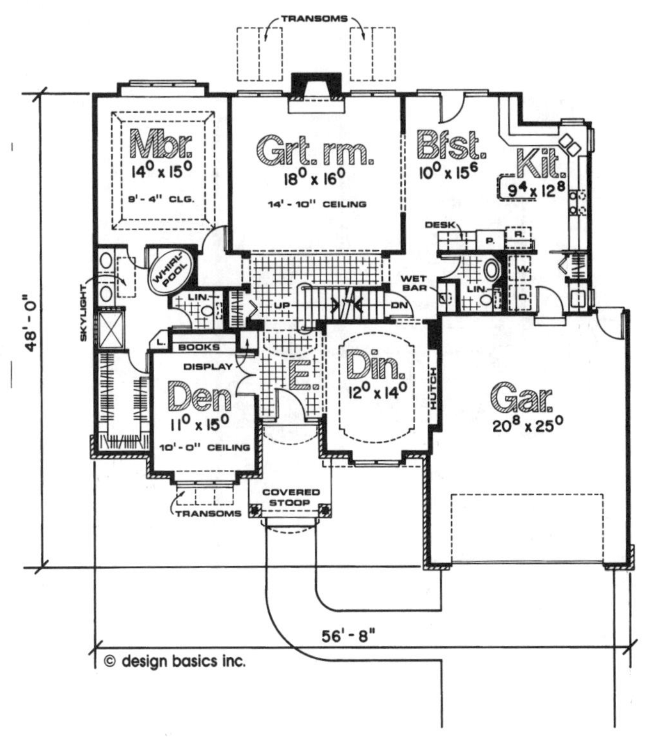
TRANSOMS
Mbr.
14^0 x 15^0
9'-4" CLG.
Grt. rm.
18^0 x 16^0
14'-10" CEILING
Bfst.
10^0 x 15^6
Kit.
9^4 x 12^8
DESK
P.
R.
WHIRLPOOL
SKYLIGHT
LIN.
UP
WET BAR
DN
W.
D.
LIN.
BOOKS
DISPLAY
Den
11^0 x 15^0
10'-0" CEILING
E.
Din.
12^0 x 14^0
HUTCH
Gar.
20^8 x 25^0
COVERED STOOP
TRANSOMS
48'-0"
56'-8"
© design basics inc.

Features

- Entry boasts impressive high ceiling, featuring built-in curio display unit.
- Elegant French doors open from entry to cozy den with built-in cabinets.
- Formal dining room presents dramatic ceiling detail and space to accommodate buffet or hutch.
- Great room has 14-foot-high ceiling and raised hearth fireplace flanked on either side by floor-to-ceiling windows.
- Private master bedroom presents vaulted ceilings, tunneled skylight above oval 2-person whirlpool.
- Large laundry room conveniently located with access from garage and kitchen.

First Floor	1,701 sq. ft.
Second Floor	639 sq. ft.
Total Living Area	2,340 sq. ft.

PRICE CODE: D

CUSTOMIZE IT!

ORDER TOLL FREE 1-800-533-4350 24-HOUR FAX ORDERING 1-800-344-4293

PLAN DB2414

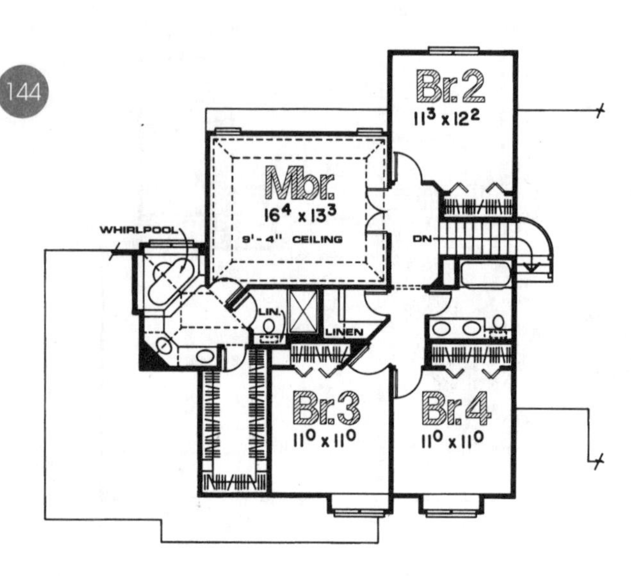

Br. 2
11^3 x 12^2
Mbr.
16^4 x 13^3
9'-4" CEILING
WHIRLPOOL
DN
LIN.
LINEN
Br. 3
11^0 x 11^0
Br. 4
11^0 x 11^0

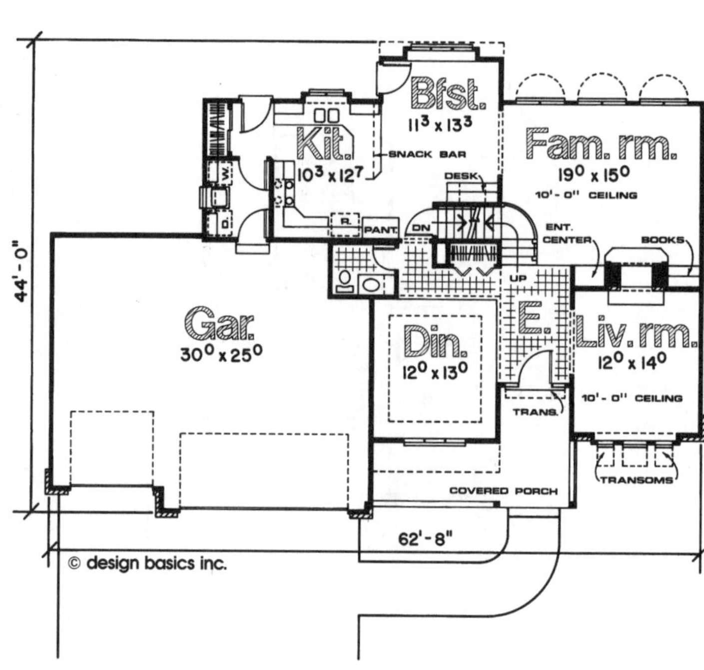

Bfst.
11^3 x 13^3
Kit.
10^3 x 12^7
SNACK BAR
DESK
Fam. rm.
19^0 x 15^0
10'-0" CEILING
W.
D.
R.
PANT.
DN
ENT. CENTER
BOOKS
UP
44'-0"
Gar.
30^0 x 25^0
Din.
12^0 x 13^0
E.
Liv. rm.
12^0 x 14^0
10'-0" CEILING
TRANS.
TRANSOMS
COVERED PORCH
62'-8"
© design basics inc.

Features

- Captivating elevation with covered porch.
- 3-car garage offers added perk.
- Entry surveys formal rooms.
- Living room with volume ceiling, elegant windows and see-thru fireplace.
- Volume family room includes repeating arched windows, see-thru fireplace, entertainment center and bookcase.
- Sunny kitchen/dinette area offers wrapping counters, snack bar, planning desk, nearby utility/laundry room and large closet.
- Comfortable secondary bedrooms serviced by walk-in linen closet and ample bath with dual lavs.
- Master suite includes French doors, vaulted ceiling, whirlpool, dual vanities and huge walk-in closet.

First Floor	1,268 sq. ft.
Second Floor	1,075 sq. ft.
Total Living Area	2,343 sq. ft.

PRICE CODE: D

PLAN DB1862

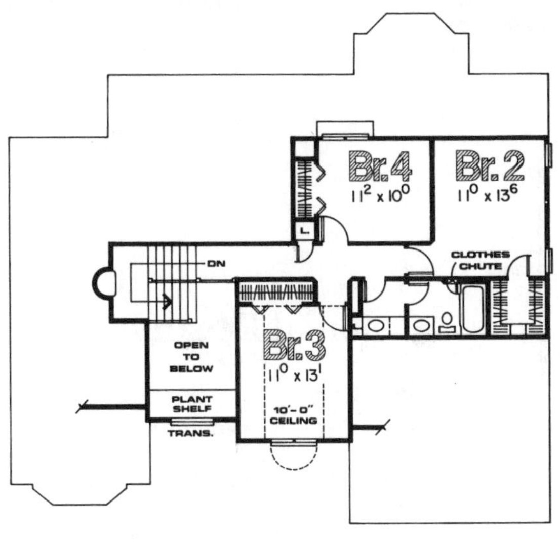

Br.4
11² x 10⁰
Br.2
11⁰ x 13⁶
DN
CLOTHES CHUTE
OPEN TO BELOW
PLANT SHELF
TRANS.
Br.3
11⁰ x 13¹
10'-0" CEILING
UP

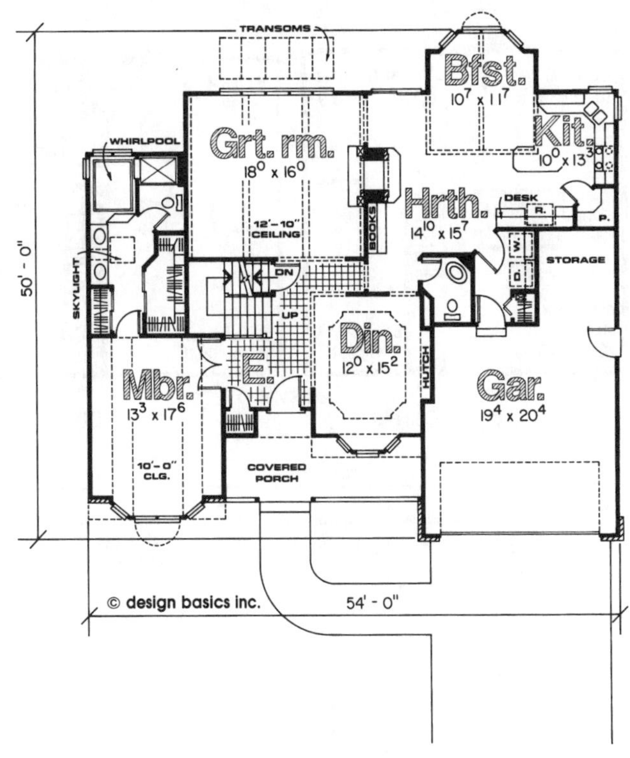

TRANSOMS
Bfst.
10⁷ x 11⁷
Kit.
10⁰ x 13³
WHIRLPOOL
Grt. rm.
18⁰ x 16⁰
12'-10" CEILING
BOOKS
Hrth.
14¹⁰ x 15⁷
DESK
P.
W.
D.
STORAGE
SKYLIGHT
DN
UP
50' - 0"
Mbr.
13³ x 17⁶
10'-0" CLG.
E.
Din.
12⁰ x 15²
HUTCH
Gar.
19⁴ x 20⁴
COVERED PORCH
© design basics inc.
54' - 0"

Features

- Covered porch and elegant arched windows highlight front elevation.
- 2-story entry showcases stairway and formal dining room with bayed window.
- Superb great room has see-thru fireplace and windowed wall for elegant rear view.
- Livable island kitchen/breakfast/hearth room features arched window, cathedral ceiling, walk-in pantry and bayed dining.
- Second level features interesting sill detail on landing and plant shelf overlooking area below.
- Comfortable secondary bedrooms share compartmented bath with separate lavs and clothes chute.
- Main level master suite with arched window, volume ceiling, dual lavs, whirlpool tub and two closets.

First Floor	1,653 sq. ft.
Second Floor	700 sq. ft.
Total Living Area	2,353 sq. ft.

PRICE CODE: D

CUSTOMIZE IT!

PLAN NPT128

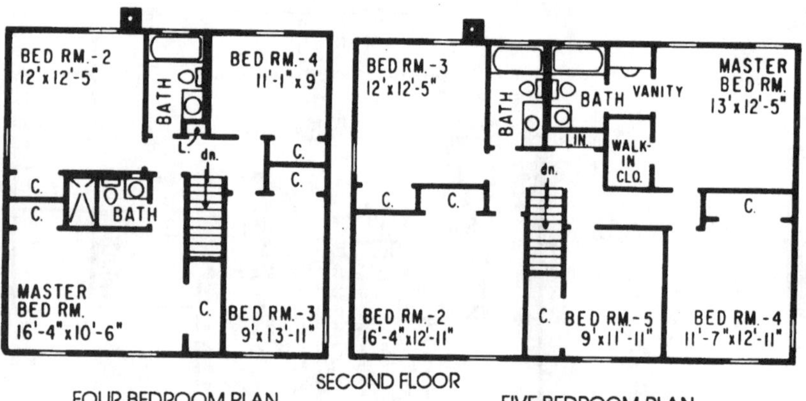

BED RM.-2 12'x12'-5"
BATH
BED RM.-4 11'-1"x9'
L.
dn.
C.
C.
C.
C.
BATH
MASTER BED RM. 16'-4"x10'-6"
C.
BED RM.-3 9'x13'-11"
BED RM.-3 12'x12'-5"
BATH
BATH
VANITY
MASTER BED RM. 13'x12'-5"
LIN.
WALK-IN CLO.
dn.
C.
C.
C.
BED RM.-2 16'-4"x12'-11"
C.
BED RM.-5 9'x11'-11"
BED RM.-4 11'-7"x12'-11"

FOUR BEDROOM PLAN

SECOND FLOOR

FIVE BEDROOM PLAN

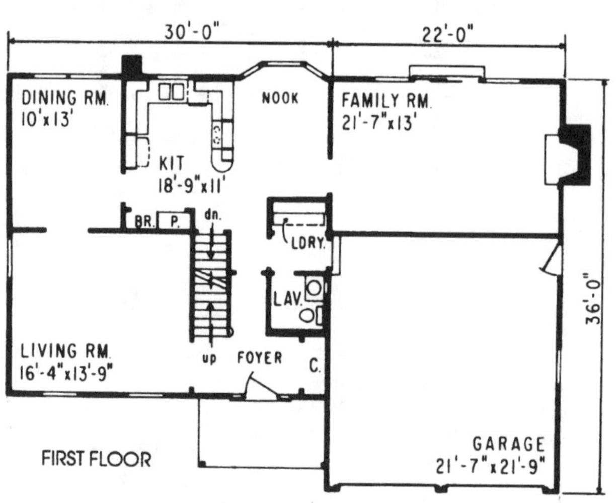

30'-0"
22'-0"
DINING RM. 10'x13'
NOOK
FAMILY RM. 21'-7"x13'
KIT 18'-9"x11'
BR.
P.
dn.
LDRY.
LAV.
36'-0"
LIVING RM. 16'-4"x13'-9"
up
FOYER
C.
GARAGE 21'-7"x21'-9"

FIRST FLOOR

Colonial Dream

Features

- Versatility is the byword for this two-story Colonial home.
- Left wing contains the living room and dining room.
- U-shaped kitchen serves the dining area with bay window.
- Adjacent to dining nook, the family room includes a fireplace.
- Upstairs, choose between a layout of five bedrooms with back-to-back baths or four bedrooms with two baths.

First Floor	1,148 sq. ft.
Second Floor	870 sq. ft.
Four Bedroom Plan	870 sq. ft.
Five Bedroom Plan	1,218 sq. ft.
Total Living Area(4)	2,018 sq. ft.
Total Living Area(5)	2,366 sq. ft.

PRICE CODE: B

PLAN NP1298

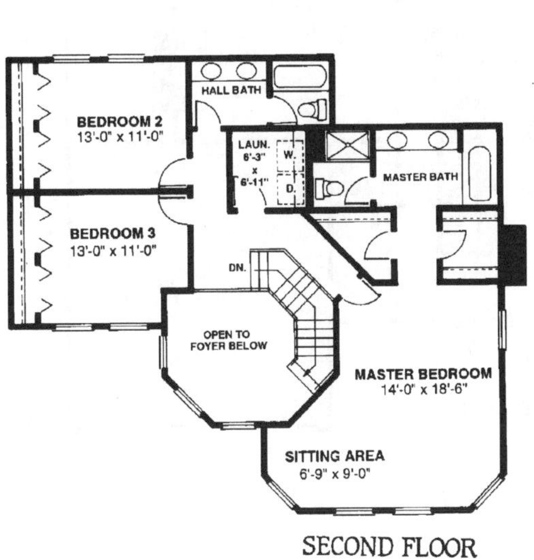

HALL BATH
BEDROOM 2
13'-0" x 11'-0"
LAUN.
6'-3" x 6'-11"
W.
D.
MASTER BATH
BEDROOM 3
13'-0" x 11'-0"
DN.
OPEN TO FOYER BELOW
MASTER BEDROOM
14'-0" x 18'-6"
SITTING AREA
6'-9" x 9'-0"

SECOND FLOOR

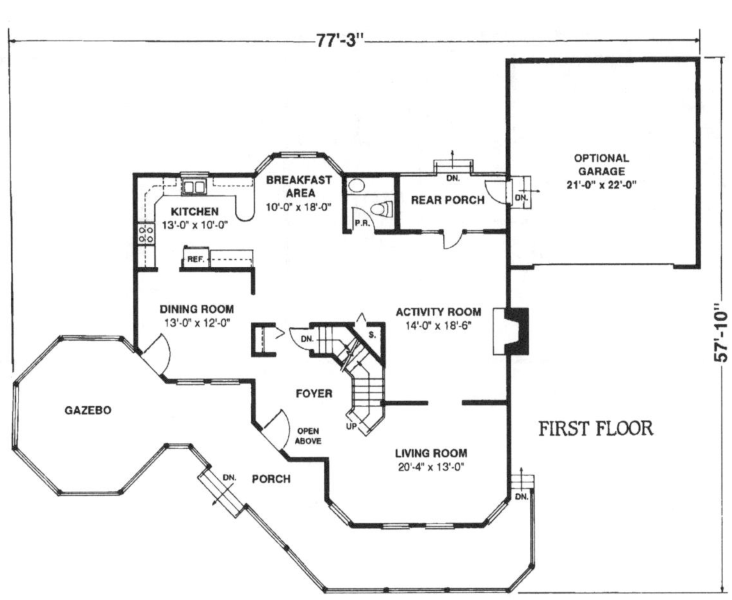

77'-3"
57'-10"
OPTIONAL GARAGE
21'-0" x 22'-0"
BREAKFAST AREA
10'-0" x 18'-0"
KITCHEN
13'-0" x 10'-0"
REF.
P.R.
REAR PORCH
DN.
DINING ROOM
13'-0" x 12'-0"
ACTIVITY ROOM
14'-0" x 18'-6"
S.
FOYER
GAZEBO
OPEN ABOVE
UP
PORCH
LIVING ROOM
20'-4" x 13'-0"

FIRST FLOOR

Castlewood

Features

- Country Victorian design with stunning exterior visual appeal.
- Geometric shapes delight the senses, with a spectacular octagonal gazebo.
- Large activity room with fireplace and access to rear covered porch.
- Dining room opens out to gazebo for inside/outside entertaining.
- Upstairs, an enormous master bedroom has a sitting area, his/her walk-through closets, and master bath with private water closet.
- Two additional bedrooms share a full bath.

First Floor	**1,281 sq. ft.**
Second Floor	**1,089 sq. ft.**
Total Living Area	**2,370 sq. ft.**

PRICE CODE: C

PLAN NP1217

148

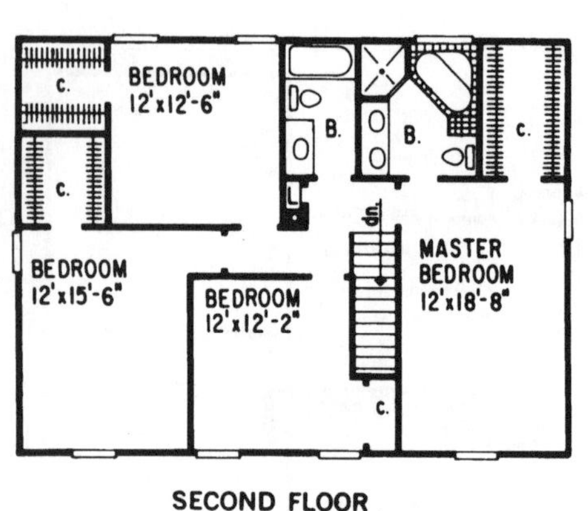
BEDROOM
12'x12'-6"
C.
C.
B.
B.
C.
BEDROOM
12'x15'-6"
BEDROOM
12'x12'-2"
dn.
MASTER
BEDROOM
12'x18'-8"
C.
SECOND FLOOR

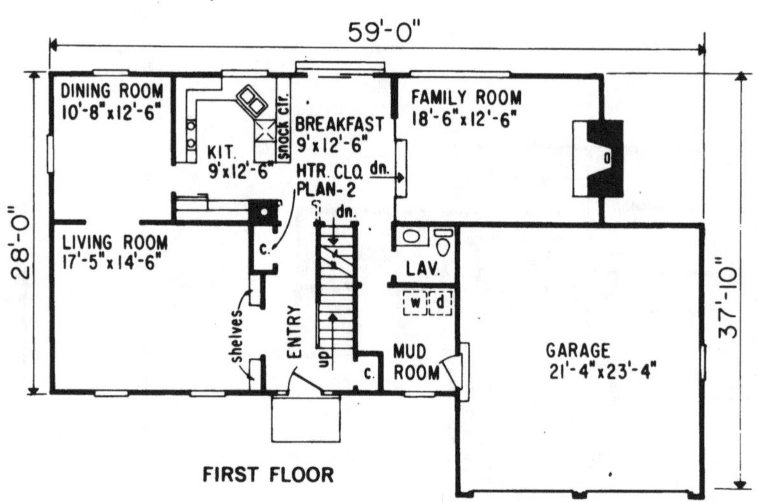
59'-0"
DINING ROOM
10'-8"x12'-6"
KIT.
9'x12'-6"
snack clr.
BREAKFAST
9'x12'-6"
HTR. CLO.
PLAN-2
dn.
FAMILY ROOM
18'-6"x12'-6"
28'-0"
LIVING ROOM
17'-5"x14'-6"
C.
dn.
LAV.
w d
37'-10"
shelves
ENTRY
up
C.
MUD
ROOM
GARAGE
21'-4"x23'-4"
FIRST FLOOR

Early American Heritage

Features

- Exterior features of this Early American home showcase its unique design.
- Second-floor overhang and gabled windows add dramatic tension to horizontal siding.
- Formal dining room is located to the left of the kitchen.
- Large sunken family room includes fireplace.
- Second-floor includes master bedroom, deluxe master bath with corner deck tub and double vanity, and large walk-in closet.
- Three additional upstairs bedrooms share a full bath.

First Floor	1,212 sq. ft.
Second Floor	1,160 sq. ft.
Total Living Area	2,372 sq. ft.

PRICE CODE: C

PLAN AM2271

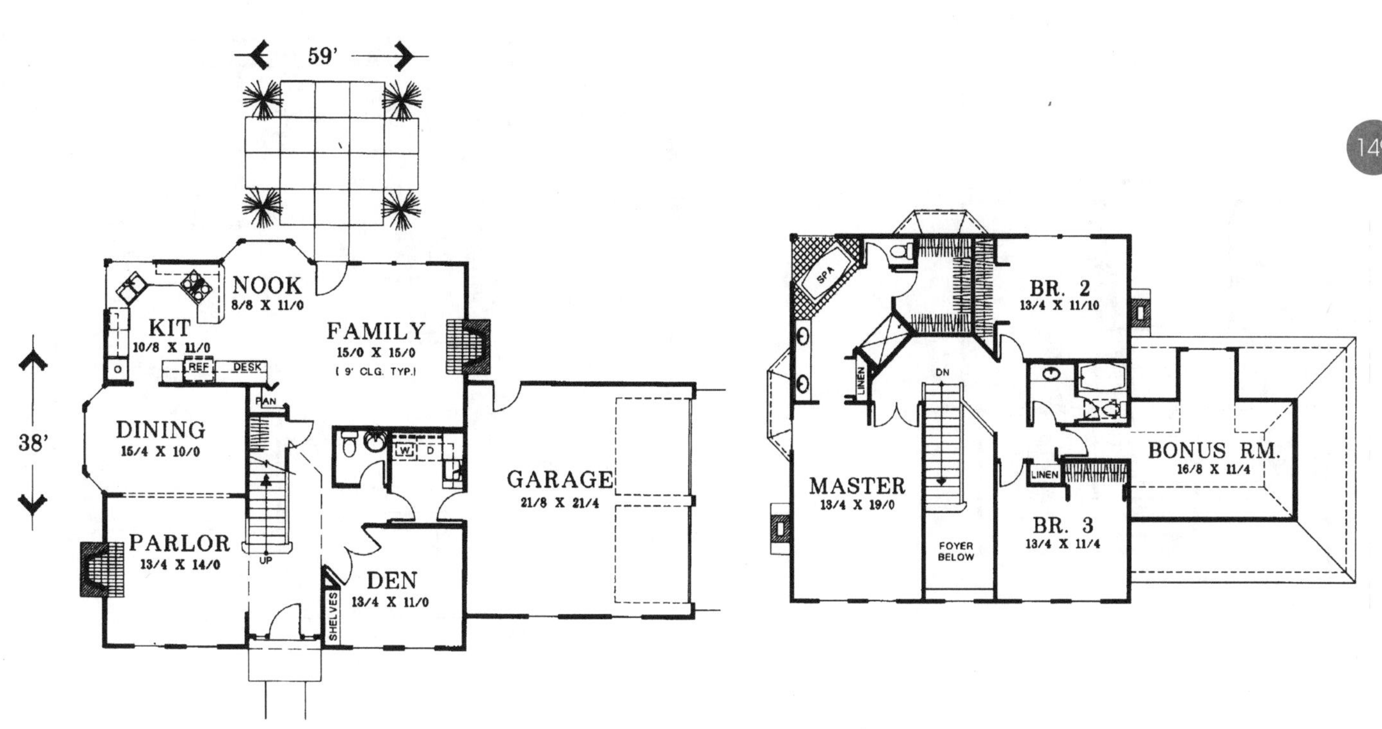
59'
38'
NOOK
8/8 X 11/0
KIT
10/8 X 11/0
REF
DESK
FAMILY
15/0 X 15/0
(9' CLG. TYP.)
PAN
DINING
15/4 X 10/0
W
D
GARAGE
21/8 X 21/4
PARLOR
13/4 X 14/0
UP
SHELVES
DEN
13/4 X 11/0
SPA
BR. 2
13/4 X 11/10
LINEN
DN
BONUS RM.
16/8 X 11/4
MASTER
13/4 X 19/0
LINEN
BR. 3
13/4 X 11/4
FOYER
BELOW

First Floor	1,285 sq. ft.
Second Floor	1,100 sq. ft.
Total Living Area	2,385 sq. ft.
Bonus Room	+238 sq. ft.

PRICE CODE: C

PLAN DB1553

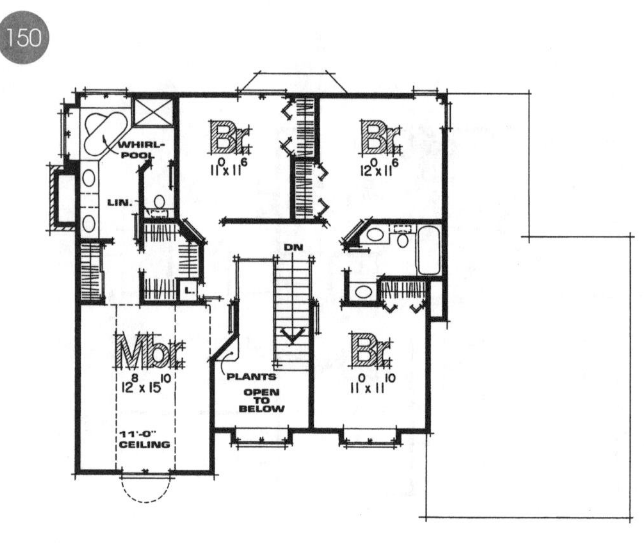

WHIRL-POOL
LIN.
Br. 11⁰x11⁶
Br. 12⁰x11⁶
DN
L.
Mbr. 12⁸x15¹⁰
PLANTS
OPEN TO BELOW
Br. 11⁰x11¹⁰
11'-0" CEILING

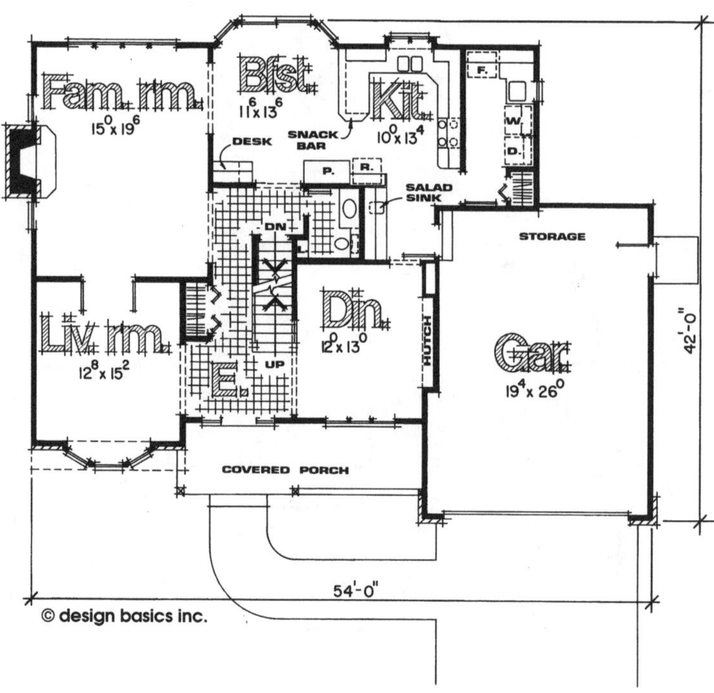

Fam. rm. 15⁰x19⁶
Bfst. 11⁶x13⁶
Kit. 10⁰x13⁴
DESK
SNACK BAR
P.
R.
F.
W.
D.
SALAD SINK
STORAGE
DN
UP
Liv. rm. 12⁸x15²
E.
Din. 12⁰x13⁰
HUTCH
Gar. 19⁴x26⁰
42'-0"
COVERED PORCH
54'-0"
© design basics inc.

Features

- Bright 2-story entry with plant shelf.
- Hard surface trafficways.
- Central hall formalizes front half of the house.
- French doors connect family room and living room with enticing bayed window.
- Efficient kitchen with snack bar and pantry is open to bayed breakfast area with planning desk.
- Salad sink and counter space doubles as servery for formal dining room.
- Master bedroom offers volume ceiling and arched window .
- Master bath features walk-through closet/ transition area and corner whirlpool.
- Interesting angles add design character to bedrooms.

First Floor	1,303 sq. ft.
Second Floor	1,084 sq. ft.
Total Living Area	2,387 sq. ft.

PRICE CODE: D

PLAN DB2208

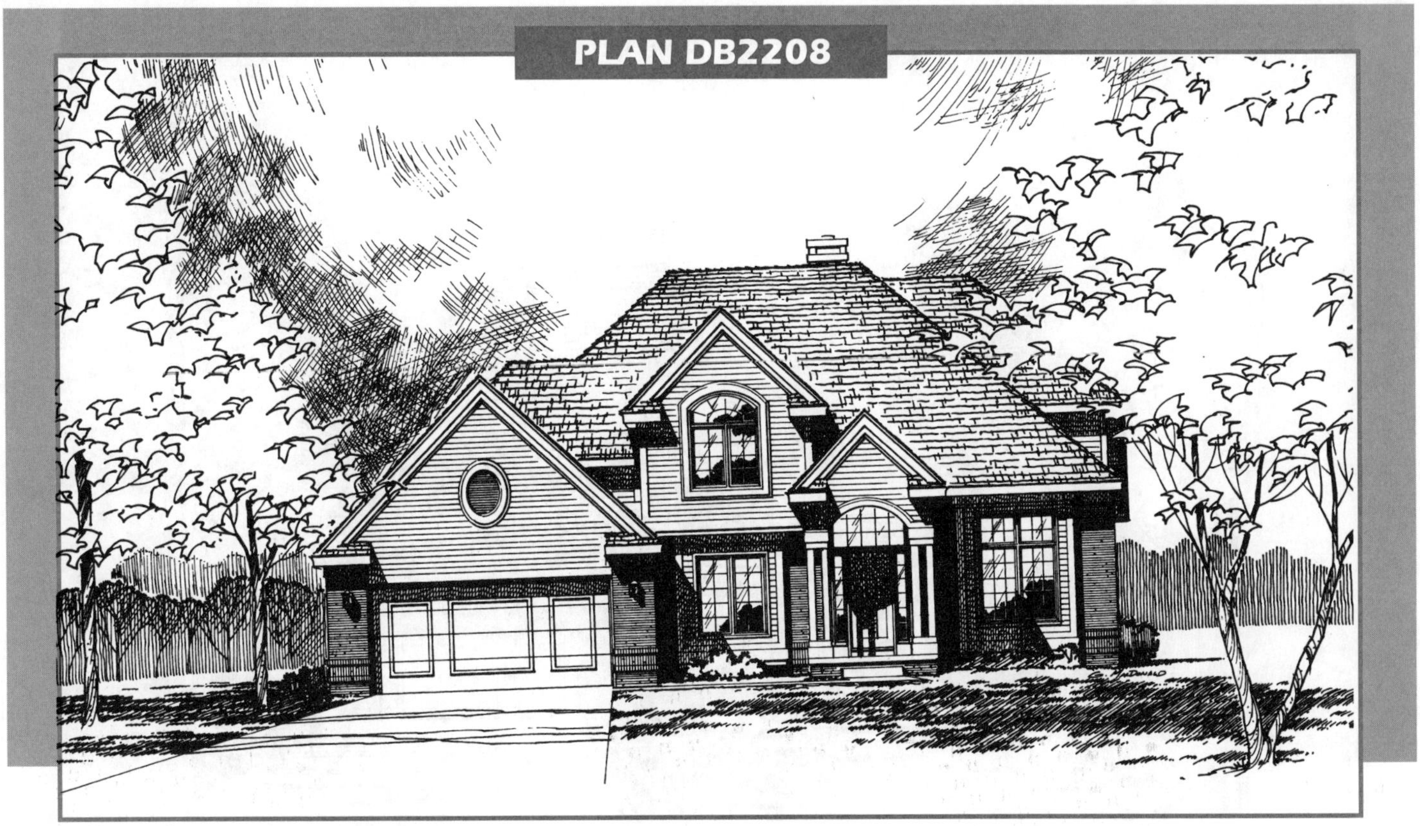

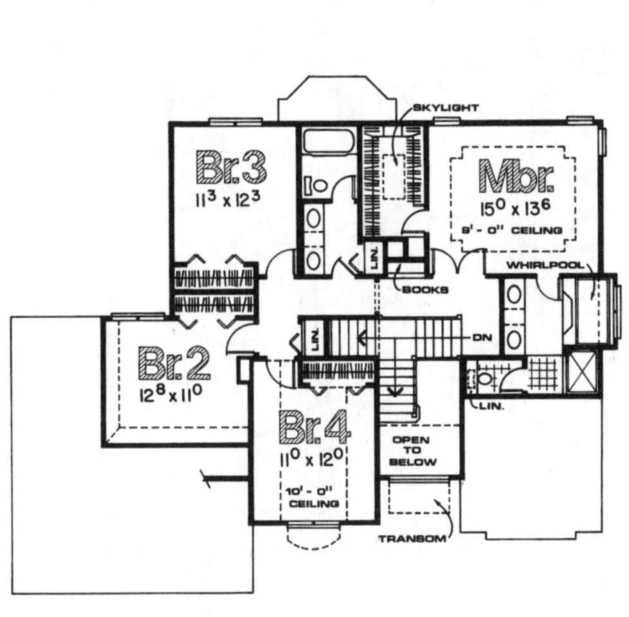
SKYLIGHT
Br. 3
11^{3} x 12^{3}
Mbr.
15^{0} x 13^{6}
9' - 0" CEILING
LIN.
BOOKS
WHIRLPOOL
Br. 2
12^{8} x 11^{0}
LIN.
DN
LIN.
Br. 4
11^{0} x 12^{0}
10' - 0" CEILING
OPEN TO BELOW
TRANSOM

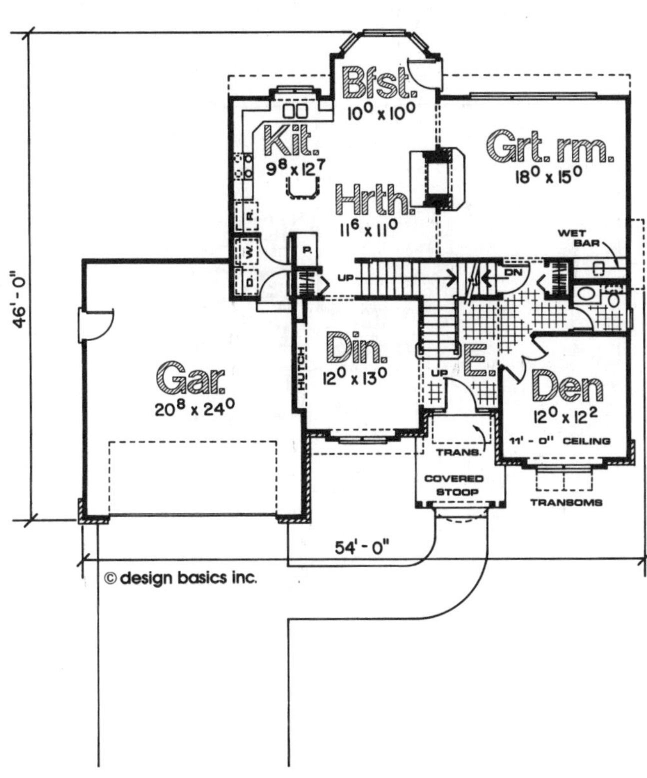
Bfst.
10^{0} x 10^{0}
Kit.
9^{8} x 12^{7}
Hrth.
11^{6} x 11^{0}
Grt. rm.
18^{0} x 15^{0}
WET BAR
R.
W.
D.
P.
UP
DN
46' - 0"
Gar.
20^{8} x 24^{0}
HUTCH
Din.
12^{0} x 13^{0}
UP
E.
Den
12^{0} x 12^{2}
11' - 0" CEILING
TRANS.
COVERED STOOP
TRANSOMS
54' - 0"
© design basics inc.

Features

- Large covered stoop at entry.
- Double doors on angle into den.
- Windows line back of open great room.
- Great room showcases wet bar and see-thru fireplace.
- Cozy hearth room shares fireplace.
- Bayed dinette and island kitchen with pantry and lazy Susan.
- T-shaped staircase for convenience.
- Compartmented bath with 2 lavs for secondary bedrooms.
- Arched window and volume ceiling in bedroom #4.
- Natural light floods whirlpool tub in master bath.
- Large walk-in closet with skylight off master bedroom.

First Floor	1,250 sq. ft.
Second Floor	1,140 sq. ft.
Total Living Area	2,390 sq. ft.

PRICE CODE: D

PLAN DB2203

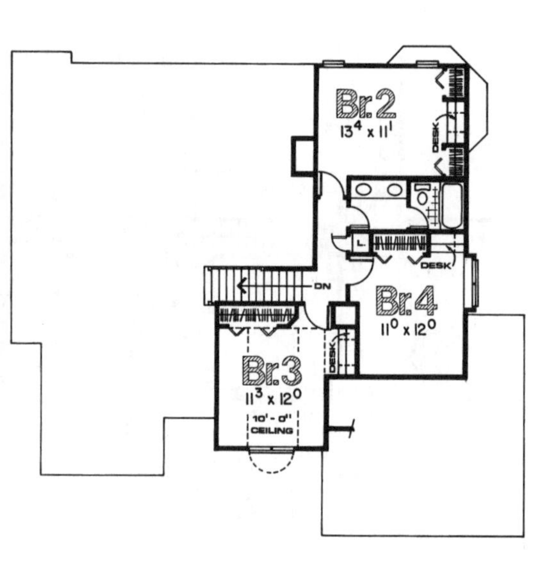
Br.2
13^4 x 11^1
DESK
L
DESK
DN
Br.4
11^0 x 12^0
DESK
Br.3
11^3 x 12^0
10'-0" CEILING

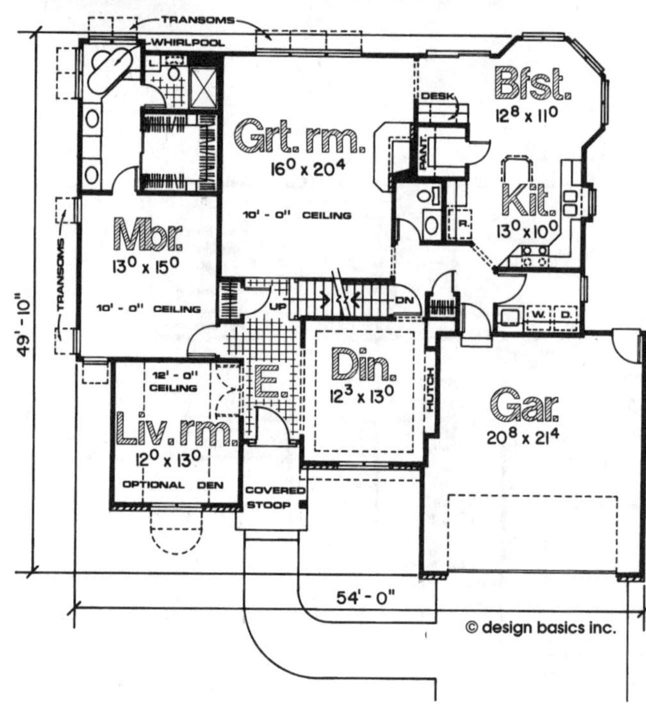
TRANSOMS
WHIRLPOOL
L
Grt. rm.
16^0 x 20^4
10'-0" CEILING
DESK
Bfst.
12^8 x 11^0
PANT.
Kit.
13^0 x 10^0
R.
Mbr.
13^0 x 15^0
10'-0" CEILING
TRANSOMS
49'-10"
UP
DN
W. D.
12'-0" CEILING
E.
Din.
12^3 x 13^0
HUTCH
Gar.
20^8 x 21^4
Liv. rm.
12^0 x 13^0
OPTIONAL DEN
COVERED STOOP
54'-0"
© design basics inc.

Features

- Entry flanked by formal rooms.
- French doors open into volume living room/ optional den with dramatic arched window under volume ceiling.
- 2-sided fireplace for the large great room and windows out the back.
- Formal ceiling and hutch space in dining room.
- Walk-in pantry, desk and island counter in kitchen open to semi-gazebo dinette.
- Convenient access to laundry room with soaking sink and window.
- Luxurious master dressing/bath area features his and her vanities, walk-in closet and corner whirlpool under windows.
- Built-in desk for each secondary bedroom.
- Compartmented bath for second level.

First Floor	1,697 sq. ft.
Second Floor	694 sq. ft.
Total Living Area	2,391 sq. ft.

PRICE CODE: D

PLAN MN2392

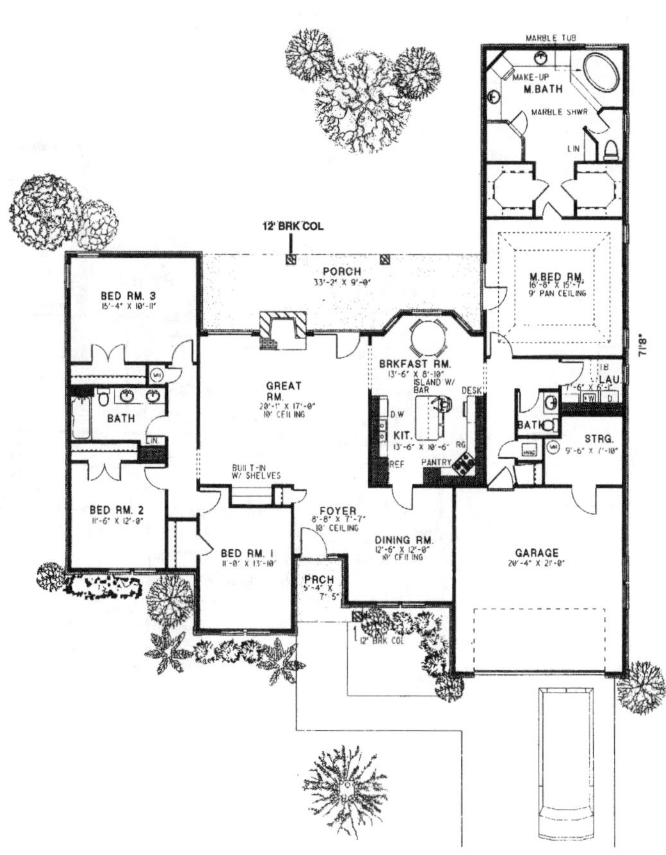
MARBLE TUB
MAKE-UP
M.BATH
MARBLE SHWR
LIN
12' BRK COL
PORCH
33'-2" X 9'-0"
M.BED RM.
16'-8" X 15'-7"
9' PAN CEILING
BED RM. 3
15'-4" X 10'-11"
BRKFAST RM.
13'-6" X 8'-10"
ISLAND W/ BAR
DESK
LAU.
7'-6" X 6'-1"
GREAT RM.
20'-1" X 17'-0"
10' CEILING
BATH
LIN
D.W
KIT.
13'-6" X 10'-6"
RG
REF
PANTRY
BATH
STRG.
9'-6" X 7'-10"
BUILT-IN W/ SHELVES
FOYER
8'-8" X 7'-7"
10' CEILING
BED RM. 2
11'-6" X 12'-0"
DINING RM.
12'-6" X 12'-0"
10' CEILING
BED RM. 1
11'-0" X 13'-10"
GARAGE
20'-4" X 21'-0"
PRCH
5'-4" X 7'-5"
12' BRK COL
7'1/8"

Total Living Area	2,392 sq. ft.

PRICE CODE: C

CUSTOMIZE IT!

ORDER TOLL FREE 1 ■ 800 ■ 533 ■ 4350 **24-HOUR FAX ORDERING** 1 ■ 800 ■ 344 ■ 4293

PLAN FD6922-L

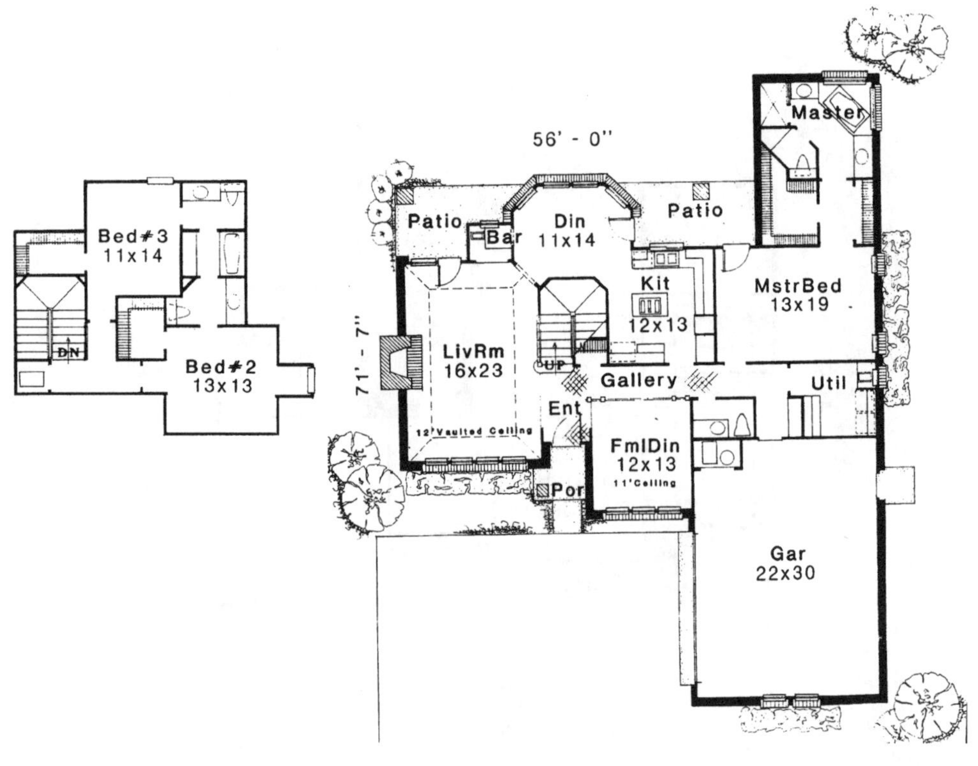

Bed#3
11x14
DN
Bed#2
13x13
56' - 0"
71' - 7"
Patio
Bar
Din
11x14
Patio
Master
Kit
12x13
MstrBed
13x19
LivRm
16x23
UP
Gallery
Util
Ent
FmlDin
12x13
11'Ceiling
12'Vaulted Ceiling
Por
Gar
22x30

First Floor	1,755 sq. ft.
Second Floor	647 sq. ft.
Total Living Area	2,402 sq. ft.

PRICE CODE: C

PLAN DB2261

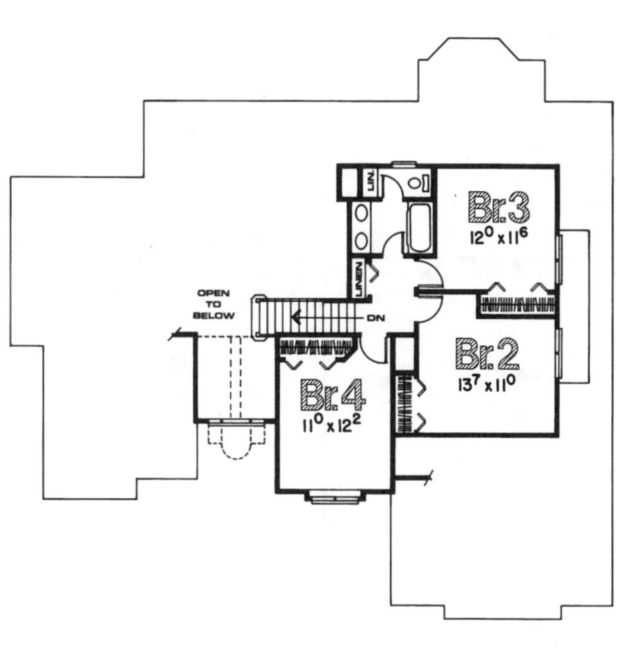

OPEN TO BELOW
DN
LIN.
LINEN
Br.3 12⁰ x 11⁶
Br.2 13⁷ x 11⁰
Br.4 11⁰ x 12²

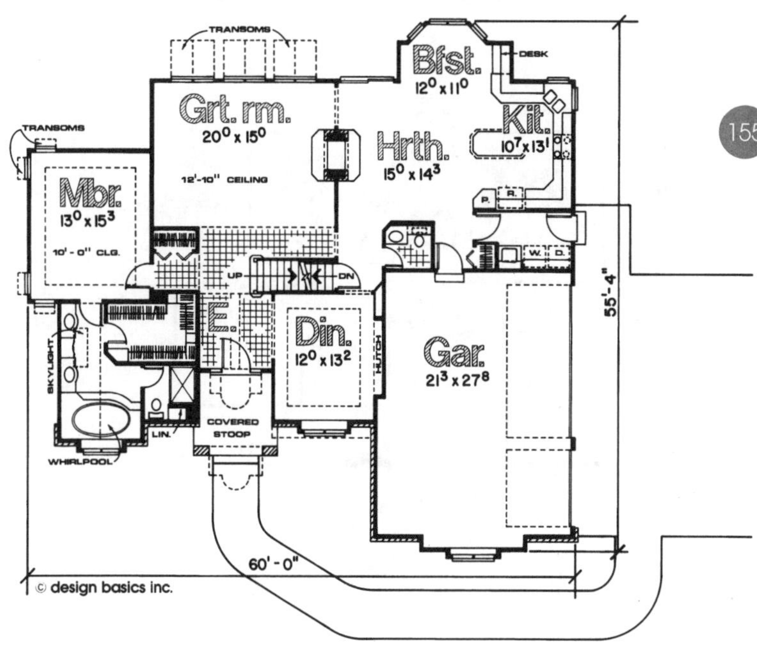

TRANSOMS
TRANSOMS
Bfst. 12⁰ x 11⁰
DESK
Grt. rm. 20⁰ x 15⁰
12'-10" CEILING
Hrth. 15⁰ x 14³
Kit. 10⁷ x 13¹
Mbr. 13⁰ x 15³
10'-0" CLG.
UP
DN
E.
Din. 12⁰ x 13²
HUTCH
Gar. 21³ x 27⁸
W.
D.
SKYLIGHT
WHIRLPOOL
LIN.
COVERED STOOP
55'-4"
60'-0"
© design basics inc.

Features

- Volume entry views formal dining room and great room beyond.
- Large repeating windows out the back of the volume great room.
- Beautiful see-thru fireplace shared by great room and hearth room.
- Gourmet kitchen with pantry, island counter and corner sink under windows.
- Separate mud room entrance.
- Secluded master suite features luxurious skylit dressing area with large walk-in closet, his and her vanities and oval whirlpool.
- Secondary bedrooms share generous compartmented bathroom.

First Floor	1,733 sq. ft.
Second Floor	672 sq. ft.
Total Living Area	2,405 sq. ft.

PRICE CODE: D

PLAN DB2919

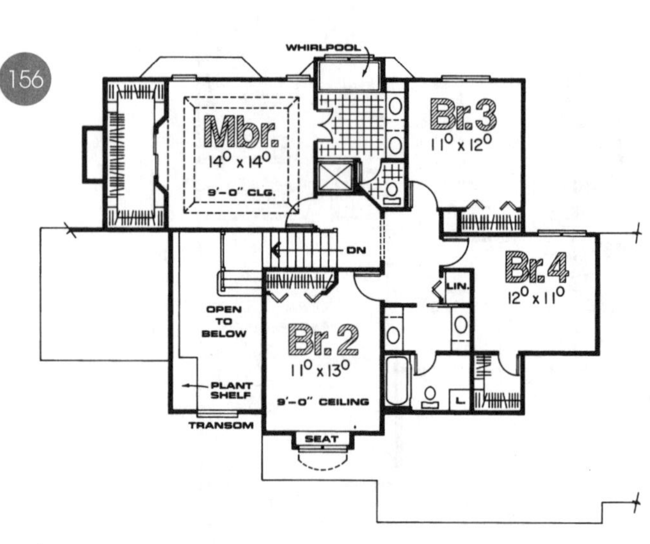

WHIRLPOOL
Mbr.
$14^{0} \times 14^{0}$
9'-0" CLG.
Br.3
$11^{0} \times 12^{0}$
DN
OPEN TO BELOW
LIN.
Br.4
$12^{0} \times 11^{0}$
Br. 2
$11^{0} \times 13^{0}$
PLANT SHELF
9'-0" CEILING
TRANSOM
SEAT

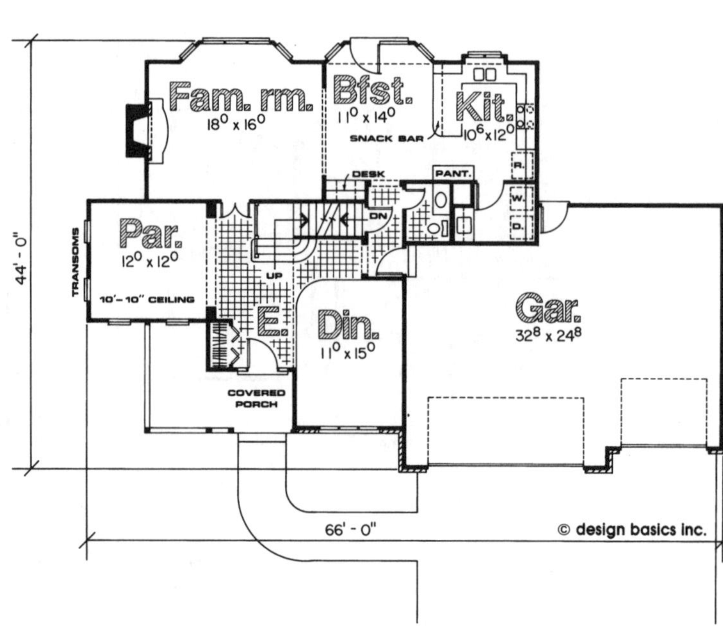

Fam. rm.
$18^{0} \times 16^{0}$
Bfst.
$11^{0} \times 14^{0}$
SNACK BAR
Kit.
$10^{6} \times 12^{0}$
DESK
PANT.
R.
W.
D.
DN
TRANSOMS
Par.
$12^{0} \times 12^{0}$
10'-10" CEILING
UP
E.
Din.
$11^{0} \times 15^{0}$
Gar.
$32^{8} \times 24^{8}$
COVERED PORCH
44' - 0"
66' - 0"
© design basics inc.

Features

- Wrapping front porch adds curb appeal .
- Formal dining room and parlor open to 2-story entry and graceful stairway.
- Efficient kitchen features lazy Susan, pantry and convenient access to laundry room.
- Bayed windows in family room and breakfast area create appealing interiors and add interest to rear elevation.
- Well-planned second level provides privacy for master suite as well as secondary bedrooms.
- Vaulted ceiling, surprising walk-in closet and spacious whirlpool bath create magnificent master suite.
- Three secondary bedrooms share easily accessible compartmented bath with dual vanities.

First Floor	1,277 sq. ft.
Second Floor	1,135 sq. ft.
Total Living Area	2,412 sq. ft.

PRICE CODE: D

PLAN NP1303

MALOU

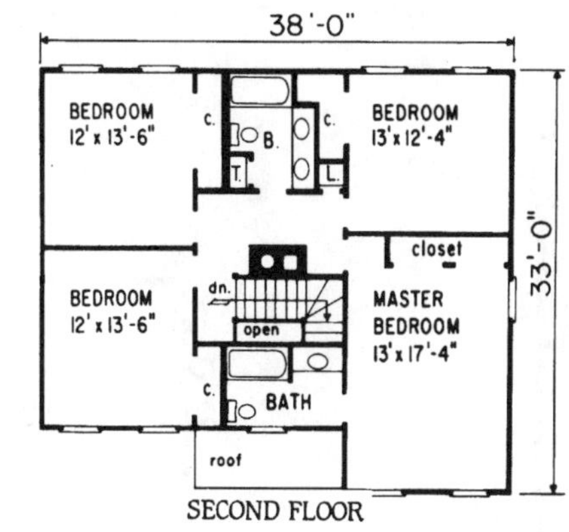
38'-0"
BEDROOM
12' x 13'-6"
C.
B.
T.
C.
L.
BEDROOM
13' x 12'-4"
closet
BEDROOM
12' x 13'-6"
dn.
open
MASTER
BEDROOM
13' x 17'-4"
C.
BATH
roof
33'-0"

SECOND FLOOR

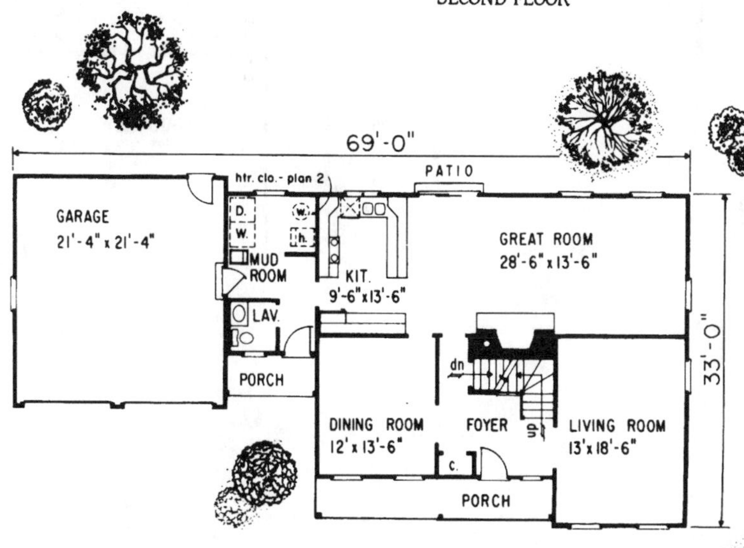
69'-0"
htr. clo.- plan 2
PATIO
GARAGE
21'-4" x 21'-4"
D.
W.
w.
h.
MUD
ROOM
KIT.
9'-6" x 13'-6"
GREAT ROOM
28'-6" x 13'-6"
LAV.
dn
PORCH
DINING ROOM
12' x 13'-6"
FOYER
up
LIVING ROOM
13' x 18'-6"
C.
PORCH
33'-0"

FIRST FLOOR PLAN 1 WITH BASEMENT
FIRST FLOOR PLAN 2 WITHOUT BASEMENT

Victorian Flair

Features

- Two-story, country Victorian home makes every bit of floor space count.
- Central foyer features an L-shpaed staircase, and access to living and dining rooms.
- Huge great room with fireplace at rear of home has sliding glass door access to backyard patio.
- Informal porch entry leads to lavatory/mud room and garage.
- Second-floor master bedroom includes private, full bath.
- Three additional bedrooms share a full bath with double-vanity

First Floor	**1,282 sq. ft.**
Second Floor	**1,132 sq. ft.**
Total Living Area	**2,414 sq. ft.**

PRICE CODE: C

PLAN AM2258C

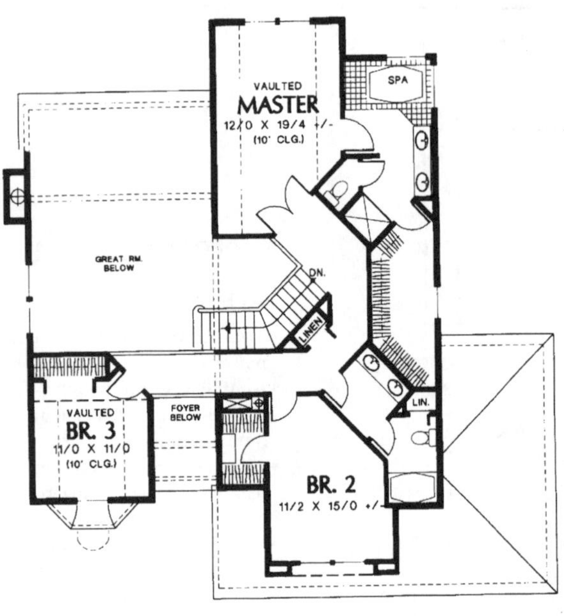
VAULTED
MASTER
12/0 X 19/4 +/-
(10' CLG.)
SPA
GREAT RM. BELOW
DN.
LINEN
VAULTED
BR. 3
11/0 X 11/0
(10' CLG.)
FOYER BELOW
LIN.
BR. 2
11/2 X 15/0 +/-

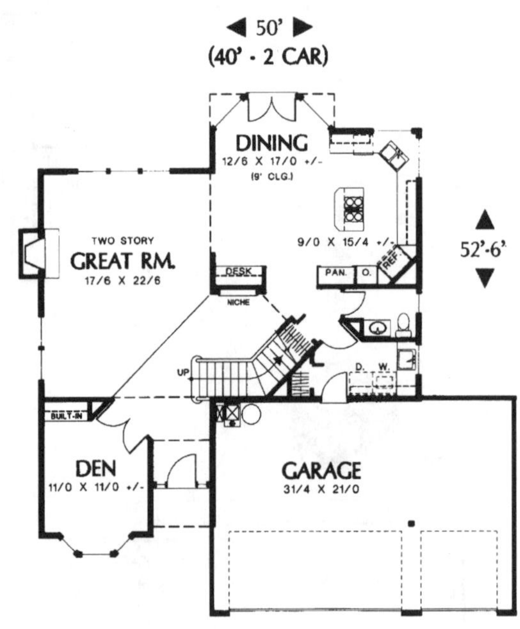
50'
(40' - 2 CAR)
DINING
12/6 X 17/0 +/-
(9' CLG.)
9/0 X 15/4 +/-
52'-6'
TWO STORY
GREAT RM.
17/6 X 22/6
DESK
NICHE
PAN.
O.
REF.
UP
D. W.
BUILT-IN
DEN
11/0 X 11/0 +/-
GARAGE
31/4 X 21/0

First Floor	1,290 sq. ft.
Second Floor	1,134 sq. ft.
Total Living Area	2,424 sq. ft.

PRICE CODE: C

PLAN FD7756B

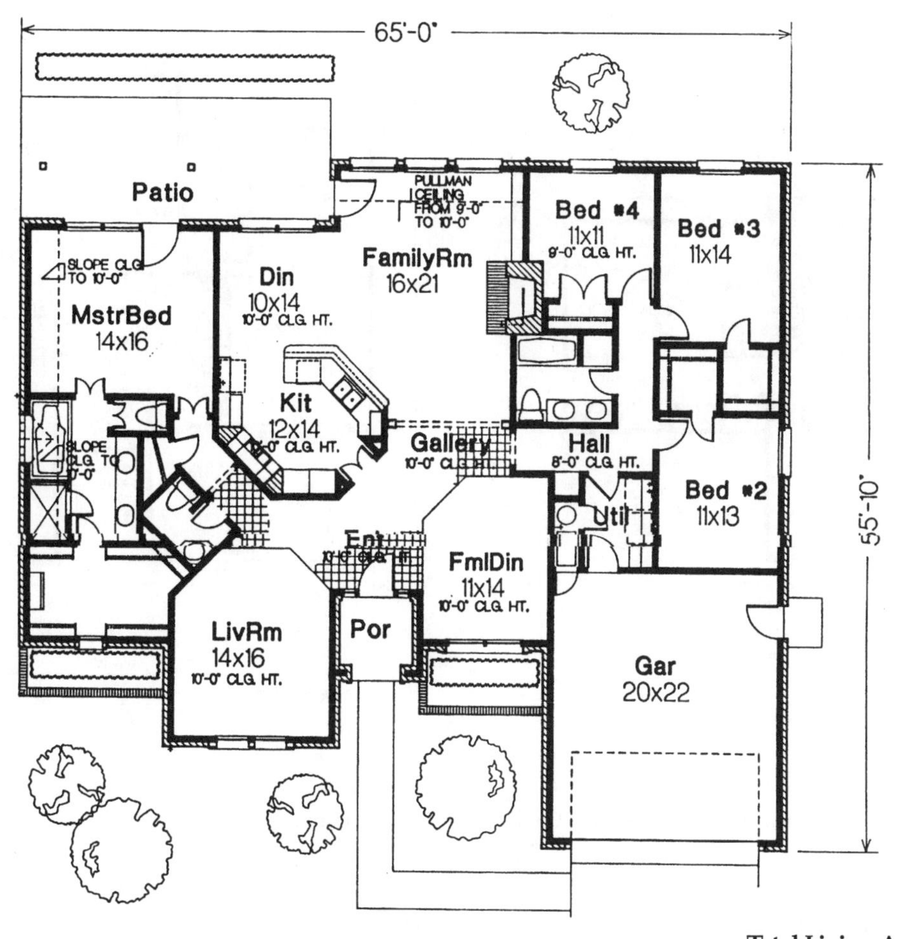
65'-0"
Patio
PULLMAN CEILING FROM 9'-0" TO 10'-0"
SLOPE CLG TO 10'-0"
MstrBed
14x16
Din
10x14
10'-0" CLG. HT.
FamilyRm
16x21
Bed #4
11x11
9'-0" CLG. HT.
Bed #3
11x14
Kit
12x14
10'-0" CLG. HT.
Gallery
10'-0" CLG. HT.
Hall
8'-0" CLG. HT.
Bed #2
11x13
Util
Ent
FmlDin
11x14
10'-0" CLG. HT.
LivRm
14x16
10'-0" CLG. HT.
Por
Gar
20x22
55'-10"

Total Living Area 2,425 sq. ft.

PRICE CODE: C

PLAN DB1033

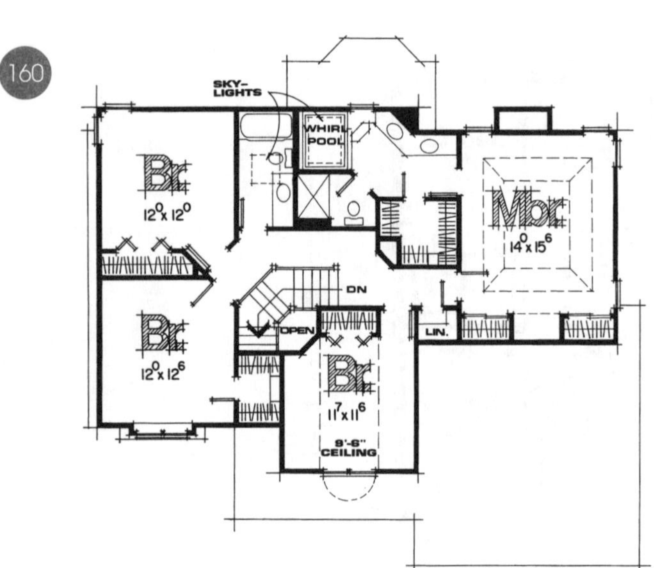
SKY-LIGHTS
WHIRLPOOL
Br.
12⁰x12⁰
Mbr.
14⁰x15⁶
DN
Br.
12⁰x12⁶
OPEN
Br.
11⁷x11⁶
LIN.
9'-6" CEILING

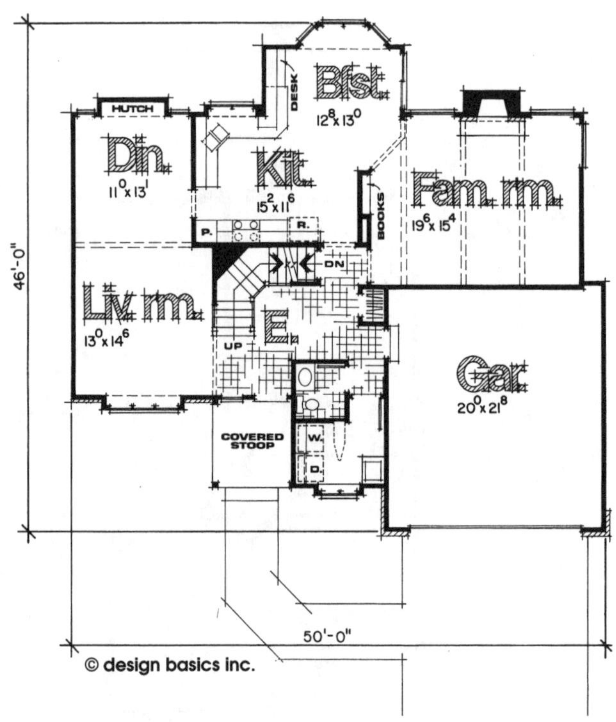
HUTCH
DESK
Bfst.
12⁸x13⁰
Din.
11⁰x13¹
Kit.
15²x11⁶
Fam. rm.
19⁶x15⁴
BOOKS
P.
R.
DN
46'-0"
Liv. rm.
13⁰x14⁶
E.
UP
Gar.
20⁰x21⁸
COVERED STOOP
W.
D.
50'-0"
© design basics inc.

Features

- Entry spotlights angled staircase and formal living room.
- Dining room with hutch space open to living room for expanded entertaining.
- Family room offers beamed ceiling, book-case and fireplace framed by windows.
- Kitchen is well planned with wrapping counter, pantry, desk and corner sink.
- Bayed window in breakfast area which provides access to the outside.
- Laundry room with sink and iron-a-way.
- Discrete main-floor powder bath.
- Master suite with his and her closets in bedroom, plus dressing/bath area featuring wrapping vanity, walk-in closet and 2-person whirlpool tub.
- Third bedroom includes walk-in closet.

First Floor	1,247 sq. ft.
Second Floor	1,183 sq. ft.
Total Living Area	2,430 sq. ft.

PRICE CODE: D

CUSTOMIZE IT!

ORDER TOLL FREE **1-800-533-4350** 24-HOUR FAX ORDERING **1-800-344-4293**

PLAN NP1292

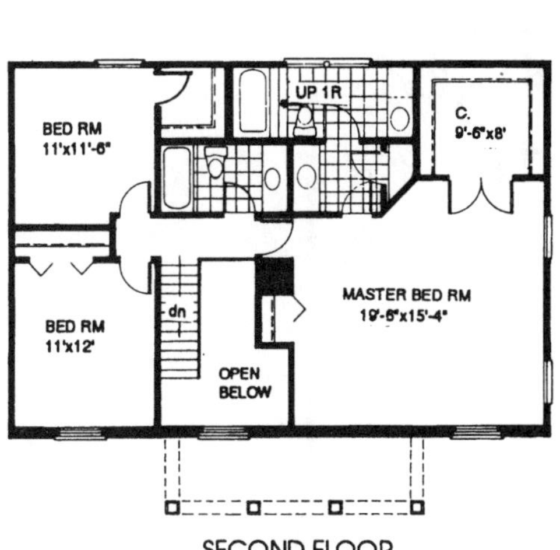
BED RM
11'x11'-6"
UP 1R
C.
9'-6"x8'
BED RM
11'x12'
dn
MASTER BED RM
19'-6"x15'-4"
OPEN
BELOW

SECOND FLOOR

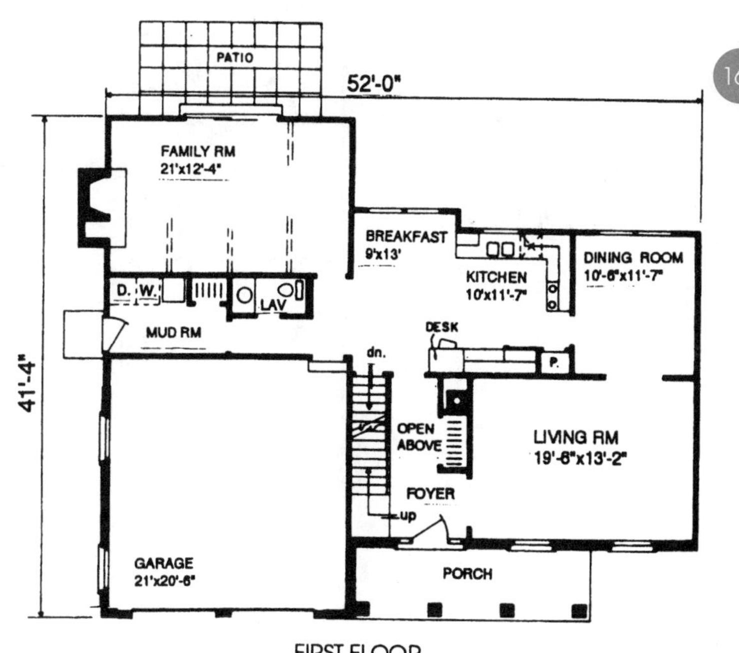
PATIO
52'-0"
FAMILY RM
21'x12'-4"
BREAKFAST
9'x13'
KITCHEN
10'x11'-7"
DINING ROOM
10'-6"x11'-7"
D.W.
LAV
MUD RM
DESK
dn.
P.
41'-4"
OPEN
ABOVE
LIVING RM
19'-6"x13'-2"
FOYER
up
GARAGE
21'x20'-6"
PORCH

FIRST FLOOR

Bountiful

Features

- Charming, traditional design of exterior is carried inside this home.
- Foyer boasts open stairway and balustrades.
- Family room has beamed ceiling and natural fireplace.
- Central hall leads to living room, large kitchen, powder room, laundry and garage.
- Second-floor master bedroom has a private bath.
- Two additional upstairs bedrooms share a full bath.

First Floor	**1,258 sq. ft.**
Second Floor	**1,176 sq. ft.**
Total Living Area	**2,434 sq. ft.**

PRICE CODE: C

PLAN MN2439

PORCH
M.BATH
BRKFAST RM.
FAMILY RM.
M.BED RM.
10' PAN CEILING
KITCHEN
REF
DW
RG
PAN
BED RM. 2
LIN
BATH
GALLERY
BATH
8" BOXED COLUMNS
FRENCH DOORS
FOYER
10' CEILING
FAMILY DINING RM.
11' BOXED CEILING
BED RM. 3
LAU.
BED RM. 4
STUDY
POR.
GARAGE

Total Living Area 2,439 sq. ft.

PRICE CODE: C

PLAN AM2233A

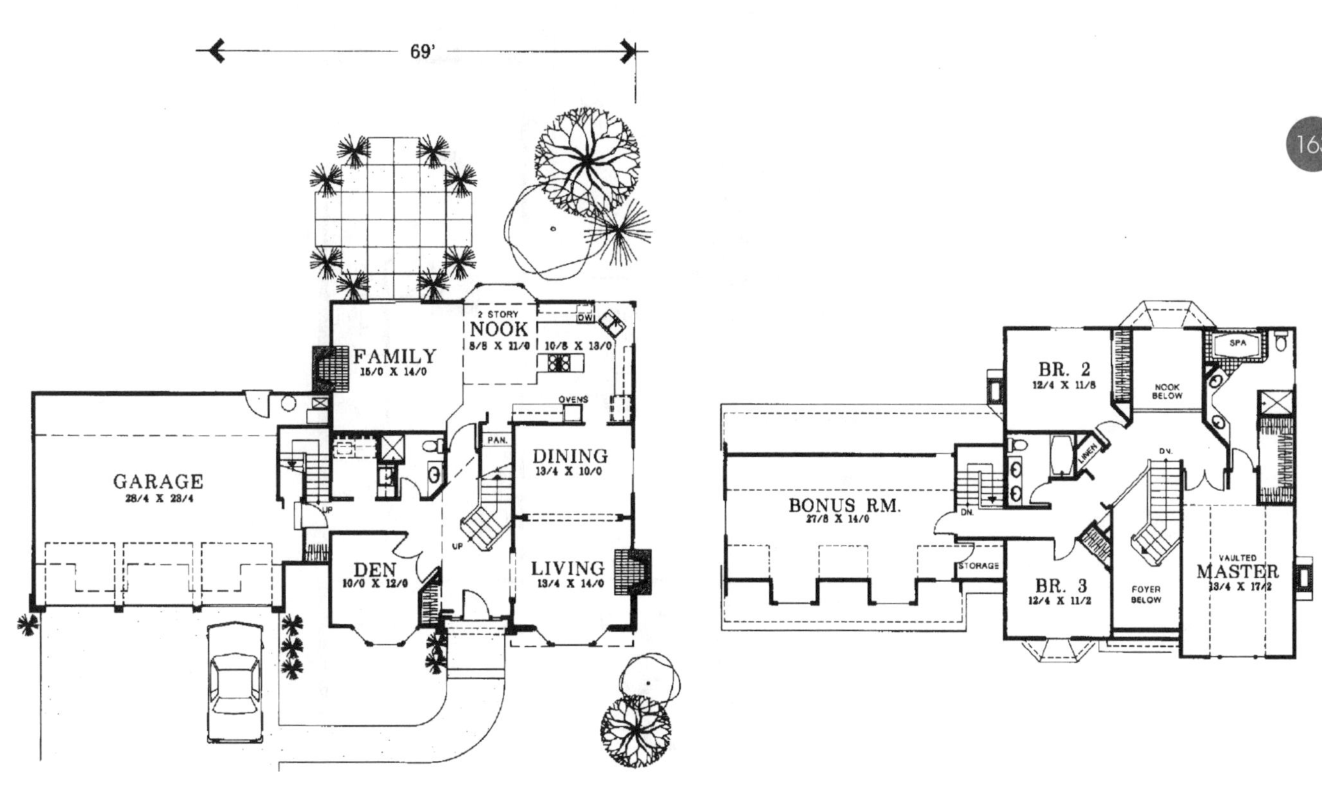
69'
40'
2 STORY
NOOK
8/8 X 21/0
10/6 X 13/0
DW
FAMILY
15/0 X 14/0
OVENS
PAN.
DINING
13/4 X 10/0
GARAGE
28/4 X 28/4
UP
DEN
10/0 X 12/0
LIVING
13/4 X 14/0
BR. 2
12/4 X 11/8
NOOK BELOW
SPA
LINEN
DN.
BONUS RM.
27/8 X 14/0
STORAGE
BR. 3
12/4 X 11/2
FOYER BELOW
VAULTED
MASTER
13/4 X 17/2

First Floor	1,360 sq. ft.
Second Floor	1,082 sq. ft.
Total Living Area	2,442 sq. ft.
Bonus Room	+482 sq. ft.

PRICE CODE: C

PLAN FD7397-L

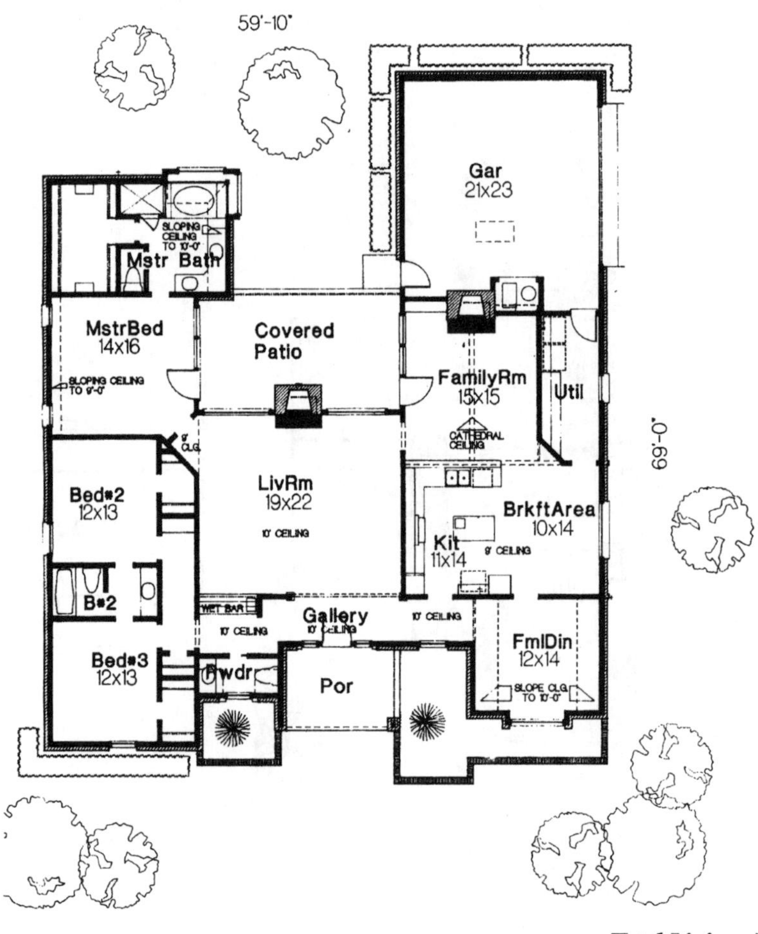

59'-10"
69'-0"
Gar
21x23
Mstr Bath
SLOPING CEILING TO 10'-0"
MstrBed
14x16
SLOPING CEILING TO 9'-0"
Covered
Patio
FamilyRm
15x15
CATHEDRAL CEILING
Util
Bed#2
12x13
LivRm
19x22
10' CEILING
BrkftArea
10x14
Kit
11x14
9' CEILING
B#2
WET BAR
10' CEILING
Gallery
10' CEILING
10' CEILING
FmlDin
12x14
SLOPE CLG TO 10'-0"
Bed#3
12x13
Pwdr
Por

Total Living Area 2,470 sq. ft.

PRICE CODE: C

PLAN DB2346

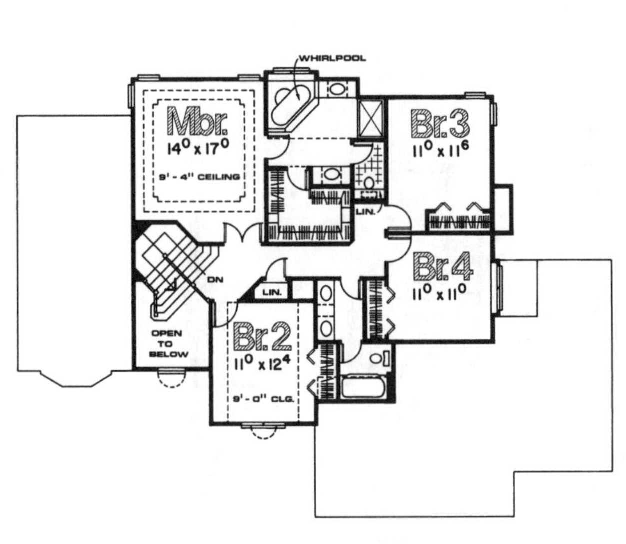
WHIRLPOOL
Mbr.
14^0 x 17^0
9'-4" CEILING
Br.3
11^0 x 11^6
LIN.
Br.4
11^0 x 11^0
DN
LIN.
OPEN TO BELOW
Br.2
11^0 x 12^4
9'-0" CLG.

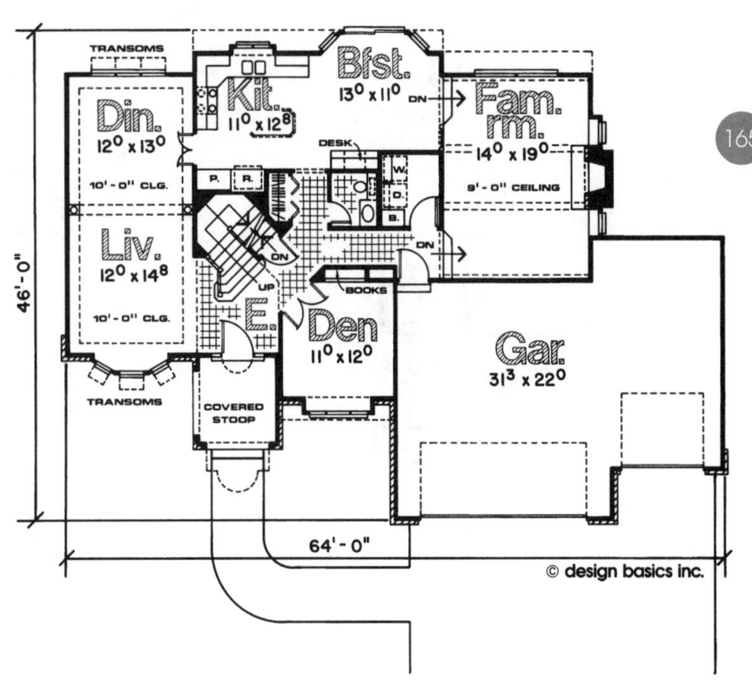
TRANSOMS
Din.
12^0 x 13^0
10'-0" CLG.
Kit.
11^0 x 12^8
Bfst.
13^0 x 11^0
DN
Fam. rm.
14^0 x 19^0
9'-0" CEILING
DESK
P.
R.
W.
D.
B.
Liv.
12^0 x 14^8
10'-0" CLG.
DN
UP
E.
BOOKS
Den
11^0 x 12^0
Gar.
31^3 x 22^0
TRANSOMS
COVERED STOOP
46'-0"
64'-0"
© design basics inc.

Features

- Magnificent elevation combines brick, wood and popular 3-car garage.
- Island kitchen and bayed dinette perfect for family pursuits.
- Adjoining living and dining rooms, ideal for entertaining, feature tapered columns and elegant windows.
- Step-down to family room with fireplace framed by windows.
- Den includes bookcase and French doors.
- Three comfortable secondary bedrooms share compartmented bath with dual lavs.
- Master suite enjoys French door entrance, tiered ceiling, large walk-in closet, his and her vanities and whirlpool.

First Floor	**1,369 sq. ft.**
Second Floor	**1,111 sq. ft.**
Total Living Area	**2,480 sq. ft.**

PRICE CODE: D

PLAN FD7904-L

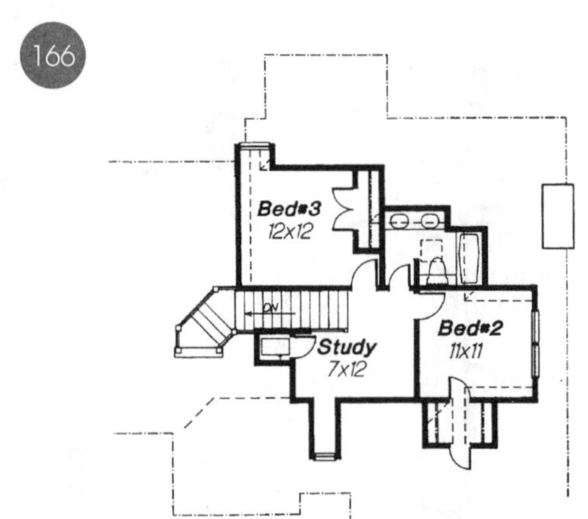

Bed#3
12x12
DN
Study
7x12
Bed#2
11x11

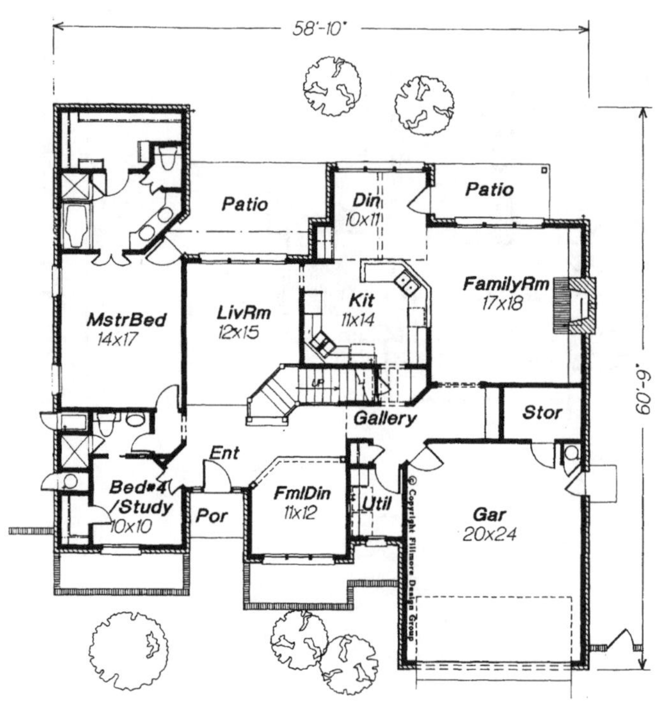

58'-10"
Patio
Din
10x11
Patio
FamilyRm
17x18
MstrBed
14x17
LivRm
12x15
Kit
11x14
UP
Gallery
Stor
Ent
Bed#4
/Study
10x10
Por
FmlDin
11x12
Util
Gar
20x24
60'-9"

First Floor	1,976 sq. ft.
Second Floor	517 sq. ft.
Total Living Area	2,493 sq. ft.

PRICE CODE: C

PLAN FD7056-LC

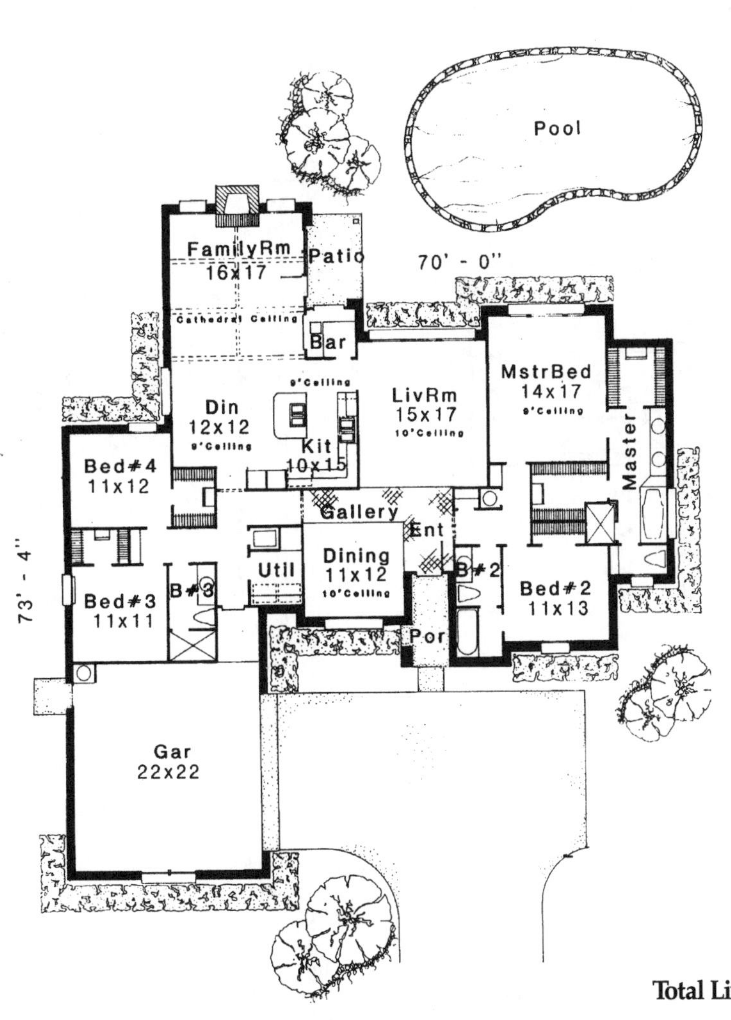
Pool
FamilyRm
16x17
Patio
70' - 0"
Cathedral Ceiling
Bar
MstrBed
14x17
9'Ceiling
9'Ceiling
Din
12x12
9'Ceiling
LivRm
15x17
10'Ceiling
Master
Kit
10x15
Bed#4
11x12
Gallery
Ent
Dining
11x12
10'Ceiling
Util
B#3
B#2
Bed#3
11x11
Bed#2
11x13
73' - 4"
Por
Gar
22x22

Total Living Area 2,495 sq. ft.

PRICE CODE: C

CUSTOMIZE IT!

ORDER TOLL FREE 1-800-533-4350 24-HOUR FAX ORDERING 1-800-344-4293

PLAN DB2898

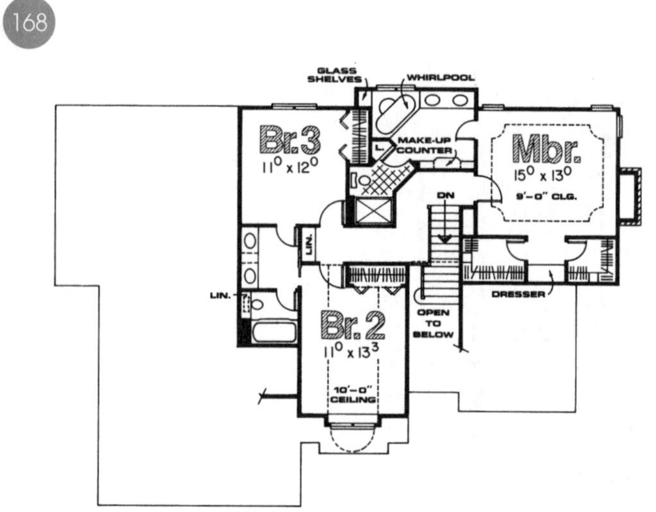
GLASS SHELVES
WHIRLPOOL
Br.3
11⁰ x 12⁰
MAKE-UP COUNTER
Mbr.
15⁰ x 13⁰
9'-0" CLG.
DN
LIN.
LIN.
Br. 2
11⁰ x 13³
10'-0" CEILING
OPEN TO BELOW
DRESSER

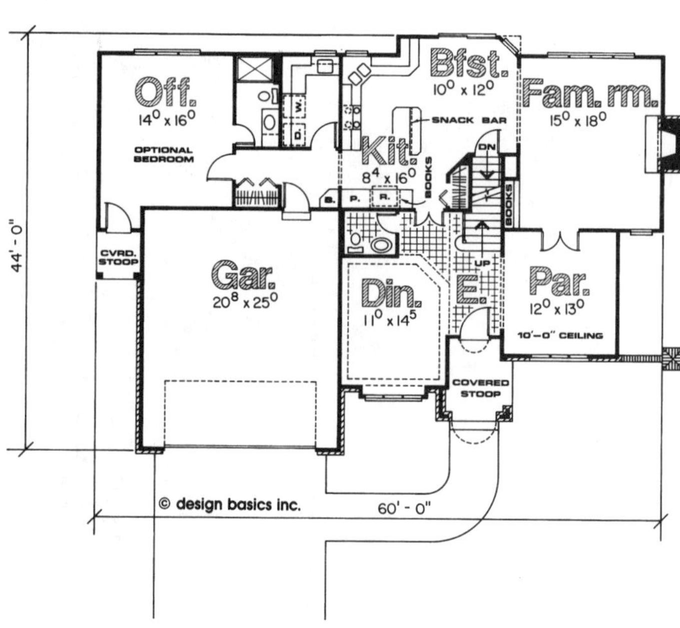
Off.
14⁰ x 16⁰
OPTIONAL BEDROOM
W.
D.
Bfst.
10⁰ x 12⁰
SNACK BAR
Fam. rm.
15⁰ x 18⁰
Kit.
8⁴ x 16⁰
DN
BOOKS
S.
P.
R.
BOOKS
44'-0"
CVRD. STOOP
Gar.
20⁸ x 25⁰
Din.
11⁰ x 14⁵
UP
E.
Par.
12⁰ x 13⁰
10'-0" CEILING
COVERED STOOP
© design basics inc.
60'-0"

Features

- Formal dining room and parlor open to 14-foot-tall entry.
- French doors between parlor and family room provide convenient expansion for entertaining and add elegance to both rooms.
- Well-integrated dinette and kitchen offers corner sink, pantry, wrapping cabinets and island snack bar.
- Versatile office or optional main level bedroom has private outside entrance and 3/4 bath.
- Upstairs, secondary bedrooms share private compartmented bath.
- Magnificent master bedroom has his and her closets and attractive ceiling detail.
- Master bath features angled whirlpool tub, dual lavs and special make-up counter.

First Floor	1,535 sq. ft.
Second Floor	962 sq. ft.
Total Living Area	2,497 sq. ft.

PRICE CODE: D

PLAN NP1415

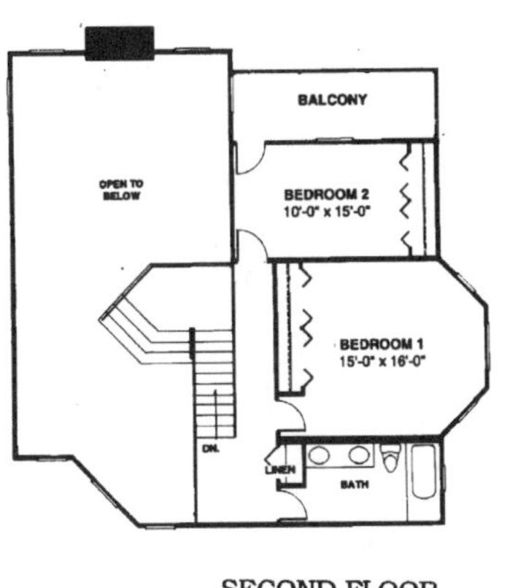
BALCONY
OPEN TO BELOW
BEDROOM 2
10'-0" x 15'-0"
BEDROOM 1
15'-0" x 16'-0"
DN.
LINEN
BATH

SECOND FLOOR

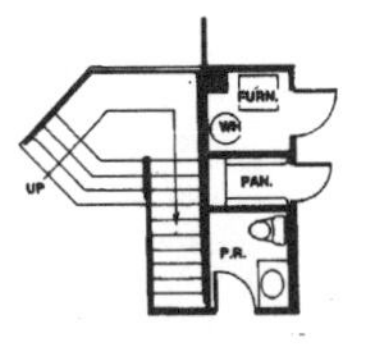
FURN.
W/H
PAN.
P.R.
UP

FIRST FLOOR
PLAN 2 WITHOUT BASEMENT

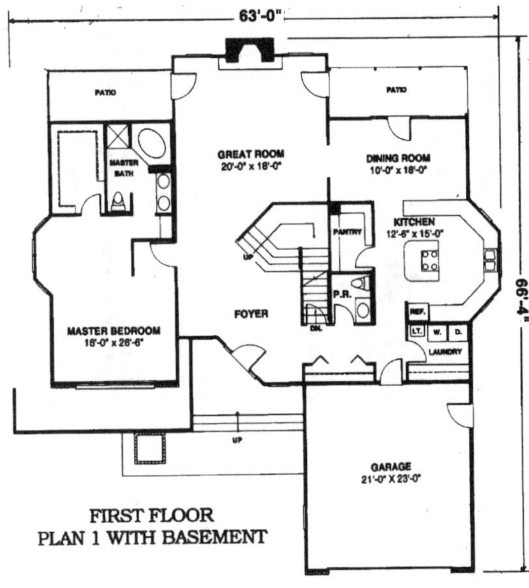
63'-0"
66'-4"
PATIO
PATIO
GREAT ROOM
20'-0" x 18'-0"
DINING ROOM
10'-0" x 18'-0"
MASTER BATH
KITCHEN
12'-6" x 15'-0"
PANTRY
UP
P.R.
FOYER
DN.
REF.
LT.
W.
D.
LAUNDRY
MASTER BEDROOM
16'-0" x 26'-6"
UP
GARAGE
21'-0" X 23'-0"

FIRST FLOOR
PLAN 1 WITH BASEMENT

Monmouth

Features

- Appearances can be deceiving -- this home looks enormous but boasts more modest dimensions inside, without sacrificing comfort.
- Columnar entrance leads into spacious foyer with dramatic, platform stairs.
- Left wing includes master bedroom suite, with dual-vanity master bath, walk-in closet, and raised Roman tub.
- Large great room with fireplace and patio access occupies the rear of the home.
- Bayed kitchen with cooking island adjoins dining room, also with patio access.
- Upstairs are two additional bedrooms that share a full bath.

First Floor	**1,854 sq. ft.**
Second Floor	**652 sq. ft.**
Total Living Area	**2,506 sq. ft.**

PRICE CODE: C

PLAN FD7852-L

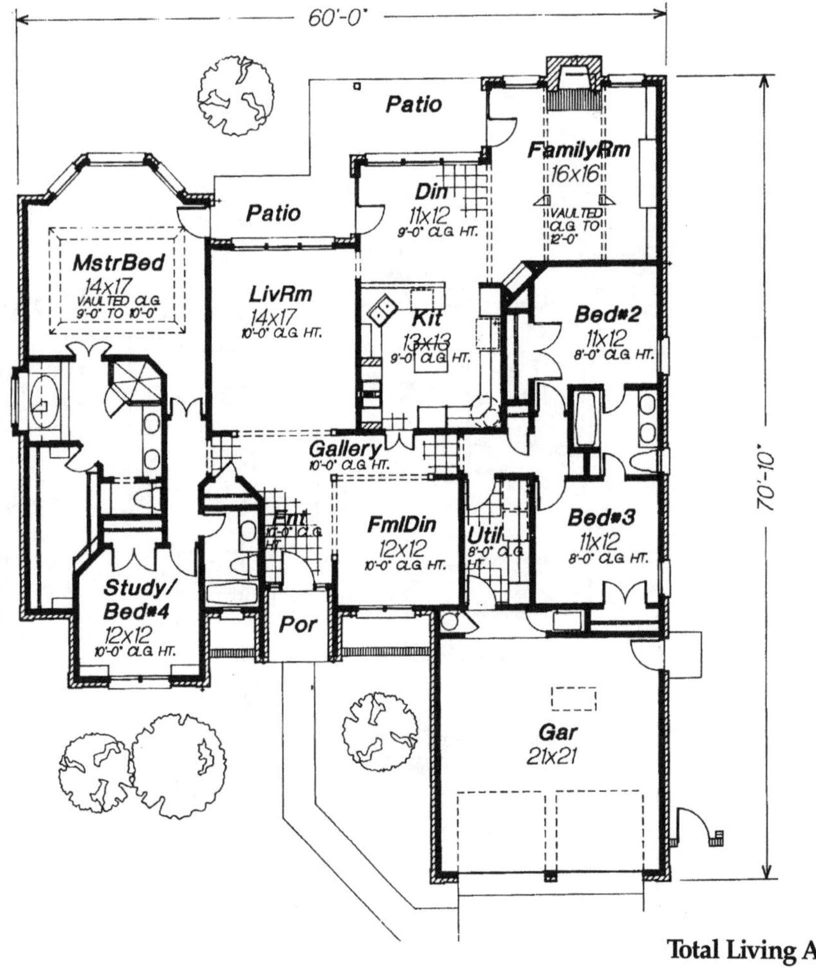

60'-0"
Patio
FamilyRm
16x16
VAULTED CLG. TO 12'-0"
Din
11x12
9'-0" CLG. HT.
Patio
MstrBed
14x17
VAULTED CLG. 9'-0" TO 10'-0"
LivRm
14x17
10'-0" CLG. HT.
Kit
13x13
9'-0" CLG. HT.
Bed#2
11x12
8'-0" CLG. HT.
70'-10"
Gallery
10'-0" CLG. HT.
FmlDin
12x12
10'-0" CLG. HT.
Util
Bed#3
11x12
8'-0" CLG. HT.
Study/
Bed#4
12x12
10'-0" CLG. HT.
Por
Gar
21x21

Total Living Area 2,506 sq. ft.

PRICE CODE: C

PLAN NP1210

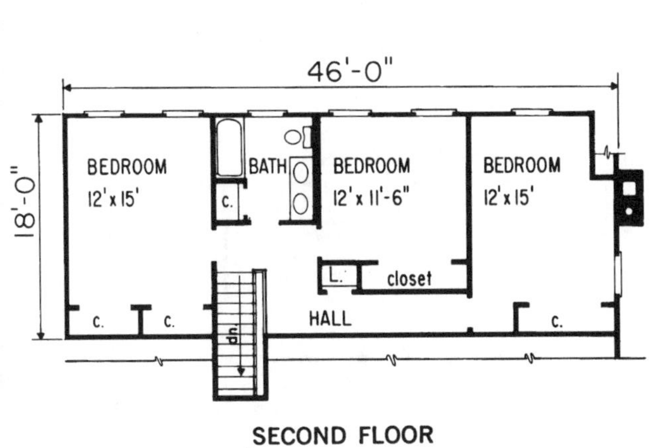

46'-0"
18'-0"
BEDROOM
12' x 15'
BATH
BEDROOM
12' x 11'-6"
BEDROOM
12' x 15'
c.
L.
closet
c.
c.
HALL
c.
dn
SECOND FLOOR

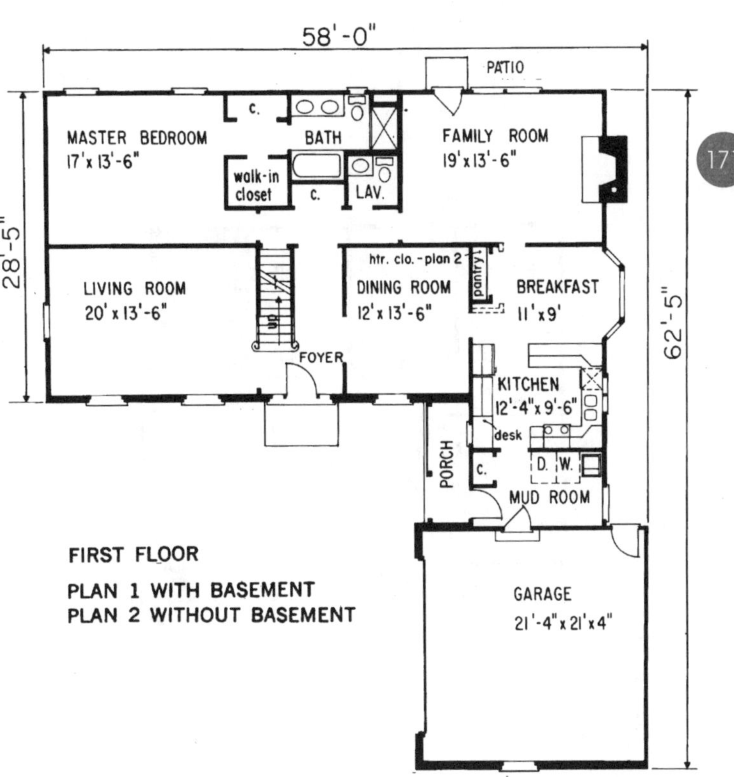

58'-0"
PATIO
28'-5"
62'-5"
MASTER BEDROOM
17' x 13'-6"
c.
BATH
walk-in closet
c.
LAV.
FAMILY ROOM
19' x 13'-6"
LIVING ROOM
20' x 13'-6"
up
FOYER
htr. clo. - plan 2
DINING ROOM
12' x 13'-6"
pantry
BREAKFAST
11' x 9'
KITCHEN
12'-4" x 9'-6"
desk
D.W.
PORCH
c.
MUD ROOM
GARAGE
21'-4" x 21' x 4"
FIRST FLOOR
PLAN 1 WITH BASEMENT
PLAN 2 WITHOUT BASEMENT

Elegante

Features

- Colonial design adds a distinctive touch to this two-story.
- Porch opens into mud room and kitchen with adjoining breakfast nook.
- Front door opens into a foyer with adjoining living room and dining room.
- First floor master bedroom with private bathroom.
- Large family room with fireplace and rear patio.
- Second floor features three bedrooms.

First Floor	1,702 sq. ft.
Second Floor	816 sq. ft.
Total Living Area	2,518 sq. ft.

PRICE CODE: C

PLAN AM2212G

172

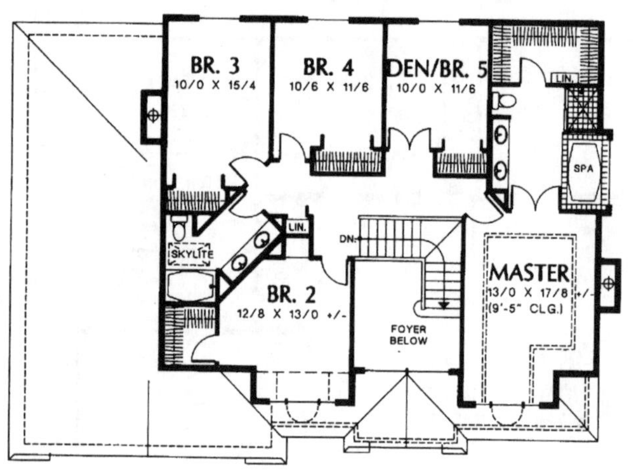
BR. 3
10/0 X 15/4
BR. 4
10/6 X 11/6
DEN/BR. 5
10/0 X 11/6
LIN.
SPA
SKYLITE
LIN.
DN
BR. 2
12/8 X 13/0 +/-
FOYER
BELOW
MASTER
13/0 X 17/8
(9'-5" CLG.)

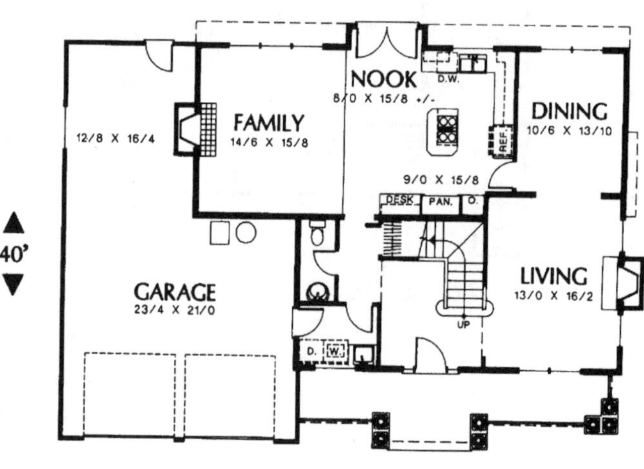
56'
40'
GARAGE
12/8 X 16/4
FAMILY
14/6 X 15/8
NOOK
8/0 X 15/8 +/-
D.W.
DINING
10/6 X 13/10
REF.
9/0 X 15/8
DESK
PAN.
LIVING
13/0 X 16/2
GARAGE
23/4 X 21/0
UP
D.
W.

First Floor	1,200 sq. ft.
Second Floor	1,339 sq. ft.
Total Living Area	2,539 sq. ft.

PRICE CODE: C

PLAN DB2229

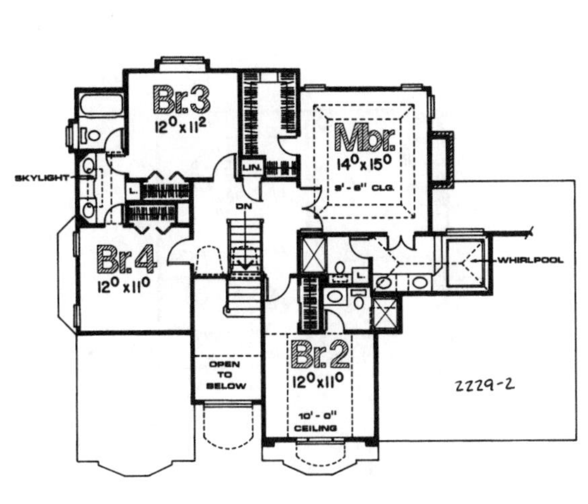

Br.3
$12^{0} \times 11^{2}$
Mbr.
$14^{0} \times 15^{0}$
9'-8" CLG.
SKYLIGHT
LIN.
DN
Br.4
$12^{0} \times 11^{0}$
WHIRLPOOL
OPEN TO BELOW
Br.2
$12^{0} \times 11^{0}$
10'-0" CEILING
2229-2

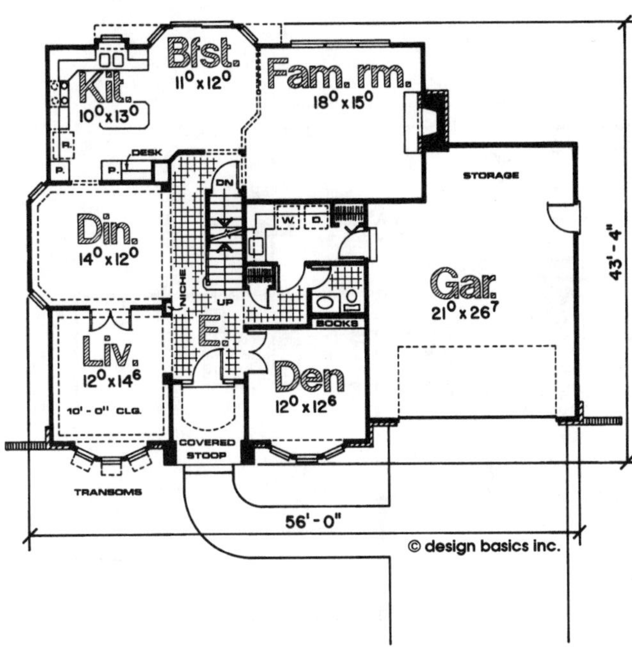

Bfst.
$11^{0} \times 12^{0}$
Kit.
$10^{0} \times 13^{0}$
Fam. rm.
$18^{0} \times 15^{0}$
DESK
STORAGE
DN
W.
D.
Din.
$14^{0} \times 12^{0}$
NICHE
UP
Gar.
$21^{0} \times 26^{7}$
BOOKS
Liv.
$12^{0} \times 14^{6}$
10'-0" CLG.
E.
Den
$12^{0} \times 12^{6}$
COVERED STOOP
TRANSOMS
56'-0"
43'-4"
© design basics inc.

Features

- Beautiful volume entry.
- Bayed windows in living room and den.
- French doors into den with built-in bookcase.
- French doors between dining room and living room.
- Large windows out the back of the family room.
- Island counter and desk in kitchen.
- Entrance through laundry/mud area containing closet and soaking sink.
- Extra storage in garage.
- Generous bathroom arrangements for secondary bedrooms.
- Double doors into the private master suite.
- Luxurious dressing area under sloped ceiling with large whirlpool and window.

First Floor	1,392 sq. ft.
Second Floor	1,153 sq. ft.
Total Living Area	2,545 sq. ft.

PRICE CODE: D

CUSTOMIZE IT!

ORDER TOLL FREE 1-800-533-4350 24-HOUR FAX ORDERING 1-800-344-4293

PLAN AM2213D

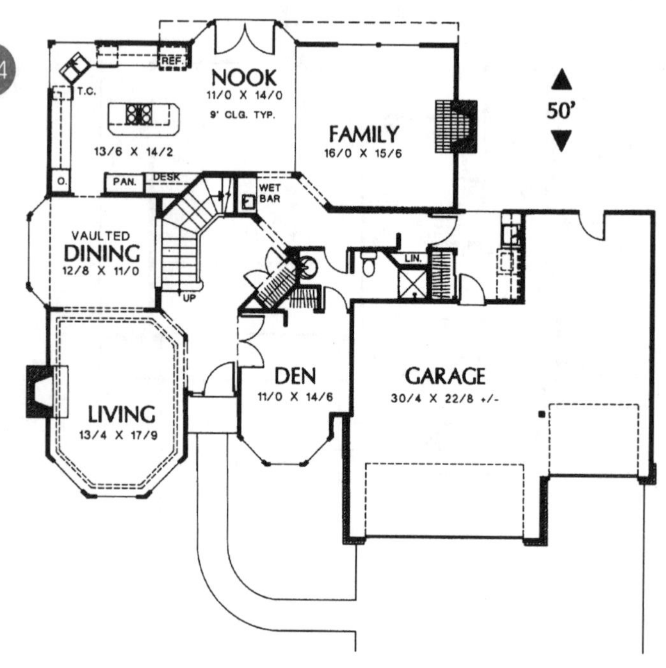
REF.
NOOK
11/0 X 14/0
9' CLG. TYP.
T.C.
13/6 X 14/2
FAMILY
16/0 X 15/6
50'
O.
PAN.
DESK
WET BAR
VAULTED
DINING
12/8 X 11/0
UP
LIN.
LIVING
13/4 X 17/9
DEN
11/0 X 14/6
GARAGE
30/4 X 22/8 +/-

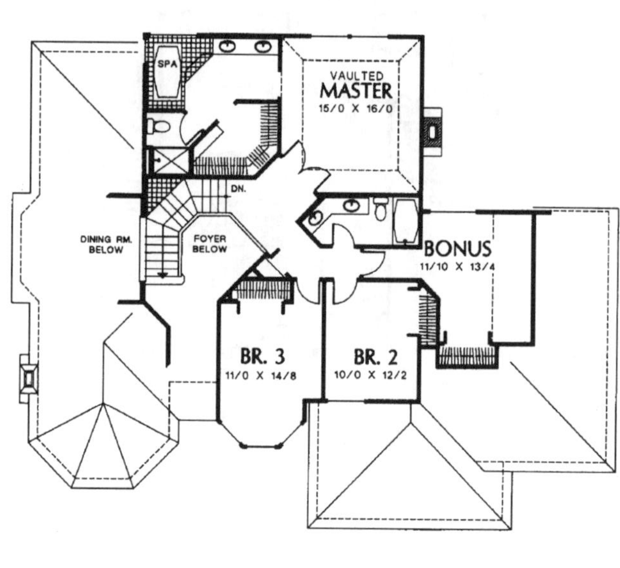
SPA
VAULTED
MASTER
15/0 X 16/0
DN.
DINING RM. BELOW
FOYER BELOW
BONUS
11/10 X 13/4
BR. 3
11/0 X 14/8
BR. 2
10/0 X 12/2

First Floor	1,586 sq. ft.
Second Floor	960 sq. ft.
Total Living Area	2,546 sq. ft.
Bonus Room	+194 sq. ft.

PRICE CODE: C

PLAN NP1213

36'-0"
38'-0"
BEDROOM 12'-10" x 11'
BEDROOM 12'-10" x 11'
HALL
B.
BATH
MASTER BEDROOM 15'-11" x 17'-7"
walk in closet
BEDROOM 13'-3" x 13'-4"
SECOND FLOOR

Scarborough

Features

- Victorian charm inside and out.
- Elegant covered front porch provides entry to either the main foyer or the mud room.
- One chimney serves cozy back-to-back fireplaces in the living room and family room.
- Sliding door in breakfast area opens .to patio.
- Large master bedroom with private bath and three bedrooms with full bath upstairs.

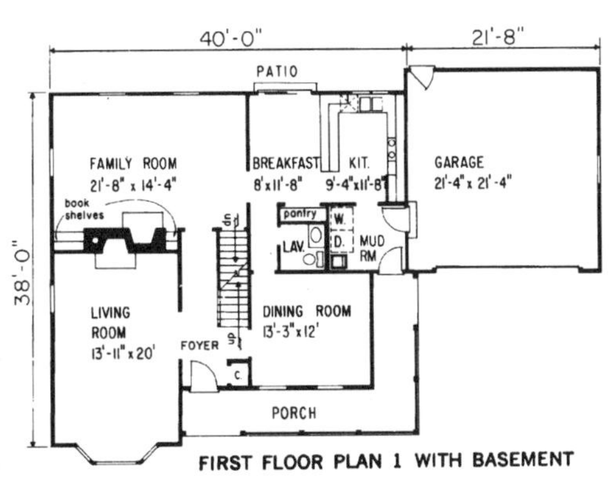

40'-0"
21'-8"
38'-0"
PATIO
FAMILY ROOM 21'-8" x 14'-4"
book shelves
BREAKFAST 8'x11'-8"
KIT. 9'-4"x11'-8"
GARAGE 21'-4" x 21'-4"
pantry
LAV
W.
D.
MUD RM
LIVING ROOM 13'-11" x 20'
FOYER
DINING ROOM 13'-3" x 12'
PORCH
FIRST FLOOR PLAN 1 WITH BASEMENT

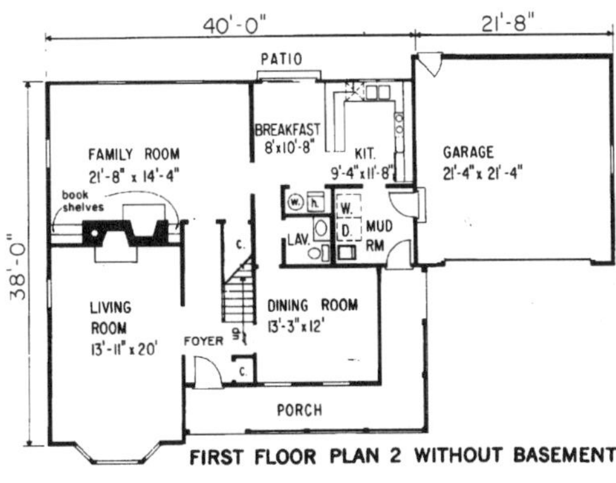

40'-0"
21'-8"
38'-0"
PATIO
FAMILY ROOM 21'-8" x 14'-4"
book shelves
BREAKFAST 8'x10'-8"
KIT. 9'-4"x11'-8"
GARAGE 21'-4" x 21'-4"
LAV.
W.
D.
MUD RM
LIVING ROOM 13'-11" x 20'
FOYER
DINING ROOM 13'-3" x 12'
PORCH
FIRST FLOOR PLAN 2 WITHOUT BASEMENT

First Floor	1,333 sq. ft.
Second Floor	1,221 sq. ft.
Total Living Area	2,554 sq. ft.

PRICE CODE: C

PLAN DB1670

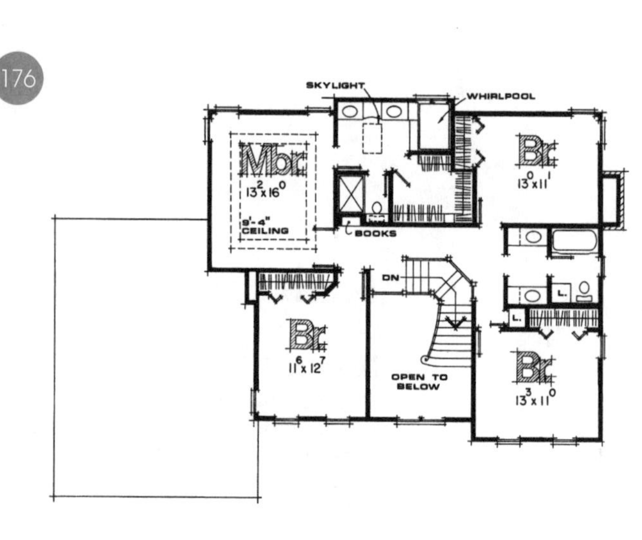

SKYLIGHT
WHIRLPOOL
Mbr.
13^{2}x16^{0}
9'-4" CEILING
BOOKS
Br.
13^{0}x11^{1}
DN
Br.
11^{6}x12^{7}
OPEN TO BELOW
Br.
13^{3}x11^{0}

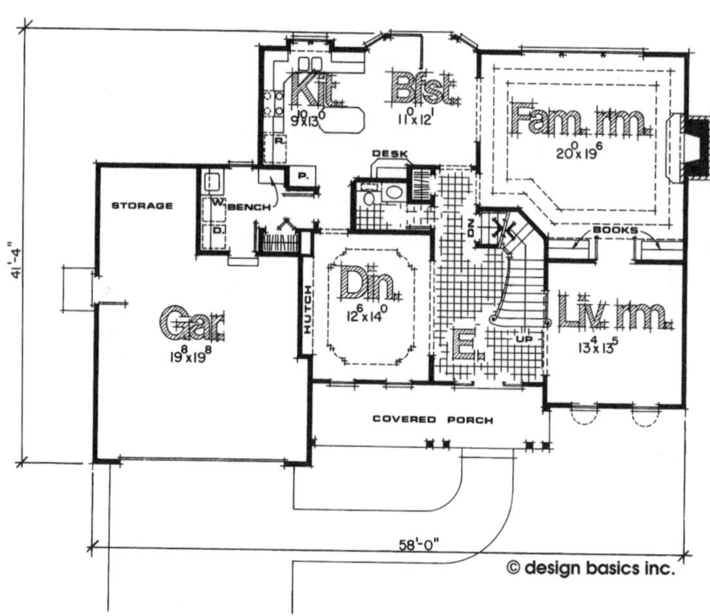

Kit.
9^{10}x13^{0}
Bfst.
11^{0}x12^{1}
Fam. rm.
20^{0}x19^{6}
DESK
P.
R.
W.
D.
BENCH
STORAGE
Gar.
19^{8}x19^{8}
HUTCH
Din.
12^{6}x14^{0}
DN
BOOKS
E
UP
Liv. rm.
13^{4}x13^{5}
COVERED PORCH
41'-4"
58'-0"
© design basics inc.

Features

- Covered front porch.
- 9-foot main level walls.
- Formal rooms flank 2-story entry with flared staircase.
- French doors connect formal and informal areas for expanded entertaining.
- Large family room with tiered ceiling, fireplace and bookcases.
- Bayed dinette adjoins kitchen with pantry and planning desk.
- Garage with extra storage accesses home through laundry/mud room with bench.
- Compartmented bath with separate vanities located for convenience to secondary bedrooms.
- Double doors lead to master suite with skylight, walk-in closet and whirlpool bath.

First Floor	1,386 sq. ft.
Second Floor	1,171 sq. ft.
Total Living Area	2,557 sq. ft.

PRICE CODE: D

PLAN AM2267G

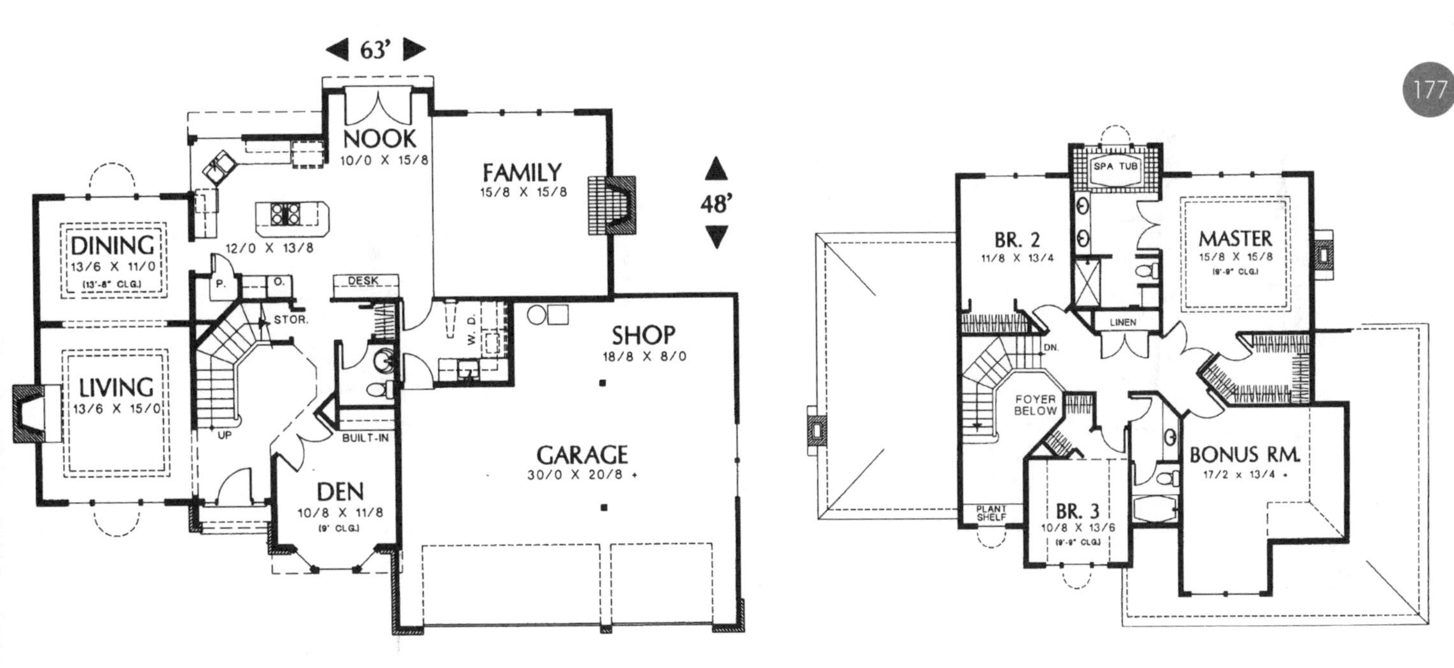

63'
48'
NOOK
10/0 X 15/8
FAMILY
15/8 X 15/8
DINING
13/6 X 11/0
(13'-8" CLG.)
12/0 X 13/8
P.
O.
DESK
STOR.
W. D.
LIVING
13/6 X 15/0
UP
BUILT-IN
DEN
10/8 X 11/8
(9' CLG.)
SHOP
18/8 X 8/0
GARAGE
30/0 X 20/8 +
SPA TUB
BR. 2
11/8 X 13/4
MASTER
15/8 X 15/8
(9'-8" CLG.)
LINEN
DN.
FOYER
BELOW
BONUS RM.
17/2 x 13/4 +
PLANT
SHELF
BR. 3
10/8 X 13/6
(9'-8" CLG.)

First Floor	1,465 sq. ft.
Second Floor	1,103 sq. ft.
Total Living Area	2,568 sq. ft.
Bonus Room	+303 sq. ft.

PRICE CODE: C

PLAN NP1427

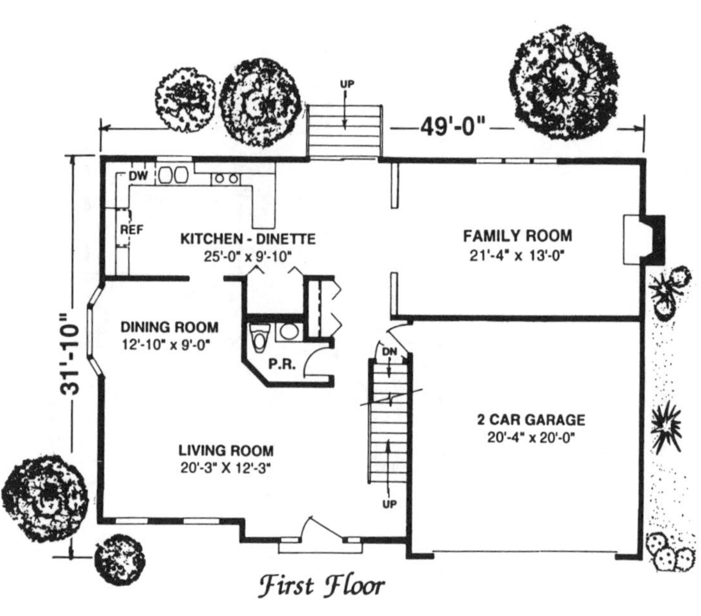
UP
49'-0"
DW
REF
KITCHEN - DINETTE
25'-0" x 9'-10"
FAMILY ROOM
21'-4" x 13'-0"
DINING ROOM
12'-10" x 9'-0"
P.R.
DN
31'-10"
LIVING ROOM
20'-3" X 12'-3"
2 CAR GARAGE
20'-4" x 20'-0"
UP

First Floor

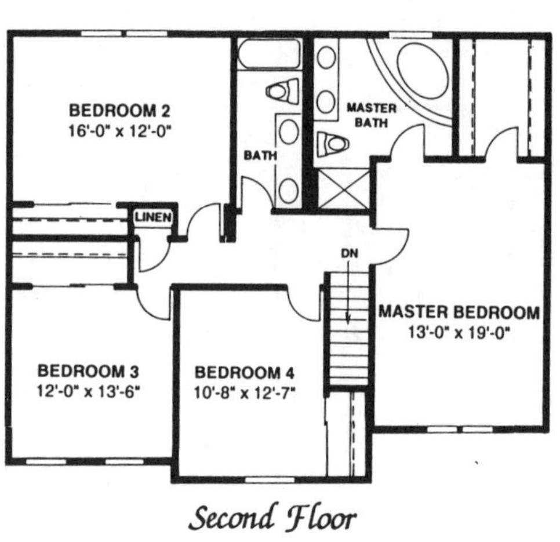
BEDROOM 2
16'-0" x 12'-0"
BATH
MASTER BATH
LINEN
DN
MASTER BEDROOM
13'-0" x 19'-0"
BEDROOM 3
12'-0" x 13'-6"
BEDROOM 4
10'-8" x 12'-7"

Second Floor

First Floor	1,168 sq. ft.
Second Floor	1,418 sq. ft.
Total Living Area	2,586 sq. ft.

PRICE CODE: C

PLAN NP1426

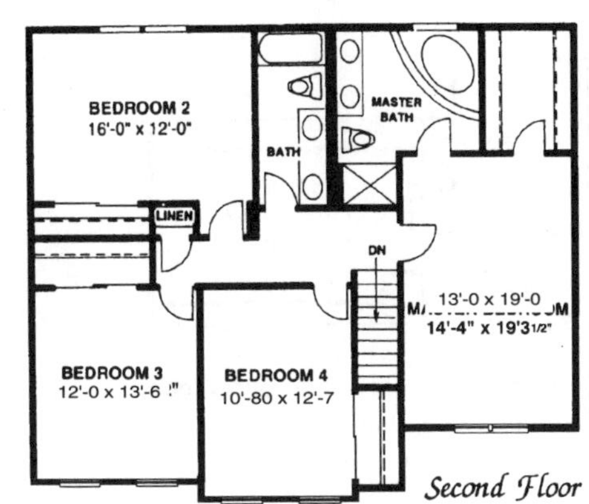
BEDROOM 2
16'-0" x 12'-0"
BATH
MASTER BATH
LINEN
DN
13'-0 x 19'-0
M/... ...M
14'-4" x 19'3 1/2"
BEDROOM 3
12'-0 x 13'-6 "
BEDROOM 4
10'-80 x 12'-7

Second Floor

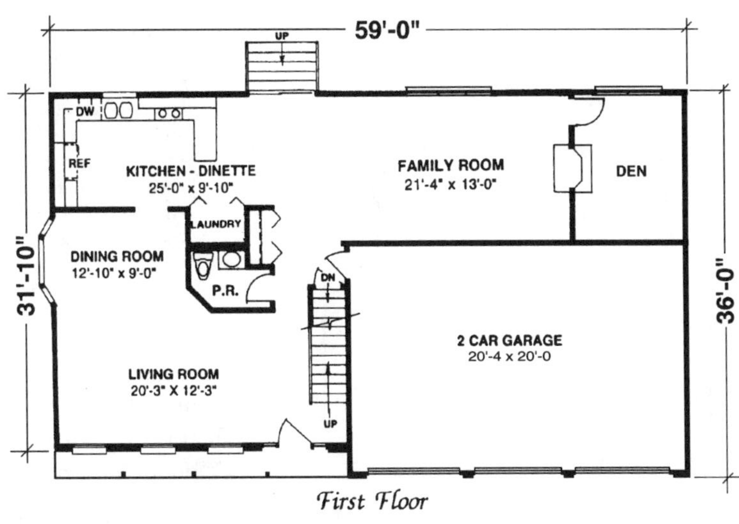
59'-0"
UP
DW
REF
KITCHEN - DINETTE
25'-0" x 9'-10"
FAMILY ROOM
21'-4" x 13'-0"
DEN
LAUNDRY
DINING ROOM
12'-10" x 9'-0"
P.R.
DN
31'-10"
36'-0"
2 CAR GARAGE
20'-4 x 20'-0
LIVING ROOM
20'-3" X 12'-3"
UP

First Floor

First Floor	1,192 sq. ft.
Second Floor	1,410 sq. ft.
Total Living Area	2,602 sq. ft.

PRICE CODE: C

PLAN NP1079

180

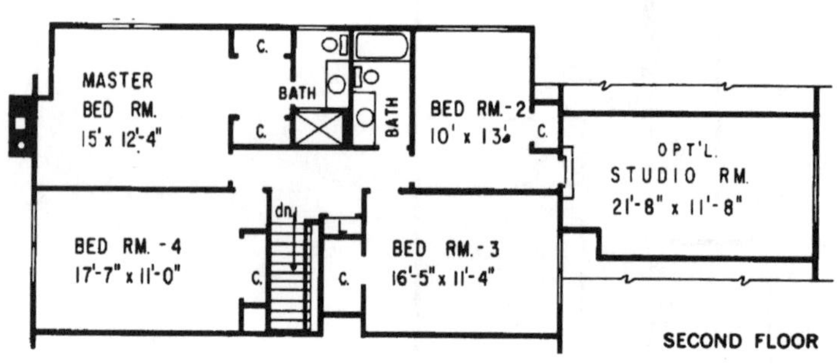
MASTER
BED RM.
15' x 12'-4"
C.
C.
BATH
BATH
BED RM.-2
10' x 13'6
C.
OPT'L.
STUDIO RM.
21'-8" x 11'-8"
BED RM. - 4
17'-7" x 11'-0"
C.
dn
C.
BED RM. - 3
16'-5" x 11'-4"
SECOND FLOOR

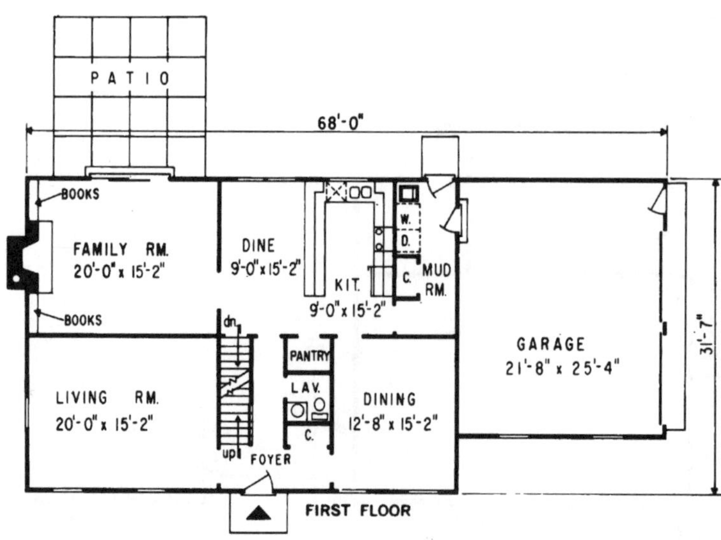
PATIO
68'-0"
BOOKS
FAMILY RM.
20'-0" x 15'-2"
BOOKS
DINE
9'-0" x 15'-2"
KIT.
9'-0" x 15'-2"
W.
D.
C.
MUD
RM.
GARAGE
21'-8" x 25'-4"
31'-7"
dn
PANTRY
LAV.
C.
LIVING RM.
20'-0" x 15'-2"
DINING
12'-8" x 15'-2"
up
FOYER
FIRST FLOOR

Country Grace

Features

- Family living was built-in to this delightful home.
- Features like a pantry off the kitchen and a mud room/laundry room off the garage highlight convenience for a busy family.
- The family room, with large fireplace, opens to a patio.
- The foyer opens to a large living room perfect for either entertaining or relaxing.
- Second-floor features three bedrooms with full bath and a master bedroom with two closets and private lavatory with shower.
- An optional studio room over the garage is available.

First Floor	1,452 sq. ft.
Second Floor	1,158 sq. ft.
Total Living Area	2,610 sq. ft.
Optional Studio	+264 sq. ft.

PRICE CODE: C

PLAN NP1425

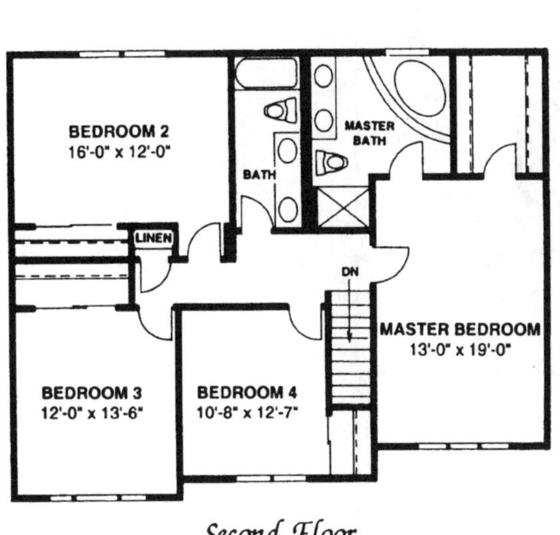
BEDROOM 2
16'-0" x 12'-0"
BATH
MASTER BATH
LINEN
DN
MASTER BEDROOM
13'-0" x 19'-0"
BEDROOM 3
12'-0" x 13'-6"
BEDROOM 4
10'-8" x 12'-7"

Second Floor

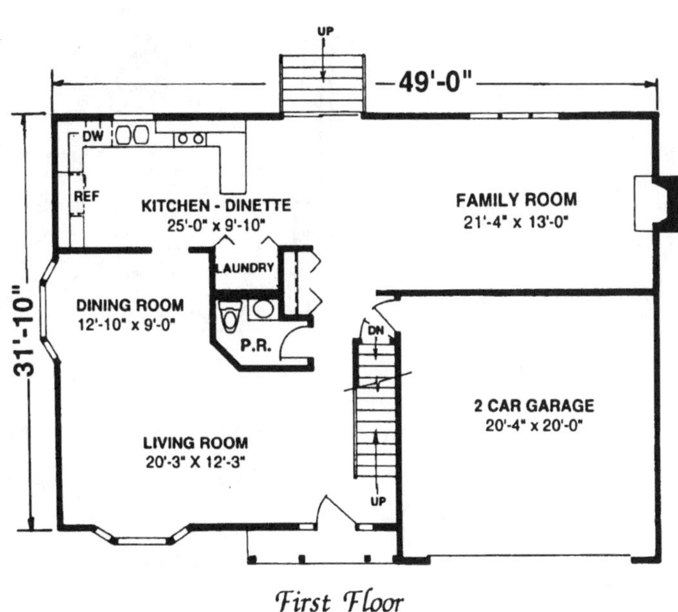
UP
49'-0"
31'-10"
DW
REF
KITCHEN - DINETTE
25'-0" x 9'-10"
FAMILY ROOM
21'-4" x 13'-0"
LAUNDRY
DINING ROOM
12'-10" x 9'-0"
P.R.
DN
2 CAR GARAGE
20'-4" x 20'-0"
LIVING ROOM
20'-3" X 12'-3"
UP

First Floor

Sunnyview

Features

- Handsome two-story design perfect for the growing family.
- Attractive porch entrance opens directly into a large family room with adjoining dining room.
- Dining room features an elegant bay window.
- Large family room with fireplace perfect for family activities.
- Upstairs, a large master bedroom with spacious walk-in closet and deluxe, dual- vanity bath with step-up tub and separate shower.
- Three additional spacious bedrooms share a full bath with dual-vanity.

First Floor	1,192 sq. ft.
Second Floor	1,425 sq. ft.
Total Living Area	2,617 sq. ft.

PRICE CODE: C

PLAN FD8037-LA

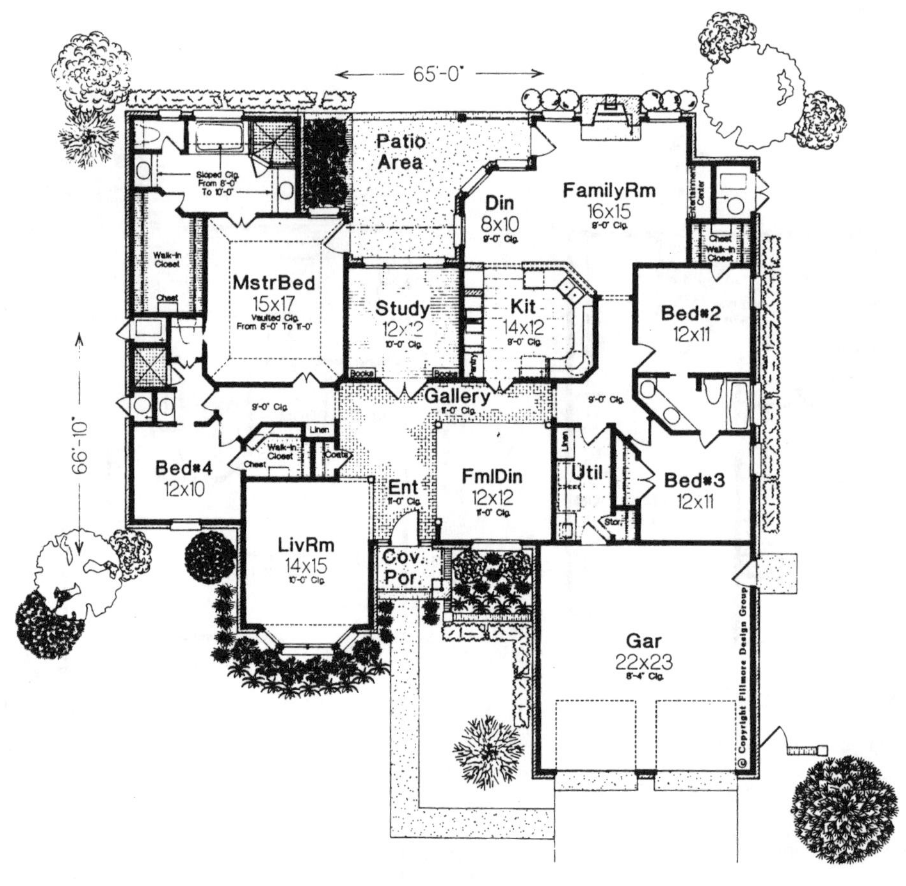

65'-0"
66'-10"
Patio Area
FamilyRm 16x15
Din 8x10
MstrBed 15x17
Study 12x12
Kit 14x12
Bed#2 12x11
Gallery
Bed#4 12x10
Ent
FmlDin 12x12
Util
Bed#3 12x11
LivRm 14x15
Cov. Por.
Gar 22x23

Total Living Area 2,626 sq. ft.

PRICE CODE: C

CUSTOMIZE IT!

PLAN AM1201

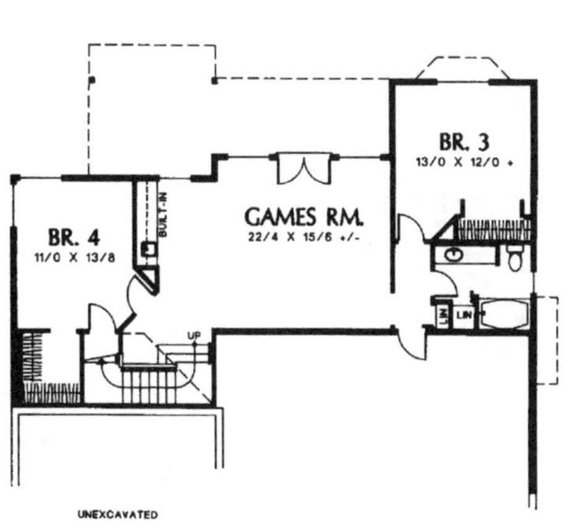
BR. 3
13/0 X 12/0 +
GAMES RM.
22/4 X 15/6 +/-
BR. 4
11/0 X 13/8
BUILT-IN
UP
LIN
UNEXCAVATED

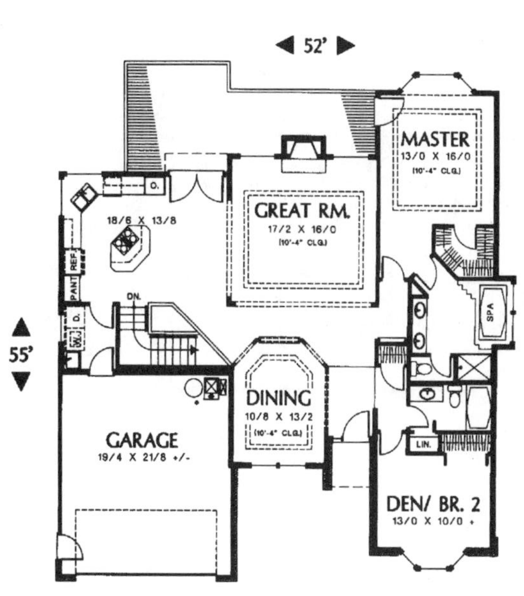
52'
55'
MASTER
13/0 X 16/0
(10'-4" CLG.)
GREAT RM.
17/2 X 16/0
(10'-4" CLG.)
18/6 X 13/8
REF
PANT
DN.
SPA
DINING
10/8 X 13/2
(10'-4" CLG.)
GARAGE
19/4 X 21/8 +/-
LIN.
DEN/ BR. 2
13/0 X 10/0 +

Lower Floor	1,012 sq. ft.
First Floor	1,644 sq. ft.
Total Living Area	2,656 sq. ft.

PRICE CODE: C

PLAN NP1072

184

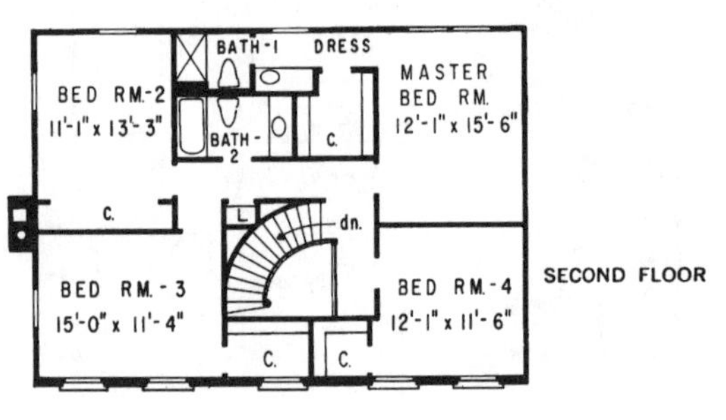
BATH-1
DRESS
BED RM.-2
11'-1" x 13'-3"
MASTER
BED RM.
12'-1" x 15'-6"
BATH-2
C.
C.
dn.
BED RM.-3
15'-0" x 11'-4"
BED RM.-4
12'-1" x 11'-6"
C.
C.

SECOND FLOOR

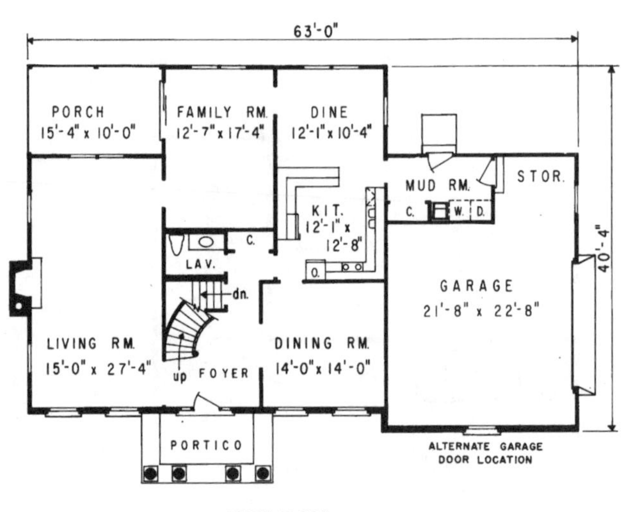
63'-0"
PORCH
15'-4" x 10'-0"
FAMILY RM.
12'-7" x 17'-4"
DINE
12'-1" x 10'-4"
MUD RM.
STOR.
C.
W.
D.
KIT.
12'-1" x
12'-8"
O.
C.
LAV.
dn.
GARAGE
21'-8" x 22'-8"
40'-4"
LIVING RM.
15'-0" x 27'-4"
up
FOYER
DINING RM.
14'-0" x 14'-0"
PORTICO
ALTERNATE GARAGE
DOOR LOCATION

FIRST FLOOR

First Floor	1,514 sq. ft.
Second Floor	1,164 sq. ft.
Total Living Area	2,678 sq. ft.

PRICE CODE: C

PLAN AM2282

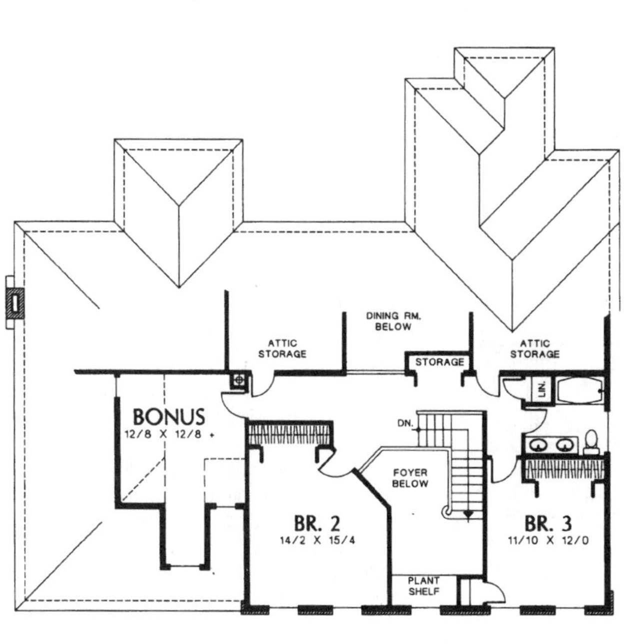

ATTIC STORAGE
DINING RM. BELOW
STORAGE
ATTIC STORAGE
LIN.
BONUS
12/8 X 12/8 +
DN.
FOYER BELOW
BR. 2
14/2 X 15/4
BR. 3
11/10 X 12/0
PLANT SHELF

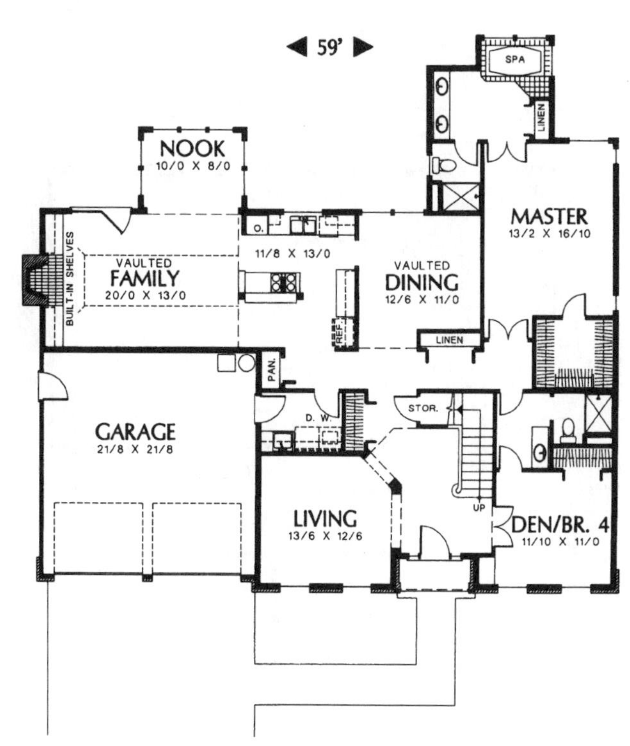

59'
SPA
LINEN
NOOK
10/0 X 8/0
MASTER
13/2 X 16/10
11/8 X 13/0
BUILT-IN SHELVES
VAULTED
FAMILY
20/0 X 13/0
VAULTED
DINING
12/6 X 11/0
REF.
LINEN
PAN.
GARAGE
21/8 X 21/8
D. W.
STOR.
LIVING
13/6 X 12/6
UP
DEN/BR. 4
11/10 X 11/0
54'

First Floor	1,992 sq. ft.
Second Floor	703 sq. ft.
Total Living Area	2,695 sq. ft.
Bonus Room	+208 sq. ft.

PRICE CODE: C

PLAN NP1243

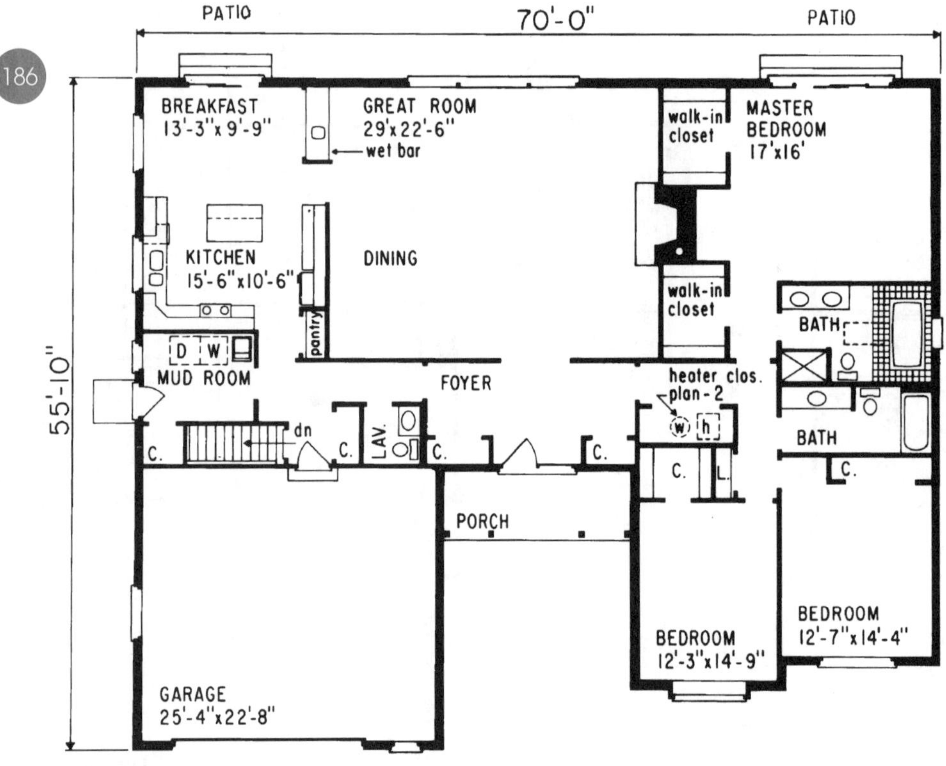
PATIO
70'-0"
PATIO
55'-10"
BREAKFAST
13'-3"x 9'-9"
GREAT ROOM
29'x 22'-6"
wet bar
walk-in closet
MASTER BEDROOM
17'x16'
KITCHEN
15'-6"x10'-6"
DINING
pantry
walk-in closet
BATH
D
W
MUD ROOM
FOYER
heater clos.
plan-2
w
h
dn
C.
C.
LAV.
C.
C.
BATH
C.
L.
C.
PORCH
BEDROOM
12'-7"x 14'-4"
BEDROOM
12'-3"x 14'-9"
GARAGE
25'-4"x 22'-8"

The Vale

Features

- Charming U-shaped home with pleasing proportions.
- Brick veneer creates a striking contrast with stucco and rough-hewn timber gables.
- Covered front porch leads to foyer hall, with great room at rear of home.
- Great room includes wet bar and fireplace on interior wall.
- Breakfast room, with access to patio, open to kitchen with island work center and pantry.
- Right wing contains master bedroom has twin walk-in closets and a full bath.
- Two additional bedrooms share a full bath.

Total Living Area 2,705 sq. ft.

PRICE CODE: C

PLAN AM2206

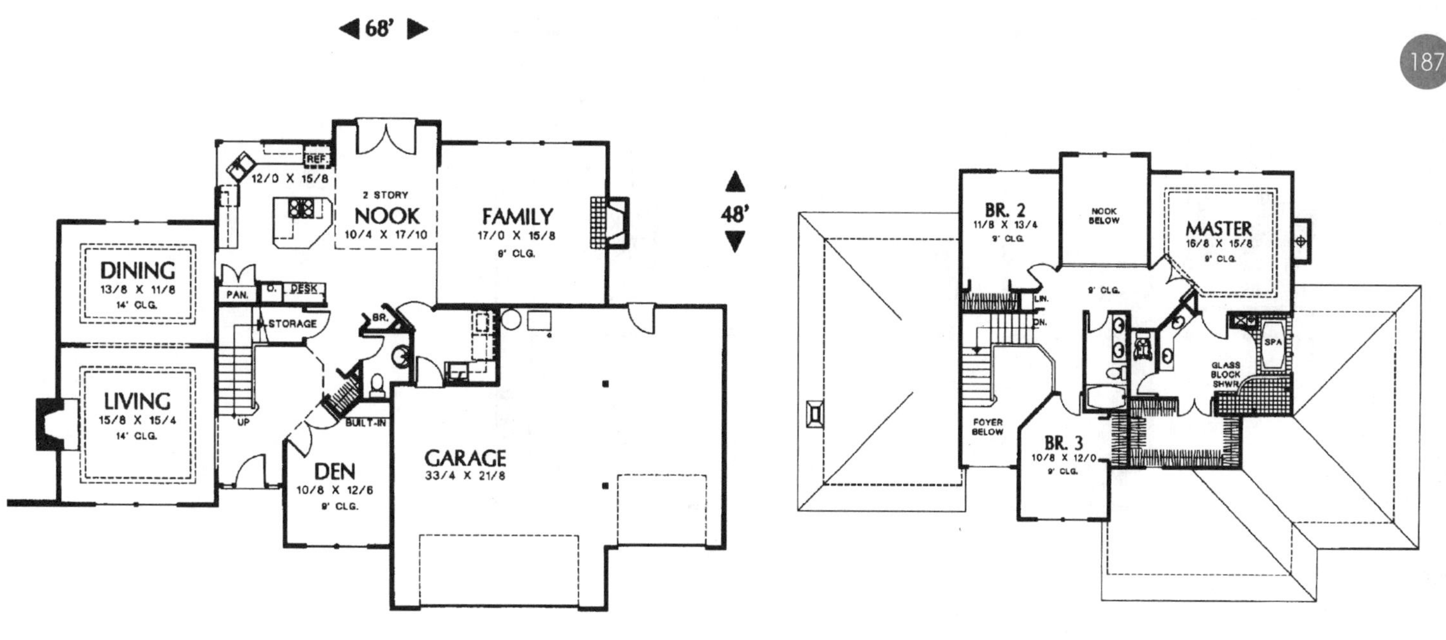
68'
48'
12/0 X 15/8
REF.
2 STORY
NOOK
10/4 X 17/10
FAMILY
17/0 X 15/8
9' CLG.
DINING
13/8 X 11/8
14' CLG.
PAN.
DESK
STORAGE
BR.
LIVING
15/8 X 15/4
14' CLG.
UP
BUILT-IN
DEN
10/8 X 12/6
9' CLG.
GARAGE
33/4 X 21/8
BR. 2
11/8 X 13/4
9' CLG.
NOOK BELOW
MASTER
16/8 X 15/8
9' CLG.
LIN.
SPA
GLASS BLOCK SHWR.
FOYER BELOW
BR. 3
10/8 X 12/0
9' CLG.

First Floor	1,600 sq. ft.
Second Floor	1,123 sq. ft.
Total Living Area	2,723 sq. ft.

PRICE CODE: C

PLAN NPES139

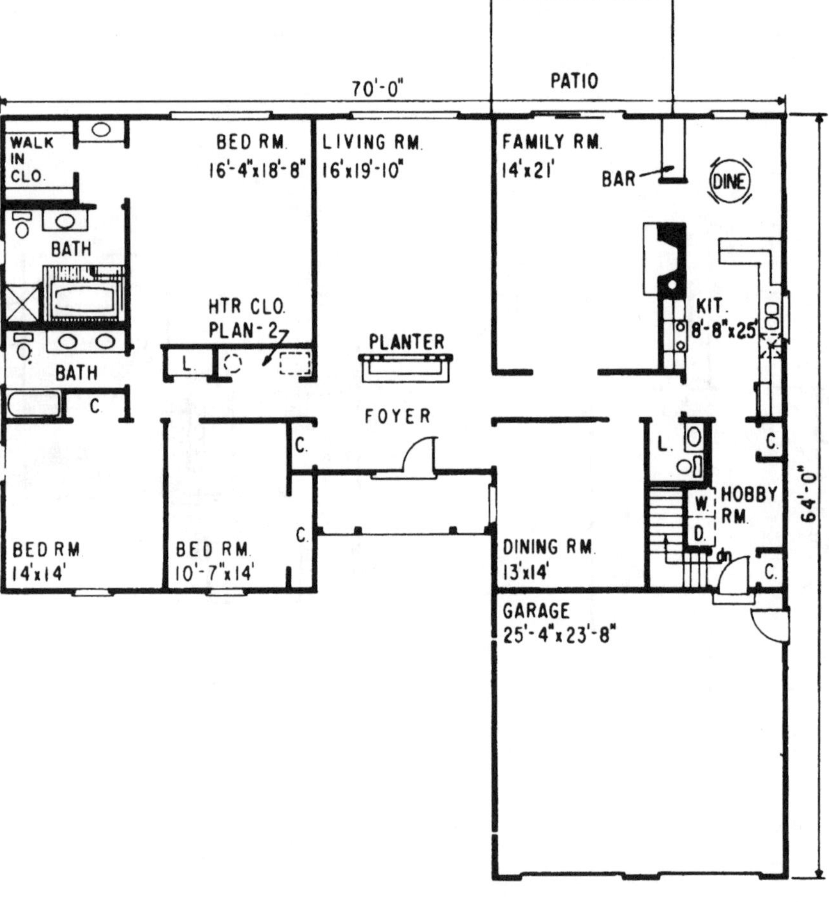

PATIO
70'-0"
WALK IN CLO.
BED RM.
16'-4"x18'-8"
LIVING RM.
16'x19'-10"
FAMILY RM.
14'x21'
BAR
DINE
BATH
HTR CLO.
PLAN-2
KIT.
8'-8"x25'
PLANTER
L.
BATH
C
FOYER
C.
L.
C.
HOBBY RM.
W.
D.
C.
BED RM
14'x14'
BED RM.
10'-7"x14'
DINING RM.
13'x14'
dn
C.
64'-0"
GARAGE
25'-4"x23'-8"

Design A / Frame Construction
Total Living Area 2,640 sq. ft.

Design B / Brick Constuction
Total Living Area 2,729 sq. ft.

PRICE CODE: C

PLAN NP1218

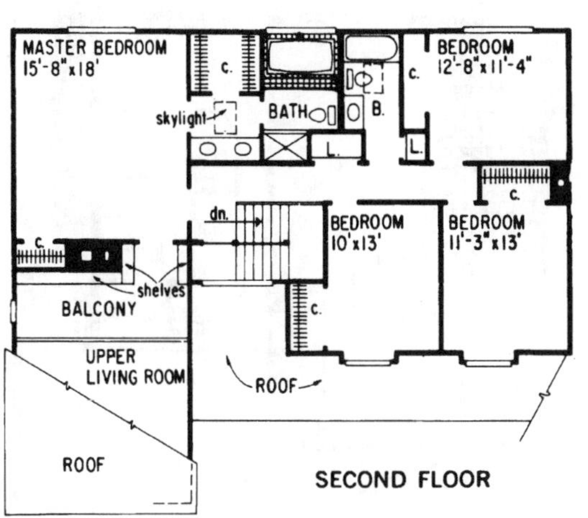

MASTER BEDROOM
15'-8"x18'
c.
skylight
BATH
B.
L.
BEDROOM
12'-8"x11'-4"
c.
L.
dn.
c.
shelves
BALCONY
BEDROOM
10'x13'
BEDROOM
11'-3"x13'
c.
c.
UPPER
LIVING ROOM
ROOF
ROOF

SECOND FLOOR

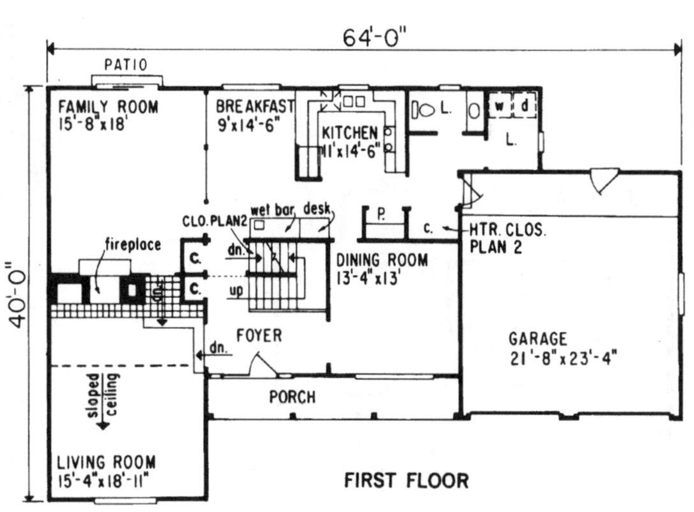

64'-0"
40'-0"
PATIO
FAMILY ROOM
15'-8"x18'
BREAKFAST
9'x14'-6"
KITCHEN
11'x14'-6"
L.
w
d
L.
CLO. PLAN2
wet bar
desk
P.
c.
HTR. CLOS.
PLAN 2
fireplace
C.
C.
dn.
up
dn.
DINING ROOM
13'-4"x13'
FOYER
dn.
GARAGE
21'-8"x23'-4"
sloped ceiling
PORCH
LIVING ROOM
15'-4"x18'-11"

FIRST FLOOR

PLAN 1 WITH BASEMENT

PLAN 2 WITHOUT BASEMENT

Camfry Contemporary

Features

- This attractive, contemporary home was designed for a large family.
- Spacious foyer allows easy traffic flow to all areas of home.
- Sunken living room with sloped ceiling leads to second-floor balcony library.
- Spacious kitchen with abundant counter space includes pantry, wet bar, and desk.
- Second-floor master bedroom suite features a dressing area, walk-in closet, and deluxe bath with skylight.
- Three additional bedrooms share a full bath.

First Floor	1,432 sq. ft.
Second Floor	1,319 sq. ft.
Total Living Area	2,751 sq. ft.

PRICE CODE: C

PLAN NP1259

190

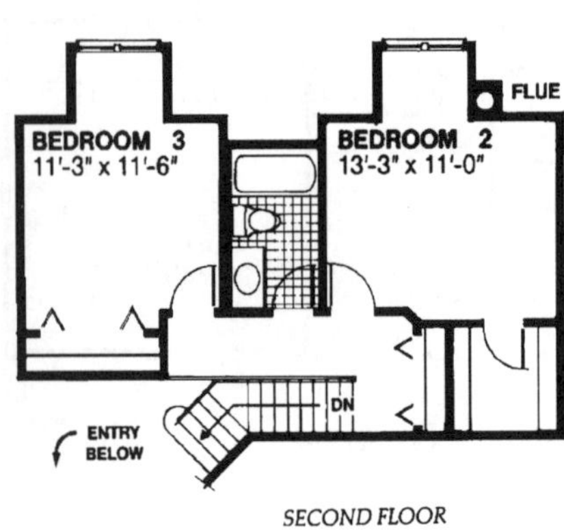

BEDROOM 3
11'-3" x 11'-6"
BEDROOM 2
13'-3" x 11'-0"
FLUE
DN
ENTRY BELOW

SECOND FLOOR

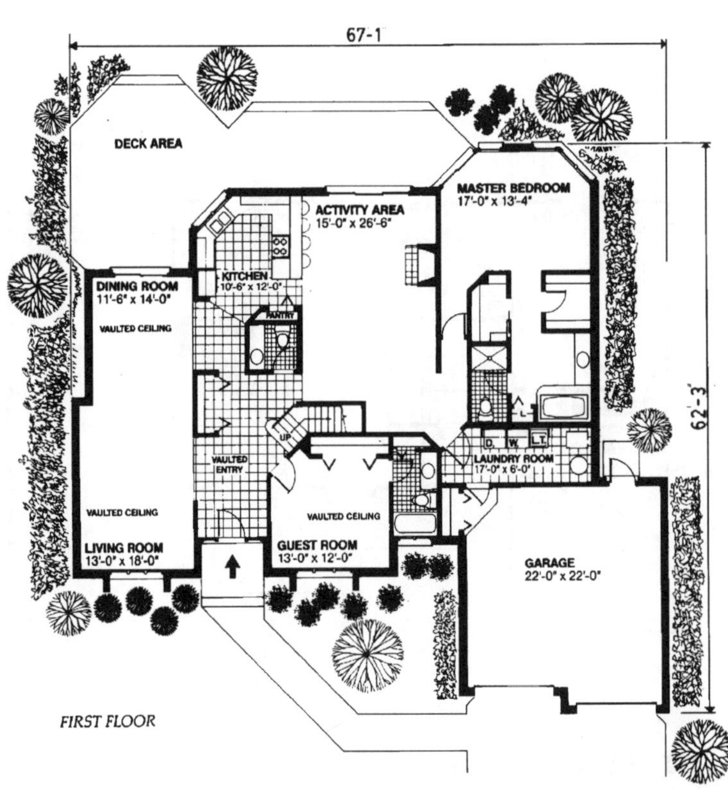

67-1
62'-3'
DECK AREA
MASTER BEDROOM
17'-0" x 13'-4"
ACTIVITY AREA
15'-0" x 26'-6"
DINING ROOM
11'-6" x 14'-0"
VAULTED CEILING
KITCHEN
10'-6" x 12'-0"
PANTRY
UP
VAULTED ENTRY
LAUNDRY ROOM
17'-0" x 6'-0"
VAULTED CEILING
VAULTED CEILING
LIVING ROOM
13'-0" x 18'-0"
GUEST ROOM
13'-0" x 12'-0"
GARAGE
22'-0" x 22'-0"

FIRST FLOOR

Homelight Estate

Features

- Brick and exposed wooden beams offer the joy of outdoor living indoors.
- A front guest room features vaulted ceiling and private bath.
- Centrally located activity room with fireplace.
- Master bedroom suite includes spa, separate shower, and access to rear deck.
- Second floor includes two additional bedrooms and a full bath.

First Floor	2,215 sq. ft.
Second Floor	542 sq. ft.
Total Living Area	2,757 sq. ft.

PRICE CODE: C

PLAN NP1208

191

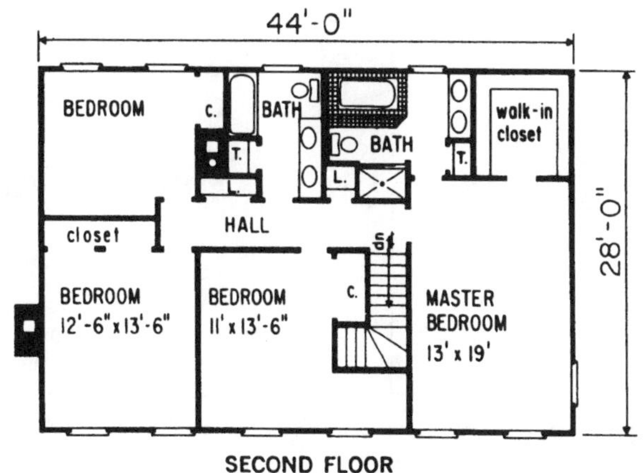
44'-0"
28'-0"
BEDROOM
C.
BATH
BATH
T.
L.
walk-in closet
HALL
closet
BEDROOM 12'-6" x 13'-6"
BEDROOM 11' x 13'-6"
C.
MASTER BEDROOM 13' x 19'
dn
SECOND FLOOR

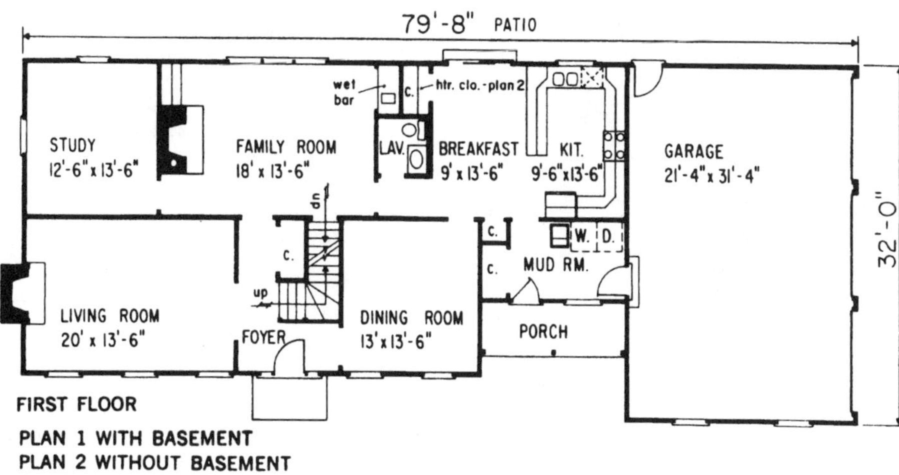
79'-8"
PATIO
32'-0"
wet bar
C.
htr. clo.-plan 2
STUDY 12'-6" x 13'-6"
FAMILY ROOM 18' x 13'-6"
LAV.
BREAKFAST 9' x 13'-6"
KIT. 9'-6" x 13'-6"
GARAGE 21'-4" x 31'-4"
dn
C.
C.
W.
D.
C.
MUD RM.
up
LIVING ROOM 20' x 13'-6"
FOYER
DINING ROOM 13' x 13'-6"
PORCH
FIRST FLOOR
PLAN 1 WITH BASEMENT
PLAN 2 WITHOUT BASEMENT

Colonial Bourne

Features

- Elegance and versatility in a classic, Colonial design.
- Two entrances grace the front of this home, a formal foyer and a porch entrance to the mud room.
- Large living room with fireplace.
- Family room with fireplace.
- Secluded study for work or relaxation.
- Upstairs, three bedrooms share a full bath with double vanity.
- Master bedroom with large walk-in closet and private bath/shower.
- Executive three-car garage.

First Floor	1,531 sq. ft.
Second Floor	1,232 sq. ft.
Total Living Area	2,763 sq. ft.

PRICE CODE: C

PLAN NP1264

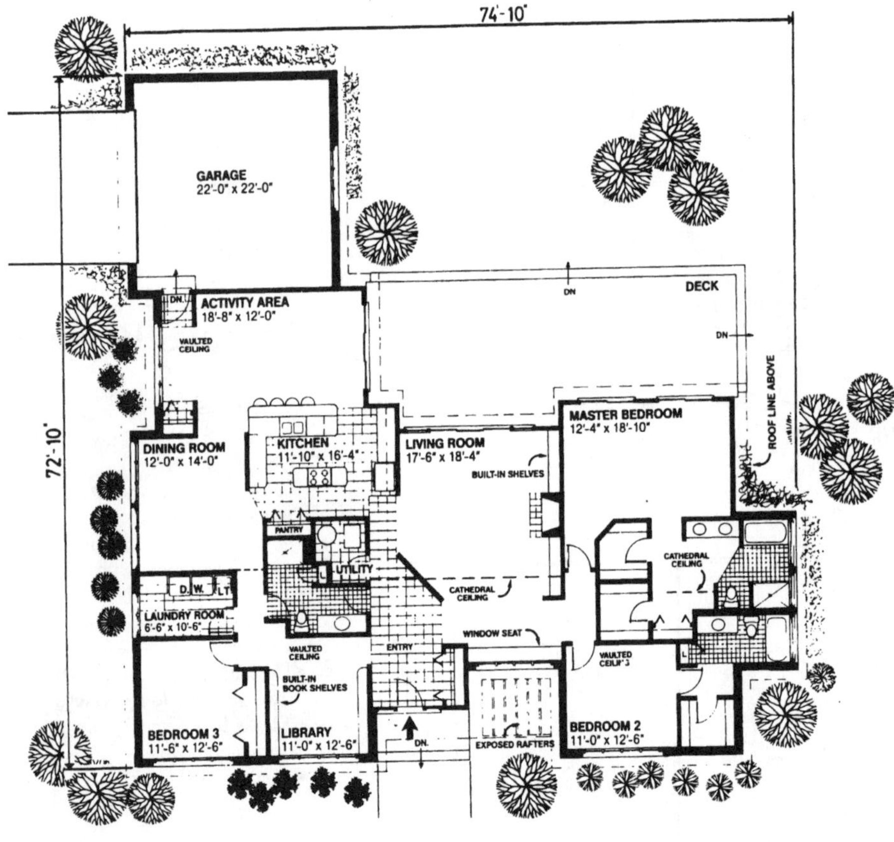
74'-10"
72'-10"
GARAGE
22'-0" x 22'-0"
DECK
DN
ACTIVITY AREA
18'-8" x 12'-0"
VAULTED CEILING
ROOF LINE ABOVE
MASTER BEDROOM
12'-4" x 18'-10"
DINING ROOM
12'-0" x 14'-0"
KITCHEN
11'-10" x 16'-4"
LIVING ROOM
17'-6" x 18'-4"
BUILT-IN SHELVES
PANTRY
UTILITY
CATHEDRAL CEILING
D.W.
LT
LAUNDRY ROOM
6'-6" x 10'-6"
VAULTED CEILING
ENTRY
WINDOW SEAT
BUILT-IN BOOK SHELVES
BEDROOM 3
11'-6" x 12'-6"
LIBRARY
11'-0" x 12'-6"
EXPOSED RAFTERS
BEDROOM 2
11'-0" x 12'-6"

Sunlight Views

Features

- Vaulted ceilings accent this one-story contemporary home.
- Foyer leads to living room on the right.
- Living room includes extras such as built-in window seats and book shelves and fireplace.
- Master bedroom at rear of right wing includes cathedral ceilings and large master bath with dressing area and walk-in closets.
- Second bedroom at right, front has walk-in closets and private bath.
- Third bedroom located in left wing with access to full bath is adjacent to the library with built-in shelving.
- Centrally located kitchen includes cooking island, pantry, and snack bar that opens to adjacent activity area.

Total Living Area 2,773 sq. ft.

PRICE CODE: C

PLAN SH91-2782

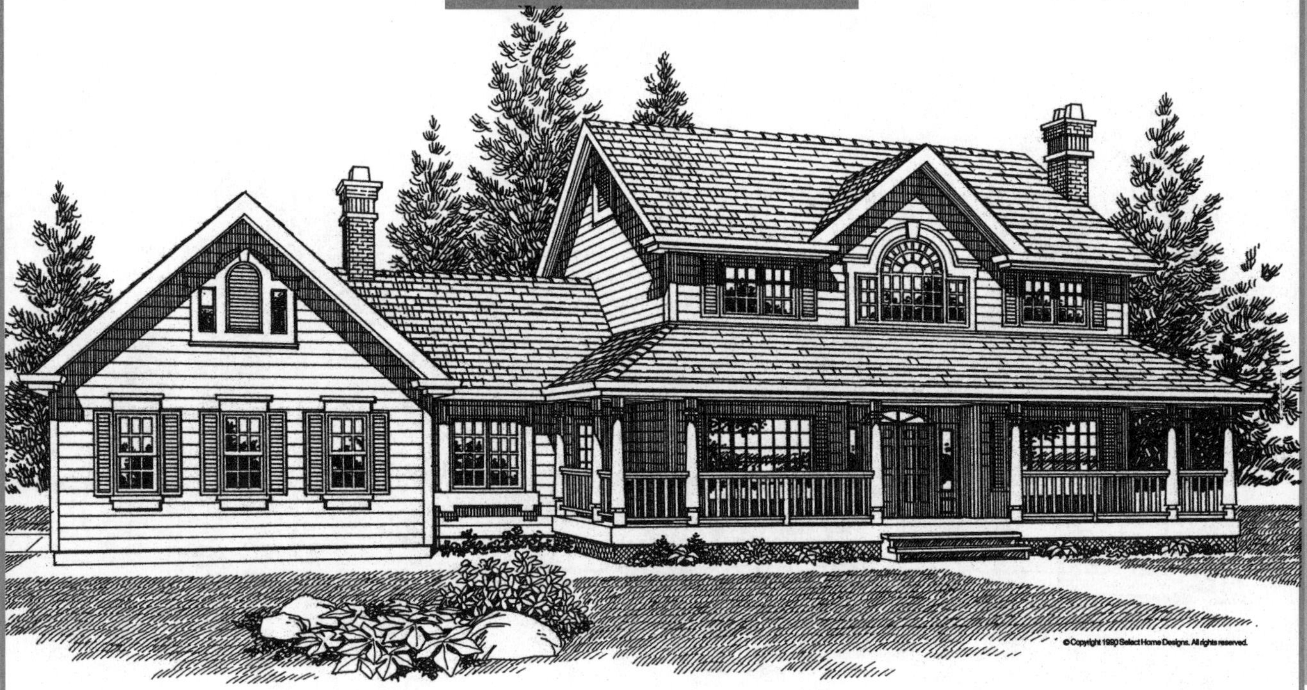

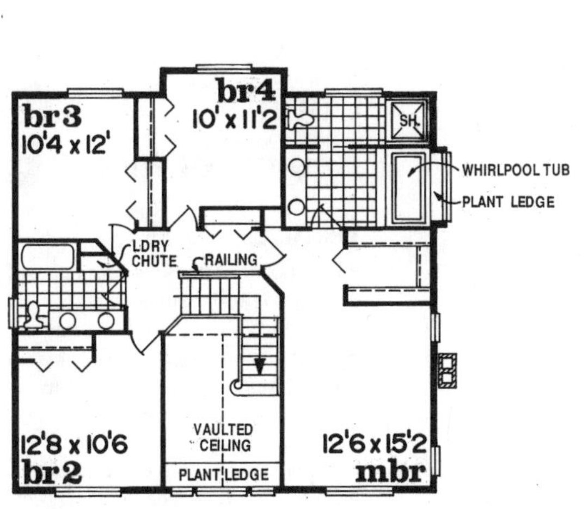
br3
10'4 x 12'
br4
10' x 11'2
SH
WHIRLPOOL TUB
PLANT LEDGE
LDRY CHUTE
RAILING
VAULTED CEILING
PLANT LEDGE
12'8 x 10'6
br2
12'6 x 15'2
mbr

second level 1160 sq. ft.

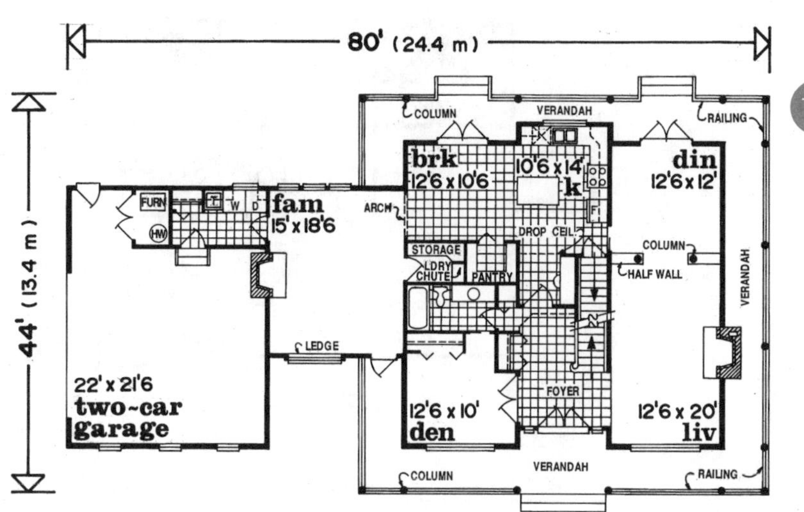
80' (24.4 m)
44' (13.4 m)
COLUMN
VERANDAH
RAILING
brk
12'6 x 10'6
10'6 x 14'
k
din
12'6 x 12'
FURN
HW
W
D
fam
15' x 18'6
ARCH
DROP CEIL
STORAGE
LDRY CHUTE
PANTRY
COLUMN
HALF WALL
VERANDAH
LEDGE
22' x 21'6
two~car garage
12'6 x 10'
den
FOYER
12'6 x 20'
liv
COLUMN
VERANDAH
RAILING

first level 1622 sq.ft.
9' CEILINGS

Features

- Grand farmhouse suits a growing family.
- Living and dining room is visually divided by half walls with decorative columns.
- Country kitchen extends to a spacious family room for informal gatherings around the fireplace.
- Master bedroom hosts a walk-in closet and divided ensuite with a whirlpool tub and twin vanity.
- Plan includes a basement and crawlspace foundation.

Total Living Area: 2,782 sq. ft.

PRICE CODE: C

PLAN NP1219

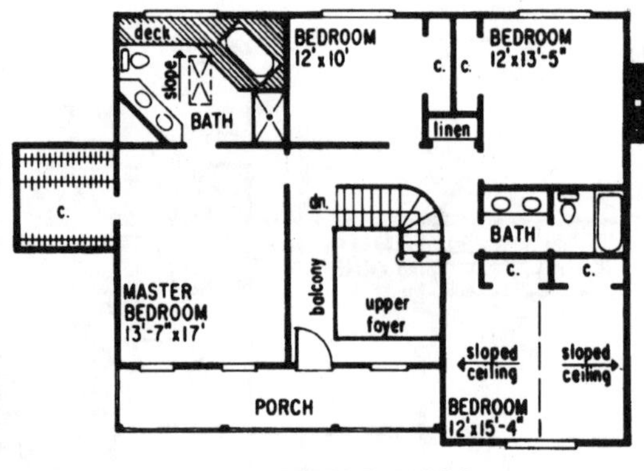
deck
BEDROOM
12'x10'
BEDROOM
12'x13'-5"
slope
BATH
c.
c.
linen
c.
dn.
BATH
c.
c.
MASTER
BEDROOM
13'-7"x17'
balcony
upper
foyer
sloped
ceiling
sloped
ceiling
PORCH
BEDROOM
12'x15'-4"

SECOND FLOOR

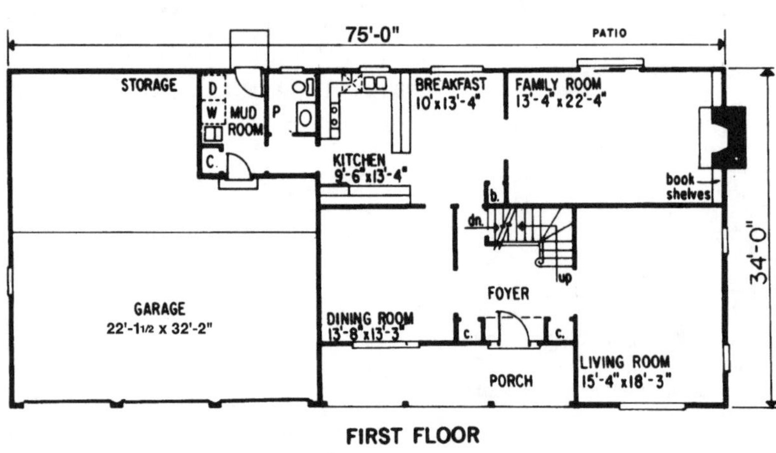
75'-0"
PATIO
STORAGE
D
W
MUD
ROOM
P
C.
BREAKFAST
10'x13'-4"
FAMILY ROOM
13'-4"x22'-4"
KITCHEN
9'-6"x13'-4"
book
shelves
b.
dn.
up
34'-0"
FOYER
GARAGE
22'-1 1/2 x 32'-2"
DINING ROOM
13'-8"x13'-3"
c.
c.
PORCH
LIVING ROOM
15'-4"x18'-3"

FIRST FLOOR

Country Remembrance

Features

- Functional porches on both floors of this home add distinction and warmth.
- Central, two-story foyer leads to living room on the right and the dining room on the left.
- A 22-foot long family room with fireplace opens onto the rear patio.
- Country-sized kitchen has adjacent breakfast area.
- Master bedroom with walk-in closet includes a deluxe bath with corner platform tub, angled vanity, and separate shower.
- Front bedroom features a vaulted ceiling and half-circle window.
- Additional bedrooms and full bath upstairs.

First Floor	1,428 sq. ft.
Second Floor	1,369 sq. ft.
Total Living Area	2,797 sq. ft.

PRICE CODE: C

PLAN AM1207

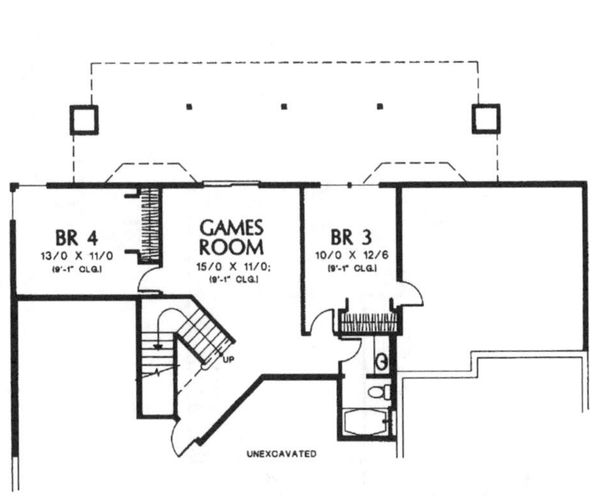

BR 4
13/0 X 11/0
(9'-1" CLG.)
GAMES ROOM
15/0 X 11/0;
(9'-1" CLG.)
BR 3
10/0 X 12/6
(9'-1" CLG.)
UP
UNEXCAVATED

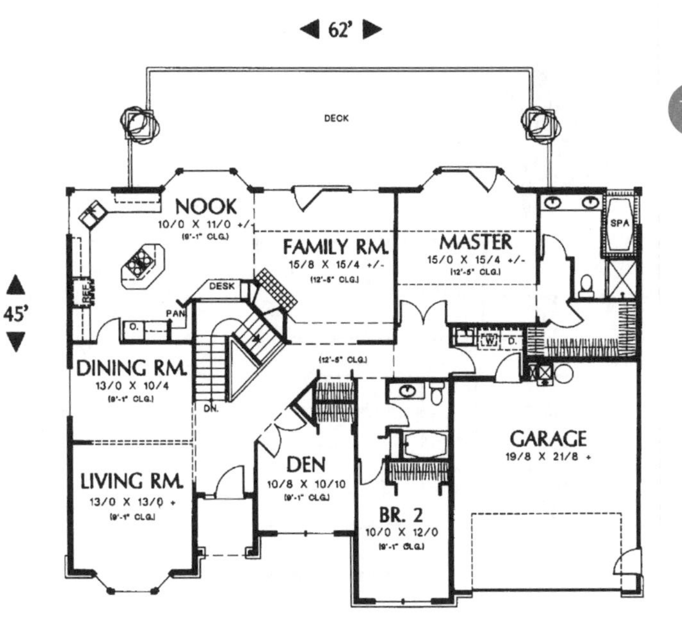

62'
DECK
NOOK
10/0 X 11/0 +/-
(9'-1" CLG.)
FAMILY RM.
15/8 X 15/4 +/-
(12'-5" CLG.)
MASTER
15/0 X 15/4 +/-
(12'-5" CLG.)
SPA
45'
REF.
DESK
PAN
DINING RM.
13/0 X 10/4
(9'-1" CLG.)
DN.
(12'-5" CLG.)
DEN
10/8 X 10/10
(9'-1" CLG.)
LIVING RM.
13/0 X 13/0 +
(9'-1" CLG.)
BR. 2
10/0 X 12/0
(9'-1" CLG.)
GARAGE
19/8 X 21/8 +

Lower Floor	837 sq. ft.
First Floor	1,972 sq. ft.
Total Living Area	2,809 sq. ft

PRICE CODE: C

PLAN MN2845

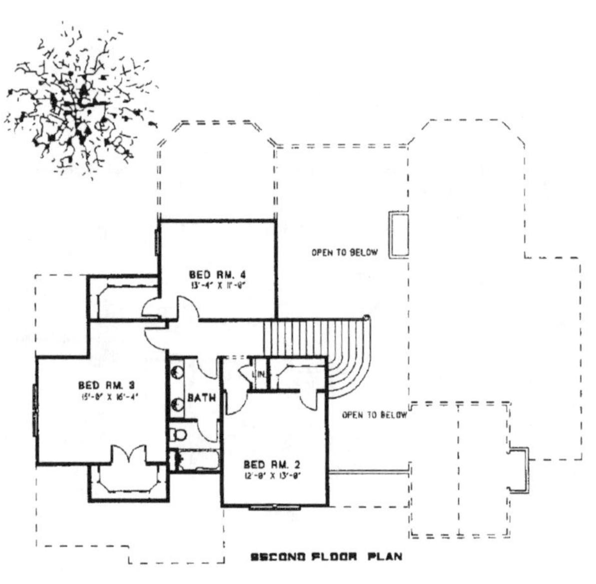

BED RM. 4
OPEN TO BELOW
BED RM. 3
15'-8" X 16'-4"
BATH
LIN
BED RM. 2
12'-8" X 13'-8"
OPEN TO BELOW
SECOND FLOOR PLAN

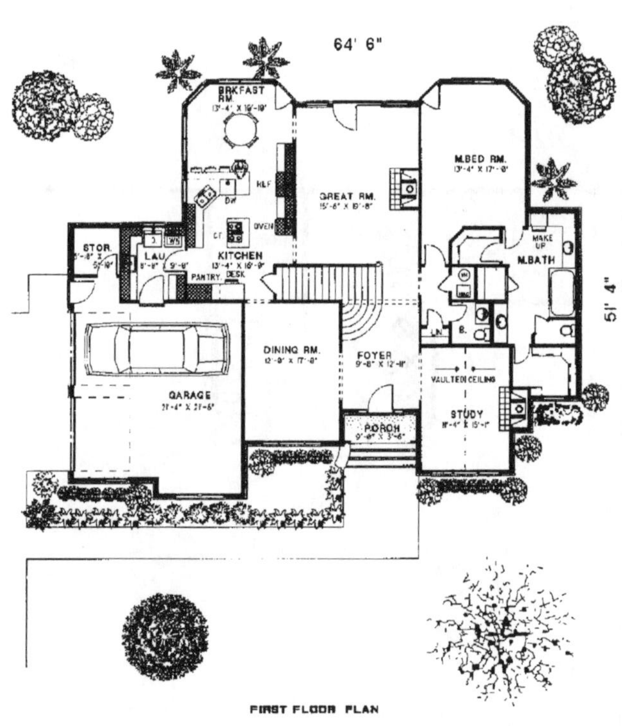

64' 6"
51' 4"
BRKFAST RM.
13'-4" X 16'-10"
REF
DW
OVEN
GREAT RM.
15'-6" X 19'-8"
M.BED RM.
13'-4" X 17'-8"
MAKE UP
M.BATH
STOR.
LAU
KITCHEN
13'-4" X 16'-9"
PANTRY
DESK
LIN
B.
GARAGE
21'-4" X 21'-6"
DINING RM.
12'-8" X 17'-8"
FOYER
9'-8" X 12'-11"
VAULTED CEILING
PORCH
STUDY
FIRST FLOOR PLAN

First Floor	**2,002 sq. ft.**
Second Floor	**843 sq. ft.**
Total Living Area	**2,845 sq. ft.**

PRICE CODE: C

PLAN NP1114

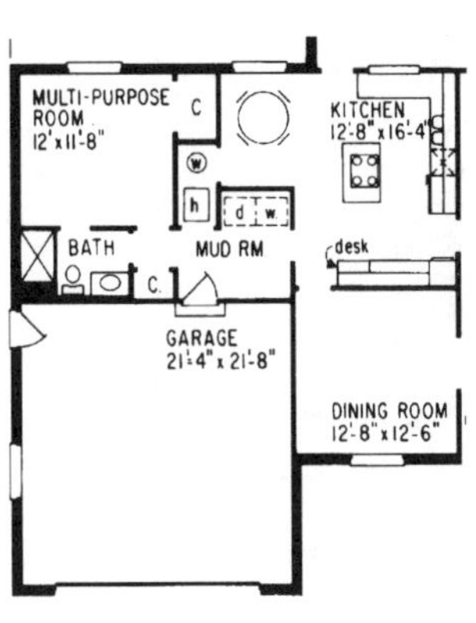
MULTI-PURPOSE ROOM
12'x11'-8"
KITCHEN
12'-8"x16'-4"
BATH
MUD RM
desk
GARAGE
21'-4"x21'-8"
DINING ROOM
12'-8"x12'-6"

PLAN 2 WITHOUT BASEMENT

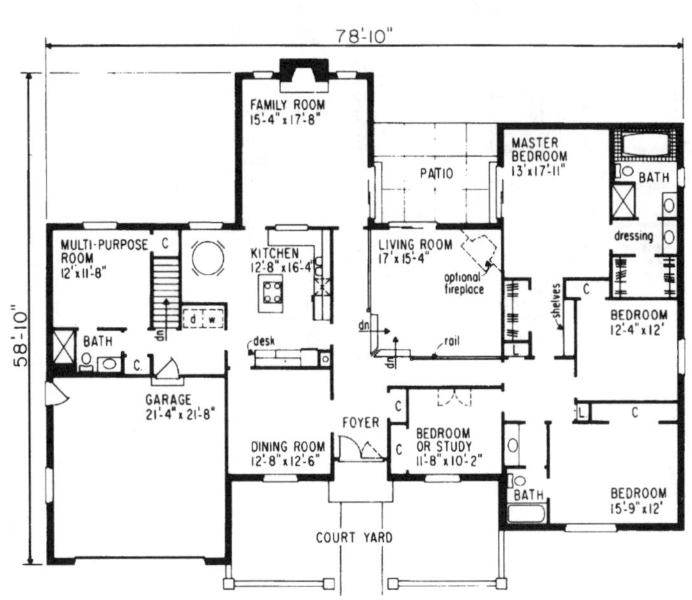
78'-10"
58'-10"
FAMILY ROOM
15'-4"x17'-8"
PATIO
MASTER BEDROOM
13'x17'-11"
BATH
dressing
MULTI-PURPOSE ROOM
12'x11'-8"
KITCHEN
12'-8"x16'-4"
LIVING ROOM
17'x15'-4"
optional fireplace
rail
shelves
BEDROOM
12'-4"x12'
BATH
desk
GARAGE
21'-4"x21'-8"
FOYER
BEDROOM OR STUDY
11'-8"x10'-2"
DINING ROOM
12'-8"x12'-6"
BATH
BEDROOM
15'-9"x12'
COURT YARD

PLAN 1 WITH BASEMENT

Courtyard Manor

Features

- This spacious home features a front courtyard and bell roof that provide an elegant, curbside look.
- L-shaped kitchen with cooking island and breakfast area is adjacent to dining room.
- Family room at rear of home includes fireplace.
- Sunken living room with optional corner fireplace and opening to patio is perfect for entertaining.
- Right wing includes master bedroom with dressing room and full bath.
- Two additional bedrooms served by one full bath round out the right wing

Total Living Area **2,851 sq. ft.**

PRICE CODE: C

PLAN DB2215

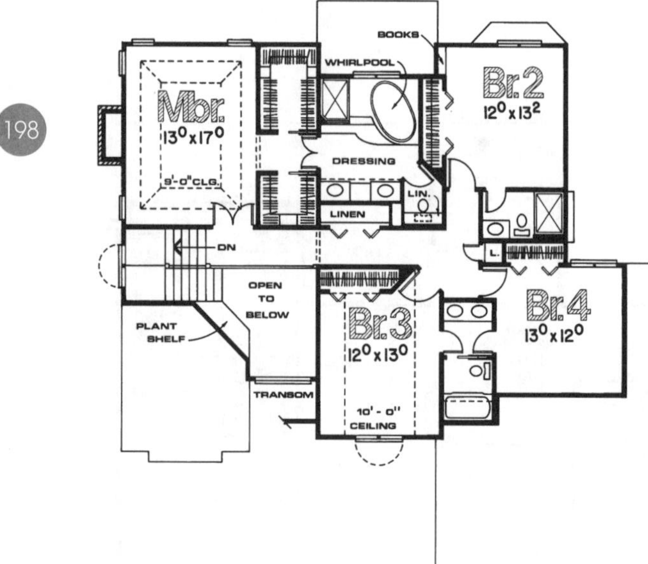

BOOKS
WHIRLPOOL
Mbr.
13^{0} x 17^{0}
9'-0" CLG.
Br. 2
12^{0} x 13^{2}
DRESSING
LIN.
LINEN
DN
OPEN TO BELOW
PLANT SHELF
TRANSOM
L.
Br. 3
12^{0} x 13^{0}
10'-0" CEILING
Br. 4
13^{0} x 12^{0}

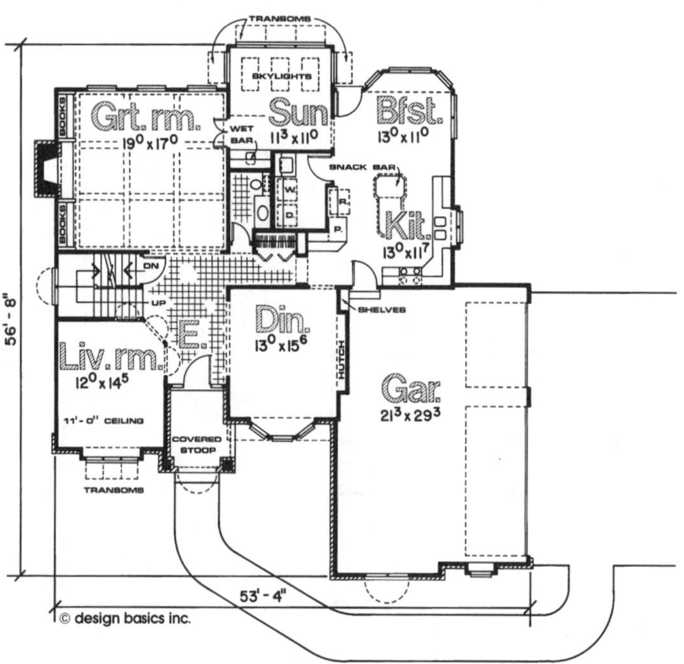

TRANSOMS
SKYLIGHTS
BOOKS
Grt. rm.
19^{0} x 17^{0}
WET BAR
Sun
11^{3} x 11^{0}
Bfst.
13^{0} x 11^{0}
SNACK BAR
W.
D.
R.
P.
Kit.
13^{0} x 11^{7}
DN
UP
SHELVES
E.
Din.
13^{0} x 15^{6}
HUTCH
Liv. rm.
12^{0} x 14^{5}
11'-0" CEILING
COVERED STOOP
TRANSOMS
Gar.
21^{3} x 29^{3}
56' - 8"
53' - 4"
© design basics inc.

Features

- 9-foot main level walls.
- Plant ledge above arched entry into volume living room.
- French doors through great room into skylit sunroom with wet bar.
- Spider-beamed ceiling in great room which also features built-in bookcases and fireplace.
- Spider-beamed ceiling in great room which also features built-in bookcases and fireplace.
- Kitchen open to dinette includes snack bar on island counter.

First Floor	1,520 sq. ft.
Second Floor	1,334 sq. ft.
Total Living Area	2,854 sq. ft.

PRICE CODE: D

PLAN AM2221B

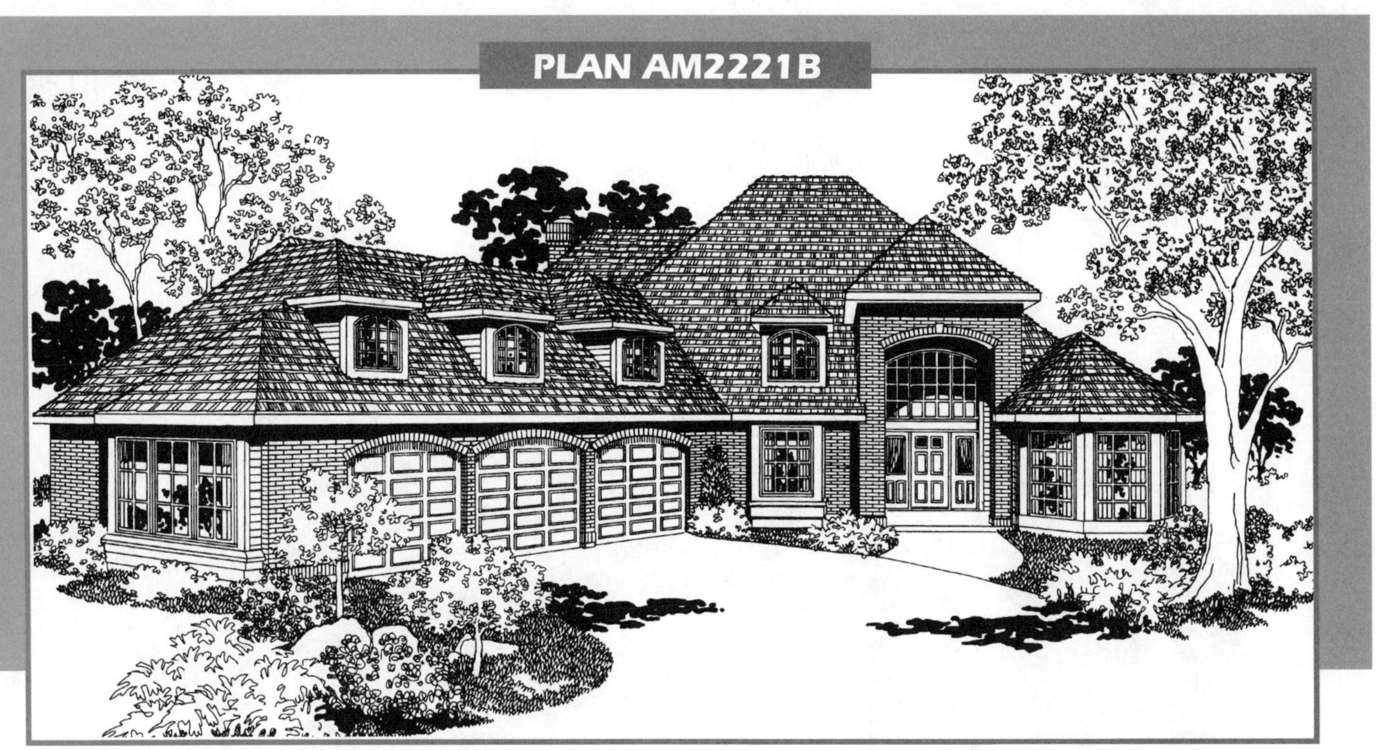

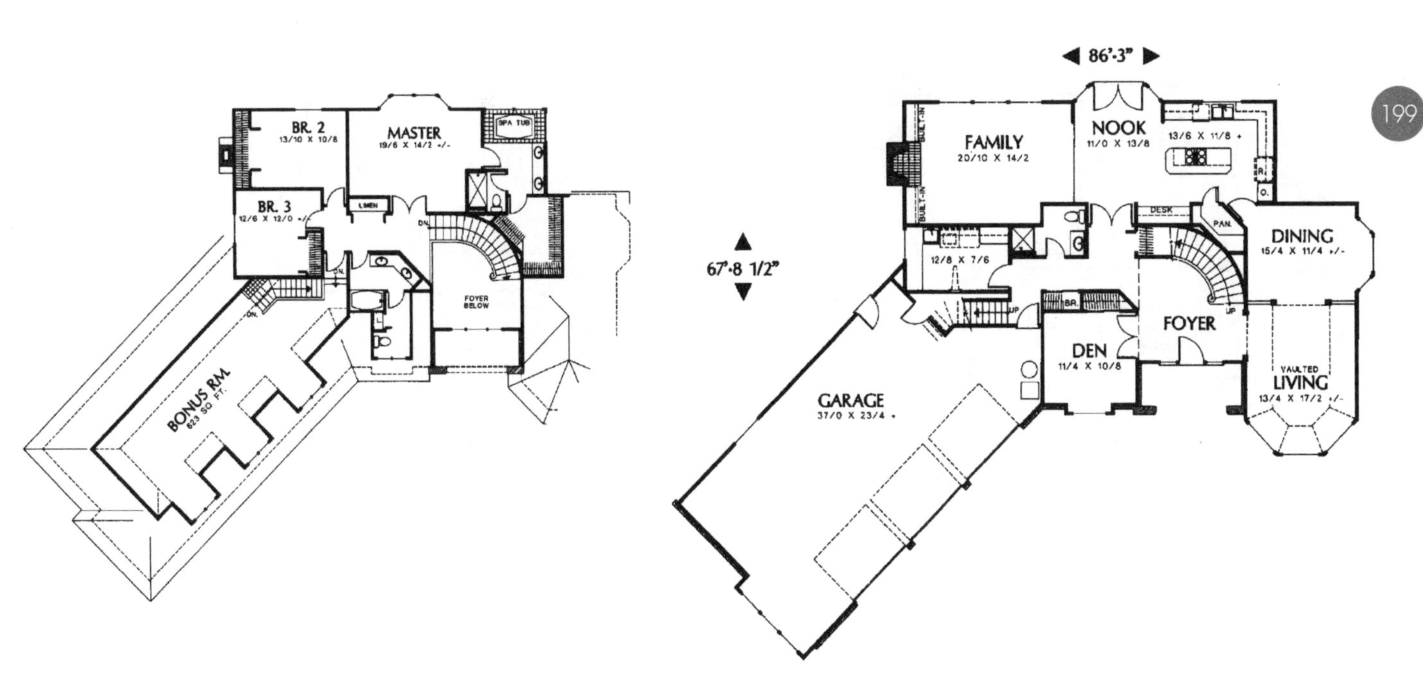
BR. 2
13/10 X 10/8
MASTER
19/6 X 14/2 +/-
SPA TUB
BR. 3
12/6 X 12/0 +/-
LINEN
FOYER BELOW
BONUS RM.
623 SQ. FT.
86'-3"
67'-8 1/2"
FAMILY
20/10 X 14/2
BUILT-IN
NOOK
11/0 X 13/8
13/6 X 11/8 +
DESK
PAN.
DINING
15/4 X 11/4 +/-
12/8 X 7/6
FOYER
DEN
11/4 X 10/8
GARAGE
37/0 X 23/4 +
VAULTED
LIVING
13/4 X 17/2 +/-

First Floor	1,758 sq. ft.
Second Floor	1,109 sq. ft.
Total Living Area	2,867 sq. ft.
Bonus Room	+623 sq. ft.

PRICE CODE: C

PLAN DB2374

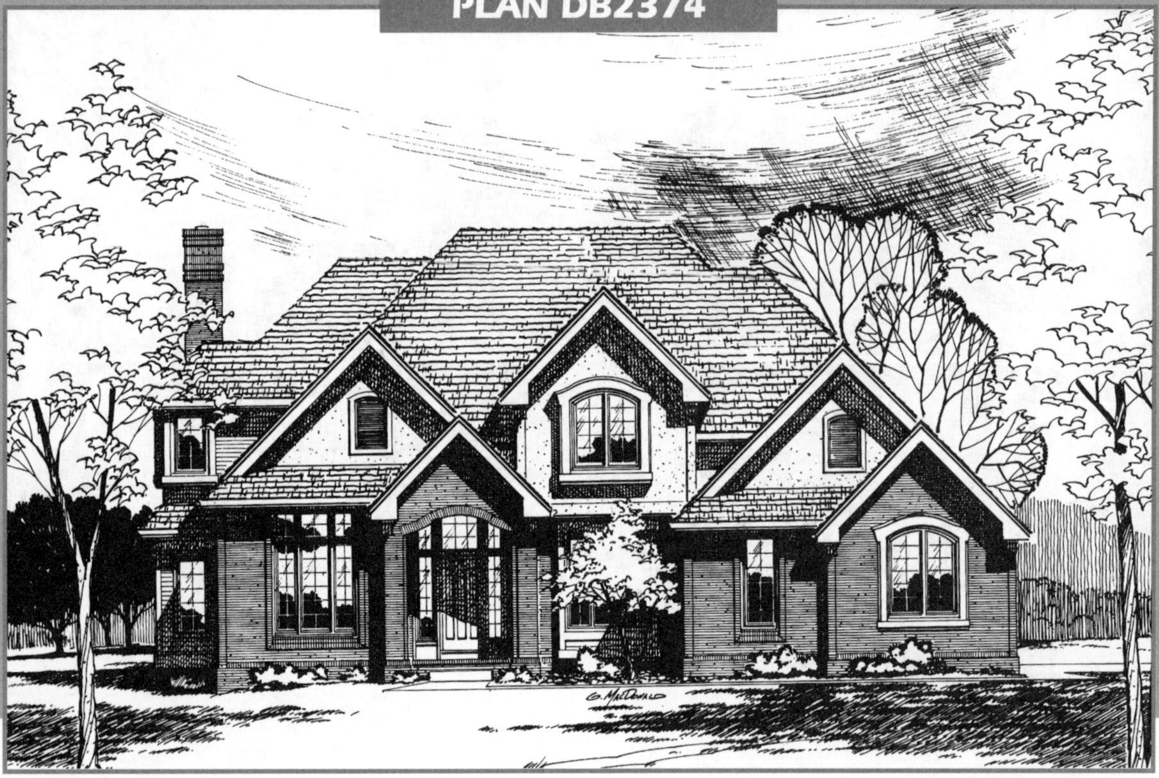

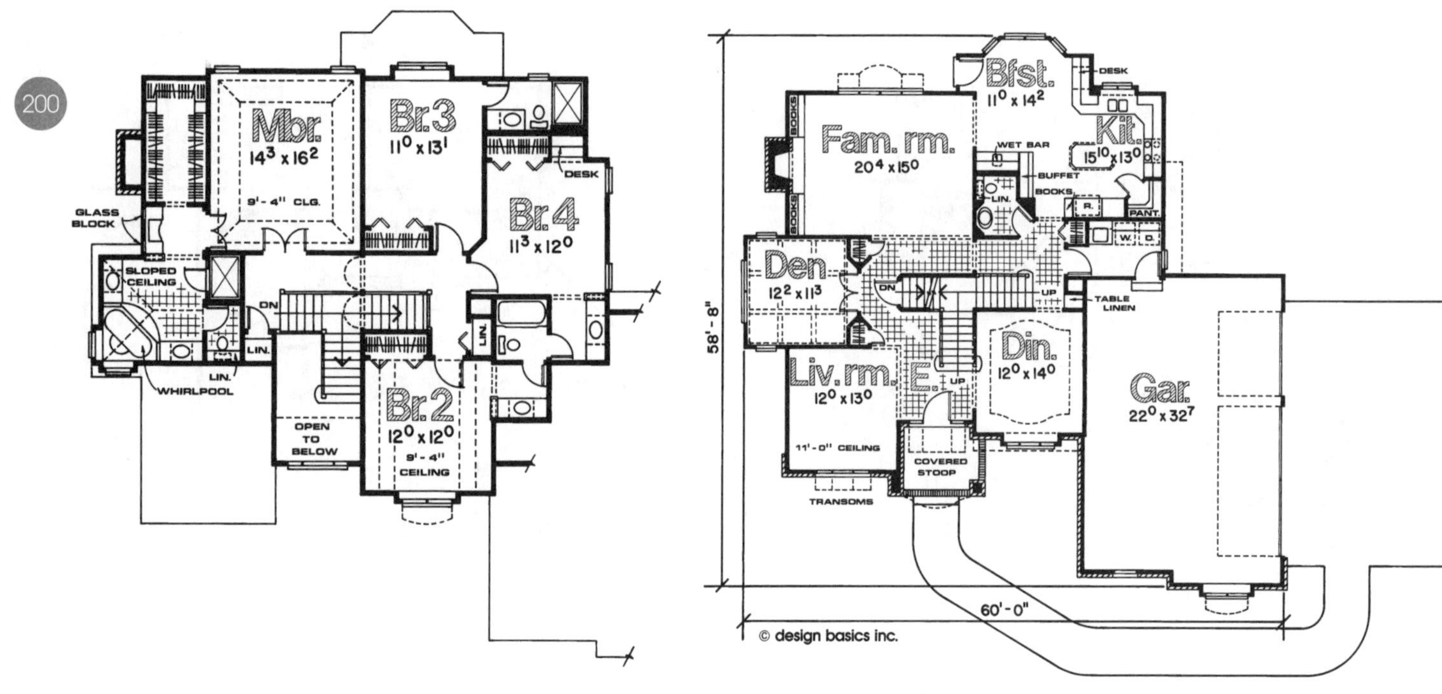

Mbr.
$14^3 \times 16^2$
9'-4" CLG.
Br.3
$11^0 \times 13^1$
Br.4
$11^3 \times 12^0$
DESK
GLASS BLOCK
SLOPED CEILING
DN
LIN.
LIN.
WHIRLPOOL
LIN.
OPEN TO BELOW
Br.2
$12^0 \times 12^0$
9'-4" CEILING
Bfst.
$11^0 \times 14^2$
DESK
Fam. rm.
$20^4 \times 15^0$
BOOKS
BOOKS
WET BAR
BUFFET
BOOKS
Kit.
$15^{10} \times 13^0$
LIN.
R.
PANT.
W. D.
Den
$12^2 \times 11^3$
DN
UP
TABLE LINEN
58'-8"
Liv. rm.
$12^0 \times 13^0$
E.
UP
Din.
$12^0 \times 14^0$
Gar.
$22^0 \times 32^7$
11'-0" CEILING
COVERED STOOP
TRANSOMS
60'-0"
© design basics inc.

Features

- Striking front elevation alludes to luxury within.
- Elegant formal room open to entry.
- 9-foot main level walls.
- Family room enhanced by arched window and fireplace framed by bookcases.
- Sunny bayed kitchen/breakfast area has wet bar/servery and walk-in pantry.
- Hollywood bath between bedrooms #2 and #4, bedroom #3 has separate 3/4 bath.
- Master suite with vaulted ceiling enjoys his/her vanity, corner whirlpool, separate make-up area and huge walk-in closet.

First Floor	1,575 sq. ft.
Second Floor	1,295 sq. ft.
Total Living Area	2,870 sq. ft.

PRICE CODE: D

PLAN DB2476

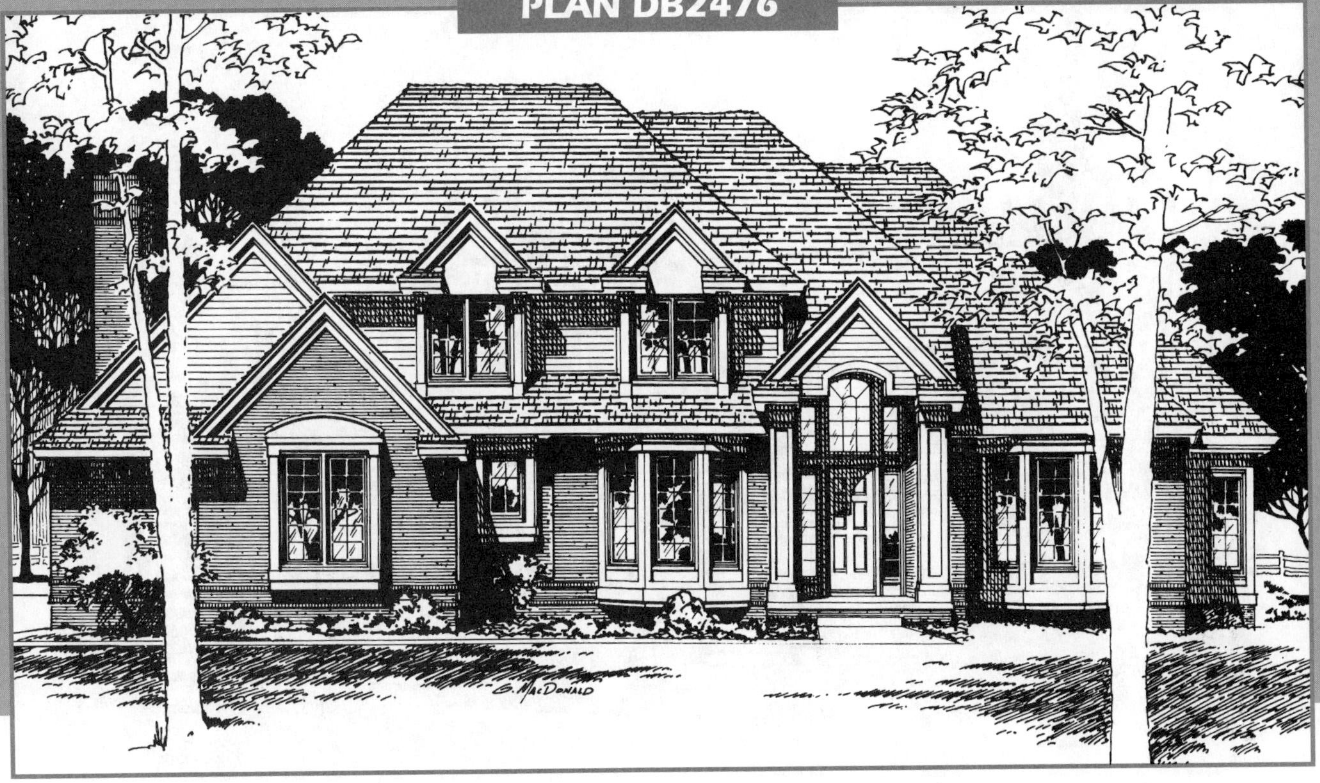

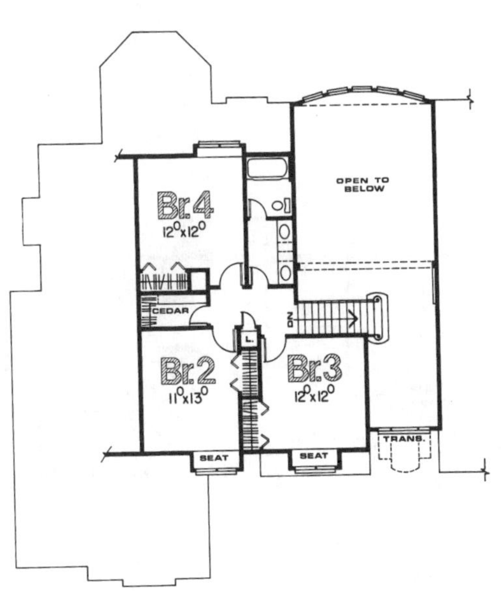

OPEN TO BELOW
Br.4
$12^0 x 12^0$
CEDAR
DN
L.
Br.2
$11^0 x 13^0$
Br.3
$12^0 x 12^0$
SEAT
SEAT
TRANS.

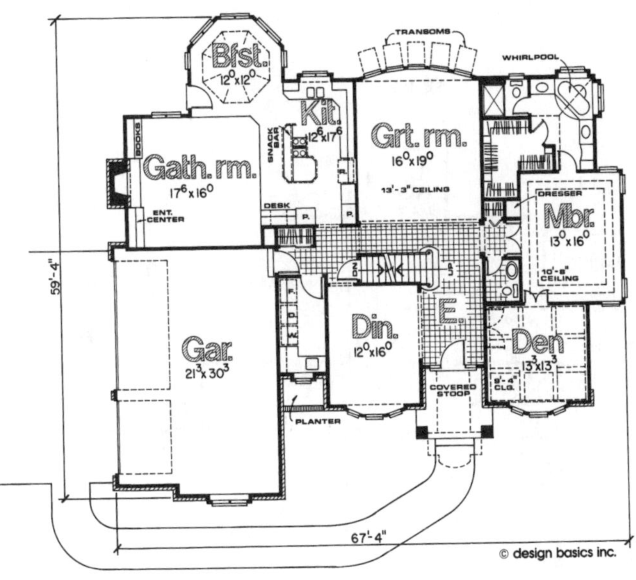

TRANSOMS
WHIRLPOOL
Bfst.
$12^0 x 12^0$
Kit.
$12^6 x 17^6$
SNACK BAR
Grt. rm.
$16^0 x 19^0$
13'-3" CEILING
BOOKS
Gath. rm.
$17^6 x 16^0$
ENT. CENTER
DESK
DRESSER
Mbr.
$13^0 x 16^0$
10'-8" CEILING
59'-4"
Gar.
$21^3 x 30^3$
Din.
$12^0 x 16^0$
E.
Den
$13^3 x 13^3$
9'-4" CLG.
COVERED STOOP
PLANTER
67'-4"
© design basics inc.

Features

- Magnificent elevation imparts grandeur and style.
- Lovely entry surveys formal dining and great room.
- Spacious great room ideal for entertaining features large bowed window for view out back.
- Splendid kitchen and sunny gazebo dinette area with island cook top, snack bar, wrapping counters, two pantries and planning desk is ideal for casual or formal pursuits.
- Secondary bedrooms #2 and #3 have cozy window seats.
- Dual lavs and compartmented bath comfortably serve upstairs bedrooms.
- Master bedroom with decorative tiered ceiling is secluded on main level affording maximum privacy.
- Pampering master bath and dressing area features huge walk-in closet, corner whirlpool and his and her vanities plus compartmented stool and shower area.

First Floor	2,183 sq. ft.
Second Floor	701 sq. ft.
Total Living Area	2,884 sq. ft.

PRICE CODE: D

PLAN AM2237K

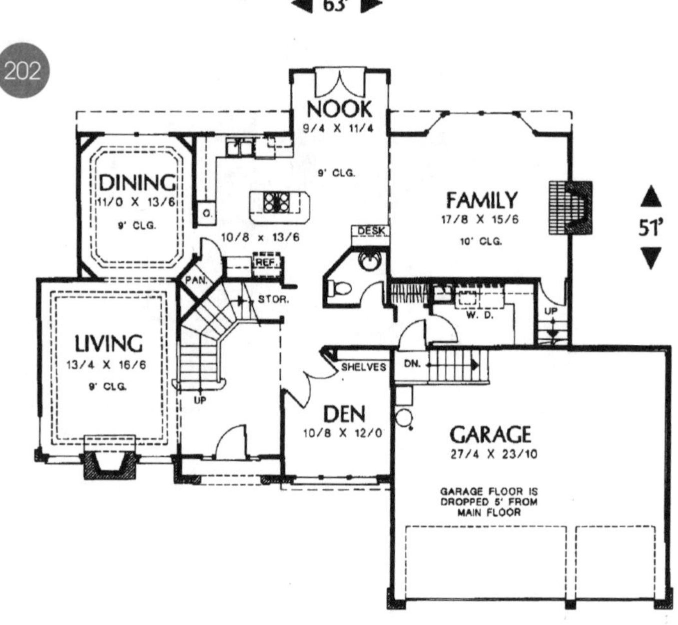
63'
51'
NOOK
9/4 X 11/4
9' CLG.
DINING
11/0 X 13/6
9' CLG.
10/8 x 13/6
FAMILY
17/8 X 15/6
10' CLG.
DESK
REF.
PAN.
STOR.
LIVING
13/4 X 16/6
9' CLG.
UP
SHELVES
DN.
W. D.
UP
DEN
10/8 X 12/0
GARAGE
27/4 X 23/10
GARAGE FLOOR IS DROPPED 5' FROM MAIN FLOOR

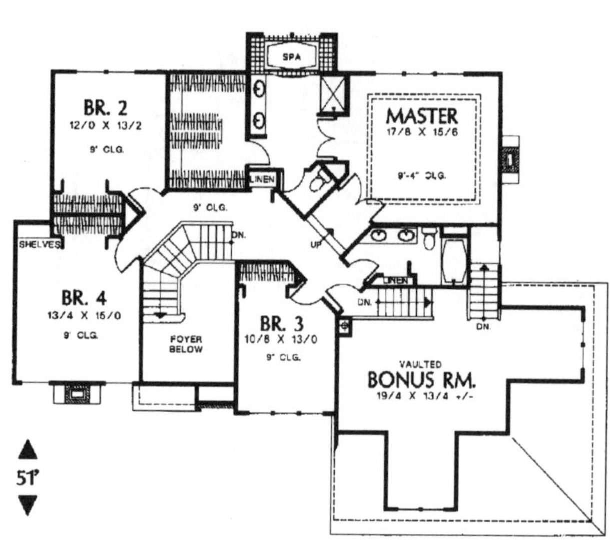
SPA
BR. 2
12/0 X 13/2
9' CLG.
MASTER
17/8 X 15/6
9'-4" CLG.
LINEN
9' CLG.
SHELVES
DN.
UP
BR. 4
13/4 X 15/0
9' CLG.
FOYER BELOW
BR. 3
10/8 X 13/0
9' CLG.
DN.
LINEN
DN
VAULTED
BONUS RM.
19/4 X 13/4 +/-
51'

First Floor	1,484 sq. ft.
Second Floor	1,402 sq. ft.
Total Living Area	2,886 sq. ft.
Bonus Room	+430 sq. ft

PRICE CODE: C

PLAN VL2888

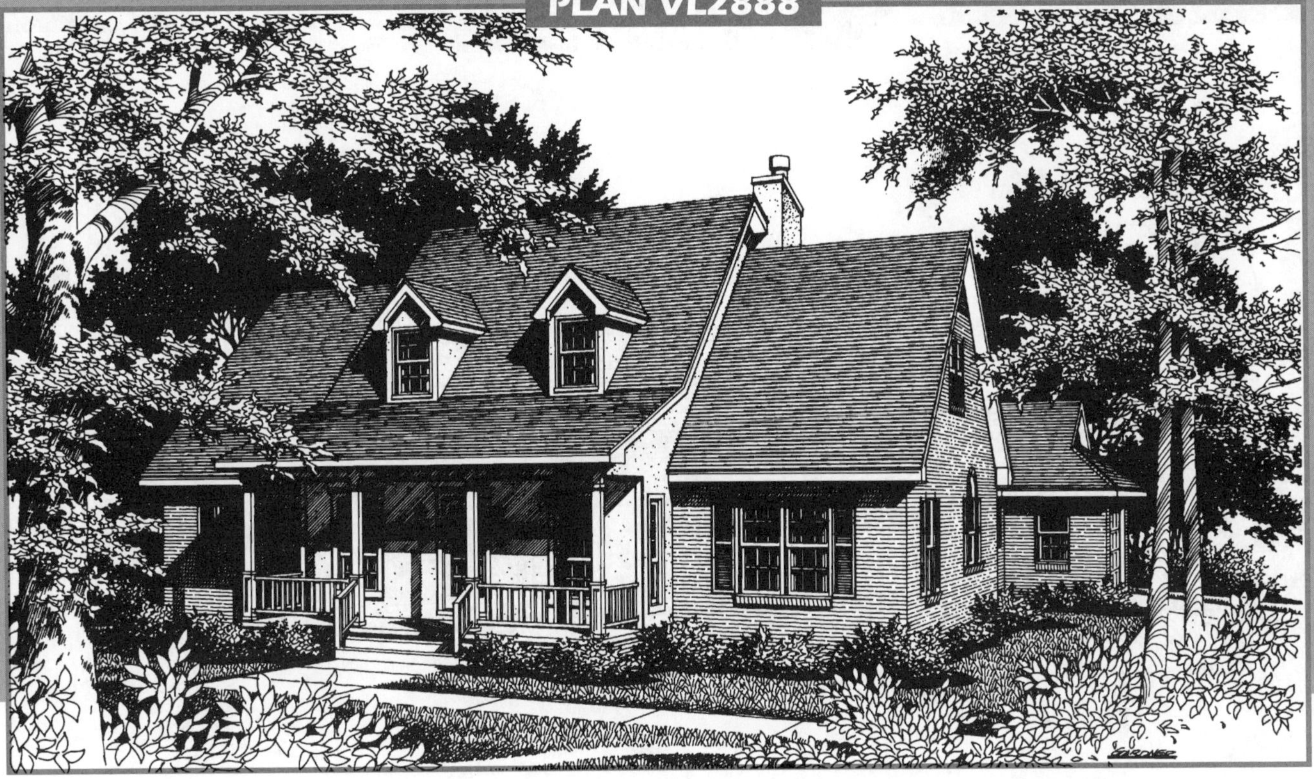

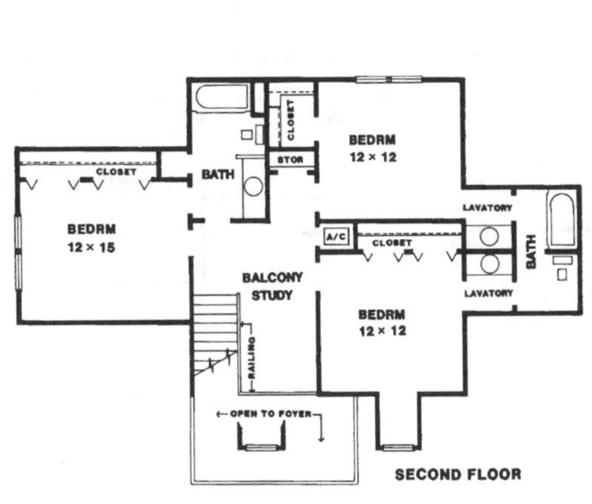
CLOSET
BEDRM
12 × 15
BATH
CLOSET
STOR
BEDRM
12 × 12
A/C
CLOSET
LAVATORY
BATH
LAVATORY
BALCONY
STUDY
BEDRM
12 × 12
RAILING
OPEN TO FOYER
SECOND FLOOR

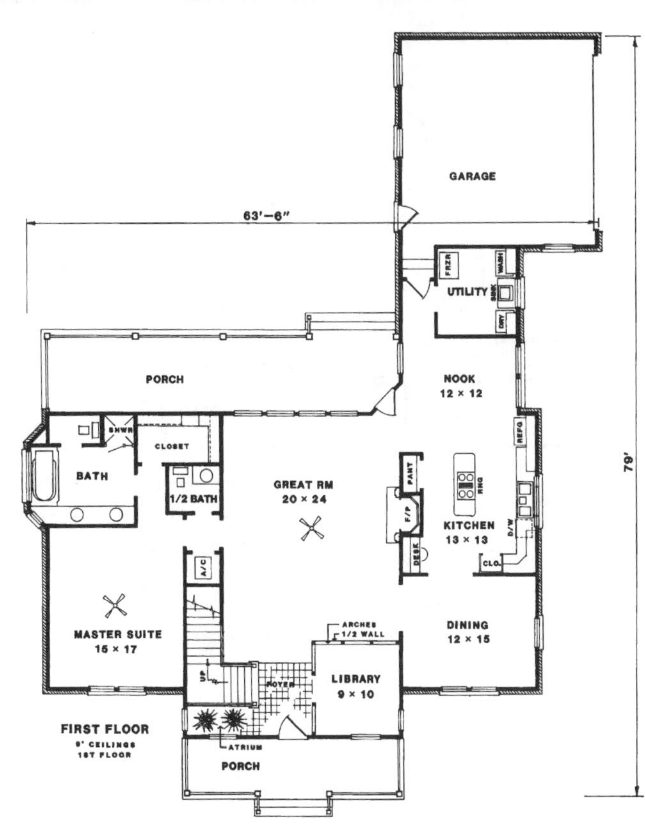
GARAGE
63'–6"
79'
UTILITY
PORCH
NOOK
12 × 12
SHWR
CLOSET
BATH
1/2 BATH
GREAT RM
20 × 24
PANT
F/P
RNG
REFG
D/W
KITCHEN
13 × 13
DESK
CLO.
A/C
MASTER SUITE
15 × 17
ARCHES
1/2 WALL
DINING
12 × 15
UP
FOYER
LIBRARY
9 × 10
ATRIUM
PORCH
FIRST FLOOR
9' CEILINGS
1ST FLOOR

First Floor	1,935 sq. ft.
Second Floor	953 sq. ft.
Total Living Area	2,888 sq. ft.

PRICE CODE: C

PLAN NP1315

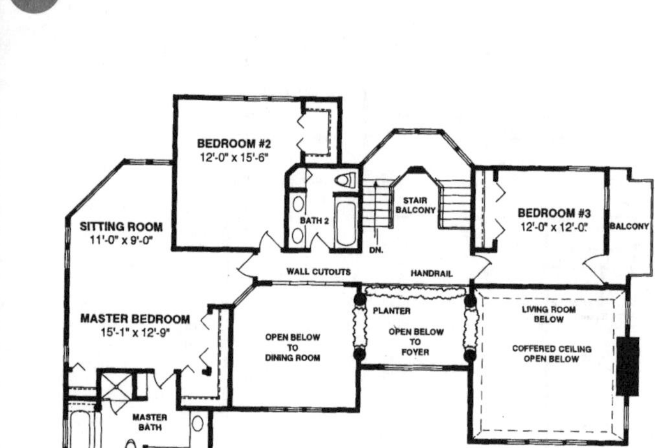
BEDROOM #2
12'-0" x 15'-6"
SITTING ROOM
11'-0" x 9'-0"
BATH 2
STAIR BALCONY
BEDROOM #3
12'-0" x 12'-0"
BALCONY
DN.
WALL CUTOUTS
HANDRAIL
MASTER BEDROOM
15'-1" x 12'-9"
PLANTER
OPEN BELOW TO DINING ROOM
OPEN BELOW TO FOYER
LIVING ROOM BELOW
COFFERED CEILING OPEN BELOW
MASTER BATH

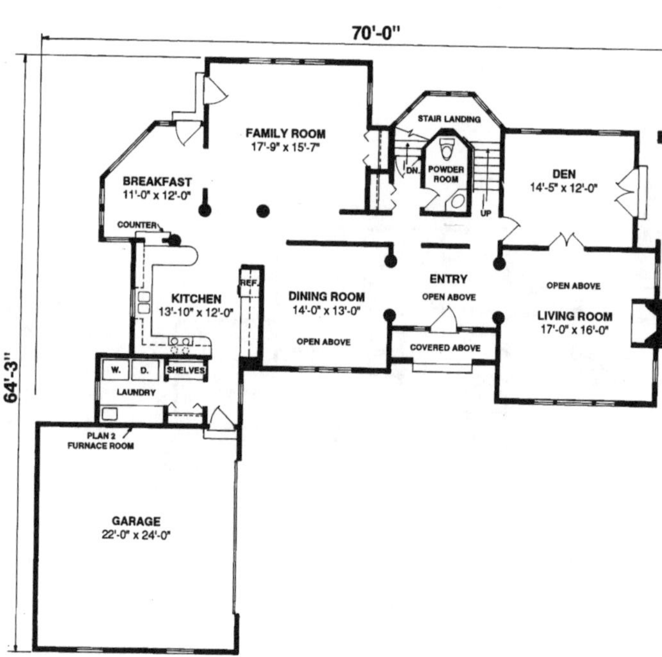
70'-0"
64'-3"
FAMILY ROOM
17'-9" x 15'-7"
STAIR LANDING
BREAKFAST
11'-0" x 12'-0"
DN.
POWDER ROOM
UP
DEN
14'-5" x 12'-0"
COUNTER
KITCHEN
13'-10" x 12'-0"
REF.
DINING ROOM
14'-0" x 13'-0"
OPEN ABOVE
ENTRY
OPEN ABOVE
OPEN ABOVE
LIVING ROOM
17'-0" x 16'-0"
COVERED ABOVE
W.
D.
SHELVES
LAUNDRY
PLAN 2
FURNACE ROOM
GARAGE
22'-0" x 24'-0"

Charmaigne Estate

Features

- Unique exterior design hints at the spacious interior of this home.
- Interior features open ceilings with wrap-around staircase and full bay windows on stair landing.
- First-floor right wing contains a den and open-ceiling living room with fireplace.
- L-shaped kitchen, and separate, sunny breakfast room.
- Second floor features a large master bedroom with equally generous sitting room for quiet moments.
- Two additional upstairs bedrooms share a second full bath.

First Floor	1,866 sq. ft.
Second Floor	1,314 sq. ft.
Total Living Area	3,180 sq. ft.

PRICE CODE: C

PLAN FD8181-L

75'-0"
62'-5"
Covered Patio
Patio
MstrBed 15x17
Din 13x10
FamilyRm 17x20
Bed#4 11x12
Bed#3 13x11
Bed#2 13x11
LivRm 13x16
Kit 13x13
Gallery
Pwdr
Util
Ent
FmlDin 13x12
Study 12x11
Cov. Porch
3-Car Gar 30x23

Total Living Area **2,945 sq. ft.**

PRICE CODE: C

CUSTOMIZE IT!

ORDER TOLL FREE 1■800■533■4350 **24-HOUR FAX ORDERING** 1■800■344■4293

PLAN VL3011

206

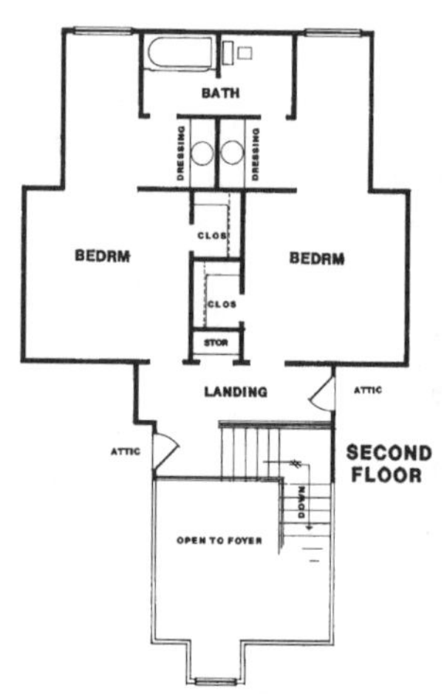
BATH
DRESSING
DRESSING
BEDRM
CLOS
BEDRM
CLOS
STOR
LANDING
ATTIC
ATTIC
SECOND FLOOR
DOWN
OPEN TO FOYER

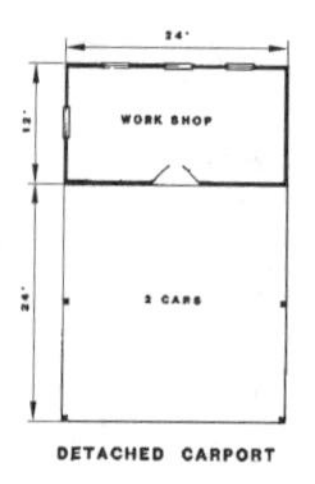
24'
WORK SHOP
2 CARS
DETACHED CARPORT

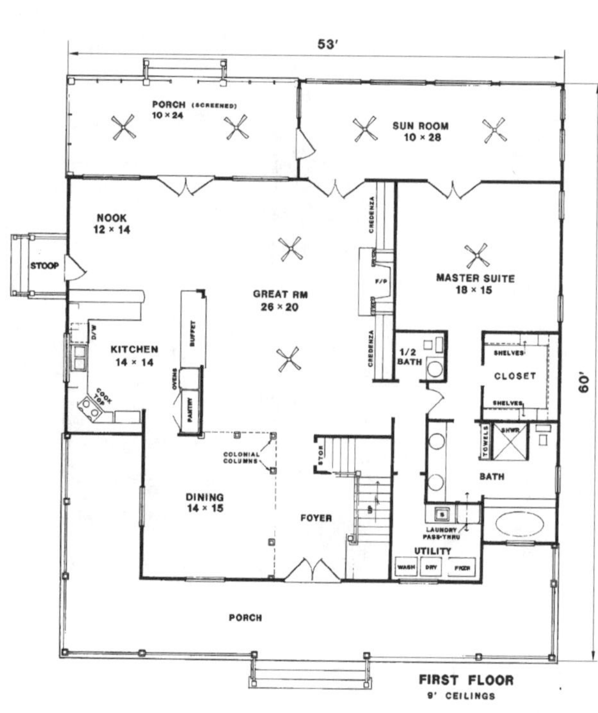
53'
PORCH (SCREENED)
10 × 24
SUN ROOM
10 × 28
NOOK
12 × 14
STOOP
GREAT RM
26 × 20
CREDENZA
F/P
CREDENZA
MASTER SUITE
18 × 15
KITCHEN
14 × 14
BUFFET
OVENS
PANTRY
COOK TOP
1/2 BATH
SHELVES
CLOSET
SHELVES
60'
TOWELS
SHWR
BATH
COLONIAL COLUMNS
STOR
DINING
14 × 15
FOYER
LAUNDRY PASS-THRU
UTILITY
WASH
DRY
FRZR
PORCH
FIRST FLOOR
9' CEILINGS

First Floor	2,361 sq. ft.
Second Floor	650 sq. ft.
Total Living Area	3,011 sq. ft.

PRICE CODE: C

CUSTOMIZE IT!

ORDER TOLL FREE 1-800-533-4350 24-HOUR FAX ORDERING 1-800-344-4293

PLAN NP1258

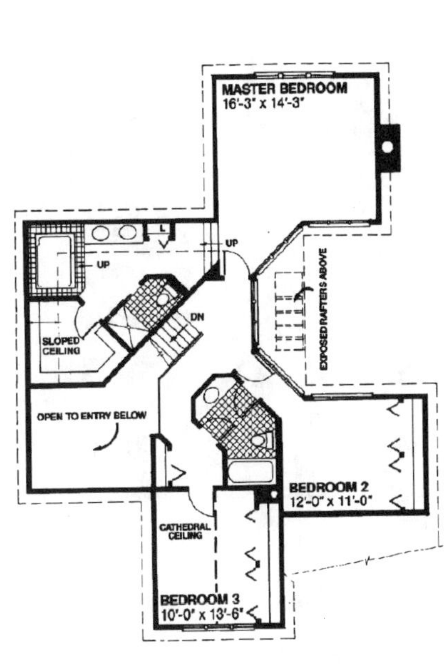
MASTER BEDROOM
16'-3" x 14'-3"
UP
SLOPED CEILING
DN
EXPOSED RAFTERS ABOVE
OPEN TO ENTRY BELOW
BEDROOM 2
12'-0" x 11'-0"
CATHEDRAL CEILING
BEDROOM 3
10'-0" x 13'-6"

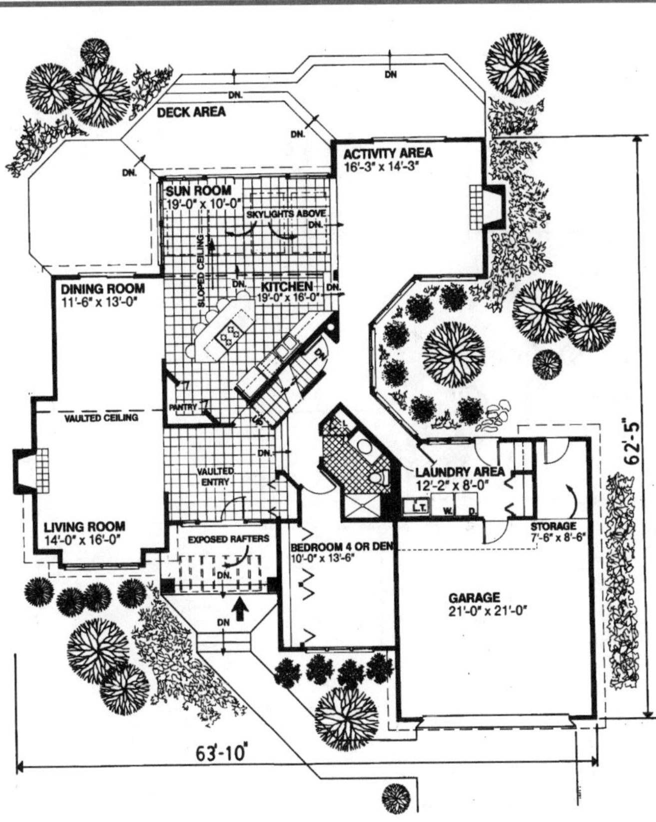
DECK AREA
DN.
ACTIVITY AREA
16'-3" x 14'-3"
SUN ROOM
19'-0" x 10'-0"
SKYLIGHTS ABOVE
SLOPED CEILING
DINING ROOM
11'-6" x 13'-0"
KITCHEN
19'-0" x 16'-0"
PANTRY
VAULTED CEILING
VAULTED ENTRY
LIVING ROOM
14'-0" x 16'-0"
EXPOSED RAFTERS
BEDROOM 4 OR DEN
10'-0" x 13'-6"
LAUNDRY AREA
12'-2" x 8'-0"
STORAGE
7'-6" x 8'-6"
GARAGE
21'-0" x 21'-0"
62'-5"
63'-10"

Garden Sanctuary

Features

- Bright and spacious living are the rule in this contemporary two-story.
- Sunlit, vaulted entrance leads to living room/dining room combination, featuring a fireplace and vaulted ceiling.
- Large sunken sun room with skylights and sloped ceilings include a garden area off the family area.
- A cathedral ceiling in one of the bedrooms provides an added touch.
- Second bedroom overlooks garden area.
- Master bedroom features adjacent spa and separate shower area.

First Floor	1,886 sq. ft.
Second Floor	1,127 sq. ft.
Total Living Area	3,013 sq. ft.

PRICE CODE: C

PLAN NP1258C

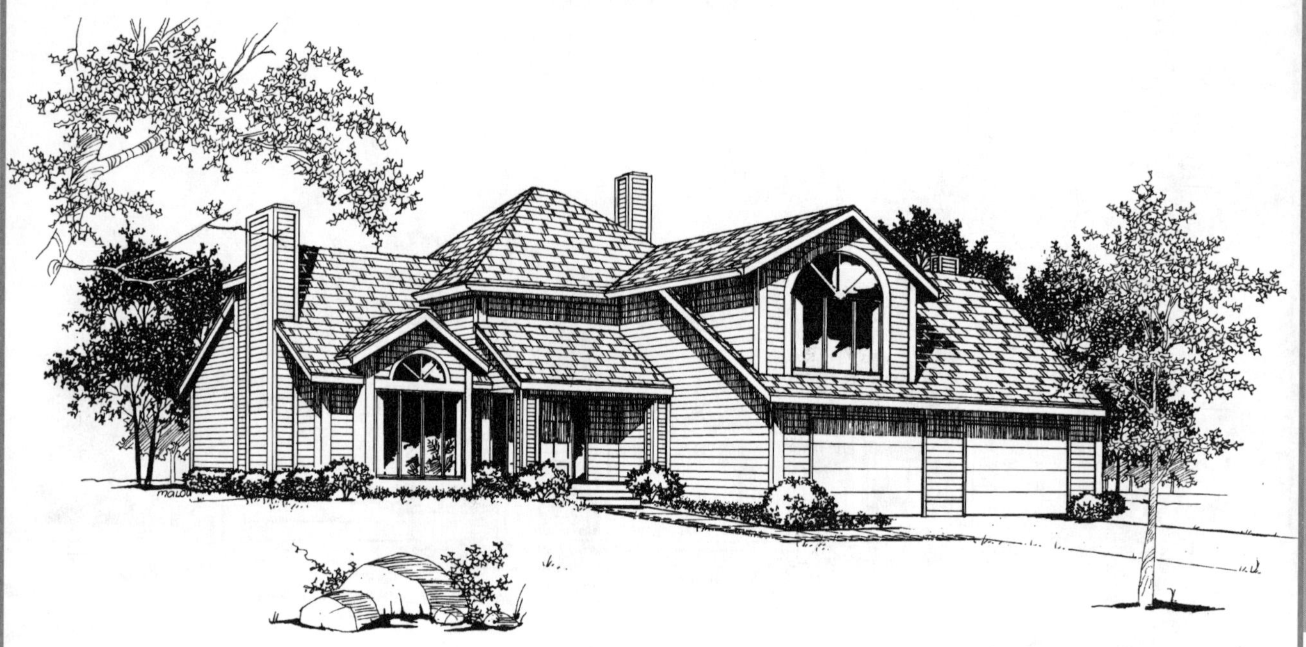

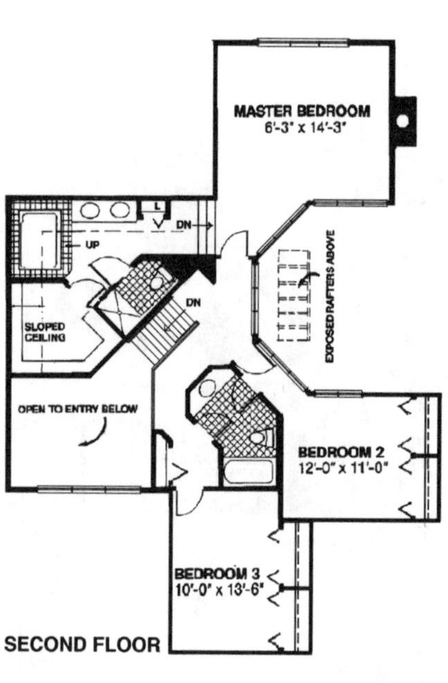
MASTER BEDROOM
6'-3" x 14'-3"
DN
UP
SLOPED CEILING
EXPOSED RAFTERS ABOVE
OPEN TO ENTRY BELOW
BEDROOM 2
12'-0" x 11'-0"
BEDROOM 3
10'-0" x 13'-6"
SECOND FLOOR

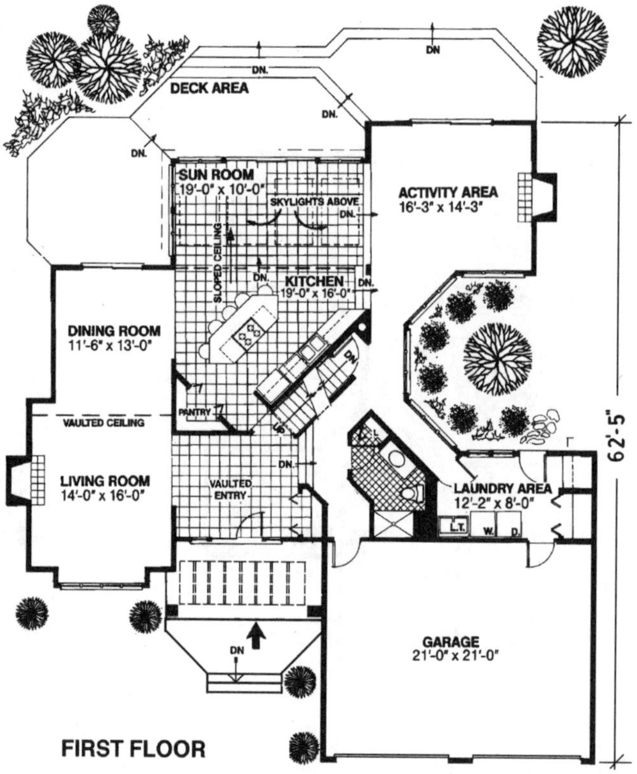

DECK AREA
DN.
SUN ROOM
19'-0" x 10'-0"
SKYLIGHTS ABOVE
SLOPED CEILING
ACTIVITY AREA
16'-3" x 14'-3"
KITCHEN
19'-0" x 16'-0"
DINING ROOM
11'-6" x 13'-0"
PANTRY
VAULTED CEILING
LIVING ROOM
14'-0" x 16'-0"
VAULTED ENTRY
LAUNDRY AREA
12'-2" x 8'-0"
GARAGE
21'-0" x 21'-0"
62'-5"
FIRST FLOOR

Contemporary Retreat

Features

- Unique two-story design.
- Exterior features overhangs, gabled vertical windows, multiple roof lines for maximum interest.
- Large sunken sun room with skylights and sloped ceiling.
- Garden area off the family room enables you to enjoy natural surroundings all year-round.
- First-floor bedroom or den with bath.
- Second floor features two bedrooms with bath and master bedroom with deluxe bath.
- Vaulted and cathedral ceilings add to the magnificence of this design

First Floor	1,699 sq. ft.
Second Floor	1,127 sq. ft.
Total Living Area	2,826 sq. ft.

PRICE CODE: C

PLAN FD8077

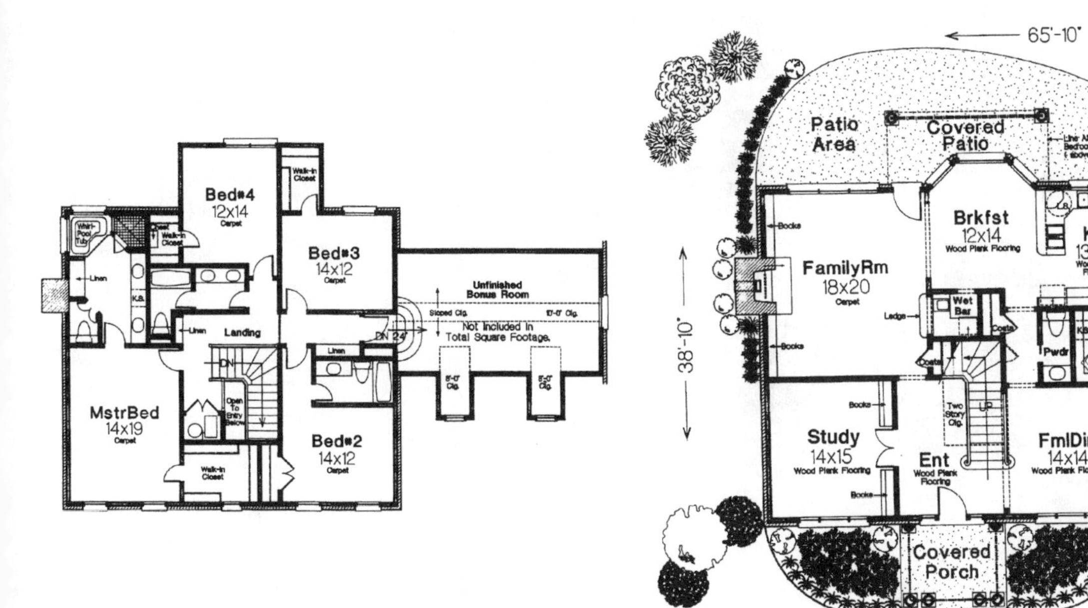
65'-10"
38'-10"
Patio Area
Covered Patio
Brkfst
12x14
Wood Plank Flooring
Kit
13x13
Wood Plank Flooring
FamilyRm
18x20
Carpet
Gar
22x24
Wet Bar
Pwdr
Study
14x15
Wood Plank Flooring
Ent
Wood Plank Flooring
FmlDin
14x14
Wood Plank Flooring
Covered Porch
© Copyright Fillmore Design Group
Bed#4
12x14
Carpet
Bed#3
14x12
Carpet
Unfinished Bonus Room
Not Included In Total Square Footage.
Landing
MstrBed
14x19
Carpet
Bed#2
14x12
Carpet

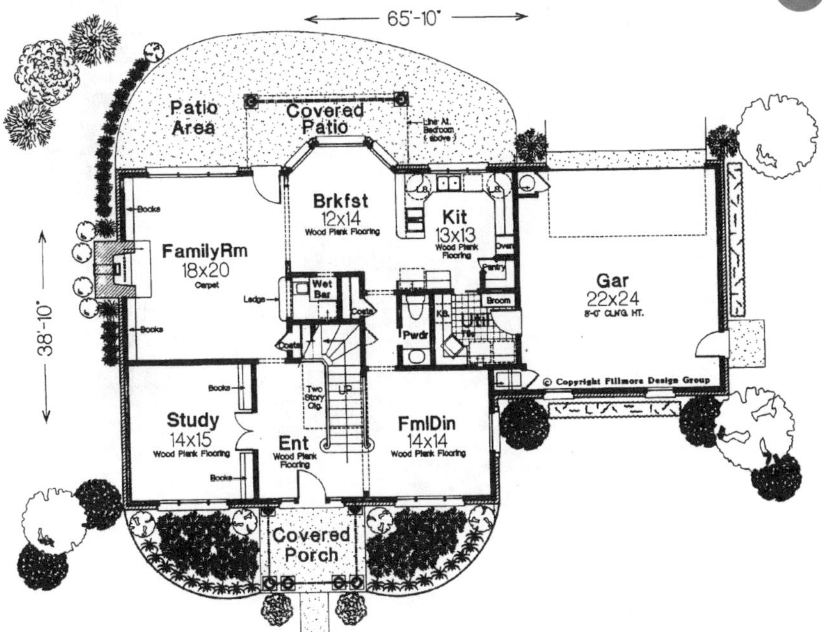

First Floor	1,573 sq. ft.
Second Floor	1,449 sq. ft.
Total Living Area	3,022 sq. ft.

PRICE CODE: C

PLAN FD6735-L

6735-L

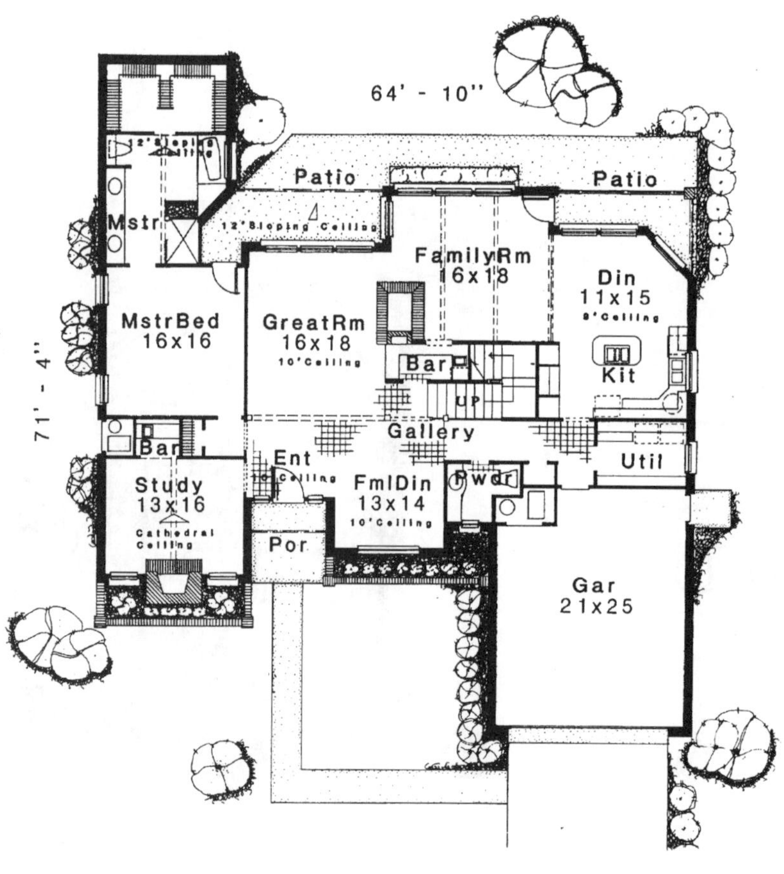

64' - 10"
71' - 4"
12' Sloping Ceiling
Patio
Patio
Mstr
12' Sloping Ceiling
FamilyRm
16x18
Din
11x15
9' Ceiling
MstrBed
16x16
GreatRm
16x18
10' Ceiling
Bar
UP
Kit
Gallery
Bar
Ent
Util
Study
13x16
Cathedral Ceiling
FmlDin
13x14
10' Ceiling
Pwdr
Por
Gar
21x25

Total Living Area 3,040 sq. ft.

PRICE CODE: C

PLAN NP1332

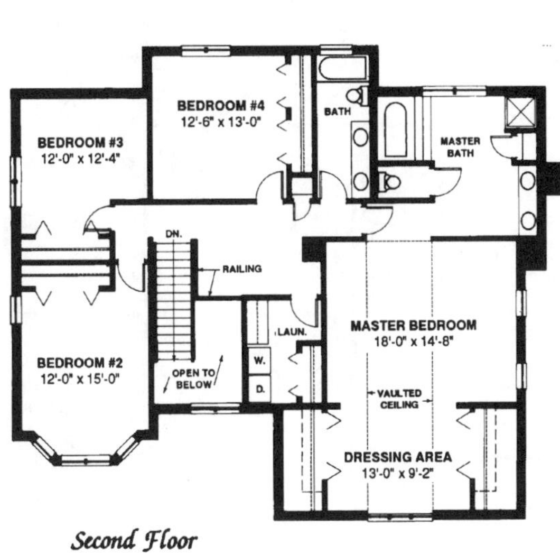
BEDROOM #4
12'-6" x 13'-0"
BATH
BEDROOM #3
12'-0" x 12'-4"
MASTER BATH
DN.
RAILING
LAUN.
W.
D.
MASTER BEDROOM
18'-0" x 14'-8"
BEDROOM #2
12'-0" x 15'-0"
OPEN TO BELOW
VAULTED CEILING
DRESSING AREA
13'-0" x 9'-2"
Second Floor

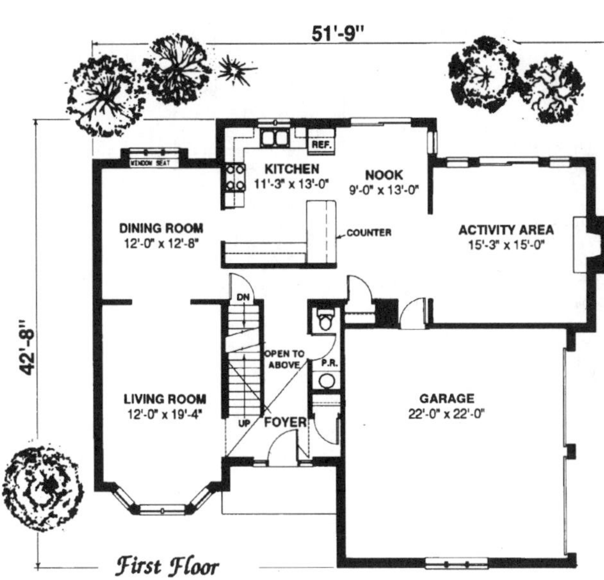
51'-9"
42'-8"
WINDOW SEAT
REF.
KITCHEN
11'-3" x 13'-0"
NOOK
9'-0" x 13'-0"
DINING ROOM
12'-0" x 12'-8"
COUNTER
ACTIVITY AREA
15'-3" x 15'-0"
DN
OPEN TO ABOVE
P.R.
LIVING ROOM
12'-0" x 19'-4"
UP
FOYER
GARAGE
22'-0" x 22'-0"
First Floor

Southern Charm

Features

- Dramatic roof lines and brick exterior make this design a stand- out.
- Cheerful entrance foyer features an open ceiling and accent windows.
- Spacious kitchen with breakfast nook.
- Activity area with fireplace.
- Large master bedroom upstairs with vaulted ceilings, separate dressing area, ample his/her closets, and deluxe master bath with private toilet.
- Three additional bedrooms upstairs share a full bath.

First Floor	1,245 sq. ft.
Second Floor	1,828 sq. ft.
Total Living Area	3,073 sq. ft.

PRICE CODE: C

PLAN AM2301

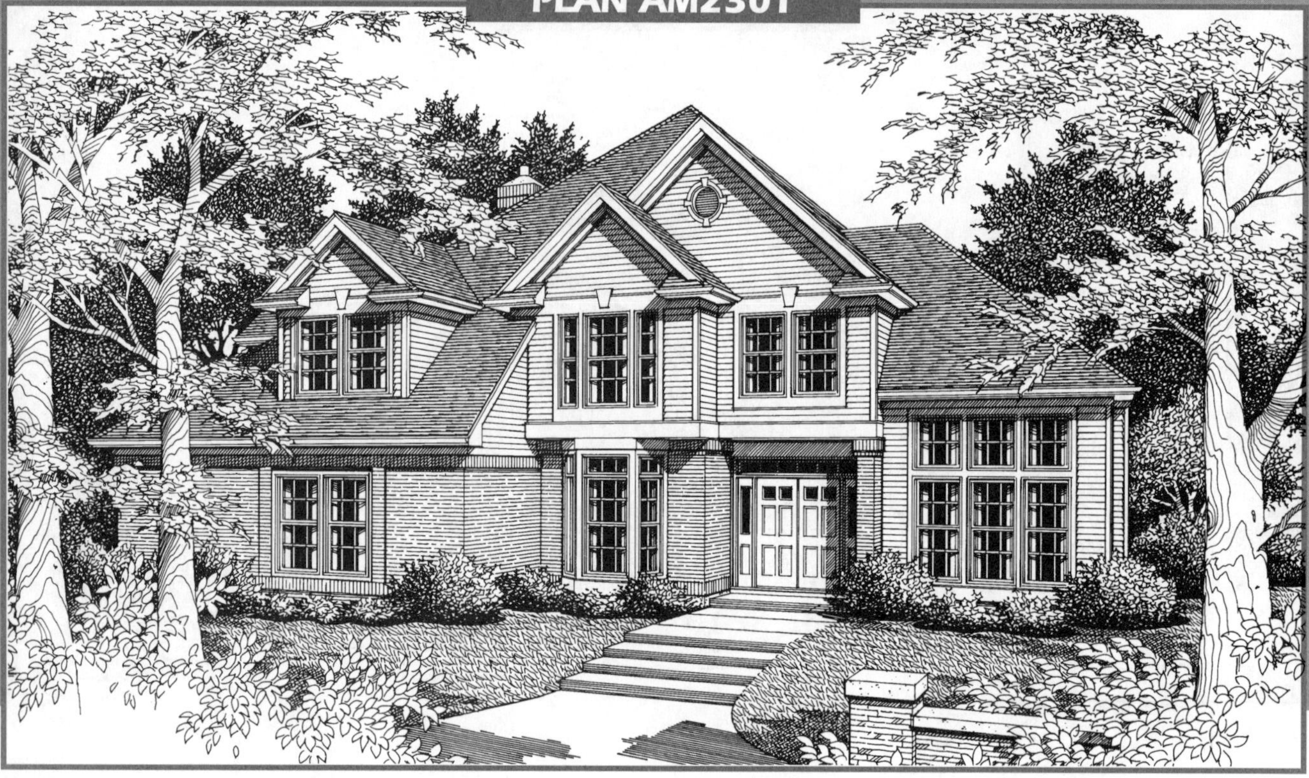

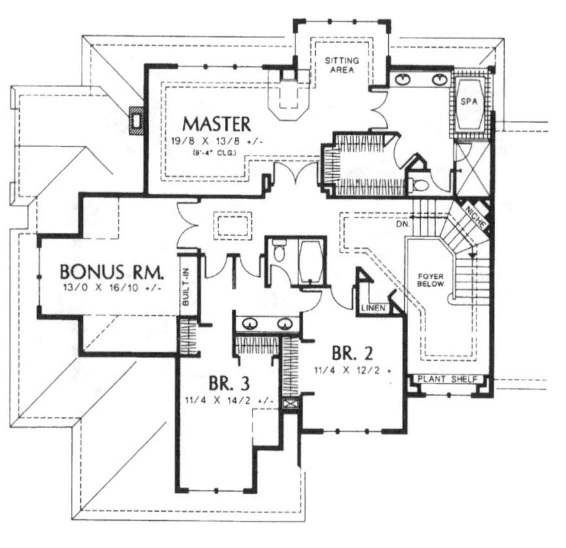

SITTING AREA
SPA
MASTER
19/8 X 13/8 +/-
(9'-4" CLG.)
DN.
NICHE
FOYER BELOW
BONUS RM.
13/0 X 16/10 +/-
BUILT-IN
LINEN
BR. 2
11/4 X 12/2 +
PLANT SHELF
BR. 3
11/4 X 14/2 +/-

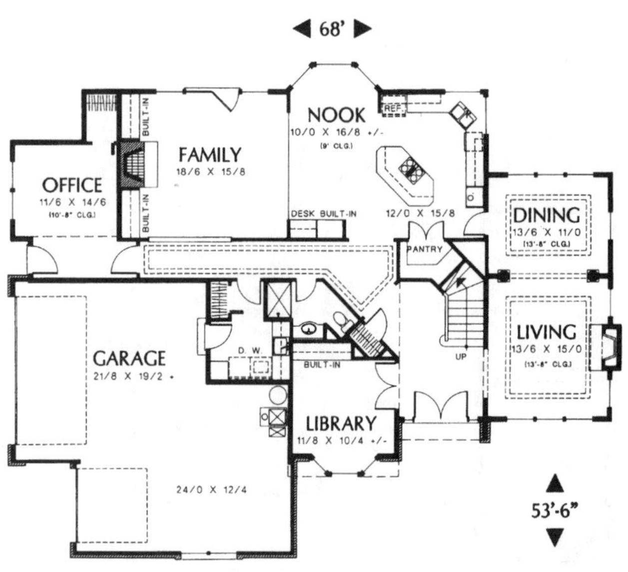

68'
NOOK
10/0 X 16/8 +/-
(9' CLG.)
REF.
FAMILY
18/6 X 15/8
BUILT-IN
OFFICE
11/6 X 14/6
(10'-8" CLG.)
DESK BUILT-IN
12/0 X 15/8
PANTRY
DINING
13/6 X 11/0
(13'-8" CLG.)
LIVING
13/6 X 15/0
(13'-8" CLG.)
GARAGE
21/8 X 19/2 +
D W
BUILT-IN
UP
LIBRARY
11/8 X 10/4 +/-
24/0 X 12/4
53'-6"

First Floor	1,779 sq. ft.
Second Floor	1,335 sq. ft.
Total Living Area	3,114 sq. ft.
Office	+209 sq. ft.
Bonus Room	+270 sq. ft.

PRICE CODE: C

PLAN FD6639

213

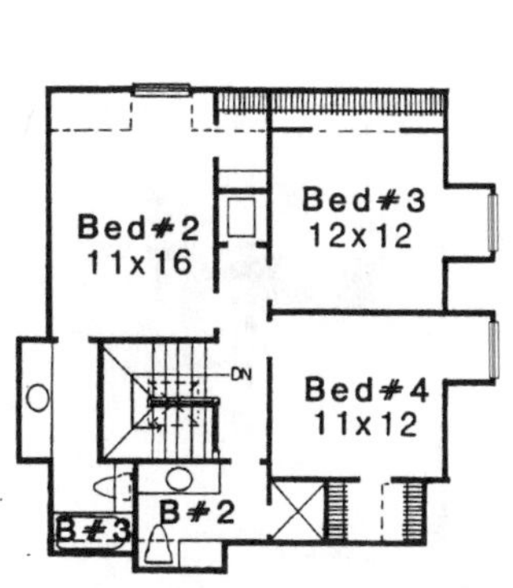
Bed#2
11x16
Bed#3
12x12
Bed#4
11x12
DN
B#3
B#2

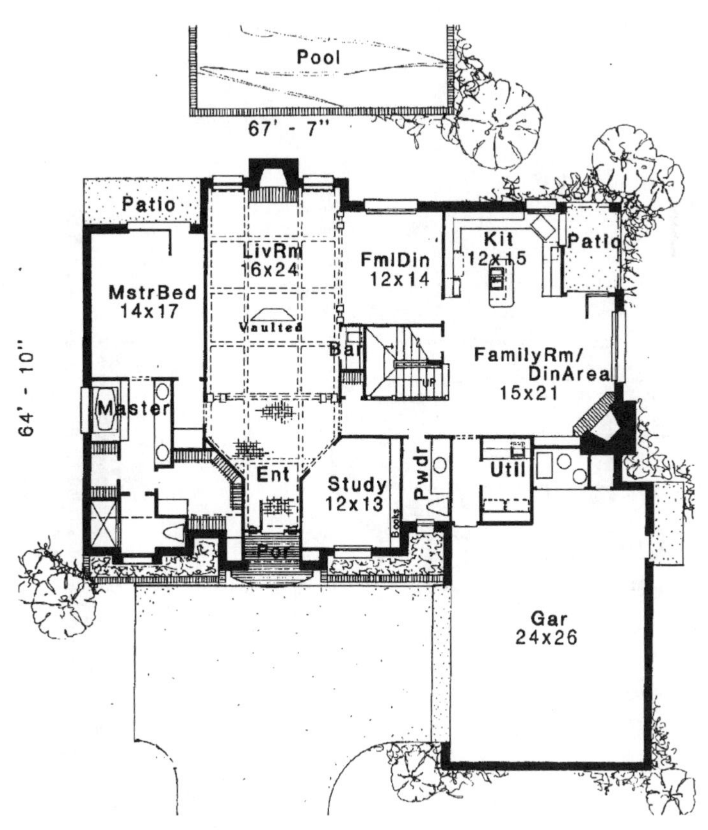
Pool
67' - 7"
Patio
LivRm
16x24
Vaulted
FmlDin
12x14
Kit
12x15
Patio
MstrBed
14x17
Bar
FamilyRm/
DinArea
15x21
UP
64' - 10"
Master
Ent
Study
12x13
Pwdr
Util
Por
Gar
24x26

First Floor	2,283 sq. ft.
Second Floor	855 sq. ft.
Total Living Area	3,138 sq. ft.

PRICE CODE: C

PLAN FD8144-L

HOLZHAUER INC. 93

214

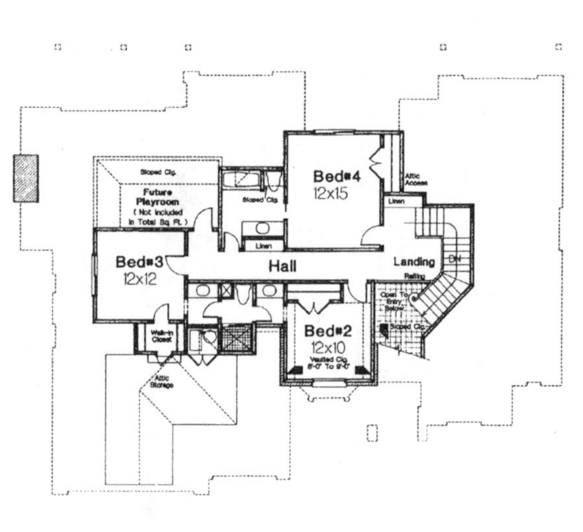

Future Playroom
(Not Included In Total Sq. Ft.)
Bed#4
12x15
Bed#3
12x12
Hall
Landing
Bed#2
12x10

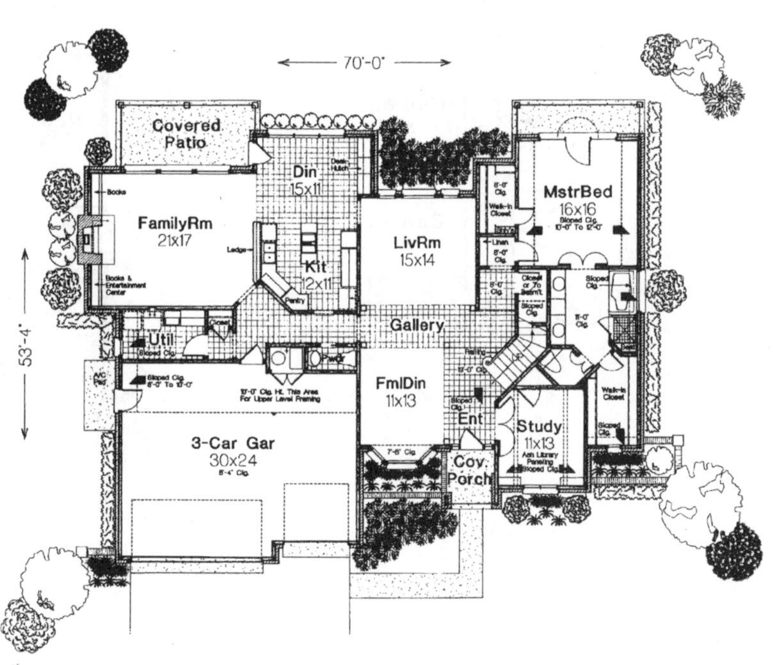

70'-0"
53'-4"
Covered Patio
Din
15x11
FamilyRm
21x17
Kit
12x11
LivRm
15x14
MstrBed
16x16
Gallery
Util
FmlDin
11x13
3-Car Gar
30x24
Ent
Study
11x13
Cov. Porch

First Floor	2,237 sq. ft.
Second Floor	907 sq. ft.
Total Living Area	3,144 sq. ft.

PRICE CODE: C

CUSTOMIZE IT!

ORDER TOLL FREE 1-800-533-4350 24-HOUR FAX ORDERING 1-800-344-4293

PLAN FD8177-L

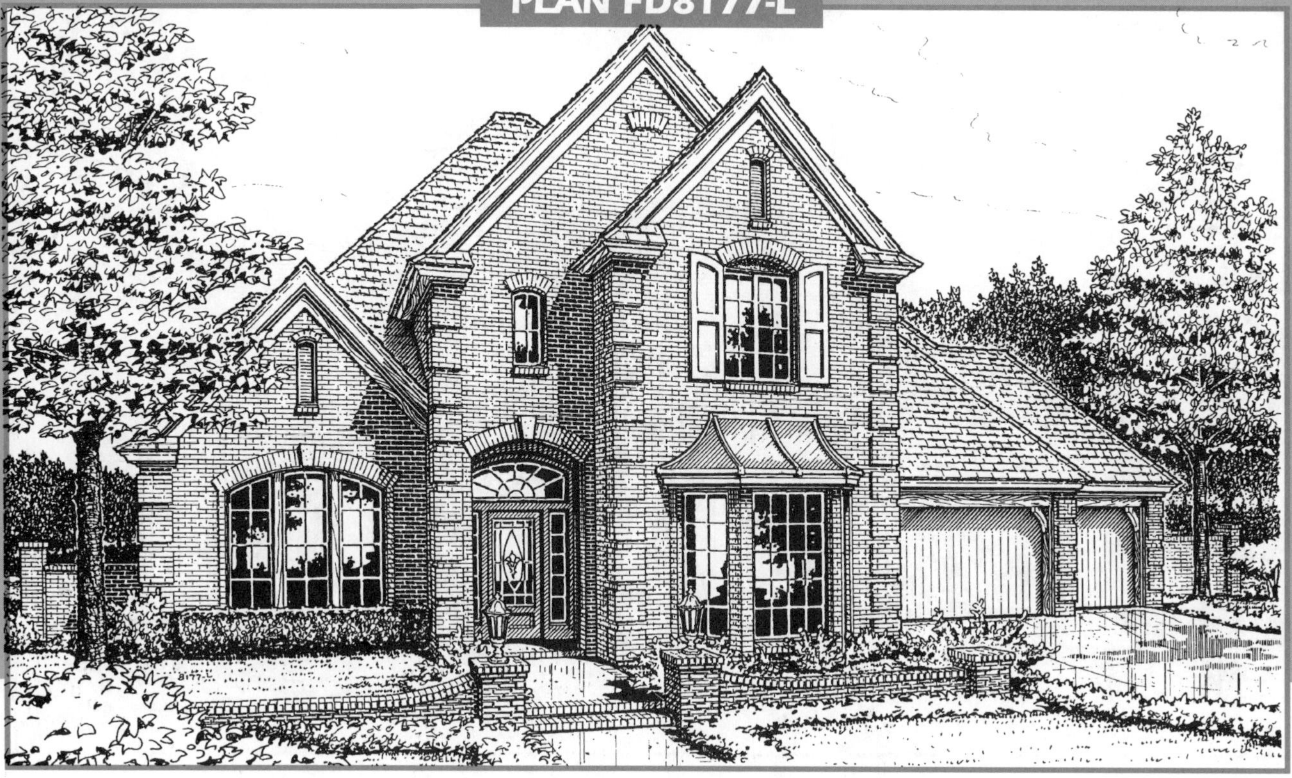

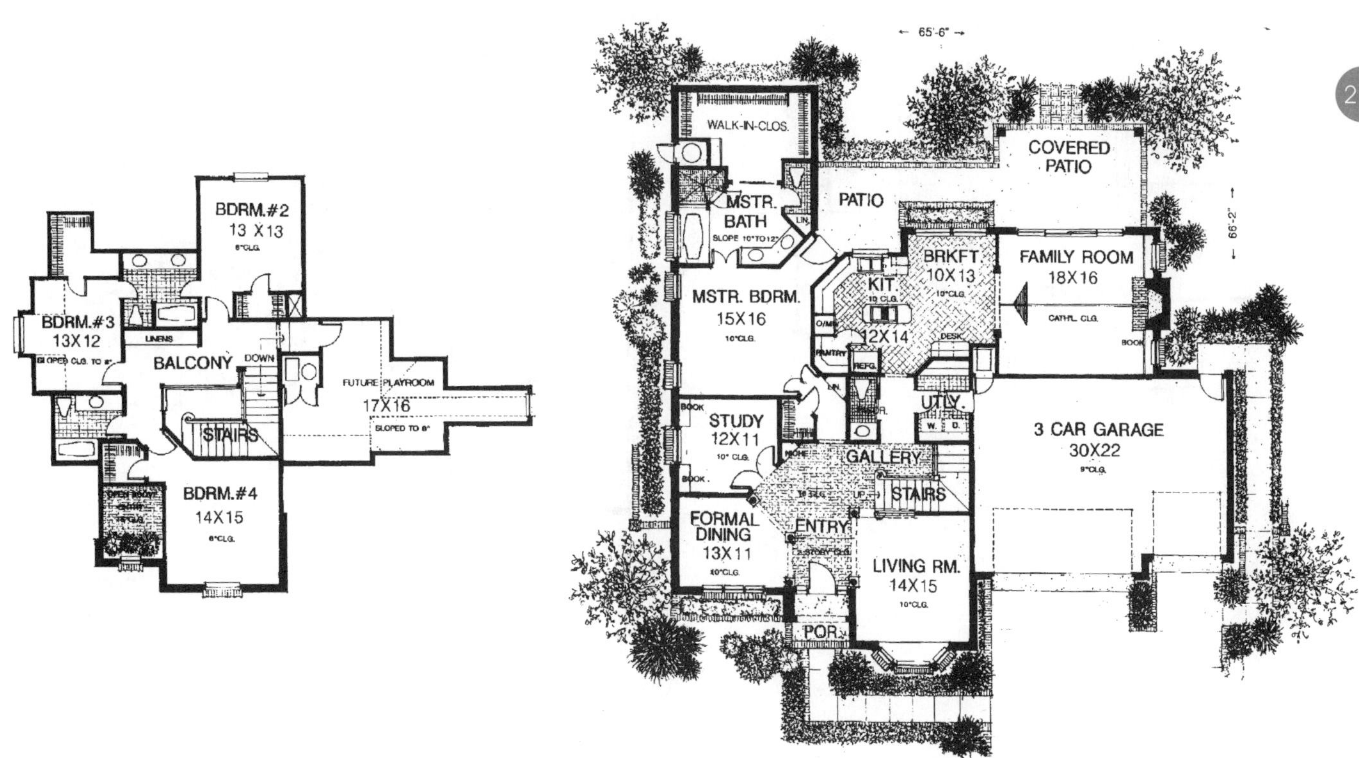
BDRM.#2
13 X13
BDRM.#3
13X12
LINENS
BALCONY
DOWN
FUTURE PLAYROOM
17X16
STAIRS
BDRM.#4
14X15
65'-6"
WALK-IN-CLOS.
COVERED PATIO
PATIO
MSTR. BATH
66'-2"
BRKFT.
10X13
FAMILY ROOM
18X16
MSTR. BDRM.
15X16
KIT.
12X14
STUDY
12X11
UTLY.
3 CAR GARAGE
30X22
GALLERY
STAIRS
FORMAL DINING
13X11
ENTRY
LIVING RM.
14X15
POR.

First Floor	2,182 sq. ft.
Second Floor	968 sq. ft.
Total Living Area	3,150 sq. ft.

PRICE CODE: C

PLAN DB1824

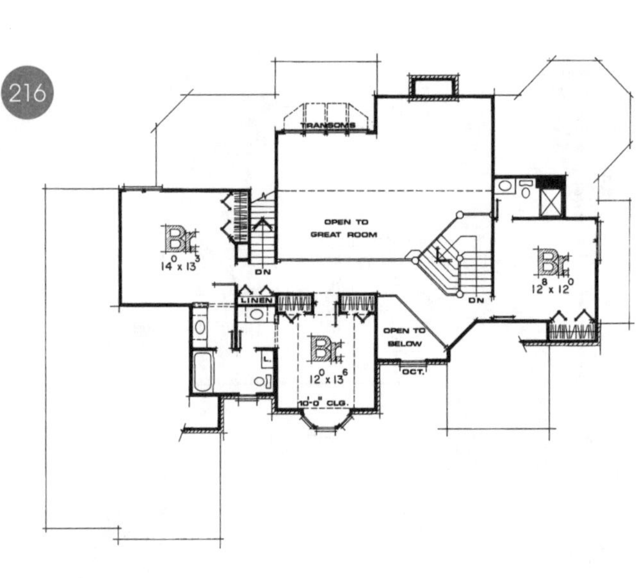

TRANSOMS
OPEN TO GREAT ROOM
Br. 14^0 x 13^3
DN
LINEN
Br. 12^8 x 12^0
DN
Br. 12^0 x 13^6
10'-0" CLG.
OPEN TO BELOW
OCT.

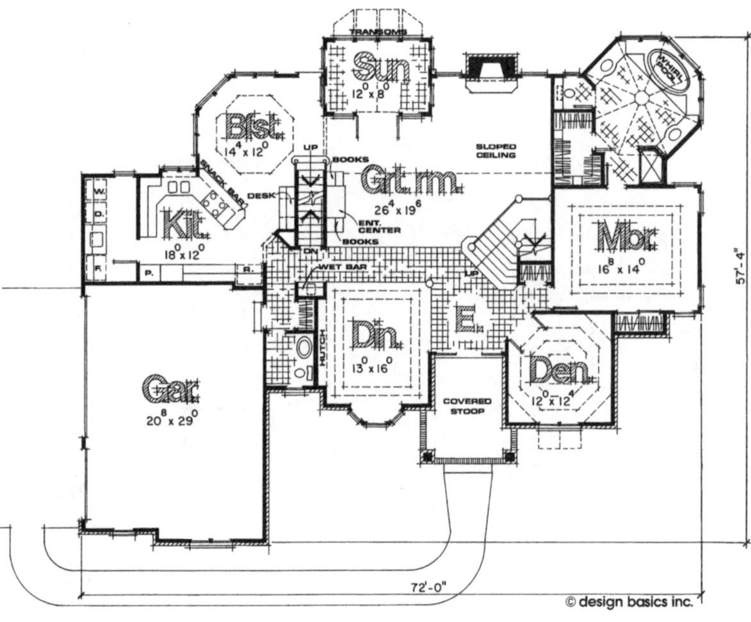

TRANSOMS
Sun 12^0 x 8^0
Bfst. 14^4 x 12^0
SNACK BAR
DESK
UP
BOOKS
SLOPED CEILING
Grt. rm. 26^4 x 19^6
ENT. CENTER
BOOKS
WHIRLPOOL
W.
D.
Kit. 18^0 x 12^0
P.
R.
WET BAR
DN
UP
Mbr. 16^8 x 14^0
HUTCH
Din. 13^0 x 16^0
E.
Den 12^0 x 12^4
COVERED STOOP
Gar. 20^8 x 29^0
57'-4"
72'-0"
© design basics inc.

Features

- Expansive views throughout.
- 9-foot main level walls.
- Private sunroom as focal point visually extends main floor living spaces.
- Back staircase for improved traffic patterns.
- Gourmet kitchen with angled counter/snack bar, pantry and desk.
- Master suite with corner windows, tiered ceiling plus his and her closets.
- Stunning gazebo master bath with oval whirlpool and his and her vanities.
- Secondary bedrooms with direct access to either shared or private baths.

First Floor	2,231 sq. ft.
Second Floor	933 sq. ft.
Total Living Area	3,164 sq. ft.

PRICE CODE: D

PLAN NP1342

malou

MASTER BEDROOM
16'-4" x 18'-10"
MASTER BATH
BATH 2
BEDROOM #2
14'-0" x 14'-0"
SITTING AREA
11'-6" x 6'-0"
W.
LAUN.
D.
L
BALCONY
DN.
STOR.
VAULTED CEILING
BONUS ROOM
15'-0" x 15'-6"
6'-0" HIGH WALL
8'-0" HIGH CEILING LINE
BATH 3
BALCONY
BEDROOM #3
14'-0" x 13'-8"
OPEN TO BELOW
STOR.

Second Floor

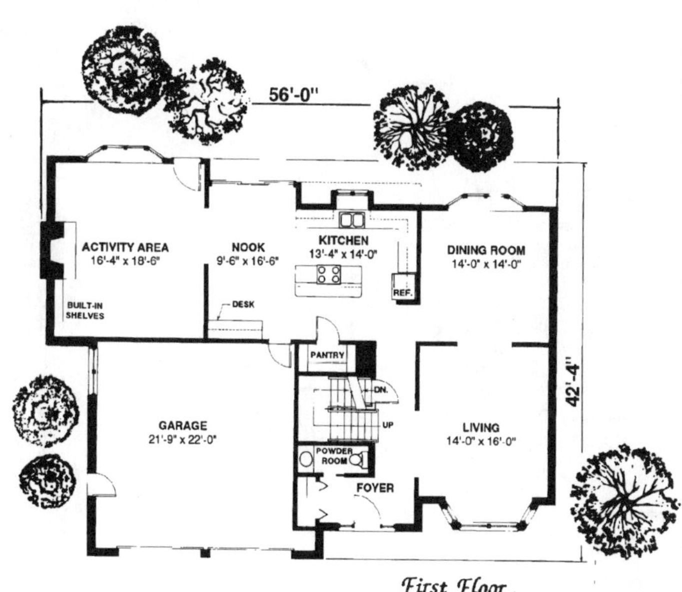
56'-0"
ACTIVITY AREA
16'-4" x 18'-6"
NOOK
9'-6" x 16'-6"
KITCHEN
13'-4" x 14'-0"
DINING ROOM
14'-0" x 14'-0"
BUILT-IN SHELVES
DESK
REF.
PANTRY
DN.
42'-4"
GARAGE
21'-9" x 22'-0"
UP
LIVING
14'-0" x 16'-0"
POWDER ROOM
FOYER

First Floor

Hearth Stone

Features

- Spacious two-story brick home offers lots of living space in an interesting design.
- Right wing showcases a large living room with bay window and formal dining room with bay window.
- Large activity area with fireplace.
- Upstairs, a large master bedroom with wood-burning fireplace, private sitting area, his/her walk-in closets, and full master bath with dual vanity and private toilet.
- Two additional bedrooms and two full baths included upstairs.

First Floor	1,478 sq. ft.
Second Floor	1,697 sq. ft.
Total Living Area	3,175 sq. ft.

PRICE CODE: C

PLAN FD8227-L

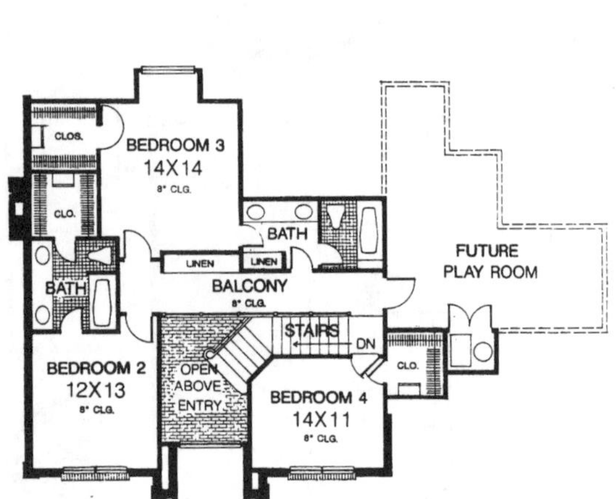

CLOS.
BEDROOM 3
14X14
8" CLG.
CLO.
BATH
LINEN
LINEN
BATH
BALCONY
8" CLG.
FUTURE
PLAY ROOM
STAIRS
DN
CLO.
BEDROOM 2
12X13
8" CLG.
OPEN
ABOVE
ENTRY
BEDROOM 4
14X11
8" CLG.

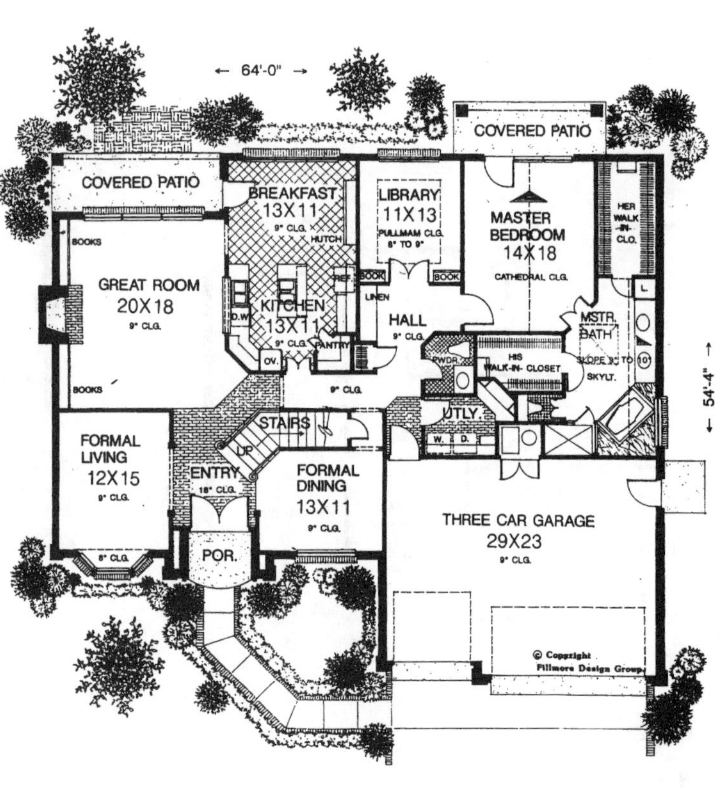

64'-0"
COVERED PATIO
COVERED PATIO
BREAKFAST
13X11
9" CLG.
HUTCH
LIBRARY
11X13
PULLMAM CLG.
8" TO 9"
MASTER
BEDROOM
14X18
CATHEDRAL CLG.
HER
WALK
-IN-
CLO.
BOOKS
GREAT ROOM
20X18
9" CLG.
BOOKS
KITCHEN
13X11
9" CLG.
D.W.
OV.
PANTRY
REF.
BOOK
BOOK
LINEN
HALL
9" CLG.
MSTR.
BATH
HIS
WALK-IN- CLOSET
PWDR
SLOPE 9' TO 10'
SKYLT.
54'-4"
9" CLG.
STAIRS
UP
UTLY.
W. D.
FORMAL
LIVING
12X15
9" CLG.
ENTRY
18' CLG.
FORMAL
DINING
13X11
9" CLG.
8" CLG.
POR.
THREE CAR GARAGE
29X23
9" CLG.
© Copyright
Fillmore Design Group

First Floor	2,236 sq. ft.
Second Floor	983 sq. ft.
Total Living Area	3,219 sq. ft.

PRICE CODE: D

PLAN AM2313A

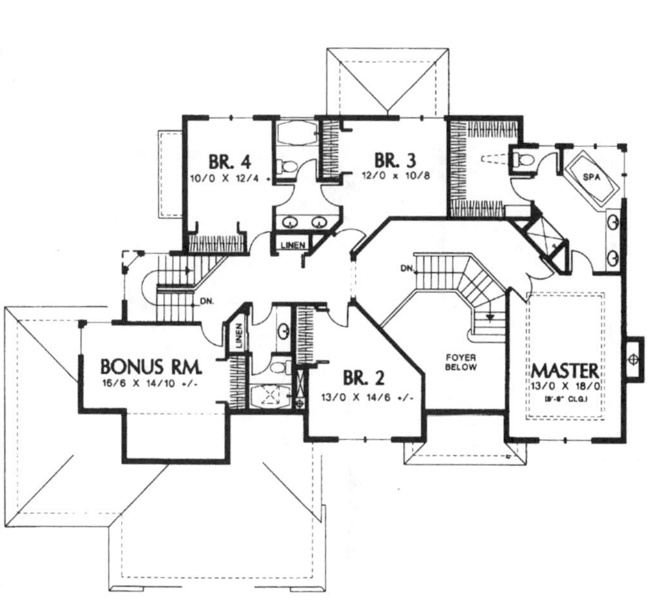
BR. 4
10/0 X 12/4
BR. 3
12/0 x 10/8
SPA
LINEN
DN.
DN.
LINEN
BONUS RM.
15/6 X 14/10 +/-
BR. 2
13/0 X 14/6 +/-
FOYER BELOW
MASTER
13/0 X 18/0

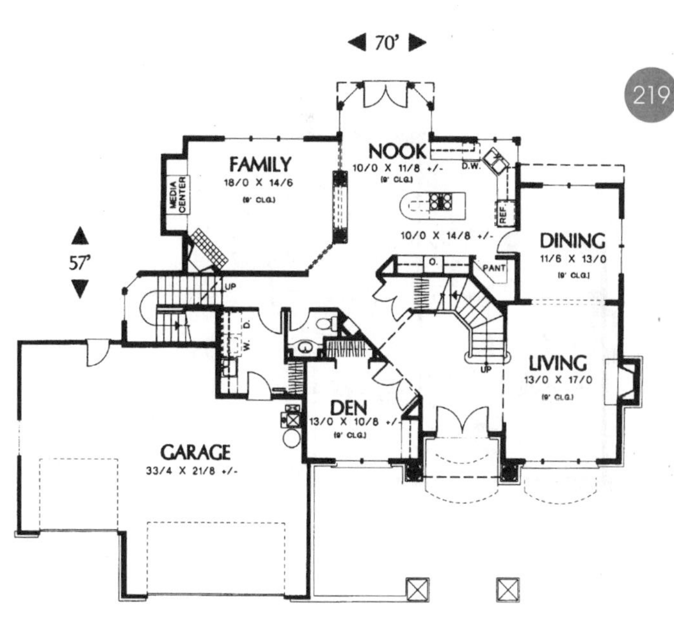
70'
57'
FAMILY
18/0 X 14/6
(9' CLG.)
MEDIA CENTER
NOOK
10/0 X 11/8 +/-
(9' CLG.)
D.W.
REF.
10/0 X 14/8 +/-
DINING
11/6 X 13/0
(9' CLG.)
PANT.
UP
W. D.
LIVING
13/0 X 17/0
(9' CLG.)
DEN
13/0 X 10/8 +/-
(9' CLG.)
GARAGE
33/4 X 21/8 +/-

First Floor	1,763 sq. ft.
Second Floor	1,469 sq. ft.
Total Living Area	3,232 sq. ft.
Bonus Room	+256 sq. ft.

PRICE CODE: D

CUSTOMIZE IT!

ORDER TOLL FREE 1■800■533■4350 24-HOUR FAX ORDERING 1■800■344■4293

PLAN FD7507

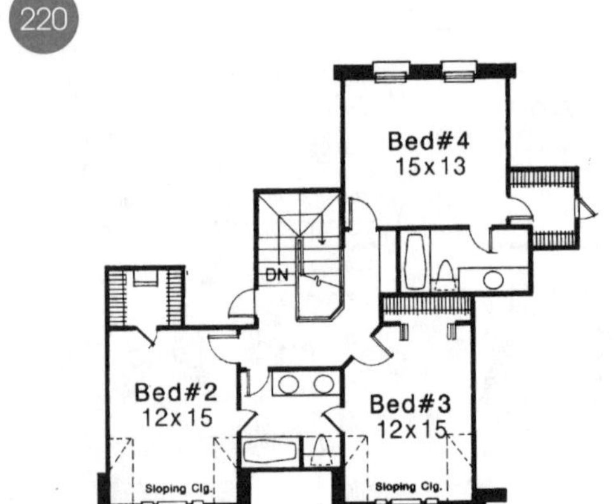

Bed#4
15x13
DN
Bed#2
12x15
Bed#3
12x15
Sloping Clg.
Sloping Clg.

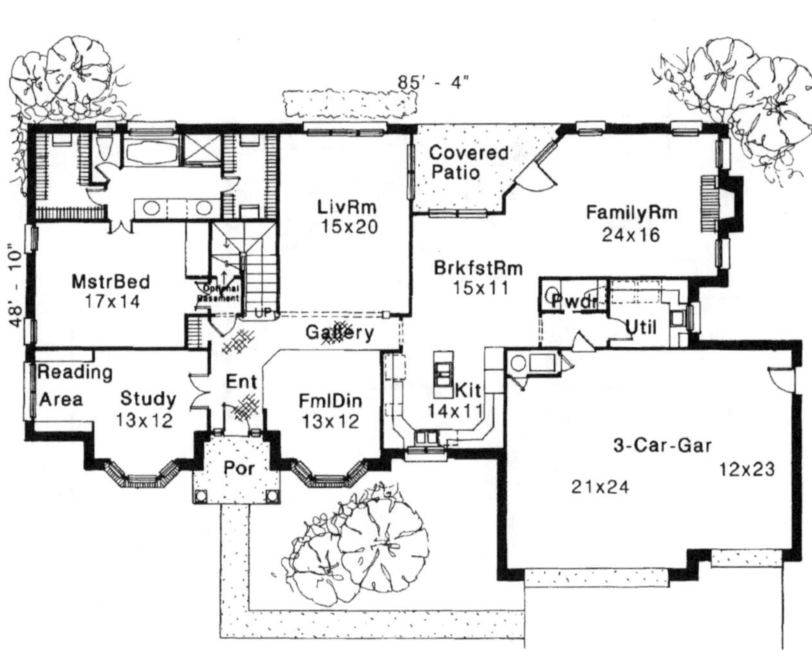

85' - 4"
48' - 10"
Covered Patio
LivRm
15x20
FamilyRm
24x16
MstrBed
17x14
BrkfstRm
15x11
Pwdr
Util
Gallery
UP
Optional Basement
Reading Area
Study
13x12
Ent
FmlDin
13x12
Kit
14x11
3-Car-Gar
21x24
12x23
Por

First Floor	2,365 sq. ft.
Second Floor	874 sq. ft.
Total Living Area	3,239 sq. ft.

PRICE CODE: D

PLAN MN3222

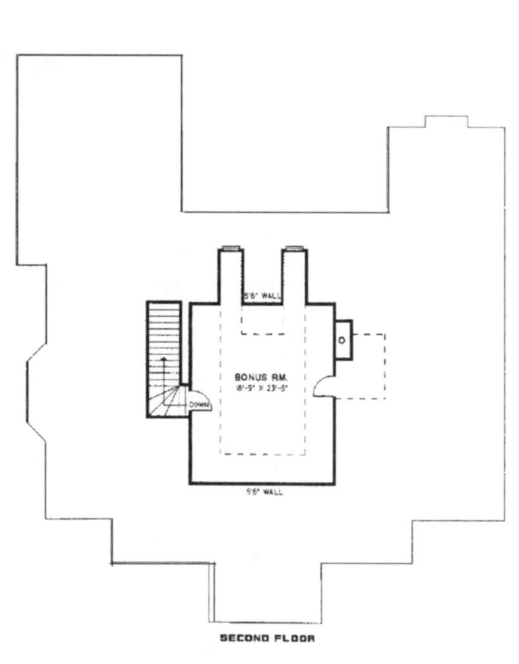
BONUS RM.
DOWN
SECOND FLOOR

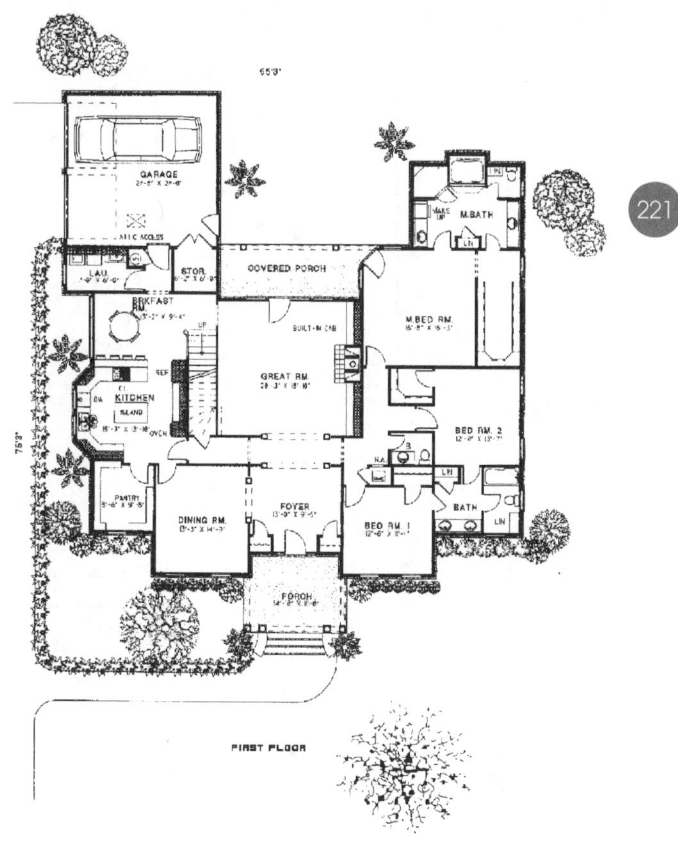
GARAGE
LAU.
STOR.
COVERED PORCH
M.BATH
BRKFAST RM.
BUILT-IN CAB
M.BED RM.
GREAT RM.
KITCHEN
ISLAND
REF
OVEN
BED RM. 2
PANTRY
DINING RM.
FOYER
BED RM. 1
BATH
PORCH
FIRST FLOOR

First Floor	2,768 sq. ft.
Second Floor	529 sq. ft.
Total Living Area	3,297 sq. ft.

PRICE CODE: D

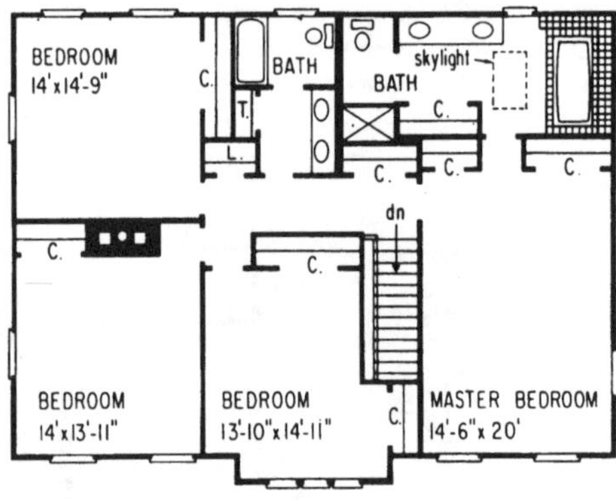
BEDROOM
14'x14'-9"
C.
T.
L.
BATH
BATH
skylight
C.
C.
C.
C.
C.
C.
dn
BEDROOM
14'x13'-11"
BEDROOM
13'-10"x14'-11"
C.
MASTER BEDROOM
14'-6"x 20'

SECOND FLOOR

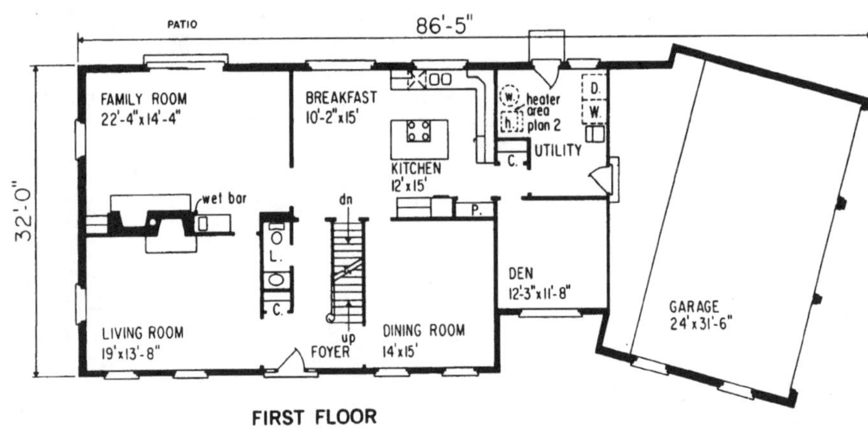
PATIO
86'-5"
32'-0"
FAMILY ROOM
22'-4"x14'-4"
BREAKFAST
10'-2"x15'
heater
area
plan 2
D.
W.
UTILITY
C.
KITCHEN
12'x15'
wet bar
dn
P.
L.
C.
DEN
12'-3"x11'-8"
GARAGE
24'x31'-6"
LIVING ROOM
19'x13'-8"
up
FOYER
DINING ROOM
14'x15'

FIRST FLOOR

PLAN 1 WITH BASEMENT

PLAN 2 WITHOUT BASEMENT

Tudor Extravagance

Features

- Traditional Tudor design on the outside is carried through to the interior of this charming home.
- Foyer with open stairway and balustrades provides formal entrance.
- Spacious family room contains beamed ceiling and natural fireplace.
- Large L-shaped kitchen with island cooking unit is open to breakfast area.
- Formal dining room off foyer.
- Large utility area accesses garage.
- A den completes the first floor picture.
- Upstairs, a large master bedroom suite with jacuzzi tub, dressing area, separate shower.
- Three bedrooms upstairs share a full bath.

First Floor	**1,810 sq. ft.**
Second Floor	**1,496 sq. ft.**
Total Living Area	**3,306 sq. ft.**

PRICE CODE: D

PLAN FD8051

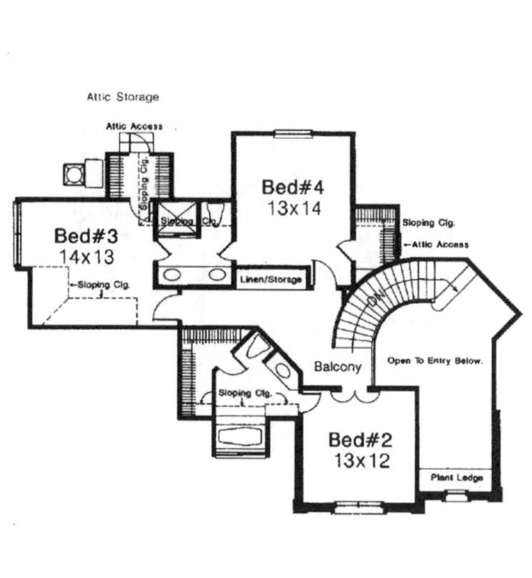

Attic Storage
Attic Access
Sloping Clg.
Bed#4
13x14
Bed#3
14x13
Sloping Clg.
Linen/Storage
Sloping Clg.
Attic Access
Balcony
Open To Entry Below.
Sloping Clg.
Bed#2
13x12
Plant Ledge

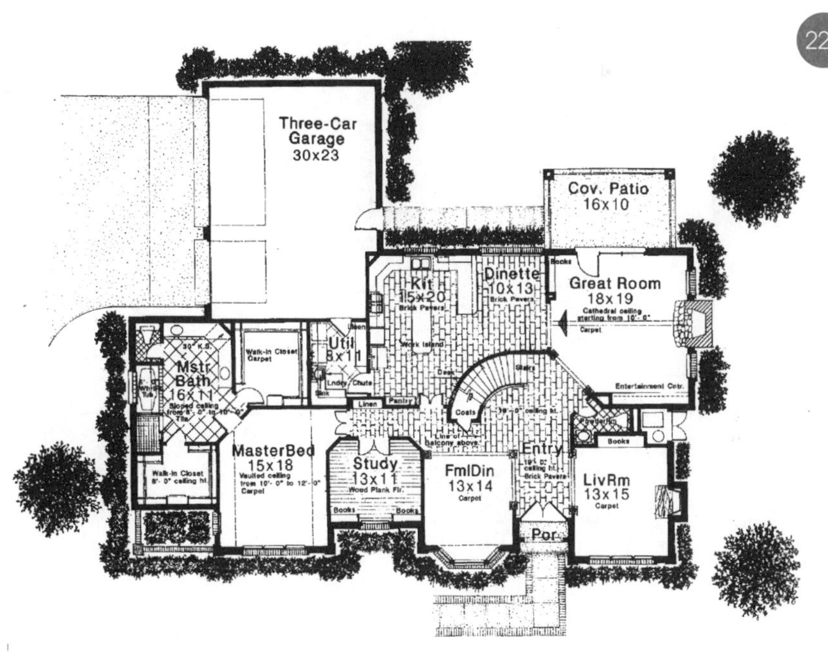

Three-Car
Garage
30x23
Cov. Patio
16x10
Kit
15x20
Brick Pavers
Dinette
10x13
Brick Pavers
Books
Great Room
18x19
Carpet
Entertainment Cntr.
Util
8x11
Walk-In Closet
Carpet
Mstr
Bath
16x11
Walk-In Closet
MasterBed
15x18
Carpet
Study
13x11
Wood Plank Flr.
Books
Books
Coats
Pantry
Linen
FmlDin
13x14
Carpet
Entry
LivRm
13x15
Carpet
Books
Por

First Floor	2,437 sq. ft.
Second Floor	922 sq. ft.
Total Living Area	3,359 sq. ft.

PRICE CODE: D

224

PLAN DB1499

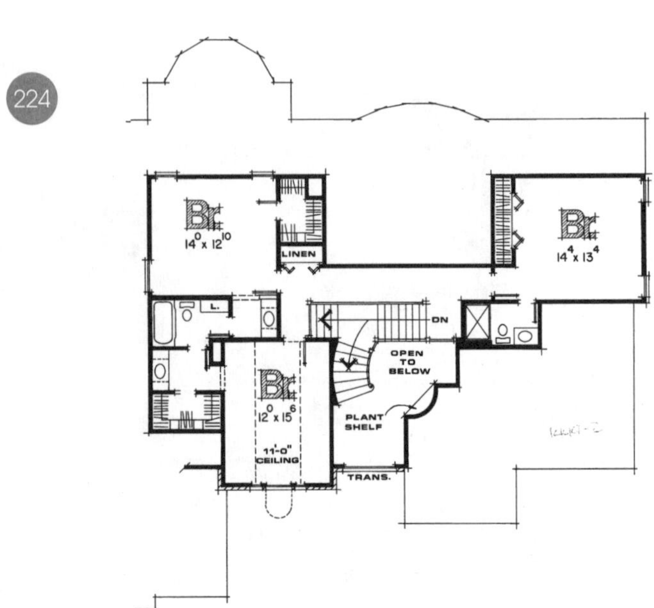

Br.
$14^{0} \times 12^{10}$
LINEN
Br.
$14^{4} \times 13^{4}$
L.
DN
OPEN TO BELOW
Br.
$12^{0} \times 15^{6}$
11'-0" CEILING
PLANT SHELF
TRANS.

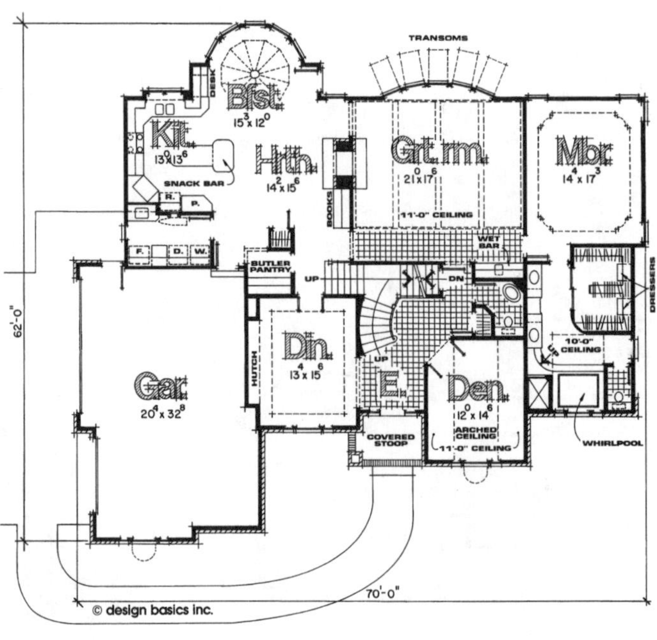

TRANSOMS
DESK
Bfst.
$15^{3} \times 12^{0}$
Kit.
$13^{0} \times 13^{6}$
SNACK BAR
Hrth.
$14^{2} \times 15^{6}$
BOOKS
Grt.rm.
$21^{0} \times 17^{6}$
11'-0" CEILING
Mbr.
$14^{4} \times 17^{3}$
WET BAR
F. D. W.
BUTLER PANTRY
UP
DN
DRESSERS
Gar.
$20^{4} \times 32^{8}$
HUTCH
Din.
$13^{4} \times 15^{6}$
E.
Den
$12^{0} \times 14^{6}$
ARCHED CEILING
11'-0" CEILING
10'-0" CEILING
COVERED STOOP
WHIRLPOOL
62'-0"
70'-0"
© design basics inc.

Features

- Decorative window and brick detailing adds grandeur to elevation.
- French doors access den with volume ceiling and lovely arched window. Dining room with hutch space and nearby hall butler pantry.
- Great room with 11-foot ceiling, see-thru fireplace and bowed transom window.
- Family living abounds in combined kitchen, breakfast and hearth room.
- Upstairs two secondary bedrooms with walk-in closets share a Hollywood bath.
- Master suite has decorative ceiling, walk-in closet with two dressers, plus step-up to shower and whirlpool tub.
- Third secondary bedroom has a private bath.

First Floor	2,375 sq. ft.
Second Floor	1,073 sq. ft.
Total Living Area	3,448 sq. ft.

PRICE CODE: E